P9-DNU-685

RENNER
LEARNING RESOURCES CENTER
ELGIN COMMUNITY COLLEGE
ELGIN, ILLINOIS 60120

Also by Christopher Collier

ROGER SHERMAN'S CONNECTICUT

Also by James Lincoln Collier

THE MAKING OF JAZZ

LOUIS ARMSTRONG: AN AMERICAN GENIUS

Decision in Philadelphia

DECISION
in
PHILADELPHIA

The Constitutional
Convention of 1787

CHRISTOPHER COLLIER

JAMES LINCOLN COLLIER

RENNER LEARNING RESOURCE CENTER
ELGIN COMMUNITY COLLEGE
ELGIN, ILLINOIS 60120

Random House
Reader's Digest Press/New York

Copyright © 1986 by Christopher Collier and James Lincoln Collier
All rights reserved under International and Pan-American Copyright Conventions.
Published in the United States by Reader's Digest Press and Random House, Inc.,
New York, and simultaneously in Canada by
Random House of Canada Limited, Toronto.
Library of Congress Cataloging-in-Publication Data
Collier, Christopher, 1930-
Decision in Philadelphia.
Bibliography: p.
Includes index.
1. United States. Constitutional Convention (1787)
2. Constitutional conventions—United States. 3. United
States—Constitutional history. I. Collier, James
Lincoln, 1928- . II. Title.
KF4520.C65   1985   342.73′024   84-45750
ISBN 0-394-52346-6   347.30224
Manufactured in the United States of America
24689753
First Edition

071465

342.73
C699d

FOR DIANE AND DICK MARGOLIS

AND

LEE LORENZ

17.45

9-18-86

I have always regarded that Constitution
as the most remarkable work known to me
in modern times to have been produced by
the human intellect, at a single stroke
(so to speak), in its application to
political affairs.

William Ewart Gladstone
in a Letter to the Committee in
charge of the celebration of the
Centennial Anniversary of the
American Constitution (July 20, 1887)

Preface

Of all the riches of human life, one of the most highly prized by human beings is freedom. The more of it we have, the more we are able to obtain the satisfaction of our other desires. In this sense freedom is the first requirement, and over the long history of humankind people have shown an astonishing willingness to risk anything, even life itself, in order to be free.

But freedom has proven, over that same long history, to be a very perishable commodity. In the world today only a minority, and not a very large minority at that, have real liberty, as it is understood in the western democracies. The freedom that exists in the United States of America, thus, is a relatively rare thing, something that most people elsewhere long for but do not really expect ever to have. Considering how rare and immensely valuable American liberty is, it is both astounding and dismaying that it should be so much taken for granted, and so little understood. Most Americans have some vague notion that they have certain "rights"—the right to say what they want, the right to a fair trial, the right to participate in government and to go to any church they choose, or to none at all. But few Americans have much idea of how their government was so carefully constructed to preserve their freedoms. Most particularly, they do not understand how the Constitution, that rock on which American freedom was built, works, what it means, and why it was put together the way it was. Indeed, even many of our recent presidents have displayed only incomplete understanding of that great document they are sworn to uphold.

This, then, is why we have written this book: to show how the American Constitution was written, and what the men who wrote it were thinking and feeling during what turned out to be a long, hot summer in Philadelphia.

Like any such book, this one was written from a viewpoint. To grossly oversimplify, over the past hundred years or so there have been two basic ways of looking at the Constitutional Convention. Some historians see it as an arena of clashing economic and sectional interests: agriculturalists versus merchants, exporting states versus ones with little export trade, the North versus the South, and so on. The historians who adhere to this interpretation see the Constitution that emerged from the Convention as the result of a whole series of compromises, and compromises of compromises, which gave the document its final shape.

Other historians view the Constitutional Convention mainly as an expression of a consensus on a group of ideals and principles widely held by thoughtful Americans of the day. That is to say, the delegates came to Philadelphia holding a more or less common world view, out of which they wrote the document. The consensus was not perfect, and ideals and ideas had at times to be compromised. But according to this interpretation, there was more agreement than conflict on basic questions of human nature and the relations of society to government in general.

We believe that both these interpretations are in part correct. It is certainly true that compromises between different interests were essential and played a large role in shaping the Constitution. It is also true that the delegates, in general, concurred on many basic philosophic questions. But we think that these two interpretations do not fully explain how the Constitution came to be. As some historians today are beginning to say, no single motivation can adequately explain the behavior of the men at the Convention—or, indeed, of people anywhere. It is our contention that these men were moved not only by economics, sectional loyalties, theories of government, and ideas about life in general, but also by springs and designs hidden deep in their personalities. The tense, quixotic Elbridge Gerry, the personally shy but intellectually bold James Madison, the clever, cautious Roger Sherman, the dogmatic Luther Martin, the brilliant but arrogant Gouverneur Morris, the majestic George Washington, the misanthropic George Mason, the openhanded John Langdon: these were human beings, with their own perceptions of the world and their own ways of dealing with it. We do not believe that we can understand why they voted as they did in Philadelphia solely by knowing where their money came from, or what parts of the country they represented. We believe that to understand how the American Constitution came to be we must know how these men *felt* about such things as power, liberty, nature, truth, God, and life itself. We are by no means attempting to write what has been called psychohistory, a discipline we view with extreme skepticism. We do think, however, that

by examining the record of what these men said and did, we can form estimates
of their attitudes and belief systems, and that the evidence will help to explain
why they took this or that position on the great issues at the Convention. Our
goal, then, has been to show who these Founding Fathers *were* as well as how
their political circumstances operated on their behavior.

The bibliography evinces our debt to the scores of historians who have made
our work possible. We wish to thank in particular George Billias, Richard
Kohn, Kent Newmyer, John O'Connor, and Paul Clemens, whose reviews of
chapters were especially helpful. Gordon Wood read the entire manuscript in
draft and some chapters again at a later stage. We are much indebted to him
for informed and always useful criticism, and are deeply grateful for his help.
Needless to say, interpretations are our responsibility.

We would also like to thank three editors: Edward T. Thompson, whose
support at the outset encouraged us to go forward; Steven Frimmer of *Reader's
Digest,* who offered much constructive criticism; and Derek Johns of Random
House, who cheerfully expedited the manuscript through publication.

Contents

Preface   xi

Part I: "OUR CASE MAY BECOME DESPERATE"   1

Chapter One: A NATION IN JEOPARDY   3

Chapter Two: AMERICA IN 1787   14

Chapter Three: THE MIND OF JAMES MADISON   25

Chapter Four: THE UNBELIEVABLE GEORGE WASHINGTON   30

Chapter Five: MADISON PLANS A GOVERNMENT   43

Chapter Six: ALEXANDER HAMILTON AND THE BRITISH MODEL   56

Chapter Seven: THE PUZZLE OF CHARLES PINCKNEY   64

Chapter Eight: MEN, MANNERS, AND RULES: THE CONVENTION BEGINS   75

Part II: THE LARGE STATES AND THE SMALL   87

Chapter Nine: ROGER SHERMAN AND THE ART OF COMPROMISE   89

Chapter Ten: WILLIAM PATERSON PICKS A FIGHT   102

Chapter Eleven: THE BATTLE JOINED   109

Chapter Twelve: LUTHER MARTIN AND A LOST OPPORTUNITY   116

Chapter Thirteen: "THE MOST SERIOUS AND THREATENING EXCITEMENT"   122

Part III: NORTH AND SOUTH   135

Chapter Fourteen: A NEW ALLIANCE   137

Chapter Fifteen: THE WESTERN LANDS   153

Chapter Sixteen: ANOTHER TRADE-OFF   166

Part IV: THE QUESTION OF POWER   181

Chapter Seventeen: BALANCING ACT   183

Chapter Eighteen: CURING THE REPUBLICAN DISEASE   195

Chapter Nineteen: JAMES WILSON, DEMOCRATIC NATIONALIST   206

Chapter Twenty: IN THE SHADOW OF WASHINGTON   217

Chapter Twenty-one: ELBRIDGE GERRY'S WAR AGAINST THE ARMY   234

Chapter Twenty-two: GEORGE MASON AND THE RIGHTS OF MAN   249

Chapter Twenty-three: "THE MOST REMARKABLE WORK"   263

Appendix A: The Articles of Confederation   273

Appendix B: The Constitution of the United States   281

Citations to Sources   293

Selected Bibliography   307

Index   323

Part I

"OUR CASE MAY BECOME DESPERATE"

Chapter One

A Nation in Jeopardy

It was all going wrong. George Washington saw it, and he wrote a friend that something had to be done "to avert the humiliating and contemptible figure we are about to make on the annals of mankind." William Grayson, a Congressman from Virginia, wrote to James Madison that if things did not change "We shall be one of the most contemptible nations on the face of the Earth." John Hancock, the governor of Massachusetts, told his legislature, "How to strengthen and improve the Union so as to render it completely adequate, demands the immediate attention of these states. Our very existence as a free nation is suspended upon it." James Madison wrote to James Monroe, "If the present paroxysm of our affairs be totally neglected, our case may become desperate."

It had seemed so promising in the beginning. They had thought they were founding a nation that would last for the ages, and when they had finally, miraculously, beaten the mightiest nation on earth and found themselves one bright morning independent, they had taken it as a sign that the Almighty was shining on them. At the end of the Revolution Americans were sure that they were a special people with a special role in history. They would "show to the nations of the Earth," wrote Samuel Adams, "what will be a most singular phenomenon amidst all the jarring interests, subtlety, and rage of politics," a people with virtue enough to practice frugality, honesty, self-denial, and benevolence, to become, in short a "Christian Sparta," a model to the world.

Their country had been formed piecemeal. The colonies were created at different times under different philosophies of life, ranging from the hard-bitten Calvinism of New England to the worldly hedonism of the Deep South. Before 1776, there was no American government as such; each colony had its own legislature, and a council and governor who were usually appointed by the Crown. Such government as there was for "America" sat in London. The Parliament and the king together could, and did, establish some general laws, having to do mostly with shipping and commerce, which applied to all of the colonies, but in a considerable measure the colonies managed to escape much of the onerous legislation and go their own way.

With the signing of the Declaration of Independence in 1776, the legal basis of all these colonial governments was undermined, and the various states set about writing constitutions and creating new governments for themselves. Each was now, in effect, an independent nation. It was, however, perfectly clear that the newly free colonies could not fight a common war against the British without some common government, and in June 1776, the delegates from the states at the Continental Congress in Philadelphia voted to draw up what one of them called "a firm league of friendship." The result was a document called the Articles of Confederation. The Articles created an organization that might be compared with the League of Nations. There was a legislature of a single house, in which each state had a single vote, regardless of its population—a system that the large states resented. There was no real executive: the President of Congress merely chaired meetings and had no powers of his own. Eventually secretaries for foreign affairs and war and a superintendent of finance were established, but these officials, however influential, had little real power. The Articles authorized the establishment of admiralty courts, and a court to deal with land disputes; but, except in one interstate land dispute, legal business was handled by state courts. The Articles could be amended only with the unanimous consent of the states, which inevitably made amendments impossible: the Articles were never amended.

The basic principle underlying the Articles of Confederation was that each state would remain "sovereign." Precisely what that was supposed to mean nobody knew, but what it did mean was that the states could ignore with impunity legislation passed by the Congress. The Congress would request the states to pay taxes, usually proportioned according to population, but it had no way of forcing the state governments actually to hand over the money. Invariably some states found excuses for not paying their share, and once one or two refused, the others would balk, saying that they would not pay until all the rest did. It was the same story with congressional requisitions on the states for bullets, wagons, blankets, and troops to fight the war. Each state sent what it thought was convenient or appropriate, which usually depended on how close to home the fighting was going on.

When peace came it brought with it problems just as trying. Among the most pressing were a congeries of difficulties with foreign nations. The British were refusing to leave their forts on the Great Lakes, as they were required to do by the Treaty of Paris of 1783, which ended the Revolution. British control of the area made it impossible for the American government to exploit the territory for the benefit of the United States.

The Spanish owned the land stretching west from the banks of the Mississippi, as well as New Orleans at the river's mouth, and were claiming a vast amount of land on the American side. As the centerpiece of a complex river system draining millions of acres of western lands, the Mississippi was the only practical means of transport out of that huge territory. It was crucial to the exploitation of the area; but in 1784 the Spanish closed the river from Natchez south.

Unfortunately, the United States could do nothing about either Spanish or English incursions, because the moment the Revolution was over, the army was disbanded: nobody wanted to pay taxes to support a standing army. As a consequence, the armed force dwindled to seven hundred ill-equipped men, and in 1787 Secretary of War Henry Knox was forced to reduce his staff to three clerks because he could not afford any more.

Then there were the Indians. Both the English and the Spanish were supplying them with arms and encouraging them to raid frontier settlements. American settlers were terrorized. In 1787 the half-breed Joseph Brant, a Mohawk chief and a captain in the British army, was organizing thousands of Indians determined to keep the Americans out of the Northwest Territory. In the South, the brilliant twenty-four-year-old Alexander McGillivray, also of mixed blood, was organizing tens of thousands of Indians who were terrorizing American pioneers with hit-and-run raids.

Many Americans were aware that the frontier battling was not primarily the fault of the Indians. Various groups of Indians were guilty of savage massacres, in which women and children were clubbed to death, but it is the general view of historians today that these assaults were usually provoked by frontier settlers, especially squatters, who were hacking farms out of the forests on land they had no legal right to, often in defiance of Indian treaties. And savagery was found on both sides. In one incident in Washington County, Pennsylvania, an American force of some three hundred men marched into a village of the Delawares. "The Americans were received in a friendly manner by the natives, and for three days they enjoyed the primitive hospitality of the Indians. Then on Sunday they gathered the villagers, about ninety in all, into their church, and while they were singing hymns, set upon them and massacred men, women, and children, only one person escaping with his life."

But in the minds of many, the question of where the fault lay was irrelevant: the main point was that the hapless American government could not control the situation. Frightened, many of the western settlers were ready to go over to the Spanish. A young American army officer from Kentucky named James Wilkinson actually took an oath of loyalty to the king of Spain in exchange for trading concessions. Wilkinson began to urge his fellow Kentuckians to set up an independent state, which could then enter into lucrative trade agreements with the Spanish. In the months leading up to the Constitutional Convention in 1787 the westerners stood, as Washington put it, "as on a pivot; the touch of a feather would turn them any way."

There was more trouble in the Mediterranean, where the Barbary pirates were preying on American shipping. The Mediterranean trade was of great importance to many of the colonies: by Thomas Jefferson's estimate the area took about one-sixth of the colonies' wheat and flour and one-fourth of their dried and pickled fish. Pirates, sweeping out of Algiers, Tunis, Tripoli, and Morocco, were capturing not only cargoes but also American citizens, whom they put into slavery or held for ransom.

In 1785 Algerians captured two ships and held their crews and passengers for ransom. The United States, with its finances in disarray, could offer only two hundred dollars a man. The Dey of Algiers sneered at the offer, and the prisoners languished in jail, some of them dying of the plague. At the same time the Bey of Tripoli offered to refrain for a year from plundering American vessels, for a payment of 12,500 guineas, which the United States government could not afford either.

Again, as the United States were now outside the British Empire, American traders were shut out of the British West Indies, with whom they had formerly carried on a lucrative trade. Shippers were eager to reopen that trade if possible, or negotiate trade treaties with other European nations to make up the loss.

There were obvious solutions to these foreign policy problems, and a firm government might have found them. But unfortunately, getting the states to agree to anything proved impossible. As one example, in 1785 Massachusetts, Rhode Island, and New Hampshire, three shipping states eager to reopen the West Indies trade, passed laws restricting British trade in their ports, hoping to force concessions from the British in the West Indies. But Connecticut, seeing a chance to draw the British trade to itself, refused to join the others, and the scheme foundered. There was a similar conflict of interest in the states' relations with Spain. States like Georgia, whose western lands, stretching to the Mississippi, would some day fill up with new arrivals, wanted the river opened and the land protected from the Spanish. States on the seacoast, with no western lands, were eager to avoid war with Spain, which might bring the Spanish fleet to shell and burn their seacoast cities and towns. Something had to be done, but what? Rufus King, a congressman from Massachusetts and later a delegate to the Constitutional Convention, summed it up succinctly when he wrote a few months before leaving for Philadelphia:

> If therefore our disputes with Spain are not settled, we shall be obliged either wholly to give up the western settlers, or join *them* in an issue of force with the Catholic king: the latter we are in no condition to think of, the former would be impolitic for many reasons, and cannot with safety be *now* admitted.

But even if treaties with Spain and England were made, there was considerable doubt that the U.S. Congress could enforce them on American citizens. The Treaty of Paris specified that Loyalists who had lost property or businesses on account of the war were to be reimbursed by the Americans who had taken over those properties or bought them from the revolutionary governments. State legislatures, however, obstructed the collection of these debts, as well as prewar debts owed to British merchants, and the inability of the United States government to enforce its own treaty was used as an excuse by the British for staying in their Great Lakes forts. Georgia and North Carolina ignored congressional treaties with Indians and supplanted them with their own. Indeed, it was the British view that "no treaty can be made with the American states that can be binding on all of them. . . . When treaties are necessary, they must be made with the states separately." The judgment certainly seemed correct. For example, in 1777 Virginia had passed acts confiscating Loyalists' lands. In one typical case an Englishman named Denny Martin, who had inherited lands from his uncle, the powerful Lord Fairfax, sued in Virginia courts for return of his lands. The Virginia courts, in defiance of the Treaty of Paris, rejected Martin's claim. Not until 1816, when the case reached the Supreme Court of the new government, did Martin win his case.

Conflicts of interest among the states made it difficult for Congress to shape a cohesive domestic policy, too. In general, the states with Atlantic ports, such as New York, Philadelphia, Boston, and Charleston, were taking advantage of their geography to tax goods imported through them by merchants in their neighboring states. New York State especially was doing handsomely, since goods bound for Connecticut and New Jersey paid duties on the way through to support the New York government. New Jersey demanded that the national government do something about the situation, and when it wouldn't or couldn't, the New Jersey legislature, in a fit of pique, voted to withhold the money requisitioned by the national government. There was an uproar in Congress; Nathaniel Gorham, a congressman from Massachusetts and later a delegate to the Constitutional Convention, said that New Jersey was on the verge of joining Connecticut in marching on New York, "and bloodshed would very quickly be the consequence." Congress was simply too weak to force a solution on the quarreling states.

Nor was it able to sort out the conflicting claims to the immensely valuable frontier lands. Connecticut had claimed the Wyoming Valley in the Wilkes-Barre area of Pennsylvania, and her settlers there had fought bloody battles with Pennsylvania troops. Indians were threatening to reclaim land they had traded away in Georgia, which was virtually defenseless. Vermont had split away from New York and established itself as an independent state, which was, however, not recognized by the national government. All of these lands were also subject to a confusion of overlapping claims by speculators, who had private deals with Indians, their own state governments, and each other. This thicket of conflicting claims had to be chopped through before Americans could capitalize on the potential wealth there. But over the years Congress had been unable to agree on several plans presented to it.

Then there was the problem of the huge debt that had piled up during the war and after. The war had been financed primarily by notes and bonds—amounting, really, to IOUs—issued both by the individual states and by the Continental Congress. Some of these notes had been bought by foreigners. Others had been given to soldiers in place of pay, and to American merchants in exchange for the pork, shoes, guns, and butter needed to fight the war. It was clear that this debt would have to be paid off if the new country was to be able to carry on trade. International commerce depended upon a flawless chain of credit, and if the credit of the United States was no good, the foreign trade of the country, on which thousands of livelihoods hung, would be badly hurt.

But once again the states were at odds. They had issued widely varying amounts of notes and had been liquidating them through a variety of mechanisms. Furthermore, some states had begun assuming portions of the national debt, also in complex ways. The situation was exceedingly confused, and nobody was able to find a satisfactory way of dealing with it.

None of these problems, foreign or domestic, was insoluble. A determined government could force the British out of the Great Lakes area and secure the nation's southern borders against the Spanish. Treaties could be negotiated to reopen the West Indies trade, or failing that, to open new markets elsewhere. The war debt could be paid—indeed, if the conflicting claims to the western lands were settled and the land was sold off to settlers, the income could go a long way to eliminating the debt.

Unfortunately, Congress was helpless to do any of these things. The problem, basically, was that the states were proving loathe to give up their precious "sovereignty." As historian Peter Onuf points out, "The Articles of Confederation were premised on the existence of thirteen distinct political communities and effectively barred a coordinated response to national political problems." In fact, many Americans believed that the diversity of interests and attitudes among the states made a national government impossible. In 1787 Pierce Butler of South Carolina, who would be a delegate to the Convention, wrote that the interests of the North and South are "as different as the interests of Russia and Turkey." Even George Washington spoke of how "different from each other in their manners, circumstances and prejudices" the states were.

Many Americans had been conscious for a long time of the inability of Congress to solve the problems facing it. According to E. James Ferguson, in an important study of the matter, a movement to reform the government had begun as early as 1780, when the states were still at war with England. The year 1780 was, Ferguson says, "in many ways the most discouraging year of the war," with military defeats, a depreciating currency, and failing morale. From that year on, there had steadily grown what historians call the "nationalist" movement, which aimed at strengthening the central government. From the moment the Articles of Confederation had been ratified in 1781, efforts had been made to improve them, and from time to time Congress had established committees for that purpose. The problems, then, had been clear to many people, and they had pressed for change. But because it took unanimous approval of the states to amend the Articles, nothing had been accomplished: any suggested change invariably gored some state's ox.

While Congress was wrestling in growing despair with these problems, yet another one appeared. At the close of the war Americans had gone on a buying spree. Eight years of privation had left them hungering for "luxuries"—clocks, rugs, glassware, and sideboards from Europe, and especially from England. They ordered goods recklessly, paying for them—or not paying for them—on credit.

It was a situation that could not continue, and it did not. Soon, British merchants began demanding payment, and by 1784 or thereabouts, currency began flowing out of the United States. Today, when we take paper money for granted, it is hard to realize that two hundred years ago it was a newfangled and suspect device. Ordinary Americans did their business in hard currency, most of it foreign money. Computations were generally done in British pounds and shillings (three shillings was a good day's pay for a craftsman), but also afloat in the country were Dutch guilders, French francs, and Spanish dollars. The latter, a silver coin, was one of the coins in widest use. It was worth eight reals and for convenience was sometimes actually cut into quarters, each worth two reals, or "two bits," a term still in use for the American quarter. This coin was the famous "piece of eight." Some states also minted coins of their own —Connecticut, for example, issued copper pennies. These state coins varied in value, and newspapers frequently ran tables of the comparative worth of state currencies. (The hundred-cent dollar became the basis of United States currency in 1792.)

A great deal of business was done without the exchange of money at all, through bookkeeping transactions, which would be balanced off at some later date. Also circulating were "bills of exchange," which were basically IOUs. That is, Farmer Smith might pay Merchant Johnson with an IOU made between Brown and White.

In any case, the supply of hard currency was finite, and as a result of the postwar buying spree it began to disappear from the country. It has been calculated that by July 1784 there was only £150,000 in the entire Commonwealth of Massachusetts—about ten shillings per person. This meant that many people had no cash and very little chance of getting any. And so began a chain of events that was to lead to a critical episode in American history, Shays' Rebellion.

To the largest part of the population, the independent farmers and their families who constituted the heart of the nation, the absence of money hardly mattered. They had never had much coin and had got along without it. Typically, a householder might see ten pounds pass through his hands each year, earned from the sale of surplus corn, cider, whiskey, or yarn spun by his wife, and spent for nails, salt, and luxuries like pewter plates. For the most part they lived by a kind of quasi barter. The merchants in the little towns would sell to the farmers on credit and eventually be paid off in cider or cordwood, which they could sell elsewhere.

But although bookkeeping barter was the basic method of commerce, people still had a need for some cash. There were taxes, which could sometimes, but not always, be worked off on the roads or paid in produce. The local shopkeeper at times had to pay cash for certain items, which in turn meant that he had to get at least some cash from his debtors.

It is obvious, then, that the disappearance of hard currency from the American states was bound to cause problems. The British manufacturers leaned on the American importers for payment, and they in turn leaned on the local shopkeepers, who leaned on the local farmers. But too frequently the farmers had no money. The storekeepers then went to court and sent sheriffs out to attach a farmer's plow or horse or even his farm; and if that was not enough, the courts might actually put the farmer in jail. From 1784 to 1786 in Hampshire County, Massachusetts, nearly a third of the males over sixteen were involved in debt cases. The figure was typical for the whole country. Sheriffs' auctions were commonplace. Here you would see for sale your neighbor's ox, your cousin's plow, your brother's barrels of cider. Farms were foreclosed and hundreds of men were thrown into debtors' prisons—seventy-three men in Hampshire County between July 1784 and December 1786.

Those in trouble were frantic, and like trapped animals, they sprang at anything that looked like a way out. They began demanding that their state legislatures save them. They asked for stay laws, which would postpone all debt collection for some period of time, typically a year. They wanted more paper money, backed only by faith, but this currency tended to depreciate even as it came from the press. They wanted tender laws, which would require creditors to accept payment in this depreciated money.

Creditors fought bitterly against these laws, which seemed to them little more than legal robbery. In states where they were able to dominate the legislatures they prevented passage of the laws. The farmers, left without legal redress, turned to illegal ones. From 1784 on, in New Jersey, South Carolina, Pennsylvania, Virginia, and Maryland, bands of insurgent farmers gathered at courts and sheriffs' auctions and closed them down. In some places they set fire to courthouses, destroying records of debt cases.

In most states, however, the authorities, backed by the militias, were able to impose order. But in Massachusetts it was a different story. There the government was in the hands of the merchants and the upper class. A good many of the towns at the western end of the state were so disaffected or impoverished that they did not bother to send representatives to the state legislature in Boston. Why spend the money to send somebody when the "money men" would control things anyway?

To make matters worse, the powers in the state had decided to levy heavy taxes in order to pay off the huge debt the state had accumulated during the Revolution. Now the farmers of Massachusetts were faced not only with the cash shortage that was afflicting people everywhere, but also with new state taxes, which they could not possibly pay.

Shays' Rebellion contains elements of what some historians have interpreted as class warfare. As we shall see in more detail later, the United States was a "deferential" society, in which a small elite of the wealthy and wellborn expected to lead, and in fact were expected by the people to do so. To a considerable extent, the very people to whom the poor farmers owed money were also the judges who convicted them and the colonels who called out the militia to enforce the decrees.

Not all historians agree with this interpretation of Shays' Rebellion; but whatever the case, the decision of the men who ruled Massachusetts to tax heavily at a moment when currency was short suggests both an ignorance of the people they governed and an indifference to their welfare. Many people were suddenly trapped, and when they found that the legislature would do nothing for them, they began to take matters into their own hands. As bands of farmers had done elsewhere, they began closing the courts and stopping sheriffs' auctions. Very quickly what had been isolated incidents became a movement, and what had been bands of men became a small army of insurgents. Leadership, almost by chance, devolved upon Daniel Shays, a hero of the Revolution who had fought at both Bunker Hill and Stony Point.

The Massachusetts government trumpeted and fussed, and eventually put together an army of its own, under General Benjamin Lincoln, which in January 1787 marched across the state to deal with the rebels. Shays led his followers in an attack on an arsenal in Springfield, in hopes of capturing weapons, especially cannon, with which to face Lincoln. The arsenal, however, was guarded by nine hundred militia, people of the same sort as Shays' men —indeed, many of them had friends with Shays—and the question was whether they would fire on their own people. They did, and left three men dead and another dying in the snow before the Springfield arsenal. There was further skirmishing, but the back of Shays' Rebellion was broken at Springfield. Shays went into hiding in New York State, and a number of the rebels were imprisoned, although all were eventually pardoned.

The impact of Shays' Rebellion on American public opinion was substantial. Today we tend to sympathize with the rebels, who seemed to have been caught in a bind by forces they were barely able to comprehend. But in 1787 they were seen by most people, even plain farmers like themselves, as a mob of murderous wild men. The cause of the rebels was perhaps just; but resorting to arms was hardly the answer, people felt. And in fact, the rebels quickly learned the lesson, sent representatives to Boston, and shortly gained through legislation a good deal of what they had tried to get by force.

If many ordinary people were upset by Shays' Rebellion, however, the people of wealth, who supplied much of the leadership for the country, were simply horrified by it. In particular, it seemed to them bizarre that the national government had stood helplessly by, lacking the legal authority to put the rebellion down.

To men like Madison and Washington, Shays' Rebellion was an imperative. It hung like a shadow over the old Congress, and gave both impetus and urgency to the Constitutional Convention. It was the final, irrefutable piece of evidence that something had gone badly wrong. For some time these men had known that the deficiencies of the American government must be remedied. Shays' Rebellion made it clear to them that it must be done *now*.

Chapter Two

America in 1787

If the nation was, as it seemed, running so rapidly into the cascades, why did not the call for a constitutional convention come earlier? Why, for example, did it not follow immediately on the signing of the Treaty of Paris in 1783? Thousands of men who fought in Washington's patched-together army, at times hungry and barefoot, must surely have known that if their government could not even provide them with shoes in winter, something was wrong.

In order to see why change was so slow in coming we must take a look at what America and Americans were like in 1787. To begin with, the country was in many respects unique among nations. It was far larger than most other countries. Its populated area stretched twelve hundred miles from north to south along the Atlantic coast and ran two hundred miles inland. Between this thin coastal strip and the Mississippi was a vast region—more than twice the size of the settled area—which was for the most part unmapped and unexplored by white men. In contrast, England would very nearly fit into New York State, and powerful Holland was smaller than any of the six largest American states.

The American giant was seen by many, both at home and abroad, as a place too large to be effectively governed as a unit. Problems of transportation and communication were staggering. Although by 1787 large sections of the settled seaboard countryside had been cleared, by far the greatest part of the country was still forest. The few interstate roads that existed were frequently nothing more than mile upon mile of mud wallow, cut by hundreds of streams, creeks, and rivers, most of which were unbridged, so that they had to be forded, or crossed by ferry. Coaches tipped over on rough roads or were mired in mud. They were washed away in swollen spring streams; it was not uncommon for travelers to be drowned. On the best routes travelers might make fifty miles a day, but more often they were lucky to cover twenty, so that it could take weeks to go from Boston to Charleston by land. (By ship the trip could be made in perhaps ten days, but there you were at the mercy of the tides and the weather.)

Mail, carried by express riders, went faster: in good weather a letter from Boston might reach Philadelphia in four days. But people living in the rough frontier town of Pittsburgh would not receive a newspaper account of an event in Philadelphia for a month: it took many Americans weeks to hear about the crucial events of the time.

The huge size of the country meant that few Americans traveled very far very often. They might, as Americans always have done, pick up and move elsewhere—from New England west, from the countryside into the city. But only the idle wealthy, and merchants on business, could afford the time and money to visit big cities like New York or Boston. For most people a journey of more than fifty miles was a rare event.

Another consequence of the vastness of the United States and the difficulties of communication was that the country was really a collection of regions, which differed considerably in economics, religion, attitudes, customs, ethnic mix, and even in some cases language. Scholars have usually distinguished six main regions: northern New England, where by the late eighteenth century poor soil and too many people for the available land produced a dependency on trade and fishing (and emigration) for survival; New York and parts of southern New England, where the soil was better and prosperity was increased by trade moving down the Hudson River and the rivers emptying into Long Island Sound; the Delaware River area around the cosmopolitan and wealthy city of Philadelphia; the fertile and populous Chesapeake Bay area, with easy river access to markets, which encouraged large-scale commercial agriculture; southern Virginia and North Carolina, with an economy based on tobacco; and South Carolina and Georgia, still sparsely populated but growing wealthy on rice and indigo plantations worked by slave labor.

These regions seemed to one another almost like foreign countries. Diaries of American travelers of the time are filled with comments about the curious habits encountered in strange places like Connecticut or Pennsylvania. They would note with surprise that here the houses were made of stone instead of wood, there the farmers plowed with horses instead of oxen. The doctrinaire Calvinism of New England, which in 1787 still prohibited Sunday travel in some places, was very different from the easy-going Anglicanism which dominated the South. The Nantucket man who got his living chasing whales lived a completely different life from that of the Georgia hill farmer, with his half dozen slaves on a frontier plantation consisting of an isolated clutch of cabins and indigo fields. It is important for us to realize that even many of the relatively sophisticated and traveled men at the Constitutional Convention felt remarkable differences between themselves and men from other sections of the country.

Then, too, there were the burgeoning settlements across the Alleghenies, whose economy combined agriculture with a hunting-gathering life-style as old as humankind. Because travel back east over the mountains was so difficult, the westerners had set their faces toward the Mississippi, to which they were connected by the Ohio and other river systems. Their loyalty to the states they had left was tenuous at best: they had no intention of obeying laws promulgated in a capital many days' travel back through trackless forests scattered with often hostile Indians, and there was no way they could be made to obey those laws.

The United States of 1787 was by no means as diverse as the bewildering ethnic crazy quilt it is today. Over 75 percent of the white population was of British and Irish stock. Among the whites, 85 percent spoke English as a first language, and although there were some Catholics and a handful of Jews, the country was overwhelmingly Protestant. Furthermore, despite the ever-increasing westward movement, the bulk of the population was clustered along the seaboard, to such an extent that in 1790 the population center was twenty-five miles *east* of Baltimore.

Nonetheless, by comparison with any one European nation, the diversity was considerable. The dominant Protestant religion was splintered into a number of sects, and mixed through the population of British descent were thousands of people from dozens of ethnic groups—Germans, Scandinavians, Spanish, French. And of course, 20 percent of the population was black.

Moreover, the United States in 1787 was far more rigidly stratified than it is today. It was, to use the historians' term, a "deferential" society, in which the populace granted certain people offices and power by right of birth. In most communities there existed a small group of men who made the basic decisions for the village or town, and who were more or less automatically elected to legislatures, judgeships, and the like. This establishment included large landowners, like Washington and Jefferson, wealthy merchants and shippers, lawyers, and in the North, ministers and theologians. There was room for bright young men to rise into it, so that there were always a few lowborn men in public office. But as often as not, the people in control of the United States were born to their stations and went on to college to prepare themselves for their roles.

This situation was not resented nearly to the degree that it would be today. The top people saw themselves as the natural leaders of their communities, and the plain people, in general, agreed with them. The belief was still widely held, if not always expressed, that the "lower orders" were somehow different sorts of creatures from "the gentry." The ordinary people viewed their "betters" much the same way as many Americans today look on the celebrated writer or television anchorman, as somebody somehow larger than life, wiser, possessed of a special knowledge or even insight handed down from above.

Even those gentlemen, like James Madison and Charles Pinckney of South Carolina, who believed in the virtues of "the people" nonetheless felt that education, wealth, and inherent quality of mind and spirit gave them the right to lead. They may have found nobility in Farmer Jones, but they were hardly about to make Farmer Jones a senator. And Farmer Jones in his turn believed that the Madisons and Pinckneys *ought* to rule. Besides, Farmer Jones had quite enough on his hands with his family, his fields, his woodlots: he was willing to let the Madisons and Pinckneys worry about running things—unless the gentlemen went too far and taxed him into poverty, as they had in Massachusetts.

What was life like for Americans in 1787? To begin with, it was mainly rural. Cities were small. Only New York and Philadelphia had populations over 25,000 people. Not more than 10 percent of the population lived in anything that could be called a city or town. By the time of the Convention only 5.4 percent of the population lived in places of 2,500 people or more.

Ninety percent of white American men were farmers. Indeed, Jackson Turner Main has calculated that most American men in 1776 owned a farm and those who did not, worked on one. Main's breakdown is this: 40 percent made their livings working their own farms. Another 30 percent worked as laborers on farms owned by others. Another, smaller, group of men owned large commercial farms or plantations. Finally, the 10 percent or so of American men who were professionals, businessmen, or urban artisans—lawyers, importers, printers—frequently owned modest farms, on which they might keep a cow or some chickens and raise vegetables for the home table. And even those townsmen who did not own farms usually kept a cow or some chickens and raised vegetables in kitchen gardens.

There was nothing unique about this. In 1787 the typical human being anywhere was a farmer, whether he was working a rice paddy in China, or watching a flock of sheep in the Yorkshire dales of England.

But the way the ordinary American farmer lived and worked was a new phenomenon. Throughout human history people have almost always clustered in small groups or communities, where everybody was in constant contact with a relatively large number of people. This is true of the hunting-gathering tribes of ancient mankind, and of the agricultural peasant villages in which hundreds of millions of people live even today.

America was different. Land has always been for human beings one of the great sources of wealth and power, and if there was anything the United States had, it was land. The Europeans pushing into the Western Hemisphere in the sixteenth century and later saw the vast, sparsely populated continent as a gold mine, open to anybody with strength and nerve to exploit it.

The earliest settlers lived in villages, perhaps enclosed by a palisade; but all that land outside the walls was too alluring, and very rapidly Americans spread out over the countryside, in most instances settling on relatively large plots of land they had bought or claimed.

In 1787 a typical independent farmer and his family owned a farm of something between 90 and 160 acres, a piece of land about a third to a half mile on a side. The result was that these independent farm families did not live cheek by jowl with their neighbors, as most other human beings did, but were isolated to a degree unusual in human societies. There were, of course, little villages, like the celebrated New England towns, with their commons, but these usually consisted of a church, a store, a tavern, and perhaps a half dozen houses, in which lived the minister, the lawyer, the storekeeper. Most people came into the village only occasionally, to go to church, attend a political meeting, or do what little business they had to do.

This does not mean that people never saw anybody but their own immediate families. There was a great deal of shared labor; two farm families might help each other to harvest the corn or sow the wheat, and of course there were those famous barn-raisings, where whole communities would gather to help a neighbor erect a building. Then, too, independent farmers frequently traded with neighbors—a keg of cider for a pig, a day's work for a barrel of apples.

Nonetheless, these early American farm families were dependent on their own resources to a far greater degree than most human beings ever had been or are today. They might spend a day helping a neighbor shuck his corn, but on most days they were alone together. Or indeed, simply alone, with the father scything hay in one field, the mother making cheese in the kitchen, the twelve-year-old daughter hoeing the squashes in the kitchen garden, the ten-year-old son picking blueberries by the swamp, and Cousin Tom mending the fence around the corn field.

Families were large by present standards. The birthrate has been calculated by one scholar as "near the biological maximum." A family was also likely to have to take in a widowed aunt, an orphaned cousin or two. It might include an indentured servant or a hired man, and of course in the South there were slaves. Thirty-five percent of Americans lived in households of seven or more, two-thirds in households of five or more. These families were young, too. In Connecticut in 1774 32 percent of the white population was under the age of ten, more than half under twenty.

For better or worse, early Americans had to rely on their families for much of their human contact. And frequently it was for worse; escape from a tyrannical husband or pathological wife was extremely difficult. A single parent could not raise a family and run a farm; it took two adults, and as a consequence, separation of husband and wife other than by death was rare.

Given the size of the farms, it is not surprising that only small portions of them were actually cultivated. The farmer might put three to five acres into grain—usually corn, which could be ground into acceptable flour, and the stalks and leaves fed to the livestock. An acre or two would be ample for the family orchard. Another dozen or so acres would be meadow, where the farmer would graze a milch cow or two, the horse or ox used for plowing, possibly a few sheep, the inevitable swine, and usually some additional livestock raised for market. In the South, with its milder climate, the livestock were usually allowed to run wild in the woods year round, foraging for themselves. In the North, the animals had to be brought into a barn, or a shed attached to the rear of the house, and kept warm and fed. As a consequence most northern families kept no more livestock than they really needed, or could take to market in the fall.

The rest of the land was left in woodlot. It is not generally realized that obtaining wood, especially in New England, was as great a problem as getting food. A Connecticut farm family would burn twenty to forty cords of wood a year, which would of course have to be cut by hand and often hauled long distances by ox sledge over snow. As the population of New England grew, the people were cutting off the wood faster than it could grow back. By 1787 southern New England was virtually denuded, a vast open landscape of fields, with a precious clump of trees only here and there. The shortage of firewood was an important factor in driving New Englanders westward.

These farm families lived, most of them, in small wooden frame houses covered with shingles or clapboard. Typically, there would be a living room with a large stone or brick fireplace at one end and a door at the other. Above would be a loft, reached by a ladder, where the lesser members of the family slept on rope beds or straw mattresses, while the parents slept downstairs by the fire. Over time a prosperous farmer would add rooms to front, back, or sides as convenient, sometimes shifting the original doors and windows around, so that when one looks at the houses that remain today, it is frequently difficult to tell what the original layout was, or what changes were made.

The cooking was done in the large fireplace. Stew bubbled in pots hanging from arms swivelling out from the sides. Bread was baked in beehive ovens built against the chimney. Chunks of meat were roasted on spits in front of the fire, and apples, potatoes, and corn were roasted directly in the coals.

Furniture was simple and sparse. A family might own a trestle table with benches, at which they ate, worked, read, prayed. There would be two or three chairs, a sideboard or cabinet to hold their utensils, pegs in the walls for clothes, and in the more affluent homes, perhaps a clock, a mirror, a small shelf of books. Eating utensils were mainly wooden, but in 1787 many farm families were acquiring a few pewter plates and forks, and a small amount of glassware.

Once agriculture was well established, famine was virtually nonexistent in the United States and ordinary hunger was rare. According to Edwin J. Perkins, Americans in 1787 were eating better—and usually far better—than the *majority* of human beings today. They ate the most extraordinary amount of meat. In 1784 one farm family of four in Whatley, Massachusetts, ate 500 pounds of pork and 200 pounds of beef, which comes out to roughly a half pound of meat a day, per person. And this was typical, not exceptional. The rich ate even more. President Washington's steward, Samuel Fraunces, usually served fish, fowl, and a roast to the president and his guests at every dinner, and at a good tavern there might be two roasts or two kinds of fowl at a meal.

One English visitor of 1806 reported that in a rough Kentucky cabin, "The dinner consisted of a large piece of salt bacon, a dish of hominy and a tureen of squirrel broth. I dined entirely on the last dish, which I found incomparably good, and the meat equal to the most delicate chicken." Henry Adams, in his classic study of American life in 1800, says, "Salt pork three times a day was regarded as an essential part of the American diet." Pork, after all, practically raised itself and was very easy to butcher and salt. To this would be added whatever fruits and vegetables were in season, and such game as could be taken locally from the forest, river, or sea: in New England, salt cod, lobster, clams; in New York, oysters and the fish that flowed into the port; in the South, partridge; in the frontier settlements, venison, squirrel, even bear. Undoubtedly because of this protein-rich diet, American men of 1787 were, according to army records, about as tall as they are today—an average of five feet eight, which was two inches taller than the average for British recruits.

If their diets were rich in protein, they were rich in alcohol, too. The amount drunk by Europeans in the eighteenth century is astonishing, and Americans were their match. A study by Mark Lender and James Martin says:

> One may safely assume . . . that abstemious colonials were few and far between. Counting the mealtime beer or cider at home and the convivial drafts at the tavern or at the funeral of a relative or neighbor, all this drinking added up. . . . While precise consumption figures are lacking, informed estimates suggest that by the 1790's an average American over fifteen years old drank just under six gallons of absolute alcohol each year. . . . The comparable modern average is less than 2.9 gallons per capita.

We must realize that the temperance movement, which culminated in the Prohibition Amendment of 1919, was a nineteenth-century development. In the eighteenth century it was generally believed that people *needed* to take in a certain amount of "spirits" every day for strength and energy: Washington, in planning one long forced march, ordered extra rations of rum for the troops as a matter of course. What is surprising is that there was not more alcoholism: it is the contention of Lender and Martin, however, that there was strong social pressure on people to avoid too-flagrant drunkeness.

Liquor was considered a blessing, not a curse. And so, contrary to what is widely believed, was sex. These early Americans were practical and unromantic in their personal lives. The choice of eligible marriage partners in a farm community of fifty or a hundred people was very limited, and so far as a second marriage went, the choice might be down to one. They were, moreover, a far more openly sexual people than we are likely to think. Sexual history is still being written, but the generally held view that all times before our own were "puritanical" is certainly not correct. In 1787 sex during the engagement was customary in some places: in one New England county, supposed to be typical, half the brides were pregnant on their wedding day during the Revolutionary era. Washington, as we shall see, was capable of writing off-color jokes; the shy

James Madison wrote pornographic verse as a college boy; and Ben Franklin was the author of a famous ribald satire, "Advice to a Young Man on the Choice of a Mistress."

In the cities, "One ever old and ever new problem was that of prostitution. One citizen of Boston declared that the increase was 'incredible' and unless stopped in the 'embryo' would have pernicious consequences." In sum, although the record is thin, it suggests that heterosexual behavior in 1787 was not much different from what it is today.

For these American farmers entertainment was infrequent and self-created. In some homes they might sing a little or dance a little for recreation. They might read aloud to each other from the Bible, or *A Pilgrim's Progress,* but other books were scarce. Mostly they were too tired in the evening for fun, and besides, candles were valuable. So they would eat, drink, perhaps pray a little, and go to bed. Only on Sundays, when they traveled into the village to go to church, would there be much variety.

Yet despite the grinding toil and the lack of amenities, Americans were fortunate people. Perkins says flatly, "The material standard of living enjoyed by the typical white family unit in the thirteen mainland English colonies was almost certainly the highest in the world by the 1770s." Outside of the cities the population was spread sufficiently thin so that Americans were not nearly as subject to epidemics, or even ordinary communicable diseases, as people in the Old World were. The air was pure; water could be drunk directly from streams and lakes. Life expectancy at birth was about thirty-five, but if you reached sixty, the odds were that you would live to seventy-five. In fact, life expectancy for a sixty-year-old man was *higher* in 1787 than it was in 1970. Our first six presidents lived to an average age of eighty, and both Washington's mother and Madison's lived into their nineties.

This was how the majority of people lived, but there were large minorities living in other, often far more unpleasant ways. For one thing, there were substantial numbers of people attached to large commercial farms and plantations as overseers, indentured servants, ordinary hired labor, or craftsmen: a large plantation would have its own carpenters, smiths, seamstresses, and the like. Another small but politically important minority lived in towns and cities, working in professions, trades, crafts, and small factories. Also in the cities was a floating population of toughs, sailors, criminals, prostitutes, and day laborers, who at times made the streets dangerous.

And finally, over 600,000 Americans, roughly 20 percent of the total, were black, most of them slaves. Ninety percent of them lived in the South, almost all of them on plantations, large or small. Most of the slaves lived in family units, although the farther south, the greater the likelihood that families would be broken up. They were treated harshly, by and large, but they were not starved: George Washington fed his slaves about 2,800 calories a day, not much less than Continental soldiers got. They were worth taking care of, for in the South they constituted 57 percent of the wealth. There were also a fair number of black freedmen scattered through the northern states, but these could not command the wages of white laborers.

What did these early Americans think and feel? They already had an inordinate sense of pride in being American. After all, they had just beaten the mightiest army on earth. They thought of themselves as virtuous, plain-living people, in contrast with the corrupt and decadent societies of Europe, where everything, they believed, was frivolity, lechery, and debauchery.

Russel Blane Nye, in a study of early American attitudes, says, "They were uniformly convinced that the United States was on the rising curve of a cycle, that its upward path was divinely ordained to be permanent, and that the entire past of the human race was only preparation for the appearance of American society. As Thomas Paine wrote in *Common Sense,* 'The birthday of the new world is at hand.' "

"Plainness" was at the heart of the American ideal. It was epitomized by Benjamin Franklin, who, in the midst of the extravagant formalities of the London and Paris societies in which he lived for twenty-five years, was admired for the simplicity, admittedly cultivated, of his dress and manner. Americans in 1787 believed that they were better than people elsewhere, and they tried to practice what they preached, and live as hardworking, God-fearing, plainspoken people.

This general picture of Americans as healthy, prosperous, hardworking, God-fearing people must be tempered by the usual exceptions. Some of them, as Shays' Rebellion makes clear, were in financial difficulties. Some were scoundrels and lunatics. But in a broad sense the picture is correct. Americans worked hard because they had to, they feared God because they were raised to do so, and they were prosperous because they were living on a continent whose resources they had hardly begun to touch.

The typical American lived on a relatively self-sufficient farm. He was independent to a degree that would have astonished a medieval peasant as much as a modern factory worker. American farmers were not constantly looking over their shoulders at village elders, headmen, overseers, the lord's reeves, shop foremen, office managers. Much of the time they perceived nobody over them but God. They could not always turn to authorities, wisemen, experts, for solutions to problems. They had to figure out a great many things for themselves, whether it was which field would do best for corn, or why God had taken a beloved child. And they could not always turn to their neighbors in times of disaster, for often their neighbors were few and far between.

The psychological effect of this way of living is hard to measure, but it must certainly have given Americans a strong feeling of self-worth and a powerful sense of their own freedom. We remember that many of them had willingly made sacrifices in order to get the British off their backs, and thousands of them had risked their lives in the actual fighting of a war that was expressly for "liberty." Their freedom mattered deeply to them; they were suspicious of authority, and quick to resent a strong hand. And how, then, were they likely to take the proposal of a new and much stronger national government, a government that might reach into their lives everywhere?

RENNER LEARNING RESOURCE CENTER
ELGIN COMMUNITY COLLEGE
ELGIN, ILLINOIS 60120

Chapter Three

The Mind of James Madison

But a few Americans recognized that unless the national government was strengthened, the factionalism, the sectional, economic, and class animosities that beset the union would soon enough have caused it to fly apart, with the pieces spinning into new orbits, with bloodshed inevitable and the country wide open to conquest. The nationalists saw this, and many of them were attempting to do something about it. But the one who saw best what to do was James Madison.

Madison has been called "the Father of the Constitution," a designation most historians would accept. The title has to be modified: in the end, the Convention fought off too many of Madison's basic ideas for him to be called its father. Indeed, he was, as the editors of his papers say, "profoundly disappointed with the results of the Convention." He wrote Jefferson as the Constitution went off to the states for ratification that the document would "neither effectually answer its national object nor prevent the local mischiefs which everywhere excite disgusts against state governments." Nonetheless, he gave to the Convention, at the outset, a philosophy that set the tenor of the meeting. Who James Madison was—how he came to feel and think the things he did —is therefore of the greatest significance.

He was born in Orange County, Virginia on March 16, 1751, into the Southern squirarchy. The first American Madison had acquired some six hundred acres in Virginia a century before James was born, and through hard work and shrewd management, subsequent generations had built up the estate to thousands of acres worked by numerous slaves. James Madison never had to work for a living; for a good portion of his life his father managed the estates, leaving James free for nation-building.

He grew up to be short, about five feet six, and slight. Someone once described him as "no bigger than a half a piece of soap." When we look at the miniature painted by Charles Willson Peale we see a sensitive face with large pale blue eyes, dark brown hair, and a small, delicate mouth. He was bookish from the first. Instead of spending his youth riding, hunting, and drinking, as his peers did, he sat in his father's rather limited library, reading.

Eventually Madison went to Princeton, then called the College of New Jersey. The philosophy that Madison was taught there combined theories of "natural rights," coming from such British thinkers as John Locke and David Hume, with a more recent Scottish school of "common sense" philosophy, which emphasized "natural" or instinctive ideas, which could be understood and even intuited by any man. Both philosophies placed a good deal of authority in the individual, as opposed to monarchs and oligarchies. The College of New Jersey, by the time Madison went there, was a seedbed of the revolutionary spirit; John Witherspoon, its president, would be a signer of the Declaration of Independence. Madison's college experience must certainly have reinforced in his mind two points: that human problems could be solved through the application of reason; and that governments should be the instruments of the governed.

Madison completed the three-year course at Princeton in two years, by curtailing his sleep and studying hard. He then stayed on for another year to study theology. Although shy, he appears to have been popular with his fellow students.

Shortly before his graduation, at which he was expected to make a speech, Madison collapsed from "over-study." He recovered easily enough and eventually was called home by his father to take over the education of his younger siblings. Once again he collapsed, this time enduring a series of attacks. These have never been accurately diagnosed, but Madison said later that they were "somewhat resembling epilepsy and suspending the intellectual functions." Thereafter Madison tended to think of himself as sickly, so much so that he felt unable to fight during the Revolution, although he did serve in the army briefly as a provisioner.

In truth, James Madison was exceedingly healthy. In a day when few diseases could be cured and most had to be allowed to run their course, Madison was rarely sick; he spent his long life in one high-pressure job after another—member of the Virginia government, congressman, secretary of state, president—and in office and out was one of the country's major politicians right to his death at eighty-five. It is the opinion of Irving Brant, Madison's most thorough biographer, that these strange attacks were "epileptoid hysteria"—that is to say, an emotional illness with symptoms resembling epilepsy.

Whatever problems Madison was suffering from, they did not prevent him from throwing himself into the great events washing over the country in the decade of the 1770s. There were the British attempts to tax the colonists, embargoes on British goods thrown up in response, the Boston massacre, in which British troops fired on the citizenry, and calls for action of one kind or another. Madison's temperament and training impelled him to join the patriot camp. When the Declaration of Independence made it necessary for Virginians to form their own government, he was one of the men elected to do the job. He never looked back: from that moment on he would spend the rest of his life in politics.

When we look at Madison's character we are struck at once by its contradictions. He was, certainly, shy. In the early stages of his political career he spoke in such a low voice that he could hardly be heard. Once, when he was over thirty and was staying at an inn in Williamsburg, somebody reached in through a window and stole his hat. Madison was so embarrassed at the idea of appearing in the streets without a hat that he stayed inside for two days, until he could buy one from a snuff dealer who happened by. One lady of his own social group observed that he was "a gloomy, stiff creature, they say he is clever in Congress, but out of it he has nothing engaging or even bearable in his manners—the most unsociable creature in existence." William Pierce, a delegate to the Convention who has left us little character sketches of the men there, described him as "a gentleman of great modesty—with a remarkable sweet temper," who was "easy and unreserved among his acquaintance. . . ."

Given this shyness, it is not surprising that he had problems with women, and apparently they began early. There is no solid evidence of a woman in his life until he was over thirty, when he fell in love with a fifteen-year-old named Kitty Floyd, the daughter of a congressman. Apparently the father, realizing that Madison would make an impressive son-in-law, encouraged Kitty to accept him, and Madison joyously announced to his friends that he was to be engaged. Thomas Jefferson, with whom he had formed a political partnership that was to lead to a deep, lifetime friendship, wrote to him, "I rejoice at the information that Miss K. and yourself concur in sentiments." However, they did not concur in sentiments. Within weeks Kitty broke off the engagement, leaving Madison both humiliated and heartbroken. Fifty years later, in going over his papers before his death, he inked out references to Kitty in his letters so heavily that they cannot be read. There is no record of another woman in his life until he married Dolley Payne Todd in 1794.

His shyness with women suggests a fear of rejection, which some of Madison's friends seem to have recognized. Elizabeth Trist, a woman who became a friend and knew him well, said that he was too sensitive to be governor of Virginia (a job he turned down). If someone attacked him in the press, she said, it would "injure his feelings and injure his health, take my word." The word his contemporaries used for him was "modest"—too modest to run for governor, too modest to speak forcefully in public, too modest to go out without his hat on.

Yet—and here is one of the contradictions in his character—James Madison was one of the main participants in America's most famous presidential love story. Dolley Madison was seventeen years younger than he, born to a good Quaker family with connections to Patrick Henry and Martha Washington. She grew up to be a charming, outgoing woman with a simple, even innocent, manner that captivated both men and women. She lost her first husband in a yellow fever epidemic that struck Philadelphia in 1793. Madison met her not long afterward, fell in love, and rushed her into a marriage she had considerable doubt about. But very quickly she grew to love him deeply, and their romance lasted the rest of their lives. They were infrequently apart, so there are few letters between them, but once, when Madison was Jefferson's secretary of state, illness kept Dolley in Philadelphia. She wrote him every day, and he wrote back nearly as frequently. She writes, "A few hours only have passed since you left me, my beloved, and I find nothing can relieve the oppression of my mind but speaking to you in this the only way. . . ." And again, "Adieu my beloved, our hearts understand each other." He is more formal: "Let me know that I shall soon have you with me, which is most anxiously to be desired. . . ." They sound like a pair of twenty-year-old lovers: she was thirty-six and he was a middle-aged intellectual and secretary of state.

The shyness so often evident in his personal relations was contradicted by a startling boldness in thought. In the quiet of his study, speaking with the silent voice of his pen to the passive audience of a piece of paper, he could be extraordinarily bold. The key to the paradox was a deep-seated fear of power that seems to have undergirt his character. He felt uncomfortable dominating and was almost inaudible when he spoke in public. But he was also afraid of domination by others, and when he felt the threat of power falling over him, he fought with vigor. He fought in the Virginia Assembly against what he conceived of as religious tyranny; he fought in his state against legislative dominance by debtor farmers eager for stay laws and paper money.

And as we shall see, throughout the Constitutional Convention he was more interested in checking power—in the states, in branches of the national government, in the church, in factions around the country—than he was in infusing the central government with energy and vigor.

This, then, was the approach he would bring to constitution-making. And he was determined that some constitution-making be done. He had come into maturity, like most other Americans, a patriot of his own state. However, as historian Lance Banning has demonstrated, in his years in the Virginia Assembly after 1783 he had become disgusted with the efforts of debtor farmers to push through paper money and scores of other ill-conceived bills, which were often repealed almost as soon as they were passed. By 1784 or 1785 he had become a member of the nationalist faction, bent on strengthening the central government.

As news of Shays' Rebellion spread through the states, James Madison concentrated his attention on politics. First he made a systematic study of the history of governments, especially republics, to see why they had worked—or more important, why they had not. He then set about writing a paper, mainly to organize his thoughts, describing what he took to be the cause of the problems with the American government. This paper was called "Vices of the Political System of the United States," and has become famous among historians as "Madison's Vices," a designation incongruous for a man who had so few of them. His analysis was astute, and the "Vices" is considered by historians to be one of the key documents in the making of the American Constitution. We shall see, in a bit, what it contained.

But James Madison was a working politician as well as an intellectual. It was well enough to analyze the problems; but the real trick was to get something done about them. And so, when he saw his chance, he seized it, expediting and directing the chain of events that led to the Constitutional Convention.

Chapter Four

The Unbelievable George Washington

The calling of the Constitutional Convention was a two-stage process, carefully maneuvered by a small group of nationalists led by James Madison, Alexander Hamilton, George Washington, and a handful of others. The first stage began with an effort to ease the movement of goods and thus facilitate commerce among the states. In the 1780s the transportation of goods in the United States was almost entirely by water. A horseman, or a small coach holding three or four people, might move over land, but the thousands of hogsheads of tobacco, barrels of rice, kegs of whiskey, and other products that constituted the commerce of the nation could only go by water. It was obvious, therefore, that if the great river systems that webbed the United States could be linked by canals, the population would spread rapidly along arteries of water, and commerce would grow dramatically.

One man who was eager to do something was George Washington. After the war, Washington had officially retired from public life, but it was deep in his nature always to involve himself in far-reaching schemes. He was particularly interested in—indeed obsessed with—a plan to build a canal through the Allegheny Mountains to connect the Ohio River system with the Potomac, which flowed into the sea. He was determined that his country should reach for the greatness he felt was its destiny; he also owned huge chunks of land in the Ohio River valley, and his farm, Mount Vernon, was on the Potomac. Such a canal might make him a fortune. He personally investigated rivers and streams that might prove useful, racing alone through rapids in a canoe, and he bored visitors to Mount Vernon with endless conversations about canals.

However, Maryland, like Virginia, bordered on the Potomac and would have to be brought into the scheme. In March 1785, commissioners from both states met at Alexandria, a new town not far from Mount Vernon, to discuss various matters concerning the Potomac. Washington was not one of the commissioners, but so keen was he on the scheme that eventually he invited them to meet at Mount Vernon, where they would be more comfortable than in a rough tavern in Alexandria. At the meeting, which became known as the Mount Vernon Conference, tolls and fishing rights were discussed, and the commissioners went home to report to their legislatures.

As it happened, the head of the Virginia Assembly's committee to deal with the commissioners' report was James Madison. In the course of the debate on the Potomac matter, the suggestion was made that there ought to be annual conferences to deal with commercial problems *in general.* Madison, whose mind raced up steps two at a time, saw in this idea something that might prove exceedingly useful to the nationalist cause. After discussing it with Washington, he went back to the Virginia Assembly and proposed that it urge Congress to take over the power of regulating American commerce. The Assembly, like most state legislatures, was jealous of its power; but eventually it approved a resolution calling for a convention of the states to make recommendations to Congress on commercial matters. "This," writes Irving Brant, "was the precipitating step toward the drafting of the Constitution."

The second stage in the process that brought about the calling of the Constitutional Convention was this conference, scheduled for the following fall, September 1786, to be held in Annapolis, the capital of Maryland. The subject would be American commerce in general, and invitations would be issued to all states. There was, however, no certainty that all the states—or any of them —would send delegates, or that whatever delegates turned up would agree on anything. Madison wrote, "Though my wishes are in favor of such an event, yet I despair so much of its accomplishment at the present crisis that I do not extend my views beyond a commercial reform."

Madison went to the conference, but Washington did not, apparently because it was felt that he should not gamble his invaluable prestige on a meeting that stood a good chance of achieving nothing. When Madison reached Annapolis on September 4, only two other delegates were present. A few others, including Alexander Hamilton of New York, arrived soon after, but in the end only Virginia, Delaware, and New Jersey delegations had quorums, and seven states were not represented at all.

Why were the states so reluctant to attend the meeting? The reasons were various, but underlying all was the pervasive fear of losing control of their own affairs. Who knew what the Annapolis Conference might agree to? It was safer not to attend.

As a result, the men who did go to Annapolis were nationalists. They had nothing to do but talk, and that, for three days, was what they did. Very little is known about the inner workings of the Annapolis Conference, because at the time, the delegates felt the necessity for keeping quiet. It is clear enough, however, that they decided to use the conference as a way to promote the nationalist cause. A steering committee was formed. As it happened, New Jersey had given its delegates authority to consider not only commercial matters but "other important matters." Broadus Mitchell, one of Alexander Hamilton's leading biographers, says, "Abraham Clark of Newark called attention to his wide option and it was determined to seize the opportunity to recommend to the states and to Congress the calling of a convention to revise the Articles of Confederation." This was not a new idea; nationalists had been discussing it among themselves since the moment the Articles had been ratified in 1781. Some historians suspect that the nationalist faction wanted the Annapolis Conference to fail so they could call for a meeting with a larger mandate. Making an opportunity out of the failure, the nationalist majority drew up an address to the states, urging them to choose delegates to

> meet at Philadelphia on the second Monday in May next, to take into consideration the situation of the United States, to devise such further provisions as shall appear to them necessary to render the constitution of the Federal Government adequate to the exigencies of the Union.

It was obvious that the states might not respond to this call for a new conference any better than they had to the call for the Annapolis Conference. But Annapolis had been a kind of caucus for the nationalists. It inspired them and gave them conhesion and a chance to work out strategy. They were young, vigorous, prestigious men who understood politics, and over the winter of 1786–1787, they constituted a powerful pressure group. They corresponded with each other, they proselytized for their cause among the important men they knew, they made speeches in the public bodies they belonged to.

Events were working for them. The economy, while basically sound, had its weak places, as farmers in debtors' prisons could testify. It was clear to more and more people that the old Congress was becoming increasingly impotent. And finally, there was Shays' Rebellion.

Nonetheless, through that winter it was far from certain that a significant number of the states would send delegations to Philadelphia. Many state legislatures were slow to vote on the issue. But Virginia was not: in October it became the first state to approve sending delegates to Philadelphia, and on December 4 its government named them. The first name on the list was George Washington.

George Washington is one of the great conundrums of American history. Loved almost to the point of veneration by the people who knew him—and those who knew him best loved him most—he has come to be seen by succeeding generations as the marble hero, as impenetrable and unlovable as the rock that famous statue in the Capitol Rotunda was cut from. As early as 1850 Ralph Waldo Emerson said about him, "Every hero becomes a bore at last." And what a bore he is! From a hundred thousand schoolhouse walls he stares blankly down on us, that dead face cut by a mouth thin and straight as a ruler. We see him as the mealy-mouthed little boy saying, "I cannot tell a lie, Pa; you know I cannot tell a lie. I did cut it with my little hatchet." We see him as the stern-visaged warrior in the bow of that rowboat crossing the Delaware, the very model of pomposity, as if he were propelling the craft through the ice floes himself by sheer willpower. Who could love a man like that?

But in life he was loved—envied by a few, hated by even fewer, but loved by most. As a boy he was favored by his mother over her other children. As a youth he was welcomed into rich and important families. As a young man barely out of his teens he was given critically important responsibilities by the Virginia government. When he was an adult people flocked to him, asking him to join in this or that project, to advise them, to act as executor of their wills —he was eventually managing the estates of so many deceased acquaintances that he said he was "deprived of every kind of enjoyment." And as a mature man he was begged by the most important people in the United States, most of whom knew him personally, to see to the fate of his country.

Nor did this veneration spring from respect for grave and noble qualities: George Washington was personally *liked*. One major biographer, James Thomas Flexner, drew a picture of him as a young country squire:

> Washington had quantities of business to shuttle him around his part of Virginia, and everywhere he rode he was entertained. In the countryside, he stayed in private houses; in town, he spent his evenings with jolly fellows at taverns where they "clubbed"—i.e., shared—the bill. He was always welcome; his popularity was great.

The extent to which Washington was genuinely loved, rather than merely respected or admired, is perhaps best illustrated by an incident usually referred to as the Newburgh Conspiracy, which occurred at the end of the Revolution. The war was winding down, and Congress was eager to send the troops home. However, the troops had not been paid, and in some instances were owed more than a year's salary. The idea was floated that they should march on Congress and demand their pay at bayonet point. Some even hoped that Washington could be persuaded to lead the revolt.

Washington stood resolute against the idea. He saw clearly that once the army, however just its cause, decided to impose its will on the civil government, democracy would slide into tyranny, and everything they had fought for would be lost. But despite him, the movement grew, and eventually a group of officers in his encampment called a meeting, with the intention of organizing a march on Congress.

Washington, it was understood, would stay away from the meeting. But just as it began, he came in through a back door. His officers were not happy to see him, and shuffled uneasily. He took the podium and began to talk, explaining to them why they should not, must not, proceed. He finished his talk. The officers stood cold and unresponsive, unmoved by his plea. "The familiar faces looking up at him were uneasy, perplexed, sullen." So he announced that he would read them a letter from a congressman, explaining how Congress was attempting to solve the problem of their pay. He took a letter from his pocket, James Flexner writes:

> And then suddenly every heart missed a beat. Something was the matter with His Excellency. He seemed unable to read the paper. He paused in bewilderment. He fumbled in his waistcoat pocket. And then he pulled out something that only his intimates had seen him wear. With infinite sweetness and melancholy, he explained, "Gentlemen, you will permit me to put on my spectacles, for I have not only grown gray but almost blind in the service of my country."

Many of the officers began openly to weep. One man who was present reported, "There was something so natural, so unaffected, in his appeal, as rendered it superior to the most studied oratory; it forced its way to the heart, and you might see sensibility moisten every eye." In that fraction of a minute Washington had broken the revolt, simply because those tough, blooded veterans loved him too much to go on with it.

The people around George Washington knew him as a man brimming with

energy, life, good spirits. One of the best horsemen in America, he was ex-
hilarated by racing at top speed through fields and over fences. He liked to
gamble, to play cards, to bet on horse races and cockfights, to dance. In one
year, when he was in his thirties, he hunted foxes forty-nine times and went
to church fifteen. He would dance for three hours at a stretch, and he loved
nothing better than to sit over dinner with old friends and new acquaintances,
drinking Madeira, cracking walnuts, telling stories, and joking. He liked fancy
clothes and was always sending to London for the latest in elegant fashion.
Even when he was in middle age his restless energy was astonishing. In 1783,
when he was over fifty and the war was over, his idea of a change of pace, after
eight terrible years of strain and exertion, was to ride for 750 miles through
the New York wilderness to scout out land for speculation.

He was, as hard as it may be to believe, capable of romantic feelings. As an
adolescent he fell in love with Sally Fairfax, the wife of a man who was both
his neighbor and close friend, and he remained platonically in love with her
all his life.

He liked an off-color joke. In middle age he wrote of one of his old aides,
Joseph Ward, who was marrying a much younger woman, that from military
experience Ward should "have learnt how to distinguish between false alarms
and a serious movement" and "like a prudent general" have "reviewed his
strength, his arms, and ammunition before he got involved in the action."
Otherwise, "let me advise him to make the first onset upon his fair del Toboso,
with vigor, that the impression may be deep, if it cannot be lasting."

He was, to be sure, reserved, aloof perhaps, which tended to make him
somewhat formal in his manner. But he was extraordinarily gregarious and
was almost always in the company of people. When he found himself alone,
he put on his hat and went in search of somebody to dine with. His diary
records that virtually every day he took tea with so-and-so, dined with such-
and-such, rode out with these and those. He kept a permanent open house at
Mount Vernon, feeding not merely distinguished visitors but any stray who
turned up at mealtime; he once remarked that he had not dined alone with his
wife for twenty years. When confronted with problems or decisions he did not
retire to his room to study the matter in books, as James Madison might do,
but gathered around him assistants, advisers, experts, and talked his way to
a solution. Despite the reserve in his makeup, George Washington all of his
life was intensely involved with people.

The details of Washington's life are well known. He was born in 1732. His
father's family had been in Virginia for three generations, and had risen into

the lower ranks of the aristocracy. They were comfortable, owned slaves and land, became lawyers and businessmen. His mother's family was newer to Virginia, but they too were people of substance. His father had been married before, and had children by his first wife who were considerably older than George. His own mother had children after him, so that he grew up sandwiched between older and younger siblings.

His mother, Mary Washington, was a peculiar woman. She was strong-minded and domineering and bullied people until she got her way. Throughout her life—and she lived until Washington was in his second term as president and himself fatigued with age—she nagged him. A single theme ran through their relationship—the shrill cry of neglect. Incredibly, while the son was leading his country in the fight for independence, was presiding over one of the most important conclaves in modern history, was struggling to keep the young nation from falling apart, she did nothing but demand to know why he was neglecting her so.

We see Washington's father less clearly. He seems to have been competent enough at business, but nothing more. Significantly, there is extraordinarily little in Washington's own voluminous writings about his father. There is instead a blank, a show of neither hostility nor affection.

When he was eleven his father died. His older half-brothers inherited the major portion of the estate, and George was left with a small plantation worked by ten slaves. This turned him into that slightly comic figure, the poor relative dependent on favors from above. It also turned him into the man of the house: his mother made George a sort of "captain" of the younger children.

Denied his patrimony, he found himself too short of cash to be educated in England, as his half-brothers had been. But he got what scrappy education he could—reading, writing, and arithmetic, probably up to the level of plane geometry.

He grew to be over six feet tall and was relatively slim, but with oversized hands and feet. His appearance was striking, especially when he was dashing about on horseback, as he so loved to do. He chose to become a surveyor, a natural route to success in a time when land was the basis of wealth. Surveyors knew better than most what land was worth and frequently were able to pyramid a small parcel into substantial holdings. At sixteen Washington got a job surveying in the Shenandoah Valley just over the Blue Ridge Mountains. Other jobs followed, and by nineteen he had managed to put together some real-estate holdings.

Then, in 1753, the French began building forts in the Mississippi–Ohio River triangle, which the English considered their own. The British government wanted somebody to investigate, and Washington was chosen because of his familiarity with the wilderness. The situation swiftly escalated into the French and Indian War. By a fluke Washington found himself with a command. His generalship was characterized more by impetuosity than by good sense, and he was driven back. But he had behaved with great personal bravery, and when the war was over, he was something of a hero, not merely in Virginia but around the American colonies and even, in a small way, in London.

He retired from the army, married a widow, Martha Custis, who brought him the estate he lacked, and took over his deceased brother Lawrence's old home, Mount Vernon. For the next seventeen years he was a gentleman farmer, experimenting with crops and breeding methods, adding to his holdings, improving his land, increasing the size of his house. He enjoyed all of this activity intensely. He liked nothing better than to saddle up at daybreak and ride through his plantations, ordering fruit trees put in here, a deer park built here. He involved himself with grandiose schemes such as the canal to connect the Ohio River with the Potomac. He was elected to the colonial legislature and carried on an enormous correspondence with people throughout the colonies and England. By the time he was forty he was a figure of consequence in Virginia, one of the state's leading men. It was not surprising, then, that in 1774, when representatives from the American colonies met to work out a coordinated response to what they were beginning to see as British tyranny, Washington was part of the Virginia delegation to the First Continental Congress.

Within a year the colonies were in open revolt, and British troops were occupying Boston. It was clear that Massachusetts could not be expected to carry the battle alone. A second continental congress was called for May 1775, in Philadelphia. George Washington was again a delegate from Virginia, and he arrived wearing his old army uniform. A decision was taken to fight. Who would lead the army? The Massachusetts men knew that it would be easier to draw the other states in if the Commander was not a Massachusetts general. Washington was one of the very few veterans of the French and Indian War young enough for the job. He impressed the other delegates as a man who was commanding, yet oddly diffident, cordial but serious. And he was, after all, wearing an army uniform. They gave him the job.

The Revolution lasted far longer than anybody would have thought possible.

The Americans suffered defeat after defeat. At first too willing to give battle, Washington quickly learned the basic lesson, which was to fight a defensive war, preserving his troops and fighting only when chances of success were good. The British never did learn the lesson, and with the defeat of Cornwallis at Yorktown in 1781, the war was suddenly over.

It was clear to the American people that Washington had worked a miracle —only he could have held his shaky army together in the face of incredible obstacles—and they offered to make him president or king, anything he wanted. Instead, refusing to take any salary, he went home, saying he had retired from public life for good, and this act of abnegation convinced the few remaining doubters that George Washington was a saint. But of course, saint he was not. What, then, was he really like?

He was blessed from birth not only with great size but with incredible strength and stamina. During his trip into the wilderness to investigate the French activity there, he underwent adventures few people could have survived. Once, when he was thrown from a raft into a river filled with ice, he swam to a little island in the middle of the river, built a fire to dry out, and slept on the frozen ground.

He was absolutely fearless and seems to have believed that he had a magical immunity to bullets. On one occasion one detachment of his troops came upon another in the dark of the woods, and shooting broke out. Washington dashed between the two lines of fire, slapping muskets up with his sword and crying for the men to desist. Fourteen of his men were killed, twenty-six wounded; Washington was untouched.

But his bravery hid a soft heart. His compassion was deep and genuine. At various points during his military career he found himself forced, for the sake of discipline, to have soldiers lashed, and on one occasion he hanged two persistent deserters from gallows forty feet high, as an example to the troops. But he frequently pardoned men other officers would have let die.

But despite his deep compassion, there was a prickly side to his nature. His position as a poor relative in youth may have had the effect of making him not merely ambitious but stridently resentful of anything he could consider a slight. Among men of Washington's social class, in America as well as in Europe, it was considered not merely correct but a matter of honor to be exquisitely precise about symbols of rank. Duels were still fought over minor insults. But Washington carried it farther than most. During the French and Indian War he chafed at being put under orders of British officers, and he once rode from the frontier to Boston to protest such a situation. His temper was always quick. If he believed he had been treated unjustly, considered his honor threatened, or felt betrayed, as he frequently did, he would burst into a rage and bellow like a bull.

According to his great biographer Douglas Southall Freeman, Washington "failed to acquire precisely the right attitude toward his superior officers . . ." and at times, "went beyond the bounds of what military etiquette of the times allowed a subordinate."

Yet he was a natural leader right from the start. Even as a young officer, when he was making tactical mistakes that frequently got men killed, he was able to command the respect of his men and the affection of his junior officers, many of them older than he was. When he finally resigned his commission after the French and Indian War, feeling somewhat cross that he had not been put in charge of things, his officers wrote him a letter begging him to stay on so they could be "led by the man we know and love."

His relationship with the officers who served under him during the Revolution is instructive. He did not bring on to his personal staff the older, more experienced soldiers, like Israel Putnam and Philip Schuyler, both of whom had fought in the frontier wars, nor Horatio Gates, who had been a major in the British regular army. Washington chose instead a group of brilliant but inexperienced young men, among them Alexander Hamilton, the Marquis de Lafayette, and John Laurens, all of them in their twenties, none of whom had had a serious command before. He treated these men like the sons he never had; he was, in fact, so much the loving but strict father that the young men discovered they could do little on their own. "Only when physically separated from the Commander-in-Chief could aides—or for that matter major generals —do much altogether on their own. And, wherever Washington acted, he dominated," says Flexner.

Another aspect of Washington's personality, which was critical to both his reputation and his success, was an immense practicality. Seventeen years as a farmer between two wars must have taught him that men and mountains could not be wished away but must be dealt with as they were. Washington seems to have been totally without the delusions, the obsessions, that afflict most people. His sight of the world was never clouded by ideology or blind faith. He had a rare ability to slice through to the heart of a problem.

This, then, was the George Washington that nature formed: a big, energetic, assertive, intelligent, and proud man, thin-skinned to criticism and quick to react to a slight; a man who liked to dominate, who was almost incapable of taking orders, but who nevertheless handled the authority he invariably sought with grace and tolerance.

But there was a second Washington, one he created himself. To understand how he came to do this, we have to take note of a concept widely prevalent in the eighteenth century. This was what was called fame. Today the word is applied to anybody who gets his name in the newspapers regularly, but in Washington's day the term had an entirely different connotation—something closer to what we would call honor. Late-eighteenth-century Americans were deeply in love with the classical societies and their statesmen, generals, historians. College students did not read English literature. They read instead Caesar's *Commentaries,* the *Orations* of Cicero, the *Politics* of Aristotle; and they constantly referred to what Polybius or Plato thought on a given subject.

This love affair with the classical world was not, of course, universal. Among deeply religious people, especially the Protestants of New England, the first authority was not Cicero, but the Bible. But even the more religious thinkers valued classical ideas. One must, Benjamin Franklin said, imitate both Jesus and Socrates.

Citizens of Rome, the Founders knew, were expected to put their duty to their country above personal interests. Love of the homeland was one of the highest goods: patriotism was not the last refuge of scoundrels but a lofty ideal that good men ascribed to.

The classical civilizations also thoroughly understood that most men seek fame. The historian Douglass Adair points out that for both the Romans and the men at the Constitutional Convention, a person earned fame by acts of virtue—at best, by living an entirely virtuous life. Desire for fame was not vulgar striving for celebrity; it was seen by Washington and the rest as a positive good, because it drove men to be virtuous. It acted as a "spur"—this metaphor was used repeatedly—that goaded men into being good. As Adair defines it, fame was "egotism transmuted gloriously into public service." We should remember that only 25 percent of the people born in Washington's generation lived past the age of twenty-six. Death was a constant companion and immortality a constant concern. Those who had an opportunity to achieve fame eagerly sought it.

But there was a virtue even higher than patriotism. As Adair points out, the great English philosopher Francis Bacon, writing in the early seventeenth century, said that the people who deserved the highest honor of all—the greatest fame—were "founders of states and commonwealths." Many educated Americans knew their Bacon and were aware of this idea. George Washington was one. He said, "The confidence and affection of his fellow citizens is the most valuable and agreeable reward a citizen can achieve."

From an early age, Washington wanted to become famous. In order to achieve this goal he had to be virtuous, and quite early in his life he deliberately set about curbing his emotions and making himself as selfless as possible, in order to act always with dignity, magnanimity, and honesty. When still a teenager, he wrote out a set of more than a hundred "Rules of Civility," which show both a sense of good manners and sensitivity to the feelings of others, coupled with an understanding of the proper deference the lower owe to the higher. Number 32 says, "You are to give the best place in your house to an equal, who should refuse it once, and then accept on the second offer." Number 36 is: "Artificers and Persons of low Degree ought not to use many ceremonies to Lords or others of high degree, but Respect and highly honor them, and those of High Degree ought to treat them with affability and Courtesie, without Arrogancy."

Neither Washington nor any of his peers saw this aspiring to virtue as in the least hypocritical or devious. They would have considered absurd today's ideal of "honestly expressing your feelings" at every turn. The idea that people were born good had not yet permeated the thinking of people in Washington's world, and it was taken for granted that most men would have discreditable desires. Throughout his life Washington fought for self-control, and more and more he gained the upper hand over his feelings, despite occasional outbursts of anger. And by sheer strength of will he made himself into an honorable, charitable, forgiving, compassionate man. Abigail Adams wrote that he "has a dignity which forbids familiarity, mixed with an easy affability which creates love and reverence." He listened to people carefully, he took what they had to say seriously, and—this was crucial—he never insisted on his own ideas simply to prove he was in charge. No wonder people loved him, and no wonder we are today baffled by his reputation: we find it impossible to believe that anyone could truly be that good.

But he was, or rather, he became so. George Washington was a great man not because he was "marble," but because he was not. He was, like any of us, wholly human; but unlike most of us, he was willing to make the unending struggle to become more than us.

Yet despite the reserve, the mantle of goodness, that increasingly characterized him, the original George Washington—the man who had fallen in love with his friend's wife, who had been reckless in battle and insubordinate toward his superior officers—still occasionally peeked out. In September 1781, when Washington was almost fifty, he found himself in Chester, Pennsylvania, waiting in fear and trembling for word of the arrival of Admiral de Grasse with the French fleet in Chesapeake Bay. Time was crucial, for an English fleet was on the way, too. If de Grasse got there first, they could lock up Cornwallis at Yorktown; if the English fleet beat them, Cornwallis would escape the trap.

While Washington waited for word of the fleet a group of top French officers, admirals and generals, left Philadelphia in a small boat to sail down the Delaware to Chester to join Washington. According to Flexner, as they came toward the town,

> they descried an amazing sight. A tall officer in blue and buff regimentals was jumping up and down, waving in one hand a hat and in the other a white handkerchief. Seen from the approaching boat, the dancing figure seemed to be His Excellency, General Washington, but, of course, that was impossible. The Frenchmen knew that Washington was (in the words of the Duc de Deux-Ponts) "of a natural coldness and of a serious and noble approach."
>
> The boat came closer: the figure was indeed His Excellency, and he was not only jumping and waving but shouting. They heard the words "de Grasse." The admiral and his fleet, Washington yelled, were in the Chesapeake. "A child whose every wish had been gratified," wrote Deux-Ponts, could not have expressed a "sensation more lively. His features, his physiognomy, his deportment," had all changed.

We cannot imagine an Eisenhower, a Pershing, a Lee, dancing with joy on a dock; but Washington did it.

Chapter Five

Madison Plans a Government

One thing clear to everybody concerned was that the Convention was unlikely to succeed at whatever it tried to do if George Washington was not present. It was not that he was a great student of political systems or would be fertile with ideas. It was simply that his presence would give the meeting legitimacy; it would assure ordinary Americans everywhere that nothing bad could come of it.

But Washington did not want to go. Washington, in fact, never wanted to attend such events. He enjoyed galloping around his farm or trekking off into the wilderness to search out likely streams for canals far more than he did sitting in stuffy rooms listening to men argue small points. Moreover, he had won the enduring gratitude of his fellow Americans and great glory around the world. In the minds of revolutionaries everywhere, he had come to be the very symbol of liberty. (When, two years after the Convention, the Bastille was flung open by the French revolutionaries, they sent the key to—of all the people in the world—the patrician George Washington.)

Washington had thus earned that fame he was so eager for; if the proposed convention dissolved in wrangling and recrimination, which it was very likely to do, his glory would be tarnished by the failure. If it succeeded, he would inevitably be drawn into whatever government came out of it, away from the countryside he loved. At fifty-five, he was getting on; why could he not spend his last years in peace?

But George Washington had spent eight tortuous years holding the states together almost by sheer willpower. His identification with his country was nearly total; he hardly distinguished between its greatness and his own. And he had a vision of a happy, prosperous America under a wise and fair government, in which people would live with each other in peace and honor, and he would do anything to achieve that vision. If his presence at Philadelphia was necessary, he would go.

But not everybody was sure that he ought to. Over the winter of 1786–1787 and into the spring, almost up to the moment when the Convention was supposed to begin, Washington was bombarded with conflicting advice. There was a great deal of feeling that the Convention was likely to fail, and that Washington should therefore keep away, to preserve the power of his reputation for use in a possible crisis, when he would be needed to pull the country together once again. Even Madison, as late as April 15, had doubts. "Would it not, however," he wrote, "be well for him to postpone his actual attendance, until some judgment can be formed of the result of the meeting?"

Meanwhile, as Washington agonized over the decision, the states began electing their delegations. Shays' Rebellion had made a difference: six months earlier less than half the states had sent delegates to Annapolis; now all but one, truculent Rhode Island, picked delegations.

As the date of the meeting approached, excitement around the United States grew. It was, in the first place, recognized very quickly that the men going to Philadelphia were an astonishing group in ability, intelligence, and character. Jefferson, John Adams, John Jay, Patrick Henry, and a dozen other famous men who were not there commented on the patriotism and talents, the ability, weight, and experience of the group that had been chosen. Through the spring, newspapers everywhere remarked on the approaching event. Said one, "The political existence of the United States perhaps depends on the result of the Convention which is to be held in Philadelphia in May next."

Although the Congress was still meeting in New York, Philadelphia was the American states' capital city in spirit and would in 1791 be so in fact. It was centrally located, it was far larger than any other American city, and it cultivated the arts and sciences. It had excellent libraries, eight newspapers, several magazines. Poets, painters, dramatists lived there. Largely because of the Quaker tone of the city, it proliferated do-good societies: for the relief of distressed ship captains, for the prevention of drowning, for the relief of widows of Episcopal clergymen, and so forth. The delegates would be meeting in an atmosphere of seriousness and high-minded intellectualism.

The city lay on the Delaware River, at a fine inland harbor, most of the time a forest of masts, through which the produce of half the continent flowed. It contained 6,651 dwellings, housing some 45,000 people. The major streets were paved with brick or stone, rare for the time. Running along both sides of the streets were sidewalks of brick, tile, or free stone, fenced off from the street by a series of posts set a few feet apart, to prevent carts and horses from running down pedestrians.

The houses were mostly brick or stone; wood, the primary building material in the countryside, was too inflammable in a city of closely spaced houses. They were usually two stories high, cut with small windows, and frequently had porches across the front, where the family might sit in the evening to chat or sing. By European standards the interiors were plain. Floors were not carpeted but scrubbed with sand, halls not papered but whitewashed. Nor were gardens as elaborate as they were abroad. Behind the house, where the kitchen was often located in a separate building, there would be a few fruit trees, and small plots of roses, lilies, tulips, sunflowers, hollyhocks, and lilac bushes.

Shops were small and specialized. Often a shop consisted of a single room. There were industries in the city, too: small factories making white lead, glue, rum, snuff, corduroy; there were thirty-four lawyers, and sixteen clergymen.

Because of the predominating Quaker tone, which opposed frivolity, Philadelphia offered fewer degenerate public amusements than did New York. Nonetheless, billiards were in vogue and horses were raced through the city streets, to the annoyance of many citizens. There was card-playing and gambling, and the lower classes enjoyed cockfighting. For more genteel entertainment people visited the galleries of the painter Charles Willson Peale, where there were displayed not only his own paintings of Revolutionary War heroes, but stuffed birds and small animals arranged in natural settings. Across the Schuylkill to the west of the city was an elaborate public garden, where visitors could wander through a huge greenhouse, ramble down flower-lined alleys, and sit in summer houses or arbors covered with vines and flowers.

As in most American towns, a good deal of life circulated around the taverns, which were more what we would think of as inns than saloons. Philadelphia had 117 of them. The one that tended to attract the delegates to the Convention was the Indian Queen, which Manasseh Cutler, a New Englander who visited the city at the time of the Convention, described as "a large pile of buildings, with many spacious halls, and numerous small apartments, appropriate for lodging room." The Indian Queen assigned Cutler a servant with powdered hair, dressed in a blue coat, buff waistcoat and breeches, a ruffled shirt, and a red cape, who brought up his luggage and two recent magazines from London, made him tea, and ordered him a barber.

All of this makes Philadelphia sound rather idyllic, but there was another side to it. The city was crime-ridden (theft, murder, mugging were common), subject to epidemics (four thousand people were to die in the yellow fever epidemic of 1793), and filled with vagrants and drunks. Directly behind the State House, where the Convention met, was the Walnut Street Jail. Here the prisoners thrust out their caps on long poles, begging money from passers-by. If no money was forthcoming they could "load you with the most foul and horrid imprecations," Cutler said. As a consequence of the numbers of criminals in the city, the streets were lit with oil lamps at night, and patrolled by constables.

In sum, Philadelphia impressed Manasseh Cutler as "large, elegant, and populous." It could not be compared with London or Paris, of course, in size, sophistication, or the extent of its criminality. But it could not be dismissed as a backyard provincial town, either; it had been, after all, one of the largest cities in the British Empire.

The Convention was scheduled to open on Monday, May 14, 1787. There was no reason to believe that it would do so, however. The uncertainties of travel, which depended so much on weather, made it hard for anyone to predict how long it would take to get from one place to another, and for some of the delegates the journey to Philadelphia would take two weeks. Besides, these were busy men, many of them members of Congress or their state governments, and they could not always get away when they wanted to. Then, too, it was a more casual time: the Convention was bound to go on for weeks; what did it matter to come a few days late?

James Madison, however, arrived in Philadelphia eleven days early. He took lodgings at a boardinghouse run by Mrs. Mary House, which the Virginians had always made a home away from home, and for the next ten days spent a good deal of time with his books and papers, thinking and making notes. He had, in fact, been doing his homework all spring and had written a number of letters to his colleagues Washington and Jefferson setting forth his basic ideas. In "Vices" he had delineated the basic difficulties: the states would not pay up when requested to; they constantly encroached on the authority of Congress; they violated at will treaties negotiated by the national government; and they trespassed on one another's rights.

What concerned Madison most in "Vices" was not only that the states were flouting national regulations, but that they were treating unjustly certain minorities within their own borders. As the modern editors of "Vices" say, "the dominant theme of the 'Vices of the Political System' was not the structural defects of the Articles of Confederation: the emphasis was rather on the deficiences and derelictions of the state governments."

Madison was especially troubled by the stay laws and tender laws and the paper money that so many of the plain people of the country were clamoring for. These laws, Madison believed, were "oppressing" the creditor minority, and if the country was to have any stability, it must have a national government capable of preventing states from passing them.

Like many eighteenth-century thinkers, Madison was not so much a pure philosopher in the modern sense of the word as a student of human nature. He accepted the idea, widely held at the time, that nations and their governments were constructed on social compacts, or contracts. The basic theory of the social contract was that power initially belonged to the people by innate, natural right. They could dispose of this power as they liked. To form a state they would contract among themselves to join together in a union. Then they would make a second contract with their rulers which would delegate certain powers but reserve all other authority to the people.

The idea of the social contract was obviously theoretical. Nations had not been formed this way, but had been put together haphazardly through the workings of history.

Madison believed, however, that the contract idea was a practical possibility. In the right circumstances, a group of people could sit down and devise a contract by which they would be governed. And he believed, furthermore, that if they did the job well, they could create a far better government than any already existing.

Second, Madison accepted the fact that human beings were by nature neither altogether good nor altogether evil but a little bit good and a little more evil. "Human beings," he maintained, "are generally governed by rather base and selfish motives, by suspicion, jealousy, desire for self-aggrandizement, and disinclination to do more than is required by convenience or self-interest, or exacted of them by force." In the famous *Federalist Papers,* published after the Convention to convince people of the virtues of the new Constitution, Madison wrote, "As there is a degree of depravity in mankind which requires a certain degree of circumspection and distrust, so there are other qualities in human nature which justify a certain portion of esteem and confidence."

One of the most important forces impelling human beings into evil, Madison believed, was the tendency to form "factions"—what we might call interest groups. Madison may have come to this belief independently, but he had certainly also found it in his reading of David Hume, the great Scottish thinker of a generation earlier, who was writing some of his major essays on the subject about the time Madison was born. According to Hume, "men are generally more honest in their private than in their public capacity. . . ." A person doing something *by himself* is likely to be held back by his conscience from doing wrong. "Honor," Hume said, "is a great check upon mankind: But where a considerable body of men act together, this check is, in a great measure, removed." In other words, members of a group who all want the same thing reinforce each other's belief in the righteousness of their cause. The members of a group, in a sense, give each other permission to do what they all want, even if it is unfair to those outside the group.

Madison believed, further, that the primary force creating factions, and putting them at odds with each other, was "the various and unequal distribution of property." "Government," he wrote flatly, "is instituted to protect property of every sort. This being the end of government, that alone is a just government which impartially secures to every man whatever is his own."

Madison was using the term "property" in a very broad sense. It meant, to him, not just money and real estate but the possession of a profession or craft, the right to bequeath real estate and other possessions, the right to learn a trade and move where it could be practiced—that is, anything that contributed to the protection or increase of material goods and economic security. He was never really very clear about how far this would extend. Nor is it clear how he distinguished between protecting property already in hand and protecting the right to acquire additional property. In truth, even though Madison struck firmly for property rights and hated the "leveling spirit" aimed at bringing down the high and raising the low, he was uneasy about great inequality of wealth. Governments should not, of course, unjustly take people's property from them; but in an ideal state things could be worked out in such a way as to "reduce extreme wealth . . . and raise extreme indigence. . . ." This could be done, he felt, because the America he envisioned would be agrarian, made up mainly of farmers, who already were the majority. There was land enough for all in this great nation; it would only be necessary to distribute it properly.

Above all, James Madison was intent on controlling power. Summing up, he said:

> If men were angels, no government would be necessary. . . . In framing a government which is to be administered by men over men, the great difficulty lies in this: You must first enable the government to control the governed; and in the next place, oblige it to control itself. A dependence on the people is no doubt the primary control on the government; but experience has taught mankind the necessity of auxiliary precautions.

Embedded in this statement, which comes from *Federalist* No. 51, is an idea that was at the heart of Madison's thinking and the personality from which that thinking sprung. This was the belief that government must be powerful enough to be effective and to control unruly factions in the society, but not so powerful as to be able to interfere with the legitimate liberties of the citizens. It was the great conundrum: how do you give government enough power, without giving it too much? This was the central issue that would face the men at Philadelphia: it was what the Constitutional Convention, at bottom, was all about.

What, in Madison's view, were the implications of all of this for government? First, it was clear that for any government to work fairly, no single faction could be allowed to dominate. Neither debtors nor creditors, manufacturers nor farmers, exporters nor landholders, should control government. This led Madison to an interesting and, for the time, novel idea.

It was widely believed that a real democracy could exist only in a very small unit, such as the city-state of ancient Greece, where it was possible for the voters to assemble in one place. Any state much larger had to be ruled, to one degree or another, by a king or legislature. Realistically, in a large state the citizens could not be consulted on every issue.

As a corollary, it was also widely believed that only a homogeneous nation with common ethics and attitudes could operate as a direct democracy, or a republic, as they termed it. A republic was a commonwealth, a nation that was organized to promote the welfare of all, and in which government was structured to reflect the will of the people—directly, if small enough, otherwise through representatives.

But it had occurred to David Hume that there might be certain advantages to largeness and diversity. In a large state the members of factions would be so spread out and remote from one another that there would be no way for them to form into unified pressure groups. (We remember how slow communication was at the time.)

How much Madison took from Hume is hard to say. But he came to believe that a republican government was not only possible in a larger unit, but would actually work better in a large state than in a small one, because in a place like America, where it took weeks to travel from one end to the next, and letters frequently never reached their destination, it would be impossible for factions to organize nationally. The farmers of western Massachusetts could cause trouble locally, but they could not form an alliance with South Carolinians with the same grievance, because the distances were too great. In general, interest groups, often representing local majorities, would neutralize one another in a national legislature. Thus despite the conventional wisdom, Madison believed that good government could work in a large country—what he termed an "extended republic."

A second virtue of the extended republic, Madison believed, was that it would certainly require the indirect election of most national office-holders, placing them a step or two away from the voters, and thus insulating them from the temporary passions of the mob.

From these ideas James Madison derived three basic principles of government, which he tucked into his hat to carry to Philadelphia. They were: the *national* principle, which said that government should arise from the people and act on them directly, rather than through the states; the principle of the *separation of powers,* which said that power should be dispersed through the government so that no single person or group of people had absolute control; and a more diffuse idea that men in power were not to be wholly trusted—they could not be expected to act in a disinterested way.

This last idea was the beginning of Madison's thinking. All people, he believed, were ultimately self-serving. They would in the end attempt to keep themselves in power as long as they could, and use that power to their own advantage, at the expense of those they governed. A government, thus, had to be constructed in such a way that nobody had complete control. One way of doing this was through the "extended Republic."

Another device for keeping any person or group of people from gathering all authority to themselves was the separation of powers. This was an old idea, fairly well known not only to intellectuals but also to the segment of the American populace who thought about these things. The government should be constructed, as Montesquieu had suggested, in such a way that its various components "checked" or "balanced" each other. This concept of the separation of powers was the second of the major ideas that Madison carried to Philadelphia.

But the most important principle was the theory that the national government must be dominant. Madison believed, along with others of the nationalists, that the power of the states must be curbed. Given his choice, he would have reduced the states to mere administrative bodies. But he recognized that this was politically impossible: in 1787 most Americans felt deep loyalties to their states, and many of them had vested interests in them, holding political office, land claims, or prerogatives of one sort or another that might evaporate with the disappearance of the state governments. Madison concluded, as he wrote to Washington, that:

> . . . [as] a consolidation of the whole into one simple republic would be as inexpedient as it is unattainable, I have sought for some middle ground, which may at once support a due supremacy of the national authority, and not exclude the local authorities whenever they can be subordinately useful.

This is a relatively rare form for a nation to take. In most countries the central government reaches down into every aspect of local community life. Counties, provinces, cities, towns, are little more than administrative subdivisions. In England, to take an example, the national government does the bulk of the taxing and spending, setting budgets for towns and cities around the country. It establishes a unified national school budget and policy. Even such lesser matters as automobile licensing, building codes, regulation of taverns— all state and local matters in the United States—are controlled from London.

The distinction between the American system and most others grew out of the recognition, right from the beginning, that the states would have to play a considerable role in the national government. The people would insist on it, and in any case, both the diversity of the nation and the difficulties of communication and transportation made a great deal of local control essential.

However, Madison wanted the states to have only such power as was "subordinately useful." He meant to lodge as much power as he reasonably could in the national government.

He justified this desire from the theoretical principle that power ultimately was lodged in the people, and only they could distribute it. From this concept flowed several other ideas. One was that, as the government drew its power from the people, it ought to operate directly on them, rather than through the states. That is to say, the national government would not, for example, have to ask the states for money, but could tax people directly in one way or another. A second notion flowing from the national concept was the idea that the legislature should be proportional to the population of the states. Under the Articles of Confederation each state had one vote in Congress, which meant that tiny Delaware had as much power in the legislature as did Virginia, with more than ten times Delaware's population. To Madison it was self-evident that this was unfair, as, during the long, hot summer, he was to point out to the delegates again and again. The states "ought to vote in the same proportion in which their citizens would do, if the people of all the states were collectively met," he said. To do anything else was "inadmissable, being evidently unjust," he insisted.

In fact, Madison's idea of "people" was not precisely what we would take the phrase to mean. Blacks would not vote, women would not vote, indentured servants would not vote, and the propertyless mob of sailors, vagrants, day laborers, and criminals who swarmed the cities would not vote. Perhaps ten percent of the population would be enfranchised; the rest were disqualified for a variety of reasons. (Actually, it was presumed that the male heads of household, who constituted the bulk of the voters, would fairly represent their families, so that in theory the franchise was much larger.)

Madison saw the states, each intent on guarding its sovereignty, as the main obstacle to a sound national government. Drawing power directly from the people via proportional representation tended to undercut the power of the states, because representatives would be responsible to their own constituents, not to their state governments.

Finally, Madison had political reasons as well as theoretical ones for wanting proportional representation. By the accident of history, the North was cut into eight states, the South into five relatively larger ones.* In a Congress where each state had a single vote, the North could dominate—and as we shall see, it had in fact used its weight to press its own interests at the expense of the South.

The North was somewhat more populous, too. However, it was widely believed that the population of the country was drifting southwestward, and that shortly the South would be more populous than the North. In fact, this never happened; the South remained less populous than the North, and in the nineteenth century would become substantially less so. But the misperception was what operated at the time. All the delegates, both northerners and southerners, believed that in a government based on proportional representation, a more populous South would eventually come to control the legislature. Madison was not a rabid partisan of the South, but others of the delegates were, and so were many of Madison's constituents back home. A plan of government that included proportional representation was bound to attract southern support. For all these reasons, proportional representation became for Madison a sine

*It was customary to speak of eight northern states, including Delaware. Seven had moved to abolish slavery; it was expected that Delaware was about to do so.

qua non of any new government, and his insistence on it would nearly break the Convention.

This line of thought led Madison to another conclusion that seemed to follow logically. If the people alone could delegate power, any new scheme of government that came out of the Philadelphia meetings would have to be ratified by them, not simply approved by state governments. Madison therefore decided that if the Convention should write a new Constitution, it should be approved by state ratifying conventions, bypassing both the old Congress and the state legislatures. This idea would seem to some illegal, even revolutionary, as it would overturn the existing government without its permission, and would violate the terms of the Articles of Confederation. But Madison's view was that nothing the properly convened people did was illegal or revolutionary; they could distribute their power as they liked, and it was part of his plan from the beginning to have the Constitution ratified by state conventions.

Yet one more notion that flowed from the national principle was the idea that the national government ought to have the power to veto state legislation. States certainly must not be allowed to pass laws that conflicted with national ones; but more than that, they must not be allowed to pass laws that were manifestly unfair, like those stay and tender laws Madison so hated.

Clearly, Madison wanted to centralize power in a new national government. But when we look at this plan closely, we see something interesting, indeed slightly peculiar: it is a plan for government that is essentially negative in its purpose. Madison believed an extended republic would curb the power of factions because they would be spread so thin they could not cause mischief; he wanted a strong national government based on proportional representation in order to curb the power of the states; he wanted the separation of powers, with its checks and balances, in order to curb the power of the national government. Everything in Madison's plan was meant to curtail, contain, constrain power wherever it might lie. The historian Bernard Bailyn has said that Madison and his political confreres saw society as "divided into two distinct, contrasting, and innately antagonistic spheres: the sphere of power and the sphere of liberty or right. The one was brutal, ceaselessly active, and heedless; the other was delicate, passive, and sensitive."

James Madison was at bottom mistrustful of power. It is a thread that runs through his entire life, both personal and political. Diffident, unassertive with women, prevented by imagined illnesses from hunting, whoring, and fighting, he was worried by power and he fought it everywhere. Before the Convention his principal battles had been against British tyranny, against the established

church in Virginia, against runaway state legislatures. In the Convention he
fought against domination of his own state by small states and northerners,
and he aimed for a government in which power was checked everywhere.
James Madison saw clearly that the great issue facing the Convention would
be the problem of adjudicating between power and liberty: the government
must have enough command to be effective, but it must be sufficiently controlled so that it could not rob the people of their liberties. Many of the men
coming to the Convention were not nearly so troubled by power as Madison
was: George Washington and Alexander Hamilton, who would dominate the
first American government, wanted a dynamic national government, which
would move with energy in many directions. Madison, too, wanted an energetic national government; but when push came to shove, he would curb power
rather than jeopardize the liberty of the citizens.

James Madison was a great political scientist, and he was also an experienced politician. He knew that in gatherings like the one to be held in
Philadelphia, the questions raised first get debated first and may swallow up
other questions that could have been asked. Madison intended to raise the first
questions.

Moreover, he felt that as the Virginians had taken the lead in calling the
Convention, they would be allowed, or even expected, to open the debate. The
other states had long tended to look to Virginia for leadership: the state was
by far the largest in size and population and had always asserted itself in
continental concerns.

So Madison urged his fellow members of the Virginian delegation to get to
Philadelphia promptly. The Virginians understood what Madison had in
mind, and they came on time. Washington, for example, arrived on Sunday,
May 13, after an almost royal progress from Mount Vernon, during which his
route was lined with cheering citizens and the carriage attended by so many
horsemen that he could not view the countryside for the dust.

He had intended to stay at Mrs. House's, with Madison and some of the
other Virginia delegates, but the moment he arrived he was scooped up by
Robert Morris, a Convention delegate, and one of the country's richest men.
During the Revolution Morris had accomplished the extraordinary task of
finding financing for the war. He had earned Washington's gratitude, and
undoubtedly Washington felt obligated to stay with him while he was in
Philadelphia.

The other members of the Virginia delegation were George Mason, a

wealthy squire who was famous for writing the Virginia bill of rights; George
Wythe, a judge of the state's highest court and professor of law at William and
Mary; John Blair, who had read law at the famous Middle Temple in London;
Edmund Randolph, governor of the state; and a doctor James McClurg, a
last-minute substitute for Patrick Henry, who opposed the whole idea of the
Convention and had refused to attend because he "smelt a rat."

Over the days until May 29, when the Convention actually got down to
business, the Virginia delegates met for two or three hours each day, thrashing
out a plan of government to present to the Convention. There were no minutes
taken at these meetings, and little came out about them later. However, it is
clear that most of the ideas came from Madison, and were then modified by
the other members of the delegation. They produced a scheme of government
that has been called by historians the Virginia Plan. It called for a legislature
of two houses, both based on proportional representation. The house would
be elected by the people, and in turn would elect the upper house. The legislature would be very powerful, and the "executive," a rather shadowy figure,
would function mainly to carry out policy set by the legislature. For example,
the legislature would set foreign policy, and appoint the national treasurer as
well as many other government officials. There would be a judiciary, which
could settle disputes among the states, and of course the national government
could veto acts of state legislatures.

The government outlined by the Virginia Plan would have cropped the
power of the states substantially. It would not, however, have led to a national
government nearly as dynamic as the American government came to be. A
weak executive dominated by the legislature could not possibly have exerted
the authority that Washington, almost from the first, commanded.

The Virginians, however, were not alone in preparing plans of government
for the Convention. Two other men—Alexander Hamilton and Charles Pinckney—eventually presented their own schemes to the Convention, and it is
worth taking a moment at this point to look at them, not so much for what
they contributed to the final document as for what they can tell us about how
the men at Philadelphia were thinking.

Chapter Six

Alexander Hamilton and the British Model

For one man at the Convention the Virginia plan was not strong enough, and he drew up a plan of his own for a government so strong that there was no chance any of the other delegates could have voted for it. The man was Alexander Hamilton—one of the most fascinating and significant people in American history. He possessed great charm and good looks: his eyes were deep blue, his hair auburn, his skin clear, his cheeks rosy, and although, at five feet seven, he was of medium height, he was small-boned and appeared delicate. He was, like Washington, physically brave to the point of foolhardiness, always ready for a duel or a battle, a propensity for which he acquired the nickname Little Mars. He was brilliant; he was not the careful craftsman of theory that Madison was, but in terms of raw intelligence he was, perhaps, the smartest man at a convention of smart men. He had raced through preparatory school and college in half the usual time, and had learned enough law in three months to gain admission to the bar. He was a man of intense passions, which, unlike Washington, he never felt called upon to check. He rushed headlong into friendships, battle, love affairs, causes—always impatient, impetuous, tempestuous. He could be wrong-headed: he frequently pushed his own ideas too hard when it would have been better to compromise. Yet this passionate man was assiduous in mastering the details of subjects set before him. Eventually, as Washington's secretary of the treasury, he would establish the supportive relationship of the government to commerce that has continued ever since. By 1787 he had married into the powerful Schuyler family of New York, and through his war record and subsequent political activity, he had become one of the most respected statesmen in the country.

But at the Convention his impact was negligible. Outvoted by the other two New York delegates, both antinationalists, Hamilton left Philadelphia on June

29, returning briefly in the middle of July after Yates and Lansing had abandoned the Convention. He was not authorized to vote alone. Broadus Mitchell, his biographer, says that his "extreme views . . . had a nuisance value," but that his real contributions to the Constitution came before and after the Convention—as a strong nationalist during the Confederation era and as a coauthor of the *Federalist Papers* in 1787 and 1788.

He was born—probably—in 1755, on the island of Nevis in the West Indies. The reasons for the obscurity of the details of his youth lie in the fact that his background was almost certainly shabbier—indeed, more sordid—than that of any other man at the Convention. His mother, Rachel Faucette, made a bad marriage, to a man who brutalized her: once, under the peculiar laws of Nevis, he had Rachel jailed, apparently for refusing him sex. Out of jail, she fled her husband, and took up with a Scotsman named James Hamilton; eventually the couple landed on St. Croix, where Alexander Hamilton grew up. Although Rachel and James Hamilton lived together for some fifteen years, they were never able to marry, owing to the legal complications of her first marriage, and their two sons were technically bastards.

James Hamilton was a classic figure out of the European eighteenth century —a highborn scapegrace fallen into the ruck and drifting around the margins of empire, vainly seeking to repair his fortune. He had been born in a twelfth-century castle in Ayershire, Scotland, the fourth son of a line descended from English dukes and barons. As fourth son he could not expect to inherit much, and in any case he apparently fell out of favor with his family and went off to the Caribbean, where he failed inexorably at a succession of business enterprises. Finally, when Alexander was about ten, James drifted away from the family.

Years later, when Hamilton was marrying into the aristocratic Schuyler family, he wrote his father, offering him a place in his new home. The father had done little for the son, had abandoned him as a boy, and had thereafter not bothered with his welfare at all. Why offer to take him in? The only plausible answer is that Alexander Hamilton was a man obsessed with status, and the connection with English nobility meant a great deal to him.

It was not much use to Rachel, however. After James left she struggled on, making some attempt to see that her clever son was educated. Then, in 1768, she died, and Alexander was now a penniless orphan entirely dependent on the goodwill of strangers. Fortunately, he was charming, bright, clearly a boy who could make his mark, and he began to attract sponsors, one of whom gave him a job in his store.

In 1772 some of these sponsors sent him to New York, where he dashed through his education at King's College, soon to be Columbia, and was taken up by important men. In the winter of 1774–1775, as the Revolution was beginning, he wrote a series of political tracts, which were widely read by people who would have been astonished to learn that the author was a teenager. When the war came on he got command of an artillery militia, read everything he could on the subject of artillery, and made himself one of the country's experts on it. Driven out of New York with the rest of the army by the British, he was taken up by yet another influential man, George Washington, who made him one of the high-spirited young men in his official family. Hamilton quickly became one of Washington's most trusted subordinates. It had been an astonishing rise; in five years the obscure schoolboy clerk had moved to the absolute center of events in his part of the world.

Hamilton fought with bravery at the battles of Trenton and Princeton, but his position on Washington's staff kept him out of most of the action. For a long time he begged and fussed at Washington to let him go out and be shot at. Eventually Washington relented and allowed Hamilton to lead a small force at Yorktown in a nighttime attack on the last British redoubt. Hamilton chose the riskiest tactic he could think of, a bayonet charge, was the first man over the barricade, and captured the redoubt. In 1780 he married Elizabeth Schuyler, and after the war he took on a number of public offices, particularly relating to financial questions, for a long time working with Robert Morris, "the financier of the Revolution." When he came to the Convention, still in his early thirties, he had become an important man in his adopted country.

He was, by this time, a man whose character was filled with puzzles. He was imperious: as a fourteen-year-old boy in the counting house on St. Croix, he had been for a period left in charge. He had glibly given orders to grizzled sea captains and fired the house attorney. As Washington's aide he had no qualms about taking to task generals twice his age.

He could behave imperiously even with George Washington. On one occasion in 1781, as Hamilton was going downstairs in the building where he and Washington worked, he ran into his commander, who said he wanted to see him. Hamilton replied that he would be right up. He was not gone for more than a minute or so, he claimed later, but when he got back upstairs he found Washington in one of his famous rages. "Colonel Hamilton," the commander in chief shouted, "you have kept me waiting at the head of the stairs these ten minutes. I must tell you, sir, you treat me with disrespect."

As Hamilton reported the story: "I replied with petulancy but with decision,

'I am not conscious of it, sir, but since you have thought it necessary to tell me so, we must part.'

" 'Very well, sir,' said he, 'if it be your choice.' Or something to this effect. And we separated."

Washington very quickly regretted having lost his temper and tried to smooth the incident over, but Hamilton would have none of it and left Washington's staff as soon as he fairly could. The argument itself was understandable: these were two high-spirited men who had been under almost constant tension for years. Hamilton's refusal to make up with Washington is not. In 1781 George Washington was perhaps the single most influential human being in the Western Hemisphere, and would have been able to get Hamilton almost anything influence could gain. Moreover, Washington felt a great deal of affection for Hamilton, as he did for all of his handpicked young men. Hamilton had earned Washington's trust and esteem: why spoil it all at a stroke? As James Thomas Flexner, one of Hamilton's biographers, writes, "Never did the megalomania that haunted the uncontrolled part of Hamilton's mind present itself more conspicuously."

Again, why did Hamilton later insist on fighting that fateful duel with Aaron Burr? Burr, of course, forced the issue, making it difficult for Hamilton to refuse to fight without dishonoring himself. But he knew that Burr intended to kill him if he could, and in view of the fact that Hamilton's son had been killed in a duel not long before, he might have found a way out of it, if only for the sake of his wife. But he did not, and was killed.

Adrienne Koch says:

> Despite his marked abilities and brilliant talents, there is an oppressive narrowness about his interests, a single-minded preoccupation with himself—his own power, ambitions, prestige, reputation, maneuvers, intrigues—that makes a striking impression upon anyone who reads his correspondence and papers after reading those of Jefferson, Madison and John Adams.

We have to see, then, that Hamilton's character included a streak of perversity. Despite his imperiousness, his way with women, his rapid rise in the world, and the immense power that he eventually came to hold, he had his black moods. In 1788 he wrote a friend, "You know the opinion I entertain of mankind, and how it is my desire to preserve myself free from particular attachments, and to keep my happiness independent on the caprice of others." Hamilton was capable of strong, sudden passions, but he was not at heart a sanguine man. He tended, in his perverse way, to disrupt relationships with people who cared for him most.

Some of this sort of mood must have been on him when he reached the Convention, for at his first opportunity to speak, while the Convention was wrangling over the Virginia and New Jersey plans, Hamilton presented a plan of his own, which he admitted in his speech "went beyond the ideas of most members" of the Convention.

To understand Hamilton's plan, we must remember that he, like most of the Founding Fathers, took a deep interest in history. In a day before modern social sciences, it was felt that the best way to understand human nature was to look at how men, and their social systems, had operated over the centuries. Douglass Adair, referring to the delegates at the Convention, concludes that the "lessons from the antique past, applied to their present situation, concretely affect[ed] their actions at Philadelphia." In fact, the founders generally believed that the way human beings behaved in ancient Greece and Rome was the way they were likely to behave in eighteenth-century America. The Philadelphia debates, for instance, ring constantly with the names of the confederacies of the days of Pericles and Thucydides—cited usually as incorporating faults to be avoided in America.

One man who especially valued the uses of history was John Adams. Adams was in London, representing Congress at the Court, but early in 1787 he published a substantial book called *Defense of the Constitutions of the United States.* In the book Adams analyzed a great many societies past and present, particularly emphasizing the classical cultures of Greece and Rome. He believed that he was writing as a scientist, not merely making intuitive guesses and hunches, but carefully weighing evidence in hopes of discovering natural laws of what we could today call political science. Adams' book was widely read by the delegates to the Convention, who found in it discussions of such principles of government as the separation of powers, and the need for a "mix" in government of both monarchial and republican principles. Although some of the men at the Convention were less interested in theory than others, most of them were familiar with ideas such as these, and many took them seriously.

However, as much enamored as these educated gentlemen were of ancient civilizations, the history they knew best was that of England and the British Empire. They knew about the Norman Conquest, Magna Carta, Common Law, and the development of the parliamentary system. Moreover, they generally believed that the English government was the *best* system of government yet developed by human beings. It was, certainly, not without its faults, but it did allow far more liberty to the people living under it than did most other systems, old or new, and it could not be denied that it worked: one had only to look at the might and wealth of the British Empire to see that. The example of the British government was constantly before these men, and we must know something about it if we are to understand the American one.

The English government as they knew it was a constitutional monarchy. What this meant, essentially, was that the king no longer possessed the authority he had had in an earlier time, but was limited by the wishes of Parliament. In theory, at least, the king had a veto over acts of Parliament, but in fact, seventeenth-century revolutions had taught English kings that they had to be cautious in disregarding the advice of the legislature: Parliament had pushed kings off the throne before—indeed, it had pushed a head off a king—and could do so again.

The Parliament and the Crown thus acted to check one another. But Parliament itself was divided into two. The lower house, the House of Commons, was elected by "the people," who in practice amounted to 5 to 10 percent of the adult male population. The upper house, the Lords, was made up of hereditary peers, some of whose families had sat there for generations. These men not only constituted half of Parliament, but almost automatically took over the most important jobs in the Church, the army, and the government.

This system had not been built on any theory of government, but had been produced by centuries of complex struggles for power. However, theorists who had analyzed it contended that by happy accident it had come out to be something highly desirable—a "mixed" government. What they meant is this: According to the theories of the classic political thinkers, there were three basic types of government: the monarchy, in which one person ran things; aristocracy, in which a group debated the laws; and democracy, in which the people directly controlled the government. The problem with all of these forms, the theorists said, was that they all tended to run off with themselves: monarchs became despots; aristocracies divided into factions, one of which gained ultimate control and formed a tyrannical oligarchy; and democracies degenerated into anarchy, which in turn gave rise to a despot.

What was to be done? The solution was to mix the three forms into one government, so that each would act as a check on the other. This, many political thinkers in 1787 believed, was precisely what happened in the English government. The principle of monarchy resided in the Crown, the principle of aristocracy in the House of Lords, and the principle of democracy in the House of Commons. The idea was that the two houses of Parliament represented two different elements of the social system—Lords, the hereditary aristocracy, Commons, traditionally, the yeoman class of small landholders, but now also the rising middle class of merchants, industrialists, and their lackeys, the lawyers. The king, it was assumed, represented the nation as a whole and would step in between the Houses of Parliament when necessary. It was a system lavish with checks and balances.

The delegates at Philadelphia had grown up under this system and knew its workings inside and out. They did not all love it—few of them wanted a government with a king and aristocracy—but they respected it, although they saw it as having been corrupted by a venal king. One man who admired it extravagantly, however, was Alexander Hamilton. This he made plain in his long speech, which lasted about five hours, on June 18.

As reported in Madison's "Notes" on the convention debates, Hamilton began by pointing out that the states "constantly pursue internal interest adverse to those of the whole." Furthermore, "Men love power," and the states were unlikely to give up their sovereignty unless they were forced to. He then went on to say that "the British government was the best in the world," and he "doubted much whether anything short of it would do in America." Men serve their avarice through the states and will keep power there and render any confederacy precarious. Complete sovereignty must therefore lie with the national government. The Congress should have the power to "pass all laws whatever," and "all laws of the particular states contrary to the Constitution or laws of the United States [would] be utterly void." The state governors should be appointed by the national government.

What were the virtues of the British system? For one thing, "Their House of Lords is a most noble institution," because it is conservative by nature, Hamilton said. Alluding to Shays' Rebellion, he insisted that when some ideas seize the "popular passions, they spread like wild fire, and become irresistible." The House of Lords forms "a permanent barrier against every pernicious innovation" brought about by "the amazing violence and turbulence of the democratic spirit." It was necessary, then, for the United States to have lifetime senators, in imitation of the House of Lords.

For another thing, "no good [executive] could be established on Republican principles. . . . The English model was the only good one. . . ." The interest of a king would be so interwoven with the interest of the nation that he would be above corruption from abroad, and inclined to do right at home. In other words, what was good for the king was good for the country, and vice versa.

America should therefore have an executive elected for life with a veto power over all legislation.

The government Hamilton was calling for was not quite the British system, but it was close to it. The crucial difference between it and the Virginia Plan was that the checks and balances were all *internal*—the executive poised against the legislature, and so forth. There was nothing *outside* of the government—such as the electorate and interest groups—checking it in turn, other than the Constitution. As the executive and senators were not subject to reelection, they could ignore the wishes of the population as they chose. This was precisely what Hamilton intended. The people at large were filled with that "amazing violence and turbulence," constantly being seized by momentary passions, and could not possibly be expected to run a just and orderly government.

The editors of his papers say this speech is "perhaps the most important address ever made by Hamilton." Another historian, Gerald Stourzh, has called Hamilton's June 18 speech "probably the greatest speech of his political career." According to Stourzh, Hamilton was not nearly so monarchial as the speech makes him appear. What he wanted was "representative democracy," in which the people would delegate their innate power to rulers best able to use it for the general good. However, whatever Hamilton thought, few of the delegates at the Convention agreed with him. They had suffered under a king and a legislature of lifetime aristocrats, and they had no intention of replacing them with those of their own devising. Furthermore, they knew perfectly well that any government such as Hamilton was proposing would send a shudder through the population and would be instantly voted down. The balance that Hamilton in his plan struck between individual liberty and power in government had little appeal to most Americans. His plan was not debated, or as Connecticut delegate William Samuel Johnson remarked, though it was "praised by every body, it was supported by none."

Chapter Seven

The Puzzle of Charles Pinckney

Alexander Hamilton, then, chose at Philadelphia to throw away his influence by presenting a plan that nobody could support, and not too long after, by simply leaving the Convention altogether. It was another man, virtually unknown today to anybody but specialists in the period, who produced a plan that would have far more appeal in many respects to the delegates than the Hamilton Plan, the New Jersey Plan of the small state caucus, or even the Virginia Plan of James Madison. The man who drew this plan had a way of thinking about the future of the United States that contrasted sharply with the outlook of Alexander Hamilton. It was this viewpoint, not Hamilton's that was finally adopted by the Convention, and eventually the country as a whole. It is therefore once again worth spending a little time with it before we look at the infighting between the big and small states.

The Pinckney Plan is, furthermore, the centerpiece of a scholarly detective story that would ultimately cast a small shadow over the reputation of James Madison. For it now appears that the little-remembered and less-regarded Charles Pinckney of South Carolina was cheated of credit for his role in modeling the Constitution by James Madison and his supporters. Though Madison's reputation went into eclipse in the post–Civil War period, when the economic thinking of Alexander Hamilton better suited the conservative mood of the country, by and large he has been the darling of generations of scholars —the modest intellectual who studied hard and thought well. Charles Pinckney, on the other hand, was ambitious, assertive, egocentric, a politician by nature—just the sort of person many scholars would find unappealing. One of them, Madison's master biographer, Irving Brant, flatly called Pinckney "a sponger and a plagiarist." Yet there is now ample evidence that Pinckney was an energetic and consistent advocate of a strong national government, who was urging reform of the Articles of Confederation before Madison himself was convinced of the need for it. Pinckney's ideas were not, in the main, original, but they were carefully thought out and logical, and they seemed to many of the delegates worth considering. At the end of his notes for May 29 Madison wrote:

> Mr. Charles Pinckney laid before the house the draught of a federal government which he had prepared; to be agreed upon between the free and independent states of America. Mr. P. plan ordered that the same be referred to the Committee of the Whole appointed to consider the state of the American union.

It is a curiously brief entry, and it was not until 1818, over thirty years later, that anyone made anything of it. By that time most of the participants at the Convention were dead, and those alive were elderly men whose memories were clouded by time and the inevitable impulse in shapers of events to enhance their own roles. In that year Secretary of State John Quincy Adams was in the process of preparing for publication a journal of the Convention. As Convention Secretary Jackson's notes merely stated that Pinckney had "laid before the house" his plan of government, without saying what was in it, Adams wrote Pinckney for details.

Pinckney, still an active politician though now in his early sixties, wrote back that he still possessed "several rough draughts of the Constitution I proposed," which he had drawn up in working out his plan. They were, he said, "substantially the same," but he could not be quite sure which was the one he had presented to the Convention. He was, however, sending along "the one I believe it was." The plan was subsequently included in Adams' book, and there the matter rested.

But then, at some point after Pinckney died in 1824—the first positive date we have is 1830—James Madison began hinting to people that there was something fishy about the copy of the plan Pinckney had sent to Adams for publication. He discussed his misgivings with Jared Sparks, one of the great nineteenth-century compilers of the history of the Revolutionary era. Sparks reported, "Mr. Madison seems a good deal perplexed on the subject." Madison's perplexity stemmed from the fact that Pinckney's draft "went to a committee with other papers, and was no more heard of during the Convention." The implication—indeed according to Sparks' diary it was more than an implication—was that Pinckney had falsified the draft he had sent to

Adams to make it more closely resemble the Constitution in its final form. Pinckney was out to make it appear that a lot of the ideas credited to the Virginia delegation—for which read James Madison—had come out of the plan he had presented to the Convention. And according to S. Sidney Ulmer, who has done a good deal of the detective work on the subject, this was only the first of many such criticisms by Madison on the Pinckney paper, which continued until Madison's death.

Madison's attacks on Pinckney's claims to authorship of at least parts of the Constitution were followed up by his admirers and subsequent generations of scholars. Pinckney, of course, was dead and could not defend himself. The case against him seemed clinched in 1908 when it was discovered that the paper that he had sent to John Quincy Adams had not been written at the time of the Convention, but in 1818, when Adams had asked for it, as studies of ink, paper marks, and the handwriting showed conclusively. Thereafter Pinckney became a footnote to history, a man soiled by ambition, who must be dishonored for attempting to reap credit that belonged to James Madison.

One thing true of history, however, is that it is impermanent. In 1903 J. F. Jameson, one of the leading historians of his day, discovered in the papers of the Pennsylvania delegate James Wilson a group of extracts from the Pinckney Plan. At almost the same moment another leading scholar, Andrew C. McLaughlin, found in the Wilson papers "an outline of the plan of a constitution presented to the Federal Convention by Charles Pinckney." After careful study of the documents, both scholars concluded that Pinckney had indeed written a comprehensive plan of government, that it had been taken up by at least one important committee, and that a great deal of it had found its way into the Constitution of the United States. According to McLaughlin, "We can say that Pinckney suggested some thirty-one or thirty-two provisions which were finally embodied in the Constitution," of which some twelve were already in the Articles of Confederation. In the 1950s Sidney Ulmer undertook a thorough investigation of the whole problem. "Madison's objectivity as a critic in the matter," he said flatly, "is corrupted beyond repair by his personal interest in every aspect of the subject."

We should understand that by 1800 James Madison had become involved in a bitter political battle to restrain what was developing into a national government far stronger than he wanted. It was very much in his interest to interpret as narrowly as possible the Constitution he had been so instrumental in making, and this meant controlling as much as he could the history of the event. When New York delegate Robert Yates published his "Notes" of the debates in 1821, Madison attacked them as erroneous, and he altered his own speeches to show himself more of a states' righter than he had actually been at the Convention.

Once again, we must bear in mind that Pinckney was not an original thinker like Madison. Most of the ideas in his plan were taken from the Articles of Confederation, the Massachusetts constitution, and especially the New York constitution: Pinckney never denied their origins. Nonetheless, his plan was not a hodgepodge but was consistent and well thought out, and through it many provisions were brought to the attention of the Convention.

What really happened? Why was Charles Pinckney so rudely handled by history?

Charles Pinckney was a member of one of the richest and most important families in the small group of wealthy planters who ran the prosperous state of South Carolina. These wealthy families lived on large farms in elegant, spacious houses fitted out with furniture, carpeting, silver, and glassware imported from Europe. Most also owned town houses in Charleston, where they maintained a glittering winter social season complete with the latest music, dances, theatrical pieces, and conversation, also imported from Europe. Intermarriage was common among these grand families: Pinckney was connected one way or another to most of the important politicians of his state.

The grand life-style of coastal South Carolina contrasted sharply with life in the western hills. There the soil was poorer, and most people followed the basic American pattern of quasi-subsistence farming, which here might include a few slaves rather than the hired man of the north. These people resented the wealthy planters of the coast, who dominated the state politically, socially, and economically. But to some extent, politicians had to take the feelings of the westerners into account.

Charles Pinckney came from the sort of background that almost inevitably produced conservative gentlemen with a nearly instinctive distrust of the mob. But for reasons we cannot discover, he grew up to be a political maverick. He was born in 1757, which made him one of the young men of the Revolution. He was educated in the law, fought the British, and in 1784 went to Congress, where he stayed almost until the opening of the Constitutional Convention. From the start of his time in Congress, Pinckney was a confirmed nationalist. At the Convention he himself said, "There is an *esprit de corps* which has made heretofore every *unfederal* [antinationalist] member of Congress, after his election, become strictly *federal* [nationalist]." Not everybody was so infected, but the younger men, especially, were likely to catch the nationalist contagion.

We know surprisingly little about Charles Pinckney—there is no full-dress biography of him. Most of what we have been told is not charitable. He is generally described as ambitious, egocentric, foppish—a lightweight attempting to make his way by maneuver and family connections. His generally sympathetic biographer in the *Dictionary of American Biography* sums him up thus: "Handsome, vain, and doubtless, something of a roué, though capable of the tenderest devotion to his three young children after the death of their mother, Pinckney possessed that iridescent genius which offends some and dazzles others. To his Federalist contemporaries he was 'Blackguard Charlie,' a demagogue, a spoilsman, and a corruptionist; to his followers he was a demi-god fit for the presidency."

At the time of the Convention, as throughout his career, he was challenging Rutledge and other Charleston powers for political dominance of the state. He was, therefore, isolated within his own delegations and was unable to count on support from the others; indeed, they often opposed his suggestions with such emphasis that it is clear they were trying to dissociate themselves from him.

He was no doubt an ambitious demagogue; his vanity caused him in later years to reduce his age at the time of the Convention from twenty-nine to twenty-four, so he would appear the youngest man there. (That distinction should have gone to Jonathan Dayton of New Jersey, who was twenty-seven.) Perhaps the best way to see Pinckney is as a politician in the modern mold. To the aristocrats, who in the main ran state governments, this sort of person was anathema. Gentlemen were not supposed to maneuver and to deceive each other. One of the constant motifs running through the Convention debates is an abhorrence of the "place men" who infested the British government, men who were always jockeying for influence in order to rise up the stairs of the British establishment and enrich themselves.

Charles Pinckney appeared to some to be a sort of place man. However, the day of government by gentlemen was dying. The new game would be party politics, as people like Washington and Madison would soon discover to their dismay. The gentleman may have disliked Pinckney for his politicking, but he was running with the stream. By the 1790s he dominated South Carolina politics, and could get elected governor, U.S. representative, or senator almost at will.

His political sense had made Pinckney an intelligent and articulate crusader for a strong national government early in the Confederation era. In 1783, when he was barely twenty-six, he published a series of pamphlets calling for strengthening the Articles—he suggested, for example, that Congress should have the power to confiscate ships of those states which failed to pay their requisitions to the national government. According to Charles Singer, "From 1784 on until the Constitutional Convention, Charles Pinckney became one of the great advocates for strengthening the Confederation." He was not the only one, or even the first, but his efforts were constant and persistent.

In May 1786, months before the Annapolis Convention, he pushed Congress into discussing a revision of the Articles. The upshot was the appointment of a committee (with Pinckney as chairman), which on August 7 offered seven amendments to the Articles. In the main these revisions were aimed at giving Congress tools for collecting money from the states, but one amendment proposed to give Congress some power to deal with maritime affairs. Congress, waiting to see what came out of the Annapolis Convention, did not debate the report. However, according to Madison's recent editors, "The movement within Congress for a convention to alter the Confederation originated with Charles Pinckney of South Carolina."

Some time before the Convention, Pinckney set down on paper a plan of government, which he intended to present to the men assembled in Philadelphia. A copy of this plan was in the hands of George Read, a delegate from Delaware, by May 21, and Read's partial description of it tallies with the plan Pinckney gave John Quincy Adams over thirty years later. And on May 29 he laid his plan before the Convention.

Unfortunately, although a number of scholars have reconstructed the Pinckney Plan from various sources, we will never know exactly what was presented to the Convention that day. We will never know, we believe, because James Madison suppressed it.

Charles Pinckney was just the sort of man James Madison would hate. Pinckney was assertive, a womanizer, vain. Madison was unassertive, shy with women, modest. Madison adhered to the code of a gentleman in his political as well as his personal behavior; Pinckney did not. Madison had served in Congress with Pinckney for several years and knew him; they were, in fact, both in the nationalist camp. Madison loathed him. Within a month of the ending of the Convention he and Washington were exchanging letters commenting in scathing terms on Pinckney's "appetite for expected praise" and his unwillingness "to lose any fame that can be acquired by the publication of his sentiments." Beyond this personal distaste was the fact that Pinckney's plan was the real rival to Madison's Virginia Plan. The Hamilton scheme was too eccentric to take seriously and the New Jersey Plan, to be discussed in

Chapter Ten, came from the opposition. But Pinckney's plan must have been a serious contender for preeminence in Madison's own nationalist camp. We cannot know what mix of jealousy and contempt brought Madison to suppress Pinckney's plan at the outset and label it a forgery thirty years later, but that is what he did.

In his notes Madison merely said that the Pinckney Plan was "laid before the house," the implication being that it was handed in written form to somebody. Robert Yates, in his notes, said flatly that Pinckney "read" his plan to the Convention. While he did so, Madison's pen lay idle. Madison admitted that he left the room from time to time, and it has been suggested by Sidney Ulmer that Madison happened to be out of the room when Pinckney read his plan. It is hard to be this charitable, however. For one thing, Madison could easily have asked Pinckney for a copy of the plan, which the egocentric Pinckney would surely have been happy to supply. For another, Madison had a second chance to include the plan in his notes, and once again omitted it.

On June 25 Pinckney gave a major speech, which has been characterized by Carl Van Doren as one of "great courage and independence" and called by Charles Warren "memorable . . . with the exception of those by Madison and Wilson, no such powerful, eloquent and brilliant contribution had been made." We will examine this speech in a moment. Yates says that at the conclusion of the speech Pinckney again outlined his plan. In his notes for that day Madison not only failed to record Pinckney's plan, he did not take down any of Pinckney's speech at all. Instead, he got it from him at some point later on. (Madison frequently did not taken notes on speeches or resolutions which he could get copies of and later transcribe into his record.) Either he asked Pinckney for a copy of the speech, or, more likely, Pinckney pressed it on him. Madison subsequently copied it faithfully into his notes—up to the description of Pinckney's scheme of government. At that point he simply said, "The residue of this speech was not furnished like the above by Mr. Pinckney."

The statement is hard to believe. Pinckney was smart and thorough as well as vain, and he would hardly have given Madison a truncated version of his speech. If he had, Madison could certainly have asked him for the rest of it. Madison was, after all, struggling to produce the most faithful record of the Convention that he could, and in similar cases he made a clear point of getting things down as fully as possible. But he did not ask Pinckney for the rest of it, either then or later. And it is simply too much to ask us to believe that both times Pinckney's plan was presented, Madison omitted it from his record of the Convention by mistake. Having omitted Pinckney's plan, he was then able to say over forty years later that it was "no more heard of during the Convention." And it also required him to say, when Robert Yates' notes were published, that Yates' notes were filled with errors.

What, then, was in Pinckney's plan? Several scholars have reconstructed it from various documents. It resembled Madison's Virginia Plan in broad outlines, but with considerable variation in detail. Pinckney wanted a "vigorous" executive consisting of a single person—not a committee, as some others advocated—who would hold office for seven years. He wanted a bicameral legislature, based on proportional representation. The legislature would have a negative over state laws; there would be a judiciary appointed by the legislature, and a council of revision which could review and veto acts of the legislature. The scheme had one interesting peculiarity: the membership of the Senate was not to be precisely proportional to the population of the states, as was the case in the other branch. Instead, the states were to be divided into three groups—small, medium, and large—with each state having one, two, or three senators according to its size. This was effectively a sort of compromise between the equal representation that the small-state people wanted and the proportional representation Madison was fighting for. It was an idea that the big-state men should have paid attention to, but they did not until it was too late.

Although not original, Pinckney's plan was well thought out and many parts of it had been tested in the states. Contrary to Madison's claim that it was "no more heard of during the Convention," it was eventually given, along with other plans and resolutions, to the Committee of Detail, which put together the first rough draft of the Constitution. Many of Pinckney's ideas, and even his language, ended up in the final Constitution of the United States. Pinckney provided the terms "president," "House," and "Senate." Also drawn from his plan were the ideas that the House should have the impeachment power; that the legislature should have the power to coin money, call up the militia, and establish post offices; and that states should not coin money or keep troops during peacetime. The concept of the president's annual State of the Union address came from Pinckney, as did the idea that the president should be commander in chief of the military. All told, some twenty-one provisions in the American Constitution appeared *first* in Charles Pinckney's plan. In addition, there are a number of other provisions that appear in the Pinckney Plan as well as in the Virginia and/or New Jersey plans, so that Ulmer was able to raise his estimate of specific Pinckney contributions to the final draft of the Constitution to forty-three.

Of course, a great many of these provisions were obvious and were the sort of thing that many of the men at the Convention would have suggested. We cannot, as Sidney Ulmer suggests, call Pinckney the Father of the Constitution, simply because he happened to commit to paper a lot of ideas that would have found their way into the Constitution anyway. Many of the delegates had worked on drafting their own state constitutions or the Articles of Confederation and had their own opinions about what should or should not go into such documents. The Pinckney Plan—it appears—provided one convenient source for members of the Committee of Detail to dip into for both devices and language; it acted as a kind of suggestion box.

But Charles Pinckney's greatest contribution to the Convention may not have been his plan. On June 25 Pinckney rose to answer Alexander Hamilton's long speech extolling the virtues of the British "mixed" system of government. The essence of Pinckney's reply was that the United States was different from any other place on earth, and that the delegates could therefore look to no other system for answers to the American problem. Charles Warren writes, "Into the debates, which had so largely turned on devotion to the States, Pinckney now breathed a spirit of Americanism." The American people, Pinckney said, were "the most singular of any we are acquainted with." And they were unique principally because there were "fewer distinctions of fortune and less of rank, than among the inhabitants of any other nation." Unlike classical societies, America was not divided into patricians and plebeians. Unlike England and France, it had neither nobility nor poor. "Our true situation appears to me to be this—a new extensive country containing within itself the materials for forming a government capable of extending to its citizens all the blessings of civil and religious liberty [and] capable of making them happy at home." Furthermore, this situation was likely to continue for several centuries, because off to the west was almost unlimited empty land, where anybody who was willing to work could make a decent living. (Pinckney, like most of the men at the Convention, tended cavalierly to dismiss the fact that there were actually tens of thousands of American Indians living in that "empty" land.)

As a consequence, Pinckney went on, the United States could not really be compared with the countries of the Old World, as Hamilton had done. In Europe there were vast gulfs between classes: the people, the nobility, the Crown. The English government was rightly drawn to reflect these divisions. In America, however, the people were more nearly equal in wealth and status. There existed no class from which to draw an analogue to the House of Lords.

Our Senate thus could—indeed, must—be built on a different foundation. It should not be made to represent the interests of an aristocracy, but should instead be a small body of wise men who would act as a check on the impetuosity of the lower branch of the legislature.

The most important point, then, is not the details of the Pinckney Plan but the attitude he expressed. Again and again he pointed to the equality that existed in the United States, compared with all other countries. Again and again, he said that with the creation of a sensible government, this equality could be preserved. "Every member of the society almost, will enjoy an equal power of arriving at the supreme offices . . . ," he said on June 25. "None will be excluded by birth and few by fortune, from voting. . . . the whole community will enjoy in the fullest sense that kind of political liberty which consists in the power the members of the states reserve to themselves, of arriving at the public offices, or at least, of having votes in the nomination of those who fill them." It was a very modern speech. Pinckney was saying precisely what later generations of Americans came to believe, that even the inhabitant of a log cabin could dream of becoming president.

It was not an idea that everybody at the Convention would relish; many agreed with Roger Sherman of Connecticut that the ordinary people were unfit to be governors and ought to elect the best among them to rule. Indeed, Pinckney himself would not have wanted to see a government in the hands of ill-educated plow-joggers. Nonetheless, he was advocating a broader political democracy than many of the men at the Convention thought wise.

The speech, moreover, was strongly nationalistic. America need make no apologies for itself, but should find its own way to fit its own circumstances. And here again Pinckney was running against the established wisdom, which said that we must learn from the experience of history. Not so, Pinckney said. America was different, and could learn only from itself.

It was a remarkable speech. Washington, Madison, Hamilton, and the rest were eighteenth-century men, reflecting an eighteenth-century world, where place and privilege went automatically with birth. Pinckney had already leapt into the nineteenth century. He was a nineteenth-century politician with nineteenth-century opinions about democracy and America's place in the world. It was a speech that Andrew Jackson could have made, fifty years later. "From the time that Pinckney spoke," says the nineteenth-century historian Francis N. Thorpe, ". . . the members must have been persuaded, if any were yet in doubt, that the Constitution which they were making must be American in character."

Charles Pinckney, contrary to what has been believed by so many commentators on the Constitution, was no mere cipher at the Convention, intent mainly on puffing himself up in the eyes of other men. He was one of the first men in the United States to work actively and continuously to bring about a revision of the Articles; he pushed Congress hard to approve the idea of making changes; he produced a useful plan at the Convention; he spoke cogently and forcefully from the floor many times; and he eventually led the fight in his home state for ratification of the final document. Whatever character flaws he may have had—the egotism, the political instincts that so many of the other gentlemen around him abhorred—he was an intelligent, experienced, clear-sighted, and convincing man whose ideas and opinions had considerable weight. The Father of the Constitution he was not; but he must be seen as one of the group, with James Madison, James Wilson, Roger Sherman, and others, who did the most in shaping it.

Chapter Eight

Men, Manners, and Rules:
The Convention Begins

The Convention had originally been called for May 14, but according to the rules laid down at the Annapolis Convention, it could not act until seven states were represented. The states had their own rules about what constituted quorums in their own delegations, and in many cases the presence of one or two delegates from a given state was not enough. But then, on Friday, May 25, when three delegates from New Jersey arrived, a quorum was reached.

It rained that day in Philadelphia, a heavy drenching rain that sluiced down the streets, shining the cobblestones and slate roofs of the houses. But rain did not deter them, and on to the State House they came, all those great names that ring in the ears of Americans—Washington, Madison, Hamilton, two Morrises, Randolph, and the rest, among them future presidents, congressmen, Supreme Court justices, cabinet members, ambassadors.

Independence Hall, or the State House, as it was called then, is one of the best-known buildings in the United States. It is a brick building, two stories high, topped by a cupola and spire double the height of the main structure. It is flanked by two smaller buildings which are joined to it by archways. It is balanced, serene, formal—precisely the sort of building in which to debate weighty matters.

The conference, for the most part, would be held in the east room, a chamber forty by forty feet, with great windows on each side and a fireplace set among much wood paneling in the back. The delegates sat grouped in threes and fours at tables the size of ordinary dining-room tables, covered with green baize. However, for part of the Convention, they met in an upstairs room similarly furnished. We are not sure why they moved, but the delegates had been keeping the windows downstairs closed so their speeches, which were sometimes orotund, would not be heard outside. It turned out to be a very hot summer: upstairs they could open the windows.

The states had picked a total of seventy-four men as delegates. Fifty-five of them actually arrived; the rest were tied up with business or family matters, or were out of sympathy with the occasion and chose not to come. Even the fifty-five who did show up were frequently absent for one reason or another; a few came late and left early. On most days there were probably not more than thirty or forty men on the Convention floor at once.

Who were these fifty-five men who would decide so much that affects how Americans live today? To begin with, they were not "typical" Americans. They were all white males, by and large Protestants, with two Catholics and a few Quakers mixed in. Only two of them were small farmers, from the class that made up 85 percent of the white population. More than half were lawyers; another quarter were owners of large commercial farms or plantations. All of them had held public office. Three of them were governors of their states, and four others had been. At least eight were judges, forty-two had been congressmen, most had served in their state governments, and a sprinkling had been speakers of their state legislatures. Eight had signed the Declaration of Independence, thirty had served in the army during the Revolution, some fifteen had seen serious action, and several were authentic battlefield heroes. Almost all of these men were known figures in their states, and perhaps a quarter of them had national reputations. It was as if today, to reach some important national decision, Americans were to bypass Congress and put together a conference of the wisest and most experienced people—college presidents, chairmen of large corporations, famous social scientists, distinguished public servants.

The historian Clinton Rossiter suggests that at most two other "teams" could have been put together to equal this one. It is true that some important men were absent. John Adams was in London representing the United States government, and Thomas Jefferson was in Paris doing the same. Sam Adams, John Jay, Dr. Benjamin Rush, and Patrick Henry did not attend for various reasons; but few other illustrious names were missing. But those who did attend were simply smarter, better educated, more experienced, and wiser than most. Jefferson, when he heard in Paris who would be at the Convention, called them a group of demigods.

These men were also, by and large, drawn from a tiny aristocracy. A few, like Roger Sherman and Luther Martin, had been born into those quasi-subsistence farm families that constituted the heart of the nation, and a few others, like Alexander Hamilton and William Paterson, had started life clerking in stores. But they had risen high (and as we shall see, these lowborn men tended to mistrust the judgment of the common people more than the aristocrats did). These were members of the establishment and they did not come to Philadelphia to overthrow the system.

Nonetheless, it is extremely important to our understanding of how the American Constitution was made to keep firmly in mind that, although the delegates in the main came from similar backgrounds, they were temperamentally as diverse as any group of people is likely to be. Some were bold, some cautious; some shy, some outspoken; some politically adept, some bristly and rancorous.

We can get a good picture of this temperamental variety by looking at the four men who made up the Massachusetts delegation. Outwardly, they appear much the same: three had gone to Harvard, two were lawyers, two businessmen, all had been in public life. But inwardly they were different. Rufus King was "handsome and ambitious, with perhaps a trace of . . . haughtiness." He was, the great speaker Daniel Webster later said, "unequalled" as an orator. By contrast, Nathaniel Gorham was a poor speaker but had an "agreeable and easy-going manner." Elbridge Gerry was likewise a poor speaker, but he was far from agreeable in his manner. He suffered from a nervous tic, and while admired for the clarity of his thought and his integrity, could be stubborn and argumentative when his mind was made up. Caleb Strong, on the other hand, was of a compromising nature. "Of simple, engaging manner, he was concilliatory toward friend and opponent."

These, then, were four quite different men, despite their common background, and at the Convention they would frequently not vote as a bloc. Indeed, at one of the most critical moments at the Convention they would split two against two, cancel their state's vote, and thus have a profound effect on American history. They would do so not out of differences in political theory, but simply because they were different men with different ways of viewing the world. We must, then, in looking at the Constitutional Convention, constantly remind ourselves that these were not gods but living, breathing human beings with their own strengths and weaknesses, their virtues and foibles.

There was one trait they held in common, however. They all believed that the system had to be made to work better, and many of them were prepared to make substantial changes in how things were done. There was a tendency for those who disapproved of the undertaking to stay away. Strong antinationalists like Patrick Henry and Richard Henry Lee of Virginia, Sam Adams of

Massachusetts, Governor George Clinton of New York, did not attend. As a consequence, the Convention had a more nationalist tone than was true of American opinion in general. For the antinationalists staying away was a bad tactical error. A handful of determined opponents of a stronger national government could have destroyed the Convention through obstructionist tactics, or by throwing their weight on the antinationalist side in closely fought issues. But they did stay away and left the battlefield to the enemy.

The delegates, then, did not accurately reflect the basic attitudes of most Americans. Although they were in grave disagreement about how it should be done, they had come to build a solid nation under a solid government. Some would have been content with tinkering, and a few had no ideas at all about what should be done, but most saw themselves as embarking on a great enterprise. It is exceedingly important to keep this in mind. Again and again in the debates they alluded to the fact that the eyes of the world were on them, that they were carrying the hopes of people everywhere in their hands. They were engaged in possibly the most important experiment a people ever undertook—to see if human beings could live in freedom under a government they would run themselves. Was it possible? Many people believed that it was not, that the common people were children and would always need over them the guiding hand of a prince, who would know what was best for them. As interested spectators around the world, especially those living under autocratic monarchs in Europe—notably in France—were acutely aware, if it could work in America, it could work elsewhere.

All of this the men at Philadelphia knew. This would be the great time of their lives, their moment on center stage, their chance to become immortal, to engrave their names in granite. Indeed, to achieve "fame." This knowledge gave their days in Philadelphia a rare intensity.

So on that rainy Friday in May they trudged or trundled in carriages to the State House. One of the most illustrious names of all, however, was missing on this day. Benjamin Franklin, aged eighty-one, and suffering from "stones" and bouts of gout, had for two weeks come to the State House each morning, brought there in the first sedan chair in America, carried by prison trusties. Franklin and Washington were the only two Americans who were as yet internationally famous. Franklin was seen as one of the great men of the age —an inventor, scientist, philosopher, man of letters, and statesman.

And it is true that Franklin was an extraordinary man. He was not merely an amateur dabbler at science but the first to show that lightning was electricity; he invented the lightning rod, a great blessing to the world at a time when lightning killed substantial numbers of people, and he refused to patent it, although by doing so he might have earned huge sums. He was generous, a prime mover in all sorts of civic projects, such as the establishment of libraries, philanthropical societies, volunteer fire brigades. (As an old man, visiting his fire brigade after an absence of many years abroad, he apologized to the members for the condition of his bucket, but said he would have it in order for the next meeting.) He was a great diplomat: his guile, intelligence, and wit were largely responsible for keeping the munitions flowing from France to Washington's army during the Revolution.

But Franklin had never chosen to make himself into a marble hero, and his vanities were apparent. He was a masterful self-publicist, constantly getting into the newspapers, some of which he published himself, and his contemporary celebrity was in part of his own contriving. By the time of the Convention Franklin was more or less chronically ill, and growing feeble, but he attended the meetings faithfully, convinced of the great importance of the enterprise. He brought to it no strong convictions, no carefully reasoned positions as to what should be done. He would accept anything that seemed reasonable, and he made it his main work to calm tempers and smooth roiled seas. His ideas were not really influential at the Convention. But the doughty presence of one of the world's great men certainly helped to maintain the tone of high seriousness with which the proceedings were carried on.

On May 25, however, he was sick, and in view of the downpour decided not to come. This was a disappointment to him. As nominal leader of the host delegation he had expected to nominate George Washington for president of the Convention himself; there was no question that Washington would be chosen. Instead Robert Morris, Washington's host, made the nomination, and Washington was duly installed in a chair in the front of the room, facing the delegates grouped around the green-baize-topped tables. The chair had a tall, elegant back, with a picture of a sun over a horizon painted on it. Washington had no table in front of him, and faced the other delegates directly.

The role of George Washington at the Constitutional Convention might surprise those who see him only in his dominating role. For parliamentary reasons, somebody else presided a good deal of the time, and Washington sat at a table with the other delegates from Virginia. He spoke formally only once, at the very end, on a small point; and such was his prestige that the delegates instantly agreed to what he wanted. Yet during that long, hot, summer, this gregarious man was constantly having dinner, tea, supper with people, and one must assume of course that he was actively promoting his positions.

According to Arthur N. Holcombe, drawing on letters of Washington, "it is clear that he wanted a general government endowed with sufficient authority to act directly upon the people of the whole country." Washington was not afraid of power. He knew how to use it well, and he was less concerned with checks and balances and building careful walls about governments than many of the other men at the Convention were. He did not want a new despotism, but neither did he want anarchy, which he believed would surely open the doors to a despot. Washington had had more experience than most in trying to work with an ineffective government. He was prepared to go farther than most of the other delegates in building strength into a new one. The few instances in which his vote was recorded show him consistently pushing for a strong executive in a strong government.

Holcombe says, "In short, it is impossible to avoid the conclusion that this strong, silent man knew how to exert a due influence in the Convention's proceedings without intervening personally in the debates on the floor." And why not intervene personally in the debates? The answer is obvious: to maintain his prestige, it was crucial for Washington to avoid being drawn into wrangling, where he might be bested in argument, or find himself too often fighting losing battles. Better to supply guidance behind the arras, and let younger men wield the swords. We must bear it in mind, then, as we follow the Convention, that looming over all the debates was the formidable figure of George Washington pressing for a strong, decisive national government.

After the installation of Washington two things of critical importance occurred on that first day. One was a deliberate move by James Madison to put himself in a good position to take notes on the Convention. At the end of his long life, he wrote, "I chose a seat in front of the presiding member, with the other members on right and left hands. In this favorable position for hearing all that passed, I noted in terms legible and in abbreviations and marks intelligible to myself what was read from the Chair or spoken by members: and not losing a moment unnecessarily between the adjournment and reassembling of the Convention I was enabled to write out my daily notes during the session or within a few finishing days after its close." It must have been a substantial chore, after sitting through hours of debate in which he played a leading role, to go back to his room each evening and write up his notes, which sometimes ran to the equivalent of ten typewritten pages for a single day.

Madison explained that he had decided to make his own notes on the Convention because he had been troubled, during his studies of earlier governments, by the difficulty—indeed impossibility—of knowing exactly what their founders had had in mind. He obviously did not trust the official secretary, twenty-eight-year-old Major William Jackson, a Continental Army Veteran, later President Washington's secretary, to keep adequate notes, and in this he was correct: Jackson recorded little more than the official votes.

But there was undoubtedly more to it than that. It is probable that Madison wanted to be prepared, later on, to defend himself if the Convention failed, or went off in some direction he did not like. Secondly, he may have realized that a time might come when politicians would try to distort the intent of the Founders, in which case a record of the debates would prove invaluable. Finally, Madison had a sense of history and his role in it. He recognized that if the Convention succeeded in reforming the nation, a record of the debates would be of extraordinary importance to historians, as in fact it is. (In the end, Madison did not permit publication of his notes until the last delegate died, who turned out to be himself.)

Madison was not the only one to make notes of the proceedings. Robert Yates, one of the future antinationalists of New York, took extensive notes through July 5, when he left; several others left much briefer accounts. But Madison's "Notes," as they are known to historians, run to over six hundred pages of printed text; they are not merely our primary source but virtually our *only* full source on the debates at the Constitutional Convention.

Yet despite the debt we owe Madison for this work, we must bear in mind that he is the major, and usually the only, reporter of an event in which he was both emotionally and politically involved. Unfortunately, many historians have accepted Madison's version of the debates uncritically. There is some basis for this view, because when Madison's report is compared with Yates' few important differences are uncovered. But most of the time we have to take Madison at his word. Nobody believes that he knowingly falsified his report of the Convention: he was far too scrupulous a gentleman, and would have scorned to do that. But if there is anything modern psychology has told us, it is that none of us is free from unconscious error. It is impossible to doubt that at times, in the quiet of his study, Madison improved his own arguments and abbreviated those of his opponents. (As we have seen, he managed to destroy the posthumous reputation of Charles Pinckney by selective reporting.) Nonetheless, on the whole, historians believe Madison's "Notes" to be unusually trustworthy.

The second important event that opening day of the Convention occurred during the reading of the credentials the delegates had brought with them from their state legislatures. Ordinarily this would have been a cut-and-dried process, something the delegates would have yawned through. But halfway down the roll call they were snapped alert by the reading of the instructions the delegates from Delaware had been given: they were on no account to agree to any change in the rules of government that did away with the one-state–one-vote principle by which the old Congress operated under the Articles of Confederation. Even if they wanted to, they could not agree to Madison's cherished principle of proportional representation. Their hands were tied, and not by accident. George Read, one of the major figures in his delegation, had specifically requested the Delaware legislature to give them this binding instruction. He had done so because, over the preceding years, he had watched the larger states attempt to maneuver the distribution of the western lands over the Alleghenies to benefit themselves at the expense of the smaller states. A few months before the Convention he wrote his colleague John Dickinson, "such is my jealousy of most of the larger States that I would trust nothing to their candor, generosity, or ideas of public justice in behalf of this State." The best thing, he wrote Dickinson, would be to have their instructions written in such a way as to forestall "disagreeable argumentation."

Behind this maneuver was a simple fact: Delaware was the smallest of the states, with a population one-tenth that of Virginia. In a legislature apportioned according to population, its delegates would be drowned in a sea of men from Virginia, Massachusetts, and Pennsylvania, Delaware's giant neighbor, whose dominance it especially feared.

When the Delaware instructions were read, nobody commented, but many were silently dismayed. The Pennsylvanians had already let it be known that they were "tired of continental gatherings in which the smallest states had exactly the same voting power as the largest," and before the Convention opened they had pushed the idea that the Convention itself ought to be run on proportional representation. Though this was Madison's sine qua non of good government, he had resisted, fearing that such a policy would drive the small states' delegates out of the Convention before it started. The Pennsylvanians dropped their demand, but the resentment against the small states was palpable; and here was Delaware announcing at the outset that it would leave the Convention rather than accept proportional representation. It was an ominous beginning, and everybody knew it, but one state, one vote was the rule adopted for the Convention.

But for the moment the big-state delegates swallowed their dismay. The Convention then appointed a committee to "prepare standing rules and orders," and adjourned for the weekend. On Monday the rules committee delivered its report, and that day and most of the next was devoted to discussing it. A good deal covered routine matters: establishing quorums and the like. A gentlemanly decorum was to be preserved, with members not gossiping among themselves, or interrupting when somebody was speaking. But on two points the delegates made decisions that were important, and perhaps critical, to the success of the Convention. These men were veterans of parliamentary debate; they knew what the risks were.

The first was a rule of secrecy: none of the delegates was to say anything whatever about what went on in the meeting room to anyone—wife, children, closest friends. There were a number of reasons for adopting this rule. One was that if it began to come out that the Convention was considering this or that course of action, there was certain to be a public uproar, which might set the country against the whole proceeding. Another was that enemies of the Convention would certainly make use of anything they heard to stir up feeling against it. A third was that the delegates wanted to be free to think out loud, to float trial balloons, to take strong positions, and to compromise. They did not want to appear to their constituencies to be flipflopping on every issue.

The delegates were astonishingly conscientious in adhering to the rule, however unfortunate that may have been for historians. It is known that in four instances delegates mentioned something about the proceedings in letters, and the French chargé d'affaires in Philadelphia sent home to his government information that was in part surprisingly accurate. But on the whole, when one considers that there were men given to talk and convivial dinners, it is astonishing how little leaked out. Not a word of what was going on in the State House appeared in any newspaper.

The seriousness with which the delegates took the rule is illustrated by a story told by Manasseh Cutler. He had wangled an invitation to visit Benjamin Franklin and felt that he was going to be in "the presence of a European Monarch." But when he went out to the garden behind the house, he "saw a short, fat, trunched old man, in a plain Quaker dress, bald pate, and short white locks, sitting without his hat under the tree." Cutler was interested in natural science, and during the course of his conversation Franklin showed him a two-headed snake, which was preserved in a jar.

> The Doctor mentioned the situation of this snake, if it was travelling among bushes, and one head should choose to go on one side of the stem

of a bush and the other head should prefer the other side, and that neither of the heads would consent to come back or give way to the other. He was then going to mention a humorous matter that had that day taken place in Convention, in consequence of his comparing the snake to America, for he seemed to forget that everything in Convention was to be kept a profound secret; but the secrecy of Convention matters was suggested to him, which stopped him and deprived me of the story he was going to tell.

About the same time, while the Virginia Plan was being debated, delegates were allowed to make copies of it to study at their leisure. One morning Thomas Mifflin, a Pennsylvania delegate, found outside the door to the meeting chamber a copy of the plan, which a delegate had dropped by accident. He picked it up and brought it to Washington. Washington pocketed it and said nothing about it until the Convention was about to adjourn. Then he rose and said in his sternest voice:

> Gentlemen, I am sorry to find that some one member of the body has been so neglectful to the secrets of the Convention as to drop in the State House a copy of their proceedings, which by accident was picked up and delivered to me this morning. I must entreat the gentlemen to be more careful, least our transactions get into the newspapers and disturb the public repose by premature speculations. I know not whose paper it is, but here it is, let him who owns it take it.

He flung the paper down on a desk, picked up his hat, and stalked out of the room, leaving the delegates cowed. William Pierce, a delegate from Georgia, who gives us this account, began feeling in his pockets to make sure that it had not been he who had carelessly dropped the paper. He was stunned to find that he did not have it. But when he went up to the desk he saw that the paper was not in his handwriting, and he was vastly relieved, when he hastened back to the Indian Queen, where he was staying, to find his own copy in the pocket of a coat he had been wearing the day before. The lost paper was never claimed.

A second wise decision made in the early days of the Convention was the adoption of a procedure under which questions that had been voted on could nonetheless be brought up again. Without this rule the Convention would have collapsed in the first week. Blocs of delegates who saw issues crucial to their states go against them, and who might otherwise have decided to walk out, could sit tight, in the knowledge that they could bring the matter up again when they thought they had a better chance. As a consequence, throughout the Convention, matters were undecided almost as frequently as they were decided. Central issues were voted on again and again.

And then, finally, on Tuesday, May 29, the delegates got down to the business of creating a new nation.

Part II

THE LARGE STATES
and
THE SMALL

Chapter Nine

Roger Sherman
and the Art of Compromise

The delegates came to Philadelphia with a wide variety of opinions on what ought to be done about the problems facing the United States, and they came in different states of preparedness. Some, like Madison, Pinckney, and Hamilton, had worked out very specific proposals; others, such as Benjamin Franklin, came prepared to support almost anything that would produce a more effective government. Some, like Roger Sherman, wanted merely to tinker with the machinery of the old government in order to remedy a few specific ills; others, like Hamilton, were ready to sweep away the old government and replace it with something radically new.

In some areas there was a good deal of consensus; for example, at the beginning most of the delegates favored a government in which the executive would be the servant of a dominating legislature, as in Madison's Virginia Plan. But in other areas there was not merely no consensus, but passionate support for opposing ideas. Such a subject was the question of how the national legislature would be constituted. The old Congress had been built on the principle of one vote per state. This, Madison believed, was patently unfair, and he put into the Virginia Plan a system of proportional representation. Madison knew that this would not be to the liking of the small states, but he believed the arguments for it were so sound that the small states would eventually have to give way before them.

But James Madison was wrong. The battle between the big states and the small states was fought with passion and dogged determination, and it came within inches of wrecking the Convention. It is to this battle that we must now turn our attention.

Like most of the great issues facing the Convention, the big-state–small-state conflict was interlocked in an exceedingly complex way with a myriad of smaller issues, so that frequently one piece of the whole could not be changed without disturbing everything around it. As a consequence, the Constitutional Convention could not, and did not, proceed in a straight line, neatly disposing of one issue after the next until all were dealt with. It moved instead in swirls and loops, again and again backtracking to pick up issues previously debated. Frequently the delegates charged breathlessly at an issue, only to realize that there was no consensus, and no hope of one at that juncture, and so they would hastily drop it. In other cases issues were so linked that when Question C was finally settled, they would discover that Questions A and B were suddenly undone and would have to be debated again.

It therefore does not make sense for us to attempt to study the Convention day by day. It will be far better to single out the major issues and follow them one at a time through the debates from beginning to end. This will mean going back to the early days of the Convention each time we pick up a new issue.

One thing that almost forces us into this procedure is a parliamentary device the Convention adopted at the beginning: to resolve themselves into a "Committee of the Whole." That is to say, the Convention voted to form a committee made up of *all* the delegates, which would, as any committee does, debate issues and make recommendations to the larger body. This was, of course, a parliamentary ruse, for the Committee of the Whole and the Convention it would make its recommendations to were identical bodies. But the device made it clear that decisions taken the first time through were only "recommendations" of the Committee of the Whole, to be reconsidered when the committee turned itself back into the Convention again. The device of the Committee of the Whole was another means for allowing the delegates to fly trial balloons and think out loud, knowing that the questions would all be debated again. It also permitted men who saw important issues go against them to bide their time in the knowledge that there would be a second chance later.

The conflict between the big states and the small ones was joined on May 29, with the presentation of the Virginia Plan, by the Virginia governor, the charming but frequently irresolute Edmund Randolph. The plan, as we have seen, called for a legislature based on proportional representation, which the small states were certain to hate.

The Virginia Plan was debated by the Convention, sitting as the Committee of the Whole, from May 30 to June 13. To the immense consternation of the small states, it was passed with no basic changes. It went through so easily because the Virginians had put together an alliance of the three most populous states—Virginia, Pennsylvania, and Massachusetts—and the three states of what was then the Deep South—Georgia and the two Carolinas.

The alliance was based in part on the misperception that with population flowing into the southwest, the Deep South states would soon be big states themselves; their interests would eventually be the same as those of the Big Three. The alliance may also have been based on a sense among the delegates from the Deep South that if they supported the Big Three on issues important to them, Virginia, Massachusetts, and Pennsylvania would not attempt to harrass the Deep South on an issue crucial to them—slavery.

Yet it was an uneasy alliance. Northerners and southerners were suspicious of each other, and their interests were opposed in a number of areas, as we shall eventually see. But for the moment the alliance held, and it was able to ram through proportional representation. But long before the ramming was done, it was clear to everybody that the Convention was faced with a deep division, which might shortly tear it apart. So strongly did men on both sides of the issue feel about it that other important issues could not be profitably addressed until this one was settled.

Today it is difficult to see why the issue should have brought such smoking ferocity to the Convention floor. Rarely in the history of the United States have the small states and the large states lined up on opposite sides of an issue. Political divisions tend to be, for example, sectional, with the South poised against the North, or the Sun Belt at odds with the Frost Belt. Or they are cut along economic lines, with city dwellers fighting farmers over, say, farm subsidies.

In 1787, however, most people felt intensely loyal to their states. As a consequence, the men from the big states could not abide the idea of the pygmies around them holding them hostage in government; and the pygmies could not, in their turn, bear the thought of a government run by the big states towering over them. The issue, then, was emotional, as well as theoretical and political.

At the outset it does not appear to have occurred to Madison that this particular issue would be so troublesome. It seemed obvious to him that the old system, which in effect gave each citizen of Delaware ten times as much weight in Congress as it gave his neighbor in Virginia, was not only manifestly unfair but philosophically unsound. James Madison's aim was not to put the big states in the driver's seat; it was instead to derive the government directly from the people, and to undercut the power of the frequently erratic state governments.

But however Madison viewed the issue, most of the other delegates tended to see it in more black-and-white terms, as big states versus small. And it took Madison some time to grasp this fact. He was not so naïve as to believe the small states would swallow proportional representation easily, but he did believe that eventually reason would force them to choke it down. He was therefore somewhat dismayed to discover that they did not mean to choke it down under any circumstances.

In their turn the men from the small states were surprised to find the big states so strongly committed to proportional representation. They knew, of course, that the big states did not like the one-state, one-vote system of voting. But the big states had accepted equality, however reluctantly, at the time the Articles of Confederation were written. The big states might fuss; but surely they recognized that they could not change the system. It was perfectly obvious, so they thought, that no small state could possibly accept a scheme of government in which the votes of their delegates would be swamped by those of the big states. The Big Three had forty-five percent of the American population. Under proportional representation they would need only one other state to achieve a majority that could run the country as it suited them. Anyone could see this, and no small-state delegate could possibly go home to his constituents with a plan for that sort of government. Both sides, then, came to the Convention expecting a fight on the issue; but neither side really expected the other to prove so determined an enemy.

The issue first came up on Wednesday, May 30, the second day of debate on the Virginia Plan. As the small states' men sat in silent dismay, the Big Three–Deep South alliance tinkered with wording in the plan to deal with the associated problem of how slaves would be counted in determining the population base for representation: the northern states, obviously, did not want them counted, the southern states did. To duck the issue for the moment, Madison proposed this wording: "that the equality of suffrage established by the Articles of Confederation ought not to prevail in the national legislature; and that an equitable ratio of representation ought to be substituted." The important thing was to push through proportional representation; the matter of how slaves would be counted could be decided later. And when he wrote up his notes later he added sourly, "This . . . being generally relished, would have been agreed to."

But it was not generally relished and was not agreed to. George Read of Delaware rose and bluntly reminded the Convention that the Delaware men were prohibited by their instructions from accepting the clause, and that if it were forced past them, "it might become their duty to retire from the Convention."

Hastily Gouverneur Morris arose and said that "so early a proof of discord in the Convention as the secession of a state would be very much regretted." Nonetheless, he did not see how they could abandon so "fundamental an article" as proportional representation. Madison then reminded the delegates that they were acting as the Committee of the Whole, and a vote on the issue would not be binding; it would be debated again. But Read was not satisfied, and the hall was filled with the feeling that the Delaware people were about to walk out. Several delegates attempted to mollify the Delaware men. In particular, it was pointed out that even if they were instructed not to *accept* proportional representation, they had not been instructed to *leave* if the Convention voted for it. But George Read would not back down, and reluctantly the big states agreed to postpone the issue.

Over the next few days the Convention wrangled over other issues concerning the national legislature, and the proportional representation issue lay quiet. Then, on June 9 William Paterson of New Jersey forced the issue. Why he did so at this point is not known, but the suspicion is that it had something to do with the arrival at the Convention that day of Luther Martin of Maryland, who would prove to be the bitterest states' righter at the Convention. Martin was by reputation one of the finest courtroom lawyers in the United States, and Paterson may have concluded that he would be able to argue the Convention out of proportional representation. And so Paterson moved that the Convention take up again the "rule of suffrage." He was seconded immediately by his colleague from New Jersey David Brearley, who went on to suggest tongue-in-cheek that perhaps the states ought to be dispensed with, and the entire country cut into thirteen equal districts. Since it would be the large states that would be cut up, while the small states would be enlarged, Brearley was attempting to carry the nationalist theory to an absurd conclusion.

William Paterson stood and in a passionate speech stated the case for the small states. Proportional representation struck at the very existence of the lesser states, he said. In joining the Confederacy under the Articles, the small states had not given up their sovereignty—ultimate and full power. In a federal system, which the confederacy under the Articles certainly was, the states, rather than the people, were the basis of government, and therefore states, rather than people, ought to have equal votes. "A confederacy supposes sovereignty in the members composing it and sovereignty supposes equality."

But beyond theoretical considerations was a practical one: the Convention was not authorized to alter the Articles dramatically. The people, said Paterson, were not prepared for anything so radical, and would not accept it. Most important of all, if the Big Three were allowed to dominate, they would run roughshod over the rest. And he concluded by alluding to:

> the hint thrown out heretofore by Mr. Wilson of the necessity to which the large states might be reduced to confederating among themselves, by a refusal of the others to concur. Let them unite if they please, but let them remember that they have no authority to compel the others to unite. New Jersey will never confederate on the plan before the Committee. She would be swallowed up. He had rather submit to a monarch, to a despot, than to such a fate. He would not only oppose the plan here, but on his return home do everything in his power to defeat it there.

The Mr. Wilson to whom Paterson referred was James Wilson of Pennsylvania. Virtually forgotten today, he was one of the great men of his time. We will learn more about him later. For the moment it will suffice to say that he had graduated from the prestigious University of Edinburgh, emigrated to America as a young man, studied law, and rapidly rose to a position of prominence in his state through the brilliance of his mind. He married into an important Pennsylvania family, which brought him into contact with leading Americans, such as Robert Morris, Washington's host during the Convention. By 1787 he was considered by his peers to be perhaps the finest legal theorist in the country.

Philosophically, Wilson was the strongest proponent at the Convention of the idea that all power resided in the people, and he worked hard to see that the people would play as direct a role in the new government as was possible. As a consequence he was a fervid believer in proportional representation.

Stung by the allusion to his own threat to organize the big states without the little ones, Wilson spoke. "Are not the citizens of Pennsylvania equal to those of New Jersey? Does it require 150 of the former to balance 50 of the latter? . . . If the small states will not confederate on this plan, Pennsylvania and he presumed some other states, would not confederate on any other."

Tempers were rising. However, Paterson realized that if the delegates voted on the issue, proportional representation would win, and he and his small-state allies would be forced either to accept the decision or leave. He therefore moved to postpone the vote until the next session. With relief the delegates agreed, and adjourned for the day.

Fortunately, the next day was Sunday, June 10. It appears that Paterson,

Roger Sherman of Connecticut, and some of the other small states' men made use of the day to meet and work out a strategy, and it is probably then that they came up with what came to be known as the Connecticut Compromise. This was a plan by which one house of the Congress would be based on proportional representation, the other on equal votes for each state.

The so-called Connecticut Compromise was devised by one of the most neglected of our Founding Fathers, Roger Sherman. There is one small town at the western edge of his home state named for him, and he appears on the two-dollar bill as one of the signers of the Declaration of Independence in John Trumbull's famous painting. Few people except students of American history know his name, and even some historians have only the vaguest idea of his importance. His role in the making of the nation was immense. Roger Sherman is the only man in our history who signed all the basic American documents. He signed the Declaration and Resolves of 1774, in which the American colonies stated their determination to resist British power, and the Association of the same year, which established the boycott of British goods. He not only signed the Declaration of Independence but was on the committee that wrote it. He was also on the committee that wrote the Articles of Confederation, which he signed; and he voted for the peace treaty with England. Finally, he would sign the Constitution. He was in the First and Second continental congresses, which organized the Revolution. He spent more time in the old Congress under the Articles than anybody else. He would be in the first United States Congress of the new government as representative, and in the second as senator.

He was, moreover, no silent witness to great events but a careful reasoner and frequent speaker. At the Convention he spoke more often than anyone other than Madison and perhaps one other, depending on whose biographer does the counting. He was considered by his peers to be one of the most influential men in the country, a clever and persuasive debater who more often than not brought people around to his way of looking at issues: things tended to go his way, because he knew how to make them do so.

He was respected by the major figures around him. John Adams called him "a solid, sensible man," and after Sherman was dead said that he "was one of the most cordial friends which I ever had in my life . . . one of the soundest and strongest pillars of the Revolution." Patrick Henry called him one of the three leading men in Congress and one of the greatest statesmen he ever knew. Thomas Jefferson once pointed him out to a friend, saying, "That is Mr. Sherman of Connecticut, a man who never said a foolish thing in his life." Even his political enemies respected and feared him. As Sherman was going off to the Convention an opponent wrote, "He is cunning as the devil, and if you attack him, you ought to know him well; he is not easily managed, but if he suspects you are trying to take him in, you may as well catch an eel by the tail." He then added that if Sherman "is stubborn he will influence too many others." In Congress one younger colleague said that if he had doubts on any issue he would watch to see how Sherman voted, with the assurance that Sherman always knew what was the right thing to do.

Why has a man so profoundly important been neglected? The answer lies in the fact that Roger Sherman was one of the most levelheaded men who ever lived. Indeed, he claimed to have gained control of his emotions by the age of twenty-one. Every statement made about him, while he lived and since, bears witness to the truth of this claim. Like Washington, he marbleized himself, but he achieved this goal at a much earlier age than Washington did. We may admire a man who never said a foolish thing in his life, but we are not likely to love him.

But the part Sherman played at Philadelphia was a major one, and we cannot understand the American government without understanding him. He was, to begin with, a devoted patriot of the state of Connecticut, finely in tune with the politics and attitudes of his fellow citizens. The New England states tended to be more democratic in the modern sense of the word than states elsewhere. Connecticut was particularly so. Its basic charter from the English Crown, which the citizens considered precious, had allowed them more self-government than existed in the other colonies. It was a state neither terribly rich nor terribly poor, a place dominated by independent farmers, with business a distinctly secondary occupation. It was, in sum, a conservative place where Calvinism still held firm and the Protestant "work ethic" was accepted as a matter of course. Connecticuters called themselves a people of "steady habits," and Roger Sherman was one of the steadiest of them all.

He was born in 1721, raised in Massachusetts, and did not move to Connecticut until he was nineteen. Not much is known of Sherman's youth, except that he grew up in the small farming community of Stoughton, Massachusetts, living the life that the vast majority of Americans lived. At the time Sherman's father died, the family owned seventy-three acres, of which it worked only a portion. The house was furnished with a few chests, chairs, tables, and one expensive mirror. There were only three beds for a family of nine. Their livestock comprised three cows, two steers, a heifer, and two sheep, a very typical assortment for the time and place.

The one element in the household that set the family a little apart from similar ones was the presence of books. Although most New Englanders of the time could read, books were not only a luxury but one which few people had time for. But young Roger developed a taste for study. Roger Sherman was determined to get on, and after his father died in 1741, when Roger was nineteen, he decided to emigrate to western Connecticut, an area that was still being settled. There was a lot of empty woodland around, and land was the fastest way to fortune. Sherman moved to the town of New Milford, borrowed some money, and bought land.

However, he was not content just to speculate in land. In his area of Connecticut, boundaries were vague and often in dispute. Surveyors were essential. Roger Sherman studied surveying, and in 1745 he was appointed county surveyor. As it had done for Washington, the job put him in a good position for making land deals. He began buying and selling; he married; he wrote and published almanacs, which not only brought him some income but gave him the beginnings of a name across his adopted colony. He studied law and was admitted to the bar. He worked his way into various municipal offices, serving at one time or another as tax assessor, sealer of weights and measures, and in 1753, just twelve years after he had come into New Milford, was elected one of five town selectmen. Two years later he was elected to the colony's legislature. In 1760 he moved to New Haven, the colony's most important trading center, which shared capital status with Hartford and was also the seat of Yale College. He continued to serve in the legislature, was appointed judge, and by the time of the Revolution was one of Connecticut's leading men.

Unlike the Washingtons and Madisons, with their plantations to support them, Sherman relied on his public salaries for an important part of his income. He was a rare, perhaps unique, figure for his era—a full-time politician. From the day he was appointed surveyor at the age of twenty-three until the moment of his death at seventy-two, he held public office without a break, a record few Americans of any time could match.

And he did it, astonishingly enough, laboring under a severe handicap. The aristocrats, who by and large ran colony governments, were usually polished gentlemen, who knew how to enter drawing rooms with maximum effect and had developed harmonious voices and a speaking style rich with literary allusion. He was self-educated. He lacked the felicitous turn of phrase, the Latinate vocabulary, the classical references that freighted—and frequently sank—the speeches of Madison, Washington, Morris. He spoke a down-home

Yankee dialect that annoyed some of the gentlemen around him and amused others.

Physically, too, he remained a plowboy. He was tall, rawboned, and clumsy. His friend and admirer John Adams said:

> Sherman's air is the reverse of grace; there cannot be a more striking contrast to beautiful action, than the motions of his hands; generally he stands upright, with his hands before him, the fingers of his left hand clenched into a fist, and the wrist of it grasped with the right.

Add to this picture the plain country dress, the short-cropped, unwigged head, the massive shoulders and tall frame, and Roger Sherman emerges as a striking if peculiar figure in a company of urbane and sophisticated men.

Roger Sherman was by nature and experience shrewd, realistic, hardheaded. Even as a young man he rarely made a misstep. He did not succeed in winning every office he sought, but he got most of them; he did not succeed in pushing through every bill he wanted, but most of the time he did. His contemporary President Timothy Dwight of Yale said he "rarely failed to convince others that he judged right."

Sherman may have had acute political instincts, but he was also a religious man, a Calvinist, a man of honor. He did not lie, he did not cheat; he knew when to speak and when to keep quiet, and never deliberately obfuscated an issue.

Nonetheless, Roger Sherman saw politics as very much "the art of the possible." He understood what his people were thinking and feeling and knew how far they could be led. He would argue his point loudly and forcefully, but when he realized the issue was lost, he would look for another way to reach his end—a committee, a compromise, a deal, that would salvage something and allow the business go to forward. He shared with Washington one rare and magnificent quality: a view of life that was utterly realistic, without ideology or dogma. He would bargain, he would compromise, he would bide his time. It is therefore not surprising that he invented the compromise that would eventually save the Convention and give the United States the Congress it has today.

The idea that two houses of a Congress could be based on different systems of representation had occurred to Sherman in 1776, at the Second Continental Congress, when the newly established states were attempting to put together the Articles of Confederation. There, as ever, the heavily populated states wanted proportional representation, the small states equal voting. During the debate on the Articles, Sherman made the point that even if the big states got proportional representation, there was no use in the Big Three ramming its ideas through, because as a practical matter the majority of small states would ignore them. This was Sherman at his pragmatic best: what was the earthly use of devising a system that would not work? Yet he understood how important proportional representation was to the big states, and he offered a solution. As reported by John Adams in 1776, he said: "The vote should be taken two ways; call the Colonies, and call the individuals, and have a majority of both." That is to say, to pass a law you would need the approval of *both* a majority of the *states* as units, and a majority of the *people* individually, through their representatives in the legislature.

But Sherman's idea of basing the legislature on two differing principles of suffrage had been too unusual for the Second Continental Congress, and it was not debated there. However, he was not one to waste a good idea, so, eleven years later he raised it once again. We have suggested that on Sunday, June 10, the day after tempers had grown so heated on the Convention floor, Sherman met with some of the other small states' men, including William Paterson, and discussed his compromise, calling for proportional representation in one house of Congress and equal voting in the other. On Monday, June 11, he presented his idea to the Convention. But the big states were not interested. Logic supported them, fairness supported them, and most important, they had the votes. Sidestepping Sherman's suggestion, James Wilson of Pennsylvania and Rufus King of Massachusetts moved that "the right of suffrage in the first branch of the national legislature ought not to be according to the rule established in the Articles of Confederation, but according to some equitable ratio of representation."

Before they could vote, however, Ben Franklin rose to say that he had written down his ideas on the subject. Wilson read Franklin's words: "It has given me great pleasure to observe that till this point, the proportion of representation, came before us, our debates were carried on with great coolness and temper." And he went on to urge more of the same. Then, in a longish speech, he offered a compromise of his own, which was so complex and impractical that historians have wondered if he was not simply stalling in order to allow the emotional heat in the room to drop. Whatever happened to the heat, when the long-postponed vote for proportional representation in the lower house of Congress was taken, the Committee of the Whole voted for it, seven to three, with Maryland divided. The big-state bloc was holding firm.

The one small state that voted with the big states was Connecticut. It did so because it was still pursuing Sherman's compromise: the state would accept proportional representation in the lower house, provided it got equal voting in the upper house. And so, shortly after proportional representation for the lower house carried, Sherman got up and moved that a vote be taken on the upper house. Everything depended on this, he said, for the "smaller states would never agree to the plan on any other principle than an equality of suffrage in this branch."

But the Big Three, with their allies from the Deep South, were determined to have proportional representation in *both* houses. They pushed their plan through on a straight party-line vote, and won six to five.

Why, when it was clear that the small states would never accept a legislature wholly based on proportional representation, did Madison and his allies insist on driving it through? For one thing, many of the big states' men were confident that, as Wilson had pointed out, if they confederated on their own, the small states would quickly be forced to come in. It is probably true that Delaware, tied commercially to Pennsylvania, would have been compelled to join. But Connecticut and Rhode Island were fiercely independent by temperament, and the New York leadership was not interested in joining any union it could not dominate. These three at least would resist pressures to join a big-state union. Furthermore, as the delegates knew, in the best of circumstances, it was not going to be easy to get the people of New York and Virginia to ratify a constitution—as, in fact, proved to be the case. Surely it would make the task almost impossible if the union was going to be only a partial one. James Madison and others of his view were almost certainly wrong in thinking that the big states could confederate successfully on their own. But it was a risk that at least some of the big states' men were willing to take, in order to form a union on what they considered sound principles.

And now we can see the value of the device of the Committee of the Whole. If this had been the final vote on proportional representation, many if not most of the small-state delegates would have walked out of the Convention. They did not because the Convention was still sitting as the Committee of the Whole, and the motions favoring proportional representation in both houses of Congress, which had just passed, were only "recommendations" and would have to be debated and voted on again when the Convention cast off the fiction of the Committee.

On June 13 the delegates finished debating the Virginia Plan. It was read out, and recommended to the Convention. It seemed to Madison and his allies that having been passed once, it could be passed again. This proved, ultimately, to be a dangerous assumption. For the next day, Thursday, June 14, William Paterson of New Jersey rose and "observed to the Convention that it was the wish of several deputations, particularly that of New Jersey, that further time might be allowed them to contemplate the plan reported from the Committee of the Whole, and to digest one purely federal, and contradistinguished from the reported plan." The battle between the big and small states was coming to its critical phase.

Chapter Ten

William Paterson Picks a Fight

The single most important element in the character of William Paterson was a fear of disorder. It manifested itself in his personal behavior, which was restrained and formal. It manifested itself in his political beliefs, which were built around the idea that "obedience to the law is the first political maxim and duty in a republican government." It manifested itself in his religious principles, which were far more concerned with hatred of licentiousness than with love of mercy. It manifested itself in his actions as congressman, governor, and justice of the Supreme Court, where he regularly demanded severe punishments for miscreants who had flouted authority and law.

He maintained a long and apparently close working relationship with William Livingston, for fourteen years governor of New Jersey, but Paterson seems to have had no other close friends. Nor was he close to his family, other than his children. At one point he lent some money to his brothers, who mishandled it; he refused to have anything to do with them afterward. He was a compulsive worker, who could closet himself with his books and papers day and night, and showed none of the gregariousness of Washington, Franklin, Hamilton, and so many of the others at Philadelphia. He married late and appears to have allowed himself no youthful indiscretions. Once, when he was a young man, an acquaintance got a girl pregnant and had to marry her, hardly an unusual occurence at that time. Paterson's response was to write a mutual friend, "For I so detest a whore, that I would not marry one of my own making," a remark that would be priggish and uncharitable coming from an aging preacher, much less a young man. As attorney general for New Jersey he was zealous in prosecuting people for fornication.

His tirades against licentiousness were endless. "Luxury effeminates and torments the opulent, and tempts the indigent," he said. As governor he supported bills to ban the playing of billiards and reduce the number of taverns in his state. As justice of the Supreme Court he bore down hardest not on ordinary criminals but on men guilty of riot and rebellion. Sitting at the trial of two unfortunate members of the Whiskey Rebellion of 1794, he virtually ordered the jury to find them guilty, and he sentenced them to death when it did. (Washington eventually pardoned them.) Even his generally sympathetic biographer John E. O'Connor says, "His position in the trials of the Whiskey Rebels . . . was and is indefensible."

Yet, despite all this, there was something oddly likeable about Paterson. William Pierce, the Georgia delegate who wrote little character sketches of his colleagues at the Convention, said that Paterson had "a disposition so favorable to his advancement that every one seemed ready to exalt him with their praises." According to O'Connor, his popularity in his home state was "phenomenal" and by the time he was forty-five he was automatically elected to any post he ran for. At the Convention he seems to have been able to work well with such diverse people as the cautious Roger Sherman and the intemperate Luther Martin.

Paterson was born in Ireland in 1745, the son of a tin-plate worker named Richard Paterson; he was the eldest of four children. In 1747, when Paterson was two, the family emigrated to America, eventually settling in Princeton, New Jersey. Here Richard Paterson opened a general store, and in a fair way prospered. The family came to occupy a large stone house with several rooms on each floor, and owned three slaves.

Paterson's father established his house and store a hundred yards from the new college campus, and as a result, Paterson was exposed, from his youth, to the high-minded intellectual patriotism and emotional uplift that characterized the college. He grew up to be a small plain young man whose "looks bespeak talents of no great extent."

Richard Paterson was not of the class of people who usually sent their children to college. But there was the campus virtually in front of his door, and the students were in and out of the store all day long—James Madison had an account there later on. It must have occurred to both Richard and his son that William was just as bright as any of the young gentlemen whom they dealt with all the time, and at the age of fourteen Paterson matriculated at the college.

At the college Paterson determined to break into the upper set, and he went about it in the usual way, learning genteel manners, dress, and form, and attempting to scrape friendships with his aristocratic fellow students. He made

his way to an extent: by the time he graduated he had developed friendships
with Luther Martin of Maryland, who was a farmer's son; Oliver Ellsworth,
from a middle-class Connecticut family; the wealthy and well-connected
Aaron Burr; and Henry Lee, from one of the great Virginia families. But the
aristocratic gentlemen did not really accept him. When, after graduation, he
wrote them, they did not always respond, and although he kept up his membership in his college clubs, it was a long time before he was able to move into
the establishment of his own state.

But the College of New Jersey at least had educated him. He got his
bachelor's degree in 1763, his master's degree in 1766, and was admitted to the
New Jersey bar in 1769. He also acquired the intellectual tenor of the college:
an evangelical Calvinism tinged with patriotism. Patriotism was the subject of
his master's speech, which contained references to the "manly and rough-hewn
virtues" of times past.

But he was unable to move onto the larger stage, perhaps from a want of
boldness, but in part from a lack of connections. Instead of choosing Princeton,
Trenton, New York, or Philadelphia, he set up practice in Hunterdon and
Somerset Counties, sparsely occupied farm country. Business was slow and to
keep himself alive he opened a branch of his father's general store; he spent
the next six years of his life as a country lawyer and storekeeper, a bored and
lonely bachelor with no particular prospects of either fame or fortune before
him. By 1775, when he turned thirty, he would not have seemed to anybody
a man destined to make a deep mark on history.

The events of 1775 changed all that. As the conflict with Great Britain led
in April to bloodshed at Concord and Lexington, the states began separately
to consider what steps they should take. New Jersey called its own provincial
congress in May, and Paterson's Somerset County farmers elected him a
representative to it. At the Congress Jonathan Dickinson Sergeant, whom
Paterson had known at college, was elected secretary. He asked Paterson to
become his assistant. Paterson accepted. Not long afterward Sergeant resigned,
and the secretaryship devolved on Paterson. William Paterson was suddenly
shoved on stage.

It was typical of the way things were getting done at the time. In 1775 most
Americans were torn about the idea of separating from England, and they
tended to let the accident of events decide for them. Paterson was no different,
and given his temperament, he could easily have joined the Tories had things
gone another way. O'Connor says, "The decision for independence that Paterson and most of his colleagues [in New Jersey] made was not the free choice

of revolutionary patriots, but the grudging recognition that there was nothing else to do."

As secretary to the provincial assembly Paterson was responsible for carrying on correspondence with the Continental Congress and signing bills and official proclamations; soon his name was known around New Jersey, and to some extent elsewhere.

With the Declaration of Independence, the old colonial governments were dissolved in a stroke, and it became necessary for the states to set up new ones. Paterson, in New Jersey's provincial congress, had shown himself to be intelligent, experienced in both business and the law, and a hard worker. His colleagues had come to respect his abilities, and through successive sessions of the New Jersey Congress he was elected secretary, named to the first legislative council, and then in the summer of 1776, was made attorney general for the state. Now, finally, he was rising, not through connections, but on sheer merit.

Paterson twice refused to serve in the Continental Congress, saying that his work as attorney general was too demanding. At least one scholar has suggested that his real reason for staying home was that he was, for a change, making a lot of money through his law practice. (Views of conflict of interest were different then, and it was acceptable for Paterson to practice law while he was attorney general.) Whatever the case, he did his work as attorney general well, prosecuted Tories as well as fornicators and debtors, and by the end of the war was a respected and well-to-do figure in New Jersey.

How, then, do we see Paterson at the brink of the Constitutional Convention? Certainly he was far less a national thinker than were Washington, Madison, and others. He had not fought in the Continental Army, nor struggled in Congress to get recalcitrant states to pay their levies. He had spent virtually all of his life in New Jersey. He was a man of his own state far more than were the men who had fought the war and run the government, and he carried to the Convention a provincial loyalty to New Jersey.

Not all of the men who came to the Convention were constantly looking over their shoulders at the people back home, but Paterson was. He said, "We must follow the people; the people will not follow us" (June 9). And again: "I came here not to speak my own sentiments, but the sentiments of those who sent me" (June 16).

Second, both nature and training had given him a profound regard for the sanctity of the law. As early as 1776, under the pressure of wartime conditions, he plunked hard for a strong executive, saying, "In the present state of warfare and confusion, we stand more in need of executive than legislative powers."

He was a law-and-order man through and through: civil rights, liberties, were less important in his political philosophy than firm government. He saw the Convention as an opportunity to curb the licentiousness of a society that had forgotten the ancient virtues of hard work and thrift. The Convention would, as Gordon Wood puts it, be the battlement from which the worthy went forth to conquer.

Third, like many if not most of the men at the Convention, William Paterson was imbued with an almost religious respect for property. The rights of property were inviolable, and he devoted a good deal of his law practice to acting for creditors against debtors. Like other political thinkers of the time, Paterson believed that in a republic, men could be free only if they were economically independent, which for most Americans meant owning a farm. This in turn meant that contracts must be inviolable, so that scheming men could not despoil others.

This congeries of beliefs contained some contradictions, and at the Convention he was tugged two ways. On the one hand his loyalty to his home state made him fear giving too much power to a national government, which might be dominated by the big states. On the other hand, his fear of chaos left him with a desire to see a firm national government take charge and regulate the country better than the old one was doing. New Jersey trade had to pass through either Philadelphia or New York City, where it could be taxed, and where middlemen could extract profits. New Jersey, as the saying went, was "like a keg being tapped at both ends." Thus, a strong national government would probably be the best protection New Jersey could have against the big states, because it would take over the taxing power itself, using the money for the general good of all states. But—and this was the essential point—a strong central government would be no protection if the big states dominated it.

Thus, on the morning of Thursday, June 14, as we have seen, William Paterson rose and asked the Convention to adjourn for the rest of the day in order that "several deputations" might have further time to "contemplate" the Virginia Plan, and "to digest one purely federal." He hoped, he said, to have such a plan ready by tomorrow.

Paterson was certainly not speaking for himself alone. Rather, he was acting as spokesman for a group of men from the small states who were horrified by the thought that a new government would be dominated by the large states. Precisely who was in this caucus of small states we do not know, but it included Paterson and Roger Sherman; the virulent states' righter from Maryland Luther Martin; either John Dickinson or George Read (or both) of Delaware, who basically favored a fairly strong national government but had the size of their state to think about; and either John Lansing or Robert Yates (or both) of New York, who were convinced that their state might be better off outside of any national scheme and were not keen to see the Convention succeed. It is probable that at least some of the other delegates from New Jersey and Connecticut joined in the caucusing.

In fact, therefore, the small-states bloc included New York and Connecticut, each with populations about the same as North Carolina. The battle lines look even less clear-cut when we remember that one member of the big-states bloc, Georgia, was among the smallest in population. What gives the division a semblance of coherence is the fact that members of the small-states group, other than New York, were geographically small, and the big states were all geographically large. It was the assumption that states with empty land would fill with people, and would fairly soon become large states by any measure. As we have seen, this assumption was incorrect, but it was almost universally believed, and it led sparsely populated states like Georgia and the Carolinas to believe that their future lay with the big states.

Secondly, the small states were all in the North, with the exception of Maryland, a border state with one foot in the South. The three Deep South states, regardless of any other considerations, were fearful of allowing the Convention to be dominated by a northern bloc, which might try to interfere with slavery.

Finally, the whole big-state–small-state conflict had got muddled with the question of states' rights—that is to say, how much power would be taken from the states and delivered to the new national government. These were not the same questions: Some of the small-state men, like Paterson, wanted a strong national government, which might protect them against the big states, *provided* that it was not dominated by the big states. But others did not. Roger Sherman, in particular, believed that each state had its particular "genius," or temperament, which expressed itself in government through the legislature. Only state legislatures could really know what was best for their constituents, and therefore the national government should be given only as much power as was absolutely necessary to put down rebellion, provide for the national defense, and regulate interstate commerce.

Sherman was one of the leaders of the small-state bloc. The other two principal figures were Paterson and Luther Martin. It is fascinating to note that all three of them were risen men. Sherman and Martin were two of the four or five delegates who had been raised on small farms; and Paterson was the son of a shopkeeper. It cannot be entirely accidental that these men came together to fight off the aristocrats from the big, wealthy states who, as it appeared to them, expected to run things.

The battle of the small versus the big states was, thus, fought out by rather odd coalitions of men with diverse motives, sometimes operating from incorrect assumptions. As a consequence, the scheme of government that the small-state caucus put together on June 14 and 15 was something of a hodgepodge, with a little something in it for everybody. It came to be called the New Jersey Plan simply because Paterson had called for it, and presented it. In it, as in the Virginia Plan, power would lie mainly with the national legislature, but there would be a single house, based on the principle of one state, one vote. There would be an executive board elected by the legislature; this board could, however, be removed by a majority of state governors. A Supreme Court appointed by the executive board would deal with impeachments of federal officers, cases involving foreigners or foreign governments, and problems that might arise under the government's right to tax and regulate trade. The plan specifically permitted the national government to levy duties on imports—this to take the taxing power away from Massachusetts, New York, and Pennsylvania and give it to the national government for the benefit of all states. It allowed the new Congress to tax state governments on the basis of population and to collect that money by force if necessary, with the consent of an unspecified number of states. Finally, it said that all acts of the Congress "shall be the supreme law of the respective states," and it specifically authorized the executive board to use force to "compel an obedience to such acts."

The New Jersey Plan, at a cursory glance, proposed a relatively strong national government but left more power to the states than the Virginia Plan did. According to Max Farrand, editor of *The Records of the Federal Convention of 1787*, it "more nearly represented what most delegates supposed they were sent to do." But because the interests of the men who worked it out were so diverse, it was filled with loopholes and exceptions intended to satisfy one or another of the small states' men, and there is some doubt as to whether it would have worked in practice. John O'Connor has suggested it was a mere stalking-horse for equal voting in Congress. We should think of it, then, as a compact hastily thrown together to give the small states a base for the fight, a standard around which the opponents of proportional representation could gather.

Chapter Eleven

The Battle Joined

On June 15 Paterson presented the New Jersey Plan to the Convention. The following day the delegates, now split into two factions, began to argue the merits of the two plans. The basic issue, which would be at the heart of the debate over the next four weeks, was, of course, whether a new Congress would be based on proportional representation or on the principle of one state, one vote, as was the old Congress, still sitting in New York.

As with so much else about the Convention, this issue dragged in with it other related issues. The first was: why have two houses of Congress at all? After all, under the Articles of Confederation, the old Congress consisted of a single house.

There was no very good answer to the question. The British Parliament had consisted of two houses for centuries, and when the original colonial governments had been set up over the seventeenth and eighteenth centuries, they, too, had involved two-house legislatures. When, after Independence, the states began forming their own governments, most, almost by habit, opted for bicameral legislatures. The idea was to have an "upper" house of experienced wise men to act as some sort of check on the intemperate voices of the people in the "lower" house. The upper house would, in this respect, function like the aristocratic House of Lords.

Not all of the delegates liked the idea of a bicameral Congress. The states' righters, who wanted the central government to continue more a league of independent states than a unified government, felt that congressmen should represent not factions in the society, but their own states, and as a consequence there was no need for two houses. Extreme democrats, like James Wilson and Charles Pinckney, felt that Congress should represent the people, and there should be no body of men, rich, wise or otherwise, checking the people's wishes. The delegates who opposed a bicameral Congress, however, were a distinct minority; the majority favored the idea of a bicameral legislature, with an upper house composed of far-seeing elder statesmen. There was one thing wrong with this idea however: nobody had ever been able to figure out how to choose people who were actually wise. Most states had a bicameral legislature, but in fact, the voters had persistently elected to the upper house the same sort of men they elected to the lower house. How, then, did you insure that the best people were chosen for an upper house?

The idea that a few states settled on was to reserve the upper house for the wealthy, who could be elected only by the relatively better-off. The theory behind this idea was that people with wealth had a substantial stake in the society and would not be prone to making dangerous experiments.

If the poor dominated the government, they would take wealth from the rich and redistribute it; if the rich came to dominate, they would turn themselves into that feared aristocracy. Therefore, this line of thought went, put people of property into the Senate, and let the common people dominate the lower house, so each could act as a check on the other.

The man who most carefully articulated this concept and most cogently presented it to the Convention was Gouverneur Morris. He had an idea about all of this that was fascinating and might have had tremendous consequences for the United States had it attracted support.

Indeed, Gouverneur Morris was one of the most fascinating men at the Convention. He was considered by his contemporaries to be one of the most brilliant men among them. Washington, that excellent judge of people, made use of his talents during the war, to help find finances and supplies, and later, to negotiate various matters with England and France. Morris was, however, also considered a rake, too public in his affairs with women, and not always very interested in the decent opinion of mankind. Morris was a clever business-man, who built a modest inheritance into a considerable fortune, and an astute politician, who knew the value of compromise and could invent formulas that men could agree on.

Roger Sherman would say of him, when Washington nominated Morris to be minister to France in 1790, that he had never "heard that Morris has betrayed a trust, or that he lacks integrity." But:

> With regard to his moral character, I consider him an irreligious and a profane man—he is no hypocrite and never pretended to have any reli-

gion. He makes religion the subject of ridicule and is profane in his conversation. I do not think the public have as much security from such men as from godly and honest men—it is a bad example to promote such characters.

Sherman's opinion was shared by others at the Convention and as a consequence Morris had less influence with the delegates than he might have had. He was, essentially, something of a lone wolf, who spoke frequently and forcefully but never quite convinced the Convention in the way that Madison, Wilson, and others did.

As it happened, Gouverneur Morris was away from the Convention, on business in New York, for the entire month of June and had lost the train of thought at the Convention. Nevertheless, on July 2, he rose to deliver a long speech on the upper house. The object of the Senate he said, was "to check the precipitation, changeableness, and excesses of the first branch," especially against abuses of personal liberty and threats to private property. This was a proposition most of the delegates agreed with.

He then went on to insist that the upper house "must have great personal property . . . aristocratical spirit; it must love to lord it through pride. . . ." Senators must serve for life. And he then made this startling statement, according to Madison: The Senate "will then do wrong, it will be said. He believed so; he hoped so. The rich will strive to establish their dominion and enslave the rest. They always did. They always will. The proper security against them is to form them into a separate interest. The two forces will then control each other." And he added: "Let the rich mix with the poor in both houses of Congress and in a commercial country, they will establish an oligarchy." That is to say, a minority of wealthy people in either house of Congress would be able to take it over through power, prestige, or outright buying of votes. The only way to check the rich from dominating a national Congress, Morris believed, was to give them their own branch, and keep them out of the other, which could then protect the interests of the common people.

Leaving aside the practicality of the scheme, it is an astonishing idea. Morris was intending to build what modern political scientists would see as a class struggle into the structure of government itself, in order to confine and control it. In any case, Morris' idea found no support. To most of the delegates, a Senate based on wealth smacked too much of the British aristocracy they had so recently thrown off at such cost. They agreed with what Washington later on said to Thomas Jefferson, when Jefferson asked why the Convention had established a Senate. "Why," Washington responded, "do you pour your coffee into your saucer?"

"To cool it," Jefferson replied.

"Even so," Washington said. "We pour legislation into the Senatorial saucer to cool it."

In other words, most of the men at the Convention were at least hopeful that a way could be found to create a Senate of wise men. And having decided that it should not be drawn from the wealthy, they took up another idea, which was embodied in the Virginia Plan: have the lower house elected by the people, and the upper house by the lower, in the hope that the legislators in the lower house would know who the wisest men in the nation were.

This idea had first come up on May 31, and it was quickly opposed by Roger Sherman, who wanted delegates to *both* houses of Congress elected by the state legislatures. The people, he said, "immediately should have as little to do as may be about the government. They want information and are constantly liable to be misled." This view of things was part and parcel of Sherman's intellectual baggage, which he shared with others of the lowborn men: the people could not be trusted to know what was best. But it was also tied to the states' rights issue. If the national government was basically to express the wishes of state governments, it ought to be elected by state governments. This, too, Sherman believed.

But Madison, as ever, was dogged. He saw that the question of how the national legislature was to be elected was attached, at least philosophically, to the proportional representation issue. "Election of one branch at least of the legislature by the people immediately," was "a clear principle of free government and . . . had the additional advantage of securing better representatives, as well as of avoiding too great an agency of the state governments in the general one." State governments, after all, were the malefactors in pushing forward those stay and tender laws through which "debtors have defrauded their creditors." If they controlled the national legislature, would it not do just the same? Again, Madison alluded to his theory of the virtues of a large, diverse nation: a legislature built on the people across the whole republic would spread factions thin, so that they could not form majorities to tyrannize minorities.

Proportional representation in the upper house would also make that house too numerous. On June 7 several suggestions were made to get around the difficulty. One was that a small state might be combined with a large one to form a single electoral district—Delaware with Pennsylvania, for example. Needless to say, the small states objected that a Pennsylvania man would invariably be chosen, and Delaware would effectively be shut out of the Senate.

In the end, the Convention failed, at this point, to settle on a method of electing the lower house. But on June 7 the Committee of the Whole voted overwhelmingly to have the upper house—the Senate—chosen by state legislatures, not by the people directly. It was a victory for the states' righters, and it might have signaled to James Madison that there was considerable sympathy for the position of the small states–states' rights delegates, and that perhaps he should look for a way to accommodate them. But he did not.

On June 15 William Paterson presented the New Jersey Plan to the Convention, and on June 16 Lansing of New York and Paterson made lengthy speeches in support of it. Lansing's main point was that the Virginia Plan went far beyond what New Yorkers had had in mind when they sent him to Philadelphia, and that it would never be ratified in his state. Paterson's principal argument was that equal voting was the established law of the land and could not be changed except, as the Articles of Confederation specified, by unanimous consent of the thirteen states.

Madison bided his time. Finally, on June 19 he made a long, carefully reasoned, and convincing speech against the New Jersey Plan. The basic thrust of his argument was that the New Jersey Plan would not cure what the delegates had been sent to heal. It was too much like the faulty Articles of Confederation and would leave the country open to the same abuses. And he concluded by begging the small states to consider the consequences of bringing the Convention down by insisting on having their own way. Suppose, in the end, there was no union. Surely the small states would be in more danger from predatory big neighbors if they were outside the protection of a national umbrella. Or suppose that the big states put together a union of their own, as James Wilson had already threatened. Surely they would not "exact less severe concessions" from the small states who eventually wanted to join than the concessions that were being suggested now.

James Madison was right. The New Jersey Plan would not have solved the problems of the old government. Madison was still unable to believe that the small states could not see this, that they would not in time listen to reason.

Some of the other delegates understood that the small states would never listen to reason. Charles Pinckney had said bluntly, on June 16, before Madison's speech, "Give New Jersey an equal vote and she will dismiss her scruples and concur in the national system." But Madison's speech was convincing to many of the delegates. On June 19, shortly after Madison finished speaking, the delegates were asked to choose between the New Jersey Plan, with equal voting, and the Virginia Plan, with proportional representation. They chose the Virginia Plan seven states to three. The alliance of the Big Three and the Deep South states was holding firm.

This vote, in effect, laid the Virginia Plan, as modified by the Convention, sitting as the Committee of the Whole, before the Convention, now sitting undisguised as itself. The entire thing would be debated again. The second half of the fight began with John Lansing, the states' righter from New York, offering a motion that would throw out the whole plan for Congress, and replace it with one more like the old Congress under the Articles. The states would never give up their sovereignty, he insisted on June 20, and even if they did, the new scheme was "too novel and complex" to work.

His motion was seconded by Roger Sherman in a conciliatory speech. Sherman saw no reason for a bicameral legislature. The problem with the old government was not that it had acted foolishly or threatened anybody's liberties, but that it had simply been unable to enforce its decrees. And he made the point, which seems not to have occurred to anybody before, that the large states had not, in the old Congress, suffered at the hands of the small states on account of the rule of equal voting. In sum, Sherman concluded, no great change in the system was needed, except to work out a scheme whereby the national government could collect its money and enforce its regulations. But he then went on to say that although he would have preferred a single legislature with equal voting, "If the difficulty on the subject of representation can not be otherwise got over, he would agree to have two branches, and a proportional representation in one of them; provided each state had an equal voice in the other."

Sherman was once again offering his compromise, but the big states were still not interested. They went on to debate again whether the first branch should be elected by the people or chosen by the state legislatures. This time direct election by the people, with its implication of proportional representation, carried, with only New Jersey and the ardent states' righter Luther Martin, voting no. Over the next few days they went on to other matters. Then, on June 27, they came once again to the election of the second branch.

They had now reached the critical point. The small states had long since signaled their willingness to accept proportional representation in the first branch of Congress, but only if they got equal voting in the second branch.

What the small states' coalition needed at this point was a carefully reasoned, well-constructed, articulate statement of their point of view. It is clear in retrospect that had they got such a speech, they just might have pulled toward them enough votes to push Sherman's compromise through at this point, and spare the Convention the crisis that nearly sank it. What they got instead was Luther Martin.

Chapter Twelve

Luther Martin and a Lost Opportunity

Luther Martin was unquestionably the most curious figure at the Constitutional Convention. Perhaps it all starts with his name, that of one of the world's great religious leaders—backwards.

Martin was sprung from generations of Colonial farmers. It is worth saying something about this. We tend to see the colonial period in American history foreshortened by time. We need to remember that by 1787 Englishmen had been living in North America for over 170 years. Some of the men at the Convention had great-great-great-grandparents who had been born Americans and who had died a hundred years before. Families like Martin's had worked farms that their grandfathers had worked, and laid flowers before gravestones that in 1787 were moss-stained and eroded by a century and a half of weather. They were not newcomers, and the intense patriotism such men felt for their country is explained in good measure by the fact that their ancestors—men and women bearing their own names—in blistering sun and stinging cold had cleared the land and built the barns and left their bones in the earth. They were thinking and feeling and working just as their forefathers had done for four and five and six generations, and out of this came not only patriotism but that conservatism that urged them to do as had been done before.

Luther Martin was the third of nine children of a back-country New Jersey farmer. His brilliance was recognized early, and at twelve he was sent off to grammar school, while his older brothers stayed home and worked the farm to help pay for his schooling. In compensation, when he later inherited a small piece of land, he turned it over to them—unlike his friend and ally William Paterson, who disowned his brothers when they mishandled some of his money.

Martin spent five years at the grammar school, and then in about 1763 matriculated at Princeton, still called the College of New Jersey. At Princeton Martin was surrounded by the sons of rich gentlemen, who would eventually inherit large estates and take their places in courts, councils, and legislatures as a matter of course. It was not surprising, then, that Martin made a good friend of his schoolmate Paterson, who was also unable to move into the center of college society occupied by the polished sons of the gentry. What did men like Martin and Sherman, who had spent their youths in cow barns and cornfields, feel about the aristocratic youths around them, who had grown up in an elegant world foreign to the experience of these country boys? We can only guess at the mix of envy, anger, and admiration in their hearts as they circled a world they could not quite penetrate.

Fortunately for Martin, he was brilliant. He was one of the top scholars in his class, first in language and possessed of an incredible memory. He began to study law, supporting himself by teaching, and eventually moved to Balti-more. In 1778, not yet into his thirties, he asked to be named attorney general in the newly formed government of the independent state of Maryland. He was nobody's first choice, but a number of others turned the position down, and eventually Martin got the job. Now, like his friend Paterson, he began a rapid rise into prominence, helped along by the wartime shortage of lawyers and the dislocations caused by the fighting. Just as Paterson did, he took private clients, fighting admiralty cases for the most part. He also served as a trooper in a company of Maryland cavalry and took part in a foray in Virginia, although he was never shot at. According to his biographers Paul Clarkson and R. Samuel Jett, he was by the end of the Revolution the best-known and most respected lawyer in Maryland, both for the meticulousness of his prepara-tion and for his skill at argument in the courtroom.

And this was despite his increasingly quixotic behavior. He drank, was slovenly, and tried the patience of his friends. Clarkson and Jett say:

> He was a familiar figure in his unpressed, unbrushed clothes, old-fash-ioned ruffles edged with lace, rich but badly soiled, at his wrists, plodding the streets from office or tavern to court and back, his nearsighted face habitually buried in a book. Baltimoreans told the story of the time that he bumped into a cow on Baltimore Street, respectfully bowed and apolo-gized to her, and absent-mindedly went on his way.

According to a friend, Joseph Story, he grew into a man of "middle size, a little bald, with a common forehead, pointed nose, inexpressive eye, large mouth, and well-formed chin. His dress is slovenly." William Pierce, in his

little sketches of the men at the Convention, said that "this gentleman pos-
sesses a good deal of information, but he has a very bad delivery, and so
extremely prolix, that he never speaks without tiring the patience of all who
hear him"—a man, it seemed, who liked the sound of his own voice.

Apparently by the time of the Convention he drank at times to the point
of making a public spectacle of himself. It was, of course, a hard-drinking age,
and the world was full of alcoholics. But gentlemen were expected both to
drink and to stay reasonably sober, and Martin clearly went beyond the bounds
of propriety.

Yet despite it all, Martin was liked in his home state for his basic decency
and vastly admired for his courtroom skills. He was generous. He habitually
gave away money by the fistful to the needy, so that even though he made a
handsome living from his law practice, he was perpetually broke. He was a
very hard worker, studying his cases assiduously. In sending him to Philadelphia the Marylanders were choosing a man they expected to prove careful in
his preparations and brilliant in debate. He would, certainly, defend the states'
interests with skill—or so they thought.

What is difficult to understand is the quality of emotion Luther Martin
brought to the defense of states' rights. He was unyielding, beyond compromise on the point, and when he spoke on the issue it was always in the strongest
terms. It became a question of principle. His friend William Paterson may have
been determined to prevent the big states from swallowing up the small ones
in the new government, but he was at least willing to compromise. Martin,
according to the Constitutional scholar Max Farrand, came to Philadelphia
"with a fixed determination to obstruct and oppose." And when the Convention would not agree with him he went home and fought ratification in Maryland. What was the motive for this passionate commitment to states' rights?
Some scholars have suggested that he operated under the thumb of Samuel
Chase, the most powerful politician in Maryland, and that for a variety of
reasons Chase and his supporters did not want a strong national government.
Philip A. Crowl, the closest student of the question, says that Martin "was
regarded by contemporaries as merely one of Chase's placemen, for Chase
secured his appointment as Attorney General in 1778 and was responsible for
his nomination as a member of the Philadelphia Convention." But it is clear
from the fervor he brought to the battle for states' rights that the issue had
become a personal one to him.

The answer to Martin's violent antinationalism probably lies in the eccentric
nature of his personality. Luther Martin was "odd," "different"—a maverick

whose behavior was frequently made even more erratic by alcohol. How much, for example, was his states' rightism motivated by resentment against the elegant gentleman from Virginia, the Deep South, and Pennsylvania who weighed so heavily on the other side? It is possible to suspect, then, that Martin —and perhaps others of the lowborn states' righters, especially Paterson— brought to the fight a certain amount of class feeling.

Yet all we can know for certain was that Martin arrived in Philadelphia determined to defend to the last the sovereignty of the states, especially his own. He appeared at the Convention on June 9. Characteristically, he got copies of various proposals that were being debated, and then on Sunday asked the Convention secretary, William Jackson, to open up the State House so he could go over the journal of the proceedings. Over the next few days he made his usual assiduous study of what had happened. Then, on June 27 he rose to speak, on the issue before the Convention—whether proportional representation or equal voting would hold in the lower house.

Whether he was acting on his own or had been given the assignment of making the defense for the small states we do not know. He may simply have been impelled by whatever tangle of emotions had pushed him into the states' rights cause. But it is more likely that the speech was part of a plan, because the moment it was over Lansing of New York and Jonathan Dayton of New Jersey made a motion for equal suffrage in the lower house of Congress. Martin had apparently been picked to make the major speech for the defense because of his reputation as a brilliant courtroom debater.

Whoever made the decision, it was a terrible mistake. The day was hot, and the delegates were tense from the steady sense of crisis that was pervading the Convention. Martin spoke, and he spoke, on and on, filling the air with long-winded locutions, arguments that wandered hither and thither and petered out in the underbrush. We have no direct statement that he was drunk, but the best respected historian of the Convention, Max Farrand, has concluded that he was. We know by Martin's own admission that he drank most heavily in hot weather—"to supply the amazing waste of perspiration," he said. The delegates yawned, shifted restlessly in their seats. The speech went on for three hours, and when it came time to adjourn, Martin said he would continue the next day. The delegates despaired. Martin did as promised, and spoke for three more hours.

In his notes for June 28, Madison reported that Martin spoke "with much diffuseness and considerable vehemence." Madison was Martin's political enemy and would not have been much attracted to him personally, either; but

Robert Yates, who was on Martin's side in the debate, reported in his notes that his arguments "were too diffuse and in many instances desultory," so that it was impossible to "methodize his ideas into a systematic or argumentative arrangement."

Yet at bottom Martin's argument was clear enough. It was not built on an appeal to natural rights and basic human nature, as the arguments of Madison, Wilson, and some of the others were. Martin had a lawyer's mind, and his argument was legalistic. It was based on Martin's firm belief in states as sovereign entities. They, not the people, were the basic building blocks in the social system. The people must act through state governments to direct the national government, and the national government must act through the state governments to direct the people. The states are therefore "equal" in the same way that people are "equal." Logically, they should have equal votes.

For Martin, the states were real beings that should not be destroyed. He was a pure federalist: the union was, and should be, a collection of governments that were joined together for certain purposes. The people had delegated power to their state governments and could not take it back without those governments' consent. The new union should be a government not of the people but of the states. He went on to insist, as Sherman had done, that the old Congress had not made unwise decisions; its weakness was that it had been unable to enforce its good ones. Nor had equal suffrage damaged the large states, whereas under proportional representation the small states would be enslaved.

The harangue, filled as it was with learned references to John Locke and ancient societies, might have impressed a jury of ordinary men dazzled by passion and rhetoric. But these were not ordinary men and they were not impressed. By itself, a long speech would not have been a problem. In a day before television and with few spectator sports, speeches were regarded as a form of entertainment. Hamilton's speech proposing an English model of government had lasted for five hours and had been listened to attentively. But Martin failed in one essential respect: he was not amusing. Later, Martin's former college classmate Oliver Ellsworth of Connecticut, a member of the small-state caucus, wrote hostilely to Martin that the speech "might have continued two months, but for those marks of fatigue and disgust you saw strongly expressed on whichever side of the house you turned your mortified eyes."

It is not difficult to imagine what Paterson, Sherman, Dickinson, and the others in the small-states camp must have thought while Martin harangued on. But there was nothing they could do about it; it was too late. Once Martin sat down, the small states could do little more than carry on a rearguard action. Sherman made a brief, cogent speech saying, "The question is not what rights naturally belong to men; but how they may be most equally and effectually guarded in society. And if some give up more than others in order to attain this end, there can be no room for complaint. To do otherwise, to require an equal concession from all, if it would create the danger to the rights of some, would be sacrificing the end to the means." But the nationalists would not give in. Wilson, Hamilton, Madison all made strong speeches for proportional representation, going over the old ground once again: equal suffrage was unjust, and illogical in a government based on the people—the small states would be making a great mistake to allow the big states to confederate without them, and so on. So they came to the vote. But before they did Benjamin Franklin, once again attempting to cool passions and unloosen intransigence, spoke. This time he proposed that as "God governs in the affairs of men," the Convention ought to have recourse to Him, and begin their sessions with a prayer. Sherman seconded the motion. But nobody else was interested, and the idea was dropped.

The vote on suffrage in the lower house came at the end of June 29. It went strictly along factional lines. On the question of equal suffrage in the first branch, Connecticut, New York, New Jersey, and Delaware voted yes. Maryland, as usual, was divided, Martin voting yes and Daniel Jenifer voting no. Proportional representation won six to four.

What would have happened if the Convention had got a thoughtful, solidly reasoned, conciliatory speech instead of Martin's endless harangue? It is, of course, impossible to say. Later events suggest that with better management Jenifer could have been brought around, and it is also possible—as later events implied—that enough of the Massachusetts men could have been swayed to bring them over, too. That would have made the vote six to five against proportional voting. But it was too late for any of that. The first branch of Congress—the House of Representatives—would be based on proportional representation.

Oliver Ellsworth rose and said that he was "not sorry on the whole . . . that the vote just passed had determined against [equal suffrage] in the first branch. He hoped it would become a ground for compromise with regard to the second branch." And the stage was set for the battle over proportional representation to be replayed, this time with respect to the Senate.

Chapter Thirteen

"The Most Serious and Threatening Excitement"

By June 30 it was clear that in the new government—should there ever be one—the branch of Congress we now call the House of Representatives would be based on proportional representation, with the result that coalitions of a few large states would be able to have things their own way. The question that remained was whether the Senate would also be based on proportional representation, or on the principle of equal suffrage under which each state got one vote.

This was the crucial issue. The delegates from the small states had been forced to accept proportional representation in one branch of Congress. The best the small states could hope for now was the Connecticut Compromise, designed by the old fox Roger Sherman, with proportional representation in the House, equal suffrage in the Senate. And they were prepared to make a fight for it.

By this time many of the men at the Convention had become emotionally entangled with the issue of proportional representation against equal suffrage. Men like Paterson and Dickinson had always been determined to save their states from domination by the big ones, and on the other side, Gouverneur Morris, James Wilson, and their allies had been convinced that equal suffrage was grossly unfair. But now, after weeks of wrangling in a hot, stuffy room, many delegates had come to see the debate as war, plain and simple. A few, especially the older sages like Sherman and Franklin, kept a handle on their passions and continued to work coolly toward a conclusion that would be generally acceptable. But most did not.

James Madison and James Wilson especially were well beyond the point where they would compromise. They were two of the most learned and intelligent men in the assembly, and they could have found some compromise everybody would accept. But they had become stubborn, and were determined to fight it out to the end.

Thus, on Saturday, June 30, as the Convention faced the final issue, there was considerable desperation among the delegates. It was another hot day, which did not help matters. The small states began the fight by pointing out that the delegates from New Hampshire had not yet arrived. Assuming that New Hampshire would join their camp, they moved that George Washington, as president of the Convention, write the New Hampshire delegates, urging them to hurry to Philadelphia. As it happened, both the New Hampshire delegates were merchants who wanted a strong central government, and they probably would not have joined the small states' bloc, but in any case, the big states were not fooled and voted down the proposal.

Then, as tempers began to rise, James Wilson stood and said, "Can we forget for whom we are forming a government? Is it for *men,* or for the imaginary beings called *states*?" As for him, if the country was going to divide over any issue, "it could never happen on better grounds." And he suggested that the large states, which comprised three-quarters of the population of the country, would go ahead and form a union of their own.

Oliver Ellsworth objected. The point was not that the majority needed protection from the minority, but that the few must be protected from destruction by the many. "We are running from one extreme to another," he said. "We are razing the foundations of the building, when we need only repair the roof."

Madison rose to answer. Ellsworth had contradicted himself on certain points, he said testily, and had got his history wrong on others. He then went on to mention that Connecticut had recently refused to authorize payment of its quota of taxes to the national government, a patent example of the abuses he wanted to correct. Ellsworth snapped back that Connecticut had always done its share, and in fact during the Revolution had had more troops in the field than Virginia.

Sherman now attempted to smooth things over. "Congress," he said, "is not to blame for the faults of the states. Their measures have been right, and the only thing wanting has been a further power in Congress to render them effectual."

Both sides were digging in their heels. Rufus King of Massachusetts announced that if the small states' men were going to be obstinate, the nationalists could be obstinate, too. He was amazed that an opportunity to provide for the happiness of the American people would be sacrificed by men adhering to a "vicious principle of representation . . . which must be as short-lived as it would be unjust." He could, he added, "never listen to an equality of votes as proposed in the motion." Dayton, from New Jersey, replied sharply, "When assertion is given for proof and terror substituted for argument, they would have no effect however eloquently spoken." Luther Martin, with uncharacteristic brevity, said flatly that he would never confederate "if it could not be done on just principles"—meaning equal votes.

By the middle of that hot Saturday it was becoming clear to Madison and Wilson that the small states' men would not budge. They were going to walk out if they lost on the issue. The main question now was whether or not to let them walk out. It was certainly preferable not to do so, however, and Madison decided to offer a concession. Early in the morning a North Carolinian, William Davie, had pointed out a major difficulty with basing a Senate on proportional representation. The Senate was supposed to be a small conclave of wise men; but under proportional representation, if tiny Delaware were to have any senators at all, giant Virginia would have to have sixteen or more, and the Senate would be huge—at least ninety members. In response, James Wilson had admitted that the problem was "embarrassing." He had proposed that one senator be elected for every 100,000 people in a state, but that the states with populations under 100,000 have a senator anyway. This proposal, in effect, would have given the small states a certain amount of extra weight.

Now Madison said he would go along with Wilson's suggestion. But it was too late. Feelings on both sides were so strong that a lot of the delegates were willing to sink the Convention rather than give in. Among them was Gunning Bedford, a fat, tempestuous delegate from Delaware. Pierce says, "He is a bold and nervous [agitated] speaker, and has a very commanding and striking manner;—but he is warm and impetuous in his temper, and precipitate in his judgment." At this moment he was precisely that.

> . . . the larger states proceed as if our eyes were already perfectly blinded. Impartiality, with them, is already out of the question. . . . Even the diminutive state of Georgia has an eye to her future wealth and greatness —South Carolina, puffed up with the possession of her wealth and negroes, and North Carolina, are all, from different views, united with the great states. . . . Pretences to support ambition are never wanting. Their cry is, where is the danger. . . . *I do not, gentlemen, trust you.* If you possess the power, the abuse of it could not be checked. . . . The small states never can agree to the Virginia Plan. . . . Is it come to this, then,

that *the sword* must decide this controversy? . . . Will you crush the smaller states, or must they be left unmolested? Sooner than be ruined, there are *foreign powers who will take us by the hand.*

This speech hinted of civil war, and could not go unanswered. King upbraided Bedford for "intemperance" and "vehemence," and was "grieved" that such a thought had entered Bedford's heart. They had reached a hopeless impasse, and adjourned. On that hot Saturday, nothing had been decided. The critical vote on proportional representation for the Senate would wait until Monday.

Once again, fortuitously, just when tempers were at their hottest, a Sunday intervened. Hopes, however, were draining away. That Sunday Gouverneur Morris stopped around at the house of his friend and ally Robert Morris (no relative), Washington's host. He found the two men "much dejected as they regarded the deplorable state of things in the Convention. Debates had run high, conflicting opinions were obstinately adhered to, animosities were kindling, some of the members were threatening to go home, and, at this alarming crisis, a dissolution of the Convention was hourly to be apprehended."

What soul-searching, caucusing, wrangling took place elsewhere on that Sunday, July 1, we do not know. We do know, however, that several men made decisions that had enormous consequences for the Convention, and over the long term, the history of the world. Three of these men were William Pierce and William Few from the Georgia delegation, and William Blount of the North Carolina delegation. None of them cut important figures at the Convention, although Pierce's little descriptions of the delegates have given him a measure of fame. All three, like several others in Philadelphia, were also members of Congress, still sitting in New York. And on that critical Sunday they boarded a coach and headed north.

The primary reason these men so suddenly left was that an issue crucially important to the South was before Congress and the vote could go their way if the Congress could get a quorum. We will deal with this matter in detail later on.

Yet another man who did some hard thinking that Sunday was Daniel of St. Thomas Jenifer, of Maryland. Jenifer was an aristocrat who had been born wealthy and remained so. He had had a long-term friendship with George Washington, had served in both state and national governments, and was an important political figure in his own state. He was the third oldest man at the

Convention—after Franklin and Sherman. Sophisticated and experienced, he was far less subject to provincialism than were Paterson and Martin, with their intense loyalties to their states. As a consequence—and the influence of Washington must have been important—Jenifer came to the Convention favoring a sound national government. He frequently voted with the nationalists, canceling the vote of the bibulous states' righter Luther Martin.

When the Convention gathered on Monday, July 2, for the crucial vote on equal suffrage in the Senate, Jenifer was absent. How many of the delegates noticed we do not know, but Luther Martin could hardly have been unaware. So the voting began. As expected, Massachusetts voted against equal suffrage. As expected, Connecticut, pursuing Sherman's compromise, voted aye for equality. New York, New Jersey, and Delaware, also as expected, voted aye. Pennsylvania voted no, with the big states. And Luther Martin, now set free by the absence of Jenifer, voted aye. In that moment the aspect of things changed. The small states suddenly had five votes, one short of a majority, and one more than they had been able to capture hitherto.

Why did Jenifer decide to absent himself on this critical day? It was clearly a deliberate choice. Jenifer had an excellent record of attendance at the Convention: he had missed few sessions, if any. Furthermore, the moment the voting was finished, he strolled calmly into the room. There can be no doubt that he stayed away on purpose, and there can be no doubt, either, that he did it to allow Martin to vote Maryland for the small states' side. Although he was from a small state, he believed that proportional representation was just: nonetheless, he would allow his state to vote against it, to save the Convention.

But the Convention was not yet saved. The small states had collected five votes, but the big states had two votes, and the four remaining votes belonged to Virginia and the Deep South. Surely the big states were safe. Virginia voted no of course. North Carolina voted no. South Carolina voted no. The vote now stood five to five, with the deciding vote in the hands of the Georgia delegation.

But with William Pierce and William Few on the way to Congress in New York, the Georgia delegation was down to two. The aristocrat William Houstoun would vote with the big states against equal suffrage in the Senate.

The other man in the delegation was different. It is of enormous consequence that Abraham Baldwin had been born, raised, and educated in Connecticut, and had moved to Georgia only three years before. Baldwin, in his own quiet way, was as remarkable as many of the more visible men at the Convention. Like Sherman, Paterson, and Martin, he was lowborn: his father was a black-smith who had educated himself and encouraged Abraham, his second son, to educate himself, too. Baldwin was born in 1754 and was thus another of the young men of the Revolution. His mother died when he was four, and his father did not remarry for ten years, so we can assume that his upbringing was not easy. He studied theology at Yale, tutored there, and became chaplain. In 1781, when he was not yet thirty, he was offered the job of professor of theology, one of the most prestigious positions in the State of Connecticut. He turned it down for reasons that are obscure but probably had to do with a general dissatisfaction with the way his life was going. He turned to the study of law, was admitted to the Connecticut bar in 1783, and then abruptly, the next year, emigrated to Georgia. Connecticut, where the nation's first law school would open in 1784, was already overpopulated with lawyers, and in fast-growing Georgia there was far more opportunity. It is significant that Baldwin chose to live in the western part of the state, among the rough farmers, who had few slaves, and who tended to be political opponents of the nabobs of the coast. By birth, inclination, training, or all three, Baldwin was somewhat "antiestablishment," which perhaps explains why he turned down the job at Yale. This attitude would certainly have made him popular among the farmers in his part of the state, and given his obvious attainments, it is not surprising that he became almost instantly a leading figure in Georgia politics. He was, furthermore, moderate, likeable, and reasonable. By 1787, when he came to Philadelphia, he was the leader of the Georgia delegation. He spoke only eight times at the Convention, but he was on four of the six "grand committees" that made important decisions, and there is no doubt that he played a more influential role in Philadelphia than his lean speaking record suggests.

But Baldwin was not, of course, acting at Philadelphia only on his own opinions. He had his adopted state to consider. Georgia had a variety of concerns at the Convention, among them fear of northern attempts to end slavery and to cut up its huge western area into additional states. Overriding everything, however, was the fact that Georgia bumped up against the Spanish south and west and was exceedingly vulnerable to attack. The Spanish were supplying the local Creek Indians with arms, ammunition, and sanctuaries in Florida. Unless the state got help from the North, an alliance of Spanish and Creeks could easily overrun Georgia's 25,000 inhabitants, burning, pillaging and scalping at will. The very lives of Georgia's citizens depended on a firm union with other states, and the Creeks may have been the principal reason why the Georgians were strong nationalists: isolated, the state was doomed.

The other Georgia delegates—Few, Pierce, and Houstoun—were as aware of this intractable fact as Abraham Baldwin was, but Baldwin had a much better understanding of an equally intractable fact, which was that the small states would walk out of the Convention if they did not get equal suffrage in one branch of Congress. Baldwin knew the Connecticut delegates personally —he used to trade at Roger Sherman's New Haven store—and although no record exists, it is hard to believe that he would not have had many conversations with the Connecticut men during those summer evenings. If nothing else, Roger Sherman would have seen to it.

So matters stood on July 2 when it came Baldwin's turn to vote on the central issue of equal suffrage for the Senate. The pressure on him must have been intense, and the strain in the hall almost unbearable. The small states had five votes; the big states had five votes, and they had half of Georgia's vote as well. But Baldwin knew that he could not allow the Convention to collapse. So he voted for equality of suffrage in the Senate, splitting the Georgia vote. With the Georgia vote null, the issue remained five to five, and in effect the big states had lost. But Baldwin had saved the Convention.

In the stunned aftermath of the vote the realization swept across the room that the small states were going to have their way on the issue—that they *had* to have their way. Jenifer had grasped it, Baldwin had grasped it, and now the bandwagon began to roll. Pinckney once more proposed his scheme of a Senate of three classes. Next, his cousin Charles Cotesworth Pinckney, also from South Carolina, rose and said that although he did not like abandoning proportional representation, some compromise had to be reached; and he suggested that a committee be formed, consisting of one man from each state, to work something out. Luther Martin was instantly on his feet, saying that he had no objection to a committee, but the small states would hold firm. They smelled victory and they would not give in now. Sherman said, "We are now at a full stop, and nobody he supposed meant that we should break up without doing something." He favored the committee. Then the parade began. Gouverneur Morris favored the committee. Edmund Randolph favored the committee, although he did not think much would come of it. Caleb Strong of Massachusetts favored it, Hugh Williamson of North Carolina favored it, Lansing favored it, Gerry favored it.

It was without question the single most critical moment at the Convention. Madison's troops were deserting him. The alliance of the Big Three with the Deep South, put together by Madison and the Virginians, which had earlier dominated the Convention and rammed the Virginia Plan through the Committee of the Whole, was collapsing with a rush. It would be a different convention, with new leaders; a convention in which no single party would dominate. It would work its way forward in jerks and hitches through ceaseless compromise. Even the Virginians, except perhaps Washington, would abandon Madison. From now on Madison, and his principal ally, James Wilson of Pennsylvania, would be fighting rearguard actions.

Both now announced that they were opposed to a committee. They knew perfectly well that the committee would recommend some modification of their cherished principle of proportional representation. But their troops had fled. The vote to put together a committee was ten to one in favor. Only Wilson's Pennsylvania voted against it. Madison could not even hold Virginia. And when the Convention chose the men who were to serve on the committee, James Madison's heart must have turned cold. The member from Georgia would be not the big-state man Houstoun but Abraham Baldwin, whose vote had beaten proportional representation. The Maryland member was Luther Martin, the New Jersey member, William Paterson, the New York member, Robert Yates. From Pennsylvania there would be not James Wilson but the evenhanded and ineffectual Benjamin Franklin. The man from his own state would be not George Washington or Madison himself but the prickly sixty-two-year-old George Mason. The member from Massachusetts would be neither of the strong nationalists, Gorham and King, but the quixotic Elbridge Gerry, who had states'-rights tendencies. The member Connecticut elected was Oliver Ellsworth, but to give the small states as much strength on the committee as possible Ellsworth became "indisposed" and Sherman substituted for him. There was, in fact, not a single one of the *leaders* of the proportional-representation side on the committee. It had been stacked, and it had been stacked deliberately by the delegates who had come to see in the course of the morning that the small states must have their way on the issue.

The Fourth of July holiday was just ahead and the members decided to take a break for a few days and come back on July 5 to hear the report of the compromise committee. To celebrate the Fourth, Washington and some of the others went to a Presbyterian church to hear a law student named James Campbell give a patriotic oration. The thrust of the student's speech was that the country, and indeed the world, was looking to the men of the Convention to produce a nation singularly happy and free. It must have given the delegates a moment of wry amusement to hear the young student declaim, "Is the science of government so difficult that we have not men among us capable of unfolding its mysteries and binding our states together by mutual interests and obligations? Methinks, I already see the stately fabric of a free and vigorous government rising out of the wisdom of the Federal Convention." Had Campbell been in the State House two days before, he would have methought him nothing of the kind.

It is doubtful that any of the members of the Grand Committee heard such orations; they were too busy elsewhere. Despite the fact that it had been loaded with small states' men, it contained a considerable number of men who had initially been in the proportional-representation camp and still, all other things being equal, preferred that system of voting. Franklin, Mason, and John Rutledge of South Carolina favored proportional representation, and Gerry and Baldwin could go either way. But the committee had been put together to compromise, and compromise it did.

On July 5, Elbridge Gerry, chairman of the committee, read the report to the Convention. It called for proportional representation in the House of Representatives, equal suffrage in the Senate. As a sop to the big states, it included a proposal that money bills must originate in the first branch. This, in theory, would prevent a consortium of small states from voting for expenditures which would have to be paid mainly by the more populous ones.

Now, of course, the compromise worked out by the committee would have to be debated, and then voted on. The outcome was predictable: the committee had made the compromise, and the Convention would accept it. But still, Madison and Wilson would not give up, and for another ten days, along with a few of their troops who had stuck with them, they continued to fight. Wilson insisted that the committee had exceeded its powers. Madison, in a long speech, pointed out that the provision calling for money bills to come from the first branch was a worthless concession, because it would be easy enough for a senator to find a representative sympathetic to a given bill who would propose it in the House. He said he refused to vote for an "injustice" in order to gratify the small states, and he added bluntly that he did not believe that the small states would try to go it alone if the big states formed their own union.

Gouverneur Morris, one of the bitter-enders who stayed with Madison, agreed that small states could not hold out against a union of the big ones. A split union could be mended only by bloodshed, in which "the stronger party will then make traitors of the weaker; and the gallows and halter will finish the work of the sword." It was an open threat that if the Convention failed, chaos would prevail, bringing tyranny in its train, in the classical mode, and representatives of moderation and order—meaning all of them there—could expect dire reprisals. Morris could hardly have been more impolitic, a characteristic his friends deplored in him, and his speech served only to make the delegates from the small states more determined.

So they wrangled on day after day in midsummer heat, mainly debating side issues. Then on July 14 Luther Martin demanded that a vote be taken on the committee's report. Once again the old arguments were thrown up. Tempers grew short; language grew strong. Martin announced that he would rather see two unions than join one formed on proportional representation; he insisted that big states were weaker and less efficient than small ones. Wilson shot back sarcastically that Martin's opinion did not surprise him, because anybody who could say that a minority should have more votes than a majority was quite able to say that a minority was stronger than a majority. Next Martin would be asserting that the minority is richer, too, Wilson added, although "he hardly expected [this view] would be persisted in when the states shall be called on for taxes and troops." (July 14)

Then young Charles Pinckney rose yet again and offered his plan for putting the states in classes, with the biggest having four or five votes in the Senate, and the smaller having fewer votes. Now, finally, Madison and Wilson were willing to go along. Wilson seconded Pinckney's motion and Madison announced that he would accept the scheme. If they had been less intransigent at an earlier moment—perhaps before positions had begun to harden around July 1—Pinckney's idea might have been acceptable to the small states' men. But now the small states knew that they could win, and they would not budge. Pinckney's proposal was voted down. The Convention adjourned, and again at a critical moment a Sunday intervened.

First thing on Monday morning, July 16, the vote on the committee report was finally taken. It was the crucial vote on the question of equal suffrage in the Senate. And to nobody's surprise, equal suffrage won, five to four, with Massachusetts split, and New York already gone from the Convention.

It is important to note that neither Massachusetts nor North Carolina voted *for* proportional representation for the Senate. In the Massachusetts delegation, the ambitious and strong-minded Rufus King was willing to "submit to a little more confusion and convulsion"—that is, sink the Convention—rather than accede to equal voting in the Senate. The easy-going Gorham, too, was willing to take the chance. On the other hand, Strong, who tended to smooth things over when possible, was ready to give in to the small states on the issue, and so was Elbridge Gerry, whose voting patterns were inconsistent. So the delegation split, and the Massachusetts vote was canceled.

The North Carolina delegation, however, voted *for* equal voting in the

Senate, breaking with its big-state allies. The main figure in the North Carolina delegation was Hugh Williamson. In a letter he later wrote to the governor of his state, Williamson spoke of "how difficult a part has fallen to the share of our state in the course of this business." Arcane matters of state politics entered into the case, but it is clear that the main reason why Williamson and his fellow North Carolinians voted with the small states against their big-state allies was to save the Convention.

The behavior of the Massachusetts and North Carolina delegates makes two important points about the Constitutional Convention. The first is that, at bottom, sectional or financial interests were again and again overridden by motives lying deep in the personalities of the delegates. Gerry and Strong of Massachusetts, and Williamson and the other North Carolinians were big states' men, some of whom had strong financial interests in fighting for a government that the big states could dominate. Yet, for different private reasons, they voted against what would have appeared to be their own self-interest. And we can assume that there were other big states' men who did likewise.

One of the most important of those reasons for voting as they did—and this is the second point that must be made about the men at Philadelphia—was that for most of them the paramount concern was to see that the Convention succeeded. The eyes of the world were on them, they believed. They, and they alone, could not only save their country but also set an example for world— as Washington put it, "raise a standard to which the wise and honest could repair." They had been charged with a great task, and they were determined, most of them, to earn that greatness. And so, when it came to the final vote, they would choose to keep the Convention intact.

The Big Three–Deep South coalition, in any case, was gone. One last desperate attempt was made to pull the coalition together again: a caucus of the big-state bloc met on the Convention floor on Tuesday morning, July 17, before the official start of the meeting for the day. Some of the big states' delegates favored going home to form their own union. Others were ready to accept the compromise as it stood. In the end, while the small states' men drifted in to listen, the big states' delegates could come to no decision. Madison wrote in his notes, "It is probable that the result of this consultation satisfied the small states that they had nothing to apprehend from a union of the larger, in any plan whatever against the equality of votes in the second branch." And so, finally, it was over.

Or almost over. On July 23 the delegates decided to allow each state two senators, voting individually. This was a radical alteration of the system under the Articles, where states could send two to seven delegates, with the delegation casting a single vote. With each senator voting for himself, the strength of state views in Congress would be greatly weakened when a delegation divided, with one senator canceling the vote of the other. But only Maryland voted against per capita voting.

Historians have seen the Convention's acceptance of equal suffrage in the Senate as a defeat for the strong nationalists. James Madison, many years later, said that that battle was "the most serious and threatening excitement" of the Convention. But was it really? The United States government had been operating for nearly a decade under a system of equal voting in a single legislature, which, moreover, did not have to contend with an executive with a veto power. It had been a government strongly states' rights in tone, very biased toward protecting the interests of the small states. The delegates from New Jersey, Delaware, Connecticut, and Maryland had come to Philadelphia expecting to get very much of the same. What they got instead was something far different, and what they not merely voted for on July 16 but actually fought for was something that on May 29, when Edmund Randolph began to read out the Virginia Plan, they could not possibly have envisioned accepting. They had surrendered almost everything but the final barricade, which they could not abandon. In the process they lost a lot of ground.

We can see, thus, how important it was to the outcome that James Madison had come to Philadelphia with a strong plan, and allies enough to push it through. By the time the initial debate on the Virginia Plan was finished on June 13, the small-state men had already given up a number of redoubts, and were aware that they were in for a desperate battle simply to avoid total defeat and unconditional surrender. Viewed from this perspective, Madison and his team of strong nationalists had won a good deal more than they had lost: it was the small-state men who had given the most ground.

What are we to make of the battle in the long view? To a considerable extent the whole issue was not real. Since 1787 there has never been a time when the big states were at odds with the small ones. Divisions have been primarily sectional—the North against the South, the Sun Belt against the Frost Belt. Or lines have been drawn on economic bases—the industrial states against the agricultural ones, the coastal states against those inland, the new West against the established East. During the fight Madison said again and again that the real division in the union was between North and South. He was right, and before the Convention was over the delegates would realize it.

Part III

NORTH
and
SOUTH

Chapter Fourteen

A New Alliance

Over the two-hundred-year history of the United States, probably no question has troubled the country as much as racial antagonism. It brought on a Civil War, which nearly wrecked the nation and left hundreds of thousands of young men dead; and it continues into the present day as a cesspool of bitterness and hatred. Good men and bad have searched desperately for a way to end the enmity between blacks and whites, and nobody has succeeded. Racial antagonism remains the most painful canker in American democracy, a wound that nothing seems to completely heal.

The problem was already evident in 1787. As the wrangling over the big-states–small-states issue moved into its final stages, it became clearer and clearer to the delegates that Madison was right about at least one thing: the major division in the country was between the North and the South. Indeed, in 1787 these two great sections of the country were already very different from each other in attitudes, life-styles, and economics. In retrospect, it is difficult to see how it could have been otherwise. In religion much of the North was dominated by the lingering effects of the Calvinist puritanism on which New England and other areas had been founded; in the South an easy-going, worldly Anglicanism, which wished to interfere with neither pleasure nor profits, held sway. In agriculture the New England states were for the most part given over to one-family farms, which produced a small surplus for trade —a few barrels of cider or whiskey, a hogshead of salted pork, a wagonload of lumber, which could be sold to raise a few shillings in cash for taxes or a new scythe blade. In the South the dominant farmers were in business; although they usually grew their own food as well, they devoted most of their land to a single cash crop—tobacco, rice, indigo—which could be sold at a profit. In the North the cash crops were cod, wheat, livestock, and lumber.

Commerce was built on a fleet of ships and a cadre of trained sailors. Economically, then, the North and South were opposite sides of a coin: the South needed the northern shippers to move their produce; the North needed southern products to trade in: they were for the moment political adversaries bound together in economic partnership.

Furthermore, although both North and South were deeply in debt, to their own citizens as well as to foreign nations, their debt was structured differently. Northerners tended to hold a great deal of national paper, while southerners held notes and bonds issued by their own states. Needless to say, the southerners did not want to be taxed by any central government to pay off the national paper held by northerners, and northerners did not want the central government to tax them in order to pay off state debts in the South.

The assumption that the future development of the union lay in what was then the Southwest—the Carolinas, Georgia, and the areas that would become Alabama, Mississippi, Tennessee, and Kentucky—created special political tensions. In designing a new government, the North had to assume that the South would soon become the dominant section of the country in both numbers and wealth. This assumption later proved incorrect, but in 1787, northerners were nervous about the possibility of a government dominated by the South.

But beyond all of these differences was one overriding one—black slavery. It defined the South. You could not think about the South without thinking first of the "peculiar institution." Economically, politically, emotionally, slavery divided the American nation into two distinct halves, and it continued to do so long after the Founding Fathers were bones in the earth. This stony fact was recognized from the start by James Madison, who in his effort to smooth over the big-state–small-state issue, said on June 30 that "the states were divided into different interests not by their difference of size, but by other circumstances; the most material of which resulted partly from climate, but principally from the effects of their having or not having slaves."

Slavery was hardly an American invention, but at least some authorities insist that American slavery was the worst the world has ever known. Slaves carried to the Americas suffered horribly during the long transatlantic voyage; many of them attempted suicide by flinging themselves overboard, refusing to eat, or clawing their throats open with their fingernails. Although a handful of blacks managed to gain their freedom and a larger number were employed in relatively pleasant tasks such as domestic service, most blacks in the South lived on plantations containing more than twenty slaves. In New England, blacks represented only 2.5 percent of the population; in the South they were

40 percent. In 1790 in fifteen out of thirty-two South Carolina counties the black population exceeded 70 percent. Sixty percent of southern families owned slaves, and it was the possession of slaves that made the South the wealthiest section of the nation.

To be black in the South was to be a plantation hand, enduring long hours of hard, tedious work, eating at subsistence levels, and coarse foods only, dressing in rags, and living a life controlled in detail from above. Some masters were relatively kindhearted, but most of the slaves were driven by overseers who at times rode among them spurring them on with the lash. For most there was no escape and little joy. In addition, all slaves could be sold away from their friends and families at the whim of cash-short masters.

The slave trade in particular was deplored by many people who condoned slavery itself. Yet the trade was locked into the institution of slavery. In the miasmic coastal lowlands the life of a slave was likely to be short, and a constant supply of new ones was needed. In Virginia, on the other hand, where blacks reproduced themselves at nearly the same rate as whites, slavery was unprofitable: it was generally believed that a slave did about 60 percent the work of a free laborer on wages, and the only way Virginians could make the peculiar institution profitable was to sell their surplus slaves to the planters of the deep South.

The foreign slave trade was of interest only to the three Deep South states; by 1779 all other states had outlawed the importation of slaves. South Carolinians imported 7,000 of them between 1783 and 1785. But in 1787 South Carolina temporarily closed down the trade, and a year earlier North Carolina had placed a prohibitive duty on slave importations. There was good enough reason to believe—if that is what you wanted to believe—that the trade was quickly drying up. (In fact, as soon as economic conditions in South Carolina improved, the trade—which had been carried on illegally—was made legal again, the greatest pressures coming from the new rich cotton areas of the west, and 40,000 new slaves were imported in the five years before 1808. As Winthrop Jordan puts it, "The way west was to be paved with Negroes.")

A good example of the southern attitude is displayed in the character of South Carolina delegate Charles Cotesworth Pinckney, cousin to the younger Charles Pinckney. The elder Pinckney was a typical South Carolina aristocrat. He was born in 1746 in Charleston, where his father was a politician and successful planter. His mother was an intelligent and strong-minded woman who was important in developing the cultivation of indigo, at the time the major source for blue dye. Pinckney moved to England with his family when he was seven, and he was educated at Oxford and then at the famous Middle Temple, where many of England's lawyers were trained.

By the time of the outbreak of the Revolution he was a major political figure in his state. He was also a patriot; he fought against the British and was captured at the fall of Charleston; his estates were confiscated. After the war he never completely recovered financially, primarily because of overoptimistic investments in one of those canal schemes that so appealed to ambitious Americans of the time, but he was, nonetheless, a wealthy man. He was also a good husband and loving father, and apparently had what his biographer Marvin Zahniser calls "an ideal marriage."

After the Revolution Pinckney went on to serve in the state legislature, and as governor, emissary to France, and candidate for the presidency. Zahniser writes that he was "not a brilliant lawyer, but learned and essentially sound," and presented "an imposing figure, genial and full of fun." He appears to have been an admirable person—intelligent, educated, patriotic, an exemplary public servant, and a devoted family man. Yet Charles Cotesworth Pinckney was implacably opposed to the abolition of slavery and the slave trade (although he supported the temporary suspension of the slave trade at moments when it suited the slaveholders). The soft feelings he had for his wife, his children, his friends, his state, did not extend to black people. Even his cousin John Rutledge, a lifelong friend and political ally, could not persuade him that trading in human flesh was pernicious. If a man like Pinckney could accept slavery—he owned forty-five slaves in 1790—what could possibly be expected of less-educated and less-sophisticated southerners?

But even those southerners who were made uneasy by slavery were not sure that anything could be done about it. Washington, who wanted to manumit his slaves, had a great deal of difficulty finding ways to set them free without throwing them out into a world that made no place for them. Southerners, by and large, believed that if slavery was abolished, their economy would collapse. Moreover, they had subtle and complex emotional ties to slavery. Not only those who owned slaves but those who did not could get from slavery a host of psychic rewards—a sense of superiority over other humans, the wielding of command, which many of them would not otherwise enjoy, and for males, an endless supply of irresponsible sex. On the debit side was considerable guilt, often unconscious, and a good deal of fear, mostly conscious, of being murdered in bed.

It should be pointed out that the lower classes of whites—indentured servants and contract laborers especially—where held in contempt by the upper crust, and in some ways were not much better off than black slaves. Nonetheless, temporary indenture is different from a lifetime of slavery.

Northerners in general disliked slavery, but not always for humanitarian reasons. Although some, especially Quakers, deplored slavery out of religious conviction, most northerners disliked it mainly because they saw blacks as less than human, somehow not nice to have around. It was clear enough to them that Africa was two thousand years behind Europe in art, literature, science, religion, invention, manners—everything that counted in the civilized world. The attitude of Ben Franklin was characteristic. He was against the importation of blacks on the grounds they might "darken" the "superior beings," namely, "the lovely white and red." This, then, was the essence of the northern attitude: slavery was no doubt immoral and reprehensible, but free or slave, Africans were not welcome, and the ultimate objective of most northerners was to purge society of their presence altogether.

Moreover, many northerners believed the horde of blacks in the South was a threat to the union as a whole. The larger the black population grew, the more likely were large-scale slave rebellions. These would certainly inspire foreign powers to take advantage of the confusion to invade the afflicted state, forcing the North, at great expense of money and life, to the defense of the South. How realistic this fear was is hard to know, but it was certainly advanced as an argument in favor of ending slave importation by men at the Convention and elsewhere.

To some extent the opposition to slavery in the North was tempered by the fact that about 200 slave ships sailed out of Boston, Newport, and other northern ports. But the presence of this fleet of slavers also meant that a great many northern men had seen the horrors of the middle passage firsthand, and many New Englanders in particular had heard the tales of slaves chained to narrow wooden bunks, drenched in vomit, blood, and excrement. Such stories were bound to increase abolitionist sentiment.

It was clear that slavery would eventually be ended in the North. By 1787 the Massachusetts courts had abolished it, and the gradual abolition of slavery in other northern states, especially Pennsylvania, Rhode Island, and Connecticut, was under way. Surely slavery was a dying institution; why cause an uproar over it when it was bound to wither away soon enough?

But slavery was not a dying institution in 1787; indeed the demand for slaves was picking up, even before the great thrust given it by the invention of the cotton gin five years after the Convention. But many Americans believed—or chose to believe—that the death of slavery would automatically follow the end of importations. And importation had already been made illegal in ten states. At any event, the human capacity for self-deception is infinite, and northerners at the Convention were so strongly committed to union that it was easy for them to believe that slavery would shortly disappear. They did not like it, but it was not something they saw as a do-or-die issue. They very quickly discovered, however, that it was so enmeshed with a host of other problems that addressing it was unavoidable.

If, for example, the new legislature was to be based on proportional representation, as Madison so fervently wished, would slaves be counted? Would they be taxed as wealth? Furthermore, it was obvious that import duties must be a key source of revenue for the new government. Would newly arrived slaves be taxed as imports? Were slaves people or property?

Then there was the question of the new states that would inevitably be cut from the western lands. Neither side wanted to admit states allied with the other, and it was generally recognized that the determining factor in the alliance would be the presence or absence of slavery. Thus, should slavery be permitted in new states? Ought northern states allow southerners to cross their borders in search of runaway slaves? Should northern states be required to hunt down and arrest fugitives? Would a black traveling with his master into a free state become free? Were slaves items of interstate commerce?

The slavery question, then, ran into everything. Moreover, the issues it touched upon were themselves intermeshed. The first of these interrelated issues to arise substantially at the Convention was the question of whether slaves were to be counted as people or property. The issue was forced up during the tense battle over proportional representation: would the South be allowed to include their black slaves?

The question of whether slaves were people or property was not new. It had arisen first in the early days of the old Confederation, when a decision had to be made about how each state's financial contribution to the central government would be assessed. It was eventually decided to base the levies on population. And how would black slaves be counted? The South, of course, wanted the count as low as possible, the North as high, and eventually the issue was compromised: one slave would equal three-fifths of a person; five slaves would count as three whites. There was no particular reason for settling on this figure —it was simply the result of compromise. Significantly, both James Madison and Oliver Ellsworth had been on the congressional committee that had proposed the figure.

At Philadelphia the situation was different. Madison and his allies were attempting to establish the principle of proportional representation. As the debate on how black slaves should be counted progressed, it became clear to the delegates that the shoes had switched feet. If representation in the new Congress was to be based on population, it was now all to the South's advantage to count as many slaves as possible. And the North, of course, now took the opposite view: slaves could be bought and sold and had no free will of their own. How did they differ from horses and mules? It was, therefore, the battle over proportional representation that first forced the slavery issue on the delegates to the Convention.

The issue arose on June 11, early in the debate over proportional representation, and it was Roger Sherman who raised it. Sherman, in the course of offering what would become the Connecticut Compromise, proposed that suffrage in the House of Representatives should be figured according to the "numbers of *free* inhabitants" in each state. This, of course, was something the southerners would not like. However, it was not a southerner but James Wilson of Pennsylvania who proposed that the proportion should also include "three-fifths of all other persons not comprehended in the foregoing description"—that is, black slaves. This was precisely the language that had been used in the old Congress in determining how state levies should be calculated. Wilson had chosen it, obviously, because it was a formula familiar to both southerners and northerners. His proposal carried nine to two. Only New Jersey and Delaware voted against it, and that was because they objected to the whole idea of proportional representation.

It is not necessary to believe that Wilson and other delegates from the Big Three had made an explicit deal with the delegates from the Deep South. At this point in the Convention, the Big Three were primarily concerned with getting proportional representation through. The delegates from the Deep South states, expecting to be big themselves soon enough, were their natural allies, and the men from the Big Three had to give them what they wanted in respect to slavery in order not to disrupt the alliance.

On June 11 few of the delegates had a clear idea of how the Convention was taking shape; they were only slowly becoming aware of the natural alliances and divisions among them. But by early in July it had become obvious to most of the delegates that the Big Three–Deep South alliance could dominate the Convention. And it occurred to Roger Sherman, if not to anyone else, that the only way his state rights–small-state bloc could avoid being crushed would be to break up the Big Three–Deep South alliance and put together a different one.

Connecticut, as we have seen, prided itself on its democratic ways. Because it was less controlled by a hereditary establishment than many other states, it had always had to govern itself by consensus. Horse-trading came naturally to Connecticut's leaders; only men who had a knack for creating consensus rose to the top in Connecticut politics. It is therefore not surprising to discover that all three of the Connecticut delegates to the Constitutional Convention were men who by temperament hated making waves.

Roger Sherman we have already come to know. The other two men in the Connecticut delegation shared his penchant for compromise. Oliver Ellsworth came from a good but not aristocratic family. He grew into a robust man, six feet two in height. He went to the College of New Jersey at a moment when Luther Martin, Aaron Burr, William Paterson, and James Madison were there, and he became friends, to an extent at least, with Martin and Paterson. He went on to study law, and eventually became one of his state's leading lawyers. He was "tall, dignified, and commanding," an effect that was some-what spoiled by his habit of taking huge amounts of snuff, so much that he was "often surrounded by a fine film of powder"; especially when he was thinking, so that his family could tell when he had been struggling over a problem by the little piles of snuff they found around the house.

Ellsworth was one of the so-called young men of the Revolution—he was thirty-one at the time of the Declaration of Independence. He held various state offices, was involved with Connecticut's attempts to raise money to support its troops during the war, and served in Congress at the same time. His experience tended to make him nationally minded, and in general he favored an effective central government. But he tended to play it safe. He was, he admitted, "unimaginative" and usually looked to Sherman for leadership. One year in Congress he voted with Sherman 78 percent of the time. When John Adams was told that Ellsworth took Sherman for his model, he remarked that it was praise enough for both. Yet Ellsworth, like another tall man at the Convention, George Washington, had a temper and could snarl sarcasms when he lost it. Highly respected, he eventually became chief justice of the United States Supreme Court.

The other Connecticut delegate, William Samuel Johnson, was by birth and training a wholly different piece of goods from Sherman and Ellsworth. He was born into a wealthy and socially prominent family, and grew up to be an elegant and sophisticated gentleman who could and did pass easily through the drawing rooms of London. Furthermore, Johnson's father was the leading figure in the Anglican Church in New England. The Anglican Church in

America was, of course, a branch of the official Church of England. It was the dominant church in parts of the country, especially the South. But in New England it was seen as suspect by the Calvinist majority.

Johnson went into law and became a leading member of the Connecticut bar. His course was not smooth, however. As a member of the established Church of England he felt considerable loyalty to the mother country. In 1766 he was sent to England to represent Connecticut. He furthered his legal studies and was awarded an honorary degree from Oxford. Both by training and temperament Johnson was a Loyalist, and although he opposed British taxes in America, he said, "British supremacy and American liberty are not incompatible with each other." An independent America would "fall into factions and parties amongst ourselves, destroy one another and become at length the easy prey of . . . the first invaders."

As a consequence, during the storms that led up to the Revolution, and in fact well into the Revolution itself, he danced gingerly from one foot to the other, attempting to avoid taking sides. Despite his equivocating he went on to become a member of the first United States Senate and, like his father, president of Columbia University.

William Samuel Johnson's neutrality during the Revolution was absolutely typical of his behavior throughout his life. He always moved cautiously; he hated controversy. He once wrote, "I must live in peace or I cannot live at all. . . . Dinner of herbs earned by the sweat of humble industry is better with love and quietness than the table of dainties accompanied by either domestic or public discord."

Johnson's physical appearance matched his delicate and charming personality. He was, wrote one observer, "*tout ensemble* of a perfect man in face, form and proportion." His portrait shows soft, dark brown eyes, and black hair (it was gray by 1787). He too was above average in height and held his body erect. He created an effect of charm and compassion controlled by intelligence and dignity—the very model of the college president he later became.

In fact, Johnson and Ellsworth were a good bit more nationally minded than was Roger Sherman, and at times forced the older man to go farther than he would have liked in the direction of a strong central government.

Men of this stripe were almost by nature bound to seek alliances to gain their ends. And in the days after the Virginia Plan was pushed through the Committee of the Whole it was clear to the Connecticut men that they would need allies on a variety of issues. Unfortunately, their natural partners, the New England states and the small-states bloc, would not do. The small states' alliance was neither large enough nor firm enough to carry the day on most issues. Massachusetts was in the big-state camp, and the other two New England states, New Hampshire and Rhode Island, were not even present. So the Connecticut men took the bold step of reaching directly into the enemy camp for an ally: South Carolina.

These two states were very odd bedfellows. South Carolina, the leader of the Deep South group, was one of the most aristocratic of states; Connecticut was the most republican. Connecticut had already provided for the gradual abolition of slavery. Half the people in South Carolina were slaves and the other half were determined to keep them that way. South Carolina, the wealthiest of all the states, was dominated by great plantations and a one-crop economy; Connecticut was a land of small family farms and diversified agriculture. But despite these differences, the two states held in common one very important, if less obvious, interest. For both, the export trade was a critical part of their economies. South Carolina lived by exporting its huge crops of rice and indigo. Connecticut families maintained a relatively high standard of living by exporting large surpluses of livestock, lumber, and foodstuffs to the West Indies. Indeed, at this time, Connecticut had about 300 ships in foreign trade and exported more to the West Indies than Boston did, and about the same as did New York—about three-quarters of a million dollars' worth of local goods.

The major trading states of Massachusetts, New York, Pennsylvania, and Virginia exported in their own ships large quantities of produce from other states as well as their own goods. New Jersey and Delaware exported and imported through Philadelphia and New York. Connecticut exported directly to the West Indies, but imported European goods through New York and Boston. South Carolina also exported directly—though not in her own ships. Thus only South Carolina and Connecticut were entirely dependent upon the direct export of their own produce. This common interest in the export trade bridged the deep division between the two states. Moreover, William Samuel Johnson's urbanity and membership in the Anglican Church made him attractive to southerners, and as a member of Congress since 1784 he had made many friends among them. And besides, Johnson owned slaves.

It is impossible for us to know exactly who of the South Carolinians brought the delegation into the alliance. However, the leading figure in the group was neither of the Pinckneys, but their cousin, John Rutledge.

John Rutledge was born in 1739. His father, a doctor, died when John was eleven, and shortly thereafter John was put into the law office of his uncle Andrew, who was Speaker of the South Carolina House of Representatives.

The uncle died when John was sixteen, but he continued his law studies, first in England and then under a man who would also become Speaker of the South Carolina House. John Rutledge thus was virtually bred into politics, and it is not surprising that at the age of twenty-one he opened his law office and got himself elected to the South Carolina legislature. He grew up to be a man about five feet eight inches tall, with reddish brown hair, wide-set blue-gray eyes, a high brow, a delicate nose. His voice was nasal, and he was said at times to speak so rapidly he was hard to understand. Yet he tended to remain silent, holding himself a little aloof, always courteous, always making sure to offend nobody and please as many people as possible. He was appointed attorney general of his state when he was twenty-five, was made chairman of the South Carolina delegation to the First Continental Congress, wrote the Constitution of South Carolina in 1778, and became governor of his state in 1782. He owned twenty-six slaves. His major clients in his lucrative law practice were the exporters and importers of his city.

His training was in the managing of men. According to one biographer, "The ruler was dominant in him. He knew the temper, the strengths, and the weaknesses of such assemblances [as the Convention]. Each was a challenge to his mastery. It had been so with him in all deliberative bodies he attended since his first appearance in the Assembly of South Carolina. Invariably, he had emerged in control." But although he held many public offices, Rutledge was happiest manipulating affairs from behind the scenes. His favorite axiom was "Care not who reigns; think only of who rules." John Adams said of him that he "maintains that air of reserve, design and cunning."

John Rutledge was precisely the sort of man Roger Sherman understood. Rutledge, moreover, had connections in the North. He had done legal business with Pennsylvania's James Wilson, and stayed with Wilson for his first few weeks at the Convention, during the time when the Big Three–Deep South alliance dominated it. His legal dealings with commercial men in Charleston had given him a national—indeed, international—acquaintance, and in 1786, the year before the Convention, he had urged his state to work for the ceding of authority over all foreign trade to the national Congress. Because of his nationalist viewpoint, he was far less a southern partisan than were most of the men from the Deep South. But neither John Rutledge nor any other southern delegate could compromise the slave interests of his state.

Precisely how and when the Connecticut–South Carolina axis was formed we do not know. It is reasonable to suppose that William Samuel Johnson acted as the go-between. Nor do we know when the two partners to the deal brought in their sectional allies—Connecticut, the New Englanders; South Carolina, the states of the Deep South. There can be no doubt, however, that an arrangement was made. A few years after the Convention the testy and independent-minded Virginian George Mason told Thomas Jefferson why he had refused to sign the final document:

> The Constitution as agreed to till a fortnight before the Convention rose was such a one as he would have put his hand and heart to. . . . The 3 New England states were constantly with us on all questions . . . so that it was these three states with the 5 Southern ones against Pennsylvania, Jersey and Delaware. With respect to the importation of slaves it was left to Congress. This disturbed the two southernmost states who knew that Congress would immediately suppress the importation of slaves. Those two states therefore struck up a bargain with the three New England states.

This was not Mason speaking but Jefferson's recollection of what Mason had told him, and it was not entirely accurate. The coalition was not a monolith. The three New England and three Deep South states did not always vote together, nor was everybody in these six delegations part of the deal. But these six states acted together to carry many crucial issues.

If we do not know how the deal was made, we have a fairly clear idea of what the terms were. At bottom, the New England states agreed to support the Deep South on slavery questions, if the Deep South would support the New Englanders on matters bearing on shipping and trade.

In making the deal, the Connecticut men were thoroughly aware that the Convention could not interfere with slavery very much, if at all, if they hoped to keep the Deep South states in the union. In agreeing to support the Deep South on slavery issues, the Connecticut men must have believed that they were bargaining off something they could not have got anyway. From their viewpoint, they were getting something for nothing.

We must remember, too, that for most of the delegates the primary goal was to see that the Convention succeeded in producing a workable government. This was the great work they were charged with, and they were prepared to bend far to complete it. So the deal was made, and the Virginia nationalists, who had dominated the Convention in June, were by August isolated with their principal allies, the Pennsylvanians.

The new dominating alliance was quite different in tone from the one James Madison had put together in May. It was characterized less by high intellectualism than by a pragmatism bent on producing a nation in which the export trade could proceed unfettered. In making this one of their major goals at the Convention, Sherman, Rutledge, and their allies were forced into theoretical inconsistency, for they wanted a national government that would on the one hand produce a sound interstate commercial system regulated by the national government, but on the other hand would leave the states free of any restrictions on exports. Instead of building a government on the foundation of a consistent theory, as Madison, Wilson, and some others wished to do, they would scratch it together piecemeal, dealing with each issue pragmatically.

This approach was not entirely to the taste of all the delegates at the Convention. The Virginians especially had come into the Convention feeling strongly that a national government must be able to control the states to a substantial degree, and throughout the Convention they would consistently vote for curbs on state powers. They were supported in this by the smaller states. Once Maryland, New Jersey, and Delaware got equal suffrage in the Senate, which would give them a fighting chance to forestall legislation they did not like, these little states were eager to see a national government that would be able to control commerce in the United States, in order to prevent the larger states around them from preying on them. But on this point their former ally, Connecticut, had abandoned them. Connecticut wanted national controls over imports only; exports were to remain unfettered.

Connecticut had abandoned its former allies on the slavery issue, too. The middle states emphatically did not want to put anything in the Constitution that would tend to prolong slavery. Many of the delegates from these states were antislavery on principle, but whatever their principles, all of them knew that a document that seemed to support slavery would be hard to push past their constituents back home. And Virginians, for their own reasons, were eager to stop the importation of slaves. This group of states in the middle of the country, then, opposed both parts of the bargain struck between the Deep South and the New Englanders, and they would fight it.

We can pick up the story on July 2, when the proportional representation crisis peaked, and the despairing delegates sent off that select committee to produce a compromise acceptable to big states and small. On July 5, the committee delivered its report, which said, among other things, that the first branch of the national legislature should be made up of one representative for every 40,000 people in each state, and included the three-fifths formula, which had earlier been generally accepted.

But the formula left some men uneasy. Among them was Gouverneur

Morris, who, as we have seen, believed that men of wealth, who had a "stake in society" and would inevitably be carrying a good deal of the expense of the government, ought to have a larger say in how their money was spent. And the next day, July 6, Morris proposed the establishment of a new committee, which would assign specific numbers of representatives to each of the thirteen states, taking into account wealth as well as population. The Convention accepted the proposal and chose for the committee Gorham and King from Massachusetts, Randolph and Rutledge from the South, with Morris as a swing vote. The composition of the committee showed how rapidly the old fight between big and small states was receding from everybody's minds: four of the five men were from the Big Three and the fifth was one of their allies from the Deep South. The balance now was between North and South.

On July 9 the committee brought in a formula that gave the North thirty-one representatives and the South twenty-five, basing the South's extra representation on the fact that it had more wealth. The debate that followed turned mainly on the question of whether wealth should be counted.

In fact, at this point in the debate the term "wealth" was being used as a euphemism for black slaves. What the argument was really all about was the extent to which the South would be allowed to count slaves when representation was calculated. If slaves were counted, it was perfectly obvious that the South could increase its number of congressmen simply by bringing in more slaves, which the Deep South states were doing in any case.

When we read the debates through July 9 we find William Paterson saying that he could "regard Negro slaves in no light but as property. They are no free agents, have no personal liberty, no faculty of acquiring property. . . ." And we find Gouverneur Morris saying that he "could never agree to give such encouragement to the slave trade as would be given by allowing [the South] representation for their Negroes. . . ."

The northerners, here, were concerned far less about the rights of blacks than to see that the South would not dominate any new Congress that came out of the Convention.

So the arguing went on. On July 9 the Convention sent out another committee, made up of one man from each state, to refigure congressional representation. The next day it brought in another set of numbers, which increased the total to sixty-five representatives but left the North-South ratio unchanged. The Convention was no better off than before, and once again the northerners set about fighting off the southerners. King of Massachusetts complained that the four "eastern" states were underrepresented in comparison with the four southernmost states. Rutledge's partner, Charles Cotesworth Pinckney, responded that he didn't demand that the South get a majority in the new legislature, but insisted that it ought to have "something like an equality." Williamson of North Carolina made the central point. "The southern interest must be extremely endangered by the present arrangement. The northern states are to have a majority in the first instance and the means of perpetuating it."

This was the crux of the problem. Everyone was aware that at the start the North would have an edge in the new Congress—in the Senate because it had more states, in the House because it was more populous. The South could accept that, and bide its time until its population grew, but it had to make certain that the North would not be able to maintain its edge forever.

To insure that this would not happen, Randolph on July 10 moved "that in order to ascertain the alterations in population and wealth"—for which read slaves—a census ought to be taken regularly and the legislature adjusted accordingly. In other words, Congress would not be allowed to reapportion itself when it saw fit, which in a Congress controlled by the North might be never, but would be constitutionally required to reapportion at regular intervals.

Morris quickly objected, again worried about populous new western states, which might come to control the Congress if reapportionment was mandatory. Better to let the Congress do as it wanted. On July 11, Sherman urged that making reapportionment mandatory was "shackling the legislature too much, we ought to choose wise and good men, and then confide in them."

They bickered on, getting nowhere, delegates from North and South one after another making one case or another in favor of their own side. As usual, James Madison made a clear and farsighted statement. Experience showed, he said, that people in power do not easily give it up. He cited the example of England. "The power there had long been in the hands of . . . the minority; who had opposed and defeated every reform that was attempted."

Of particular interest were two short speeches made by Roger Sherman, both on July 11. The first came after Rutledge spoke in favor of mandatory reapportionment. As soon as he sat down Sherman rose to say that although he had originally been against the rule requiring reapportionment, he had been convinced by "the observations" of the southerners to change his mind. The second occurred later in the day, after King of Massachusetts objected to the formula for reapportionment the last committee had brought in, with its overrepresentation for the South. Once again Sherman quickly rose to support the formula, breaking ranks with his fellow New Englanders. "In general the allotment might not be just, but considering all circumstances, he was satisfied with it." By "all circumstances," Sherman simply meant that the South was going to have to be given extra weight if the business was to go forward. The Connecticut–South Carolina axis was by this moment surely in place.

But it was not yet in control. On the eleventh, the northern bloc pulled itself together and voted not to allow the South to count their slaves in the calculation at all—not as three-fifths, not as one-half, not as anything. The one northern state to break with its fellows and vote to keep the three-fifths formula was Connecticut.

Once more a divided Convention was rushing toward a showdown that might destroy it. But then, on the very next day, July 12, the Convention, apparently without reason, reversed itself. It took a bit of clever historical detective work by a twentieth-century historian to find the solution to the mystery.

Chapter Fifteen

⬿⬾

The Western Lands

The mystery surrounds yet another trade-off involving black slaves. To penetrate it, we must have a look at the problem of the "western lands"—that is, the land west of the Allegheny Mountains.

When the Atlantic Coast of North America was colonized in the seventeenth century, there was in Europe no very accurate understanding of the geography of the New World. As various governments, mainly English, empowered groups to establish settlements there, they made huge, frequently overlapping grants of land, described in loosely worded documents that made more sense in relation to the inadequate maps of the time than in relation to the land itself. Some of these grants stretched to the Pacific Ocean. Some colonial borders remained vague until nearly the end of the eighteenth century, and inevitably, colonial governments squabbled endlessly over land claims. As late as the 1780s Connecticut settlers fought an actual war with Pennsylvania over disputed rights in the Wilkes-Barre area.

The Treaty of Paris, which ended the Revolution, set the western border of the United States at the Mississippi. The land beyond the Mississippi was the vast Spanish-owned Louisiana Territory, most of which had never been seen by Europeans. To the north the British held Canada; to the south the Spanish owned the Floridas and the territory along the Gulf of Mexico.

The land that the United States now held between the Alleghenies and the Mississippi covered a huge area, far larger than the original thirteen states. It was of enormous potential value because of the richness of the soil, the abundance of game in the forests and fish in the rivers, the minerals assumed to be underground, and the network of rivers that ran unhindered by mountains to the Mississippi, composing a great natural transportation system. There were problems: the Indians would fight to keep the whites out; foreign nations were eyeing the area covetously; and of course, the land had to be cleared, roads sliced through, houses, villages, towns built. But the potential was clear.

This vast western land was divided politically into two pieces. In the South the states of Virginia, North Carolina, and Georgia, according to their original grants, ran all the way to the Mississippi River. Below the Ohio River, therefore, the western land was at least theoretically already part of the United States, and under control of existing state governments. In practice, however, it was recognized that the western sections of these three southern states would have to be hived off as separate states (eventually this area would become Kentucky, Tennessee, Alabama and Mississippi). The difficulties of transportation and communication would make it impossible for state governments on the seaboard to control what people were doing in the Mississippi Valley a month's journey away. The settlers across the Alleghenies had come from all over the union and did not feel any special loyalty to Virginia or North Carolina, and even by 1787 they were clamoring for statehood. They would have to be given their way, and this fact was generally accepted. How these states were to be cut up, and who was to have the say about it, however, was distinctly another question.

It was another question because some of the states, like New Jersey, Maryland, and Delaware, had no direct claim to western lands. For years one of the major conflicts among the United States was between these "landlocked" states and the ones with huge western holdings. The "landlocked" states insisted that western lands ought to be turned over to the national government, which would dispose of them for the benefit of the union as a whole. Maryland in particular was adamant on the issue, because many influential men in the state had bought large speculative tracts directly from the Indians in areas claimed by other states. The western lands north of the Ohio posed less of a problem, because although speculators had been active in them for years, the states claiming them had ceded them to the national government.

This whole vast western territory, both north and south, acted as a powerful magnet on people back east. To all those landless sons in Connecticut, indentured servants in Pennsylvania, sailors in Boston tired of the sea, and of course the endless stream of new immigrants, the huge stretches of empty land across the mountains exerted an almost irresistible pull. In 1787 the western lands were still very sparsely populated. Some 96 percent of the population lived on the eastern seaboard, with only about 150,000 people scattered across the vast millions of acres between the Alleghenies and the Mississippi. But Americans were flowing across the mountains at an accelerating rate. For example, the area that would become Tennessee grew from 1,000 to 10,000 people in the decade of the 1770s, more than tripled in the next decade, and tripled again in the decade following.

To everybody it was evident that the western movement was of boom proportions. As the land was cleared, the Indians driven out, roads cut through forests, and towns built, land prices could only rise and rise again. The sums of money that could be made from even small claims dazzled men's eyes, until even the sanest of them could see nothing but streaming gold. All sense of reality fell away. Even the most commonsensical people, including George Washington and Benjamin Franklin, were drawn in, and at least two of the Founding Fathers, James Wilson and Robert Morris, would be driven into debtors' prison by land speculation.

Of course in order to speculate, you had to own land. By 1787 the western lands were a patchwork of claims, some to huge parcels that ran to millions of acres, whole counties, even substantial chunks of what would become states. These claims had various bases. In some cases speculators had made deals— often of dubious legality—with one or another group of Indians, whose authority to sell the land was frequently just as dubious. In other cases states had allotted land to various groups of speculators. In still other cases squatters had simply gone west and begun farming wherever it suited them.

But however confused the claims were, one thing was clear: the western lands were the greatest asset the new country had, and could be sold to pay off the huge debt that had accrued during the Revolution. National organization and sale of the land would inevitably accelerate the flow of people across the mountains into the virgin forests, and shortly these people would begin clamoring for statehood.

And then what? Would new states be brought in on an equal basis with the old states? Would the speculators' claims be honored? Many of the speculators were rich and powerful men, frequently holding political positions in their own states, or even the national government, and they were hardly likely to give in quickly to annulment of their claims. And what about slaves? It was assumed that a new state with an economy built on slavery would vote with the South on basic issues; states without slavery would vote with the North. One way or another, the balance in Congress between North and South could be upset by the admission of new states. Thus, leaving aside all other considerations, the question of whether new states would be free or slave had critical political implications.

As it happened, the western lands of the southern states were filling more rapidly than the Northwest Territory above the Ohio River. The areas of Kentucky and Tennessee would be ready for statehood sooner than whatever new states were to be cut out of the Northwest Territory, and as a consequence, southerners favored easy and equal admission terms for new states. Northerners, on the other hand, were in no rush to let new ones in.

The old Congress had begun dealing with the problem of the western lands in 1784, when Virginia ceded to the national government its claims in the Northwest Territory. A committee, with Thomas Jefferson at its head, was established to work out a plan for all the western lands, north and south of the Ohio River. The plan that emerged, largely Jefferson's work, called for cutting the area into fourteen states. Slavery was to be prohibited, and the states would be self-governing.

The plan was never adopted by Congress. Some congressmen from the old states felt that the westerners tended to be unruly and would start wars with the Indians, wars that the old states would have to fight. Others were afraid that the westerners, who would be mostly farmers, would gain power in the national government and heavily tax the eastern commercial interests. Still others were concerned that numerous new states would give the West far too much weight in the government, which was based, of course, under the Articles of Confederation, on equal voting by states.

In particular, congressmen wanted to make sure that the claims of people from their own states were secured—hardly surprising in view of the fact that many of the legislators from these landless states were the very speculators whose lands they sought to protect. In the wrangling, Jefferson's plan went by the boards. Other plans were brought forward in its place, but for the time being, the old Congress failed to agree on any of them, despite the fact that the western lands had become its major preoccupation.

Then in 1786 another element was added to confuse the issue further. This was an attempt by the northern states to abandon to Spain the right to navigate the Mississippi, in exchange for a commercial treaty. Northerners had little interest in the Mississippi. Indeed, they believed that the opening of the West would draw away their population, reducing real-estate values and diminishing markets for their goods. Closing off the Mississippi would slow the movement west, and a trade agreement with Spain would open up Caribbean markets to their ships.

Southerners were aghast. The value of the huge western portions of their states depended to a great extent on access to the Mississippi, in order to move their goods to market—corn and other grains, skins, tobacco, and eventually cotton. The Virginian James Monroe spoke for many when he accused eastern congressmen of trying to break up the western settlements, prevent any new ones, and thus "throw the weight of the population eastward and keep it there."

But in the old Congress, the North had an eight-to-five majority, and in 1786 it pushed through a bill authorizing Secretary of Foreign Affairs John Jay to make the swap of Mississippi navigation rights for a trade treaty with Spain. The southerners, however, fought delaying actions and were able to stall the bill because frequently so many congressmen were absent that the Congress could not make a quorum. At times as few as three of the thirteen states were represented. It strikes us as peculiar today that so many congressmen would not even bother to show up. The point was that being a congressman was never expected to be a full-time job. It had been assumed that Congress would meet once or twice a year for a period of a few weeks to settle matters brought before it, and then adjourn. Congressmen were, by and large, busy and important men, with businesses to run and political matters to attend to in their home states. In fact, because the national government was so limited in what it could do, state business was often the more important. Frequently congressmen simply packed up and went home for months at a time when it suited them.

At the moment that the Convention began to gather in Philadelphia in May of 1787, so many northern congressmen had left New York City that the South had a temporary majority, and it reversed the instructions to Jay. This for the moment put the fracas into suspension, though it prompted serious talk of disunion among New Englanders. Not long afterward Congress lost its quorum altogether, in part because fifteen congressmen were also delegates to the Convention. This was the situation when the Convention began to contend over the issue of the western lands.

We remember that on July 2, on the eve of the crucial vote on proportional representation, when the Convention was on the verge of collapse, William Few and William Pierce of Georgia, and William Blount of North Carolina, had left the Convention and gone north to Congress, sitting in New York. As we have seen, the defection of Few and Pierce allowed Abraham Baldwin, who voted with the North, to split the Georgia delegation, tie the vote on proportional representation in the Senate, effectively killing it, and save the Convention by giving the small states their necessary victory.

Why would these three southerners have left the Convention at so critical a juncture? The answer is that they had something more important to do in New York. We can understand what it was by having a look at the character

of William Blount of North Carolina, one of the most obscure delegates to the
Convention. Blount was a curious figure to find in the company of the noble
Washington, the honorable Madison, the sensible Sherman. He was a liar, a
cheater, and a thief, and was the subject of the first impeachment trial ever held
by the United States government. But Blount was a classic American figure
—a man motivated solely by the love of money. He had no interest in enduring fame, which drove men like Washington, no concern for status, which
was important especially to the lowborn men like Hamilton. Money was
what he wanted, and it did not matter to him in the slightest what he had to
do to get it.

William Blount was descended from a line of lesser English nobility who
could trace their ancestry back to the Norman Conquest. They had come to
Carolina in 1664. They proved to be aggressive and shrewd, and over the years
had become major plantation owners, with holdings in various parts of North
Carolina. By the time William was born in 1749 they were a wealthy and
respected family, members of the colony's ruling gentry.

Blount, however, did not receive quite the education usually given a southern gentleman. According to his biographer William H. Masterson, the Blount
family was not able to persuade a school teacher to come into their roughly
settled area until William was fifteen, a time when most boys' schooling was
over.

His father, Jacob Blount, was a plantation owner with a good many business
interests, and consequently, what William Blount learned as he was growing
up was not the moral perorations of Cicero, or the political thought of Hume,
but how to make money.

It became his obsession, and although he owned plantations, mills, forges,
and ships, increasingly he saw speculation in western lands as the best route
to enormous riches. Together with like-minded members of his family, he
bought a piece of Transylvania, in the western part of what would become
Kentucky and Tennessee. Over the years he continued to buy and sell land,
getting himself involved in ever-larger speculations, which in the end
amounted to millions of acres.

Blount was quite open about his willingness to lie, cheat, and bribe to get
what he wanted. For example, it had been agreed, when the British turned
Savannah back to the Americans at the close of the Revolution, that the British
merchants would have six months' protection for their goods there. Blount
found a loophole in the agreement and wrote to his brother, urging him to find
a sea captain who would capture one of the British merchant vessels anchored

there: ". . . employ who you wish," he wrote, "let the commission be in his name and all the business in his name but take care that you have sufficient instrument of writing whereby you will come in for a good share of the profit. . . . it may be necessary for you to go on to Savannah under pretense of some other business and you may stand behind the curtain and give the necessary directions. . . . if it's possible to have [the captured ship] condemned in Georgia either by party, bribery, or other way it will be best."

On another occasion, when he wanted to buy up land in defiance of a law that limited the amount a person could purchase, he advised one of his partners to "make use of any name fictitious ones will do I suppose, if not you may use the names of Blount, Williams, Johnson, Allen, Winna, Ogden, and almost any other name you please adding such Christian names to them as you please and you need not fear but I can find the people to transfer their rights to the company." And in respect to the same purchase, he offered the land commissioners, who supposedly protected the public interests, participation in the deal, on the assumption that they had accepted their posts for "*private emolument* and in order that we may both obtain our *purposes* it is necessary we should understand each other that our acts should tend to our mutual advantage. . . . Such another opportunity may never present itself of making a spec and there's an old proverb which says, 'make hay while the sun shines' . . . I wish you an agreeable journey and great choice and great plenty of Cheekamagga Squaws." When Blount's accounts were finally checked, it was discovered that his companies owned "upwards of 100,000 acres" based on forged warrants. And in 1797, after he was caught conspiring with the British to mount an attack on Spanish Florida, he was impeached and expelled from the United States Senate.

William Blount had been in politics one way or another for most of his adult life, beginning in 1776, when he became paymaster for North Carolina's troops, and ending just before his death, in 1800, when he was Speaker of the Tennessee House. But, says Masterson, Blount "was a businessman in politics for business." His sole interest in serving in the state legislature, in Congress, as governor of Tennessee, was to see that matters were arranged to advance his own interests. And in 1787 these interests were mainly in the western lands he owned so many claims to.

William Blount was at the Convention because North Carolina, for reasons of economy and efficiency, had made its congressmen double as Convention delegates. Parenthetically, it is worth noting that there is no record of Blount's ever having said anything at the Convention. He thus becomes the exception that proves the rule: even this dishonorable man was sufficiently awed by the historical importance of the event to keep his mouth shut and eschew his usual rascality. He was not, however, sufficiently impressed to stay there when there was a chance to advance his fortunes elsewhere. Sometime on July 1 or 2, Blount, along with two other Deep South congressmen at the Convention, Few and Pierce, and another North Carolina congressman, Benjamin Hawkins, learned from congressional Secretary Charles Thompson that if they came back to New York, Congress would have a quorum and could handle some important business. That business was the report of a committee on the Mississippi question. The report had been written by southerners and would urge a strong stand against Spain in favor of free navigation on the Mississippi. As it happened, a number of northern delegates were absent at the moment—six of them were at the Convention in Philadelphia—and the South would have a majority. It was an opportunity to kill the nefarious trade treaty with Spain and reaffirm American determination to gain rights to navigate the Mississippi and ship out of New Orleans, rights that were so important to the ultimate value of the western lands. So William Blount and the others left, and in effect allowed Baldwin to defeat proportional representation.

The defection of Blount, Few, and Pierce was the first act in that mystery which has been sleuthed out by historian Staughton Lynd in the course of studying the effect of the Convention on black rights. The three men were still in New York when the Convention voted down—for the time being—the three-fifths clause, which would have allowed the southern states to count their slaves toward representation. Then, on July 10 or 11, Alexander Hamilton apparently left New York for Philadelphia, probably arriving on the twelfth. On that day, Manasseh Cutler, to whom Benjamin Franklin told his little parable of the two-headed snake, also arrived in Philadelphia. Cutler was the spokesman and chief lobbyist for the Ohio Company, a New England concern that was trying to get Congress to grant it six or seven million acres in the Northwest Territory. Cutler was, of course, intensely interested in any legislation affecting the Northwest Territory, and he played a major part in framing its terms.

What caucuses, conferences, hasty meetings were held the night of July 11 we have no idea. We do know, however, that first thing in the morning on Thursday, July 12, Gouverneur Morris rose and offered a resolution providing that in the new government "taxation shall be in proportion to representation." That is to say, the more congressmen a state had, the more taxes it would pay. It was an extremely clever idea, because if the South knew that its taxes would go up as the number of its congressmen was increased, it would be less likely to press hard for all the congressmen it was entitled to on the basis of its population. This would amount to some protection for the North. Instantly, several of the major figures at the Convention, both northerners and southerners, rose to debate Morris' idea. There followed a blunt and outspoken discussion, which grew heated at times, on the whole slavery question. William Davie of North Carolina began by saying that "it was high time now to speak out. He saw that it was meant by some gentlemen to deprive the southern states of any share of representation for their blacks. He was sure that North Carolina would never confederate on any terms that did not rate them at least as three-fifths. If the Eastern states meant therefore to exclude them altogether the business was at an end."

The Connecticut delegate William Samuel Johnson rose immediately, not just to support the South on this issue, but actually to propose that blacks be counted as people, like whites, at 100 percent, a clear manifestation of the Connecticut–South Carolina alliance. But there was no likelihood that a majority of northern delegates would accept this idea, as Gouverneur Morris now made clear. The northerners had gone along with mandatory reapportionment. What more did the southerners want? he demanded.

What they wanted, Charles Cotesworth Pinckney said, was "that property in slaves should not be exposed to danger under a government instituted for the protection of property." The obduracy of the South was plain. Nobody was pussyfooting anymore. Southerners must have their slaves, and they must have enough weight in Congress to prevent it from taking their slaves from them. The northerners knew that they would have to give way on the point, and they did. The compromise was carried: at the end of the day the Convention voted to tie taxation to representation, as Morris had suggested, with each slave to be counted as three-fifths of a person, and a census with mandatory reapportionment required of Congress every ten years. New Jersey and Delaware voted no, and Georgia was divided because some of its delegates were holding out for counting blacks at 100 percent. Only in Massachusetts did any significant abolitionist sentiment show: the delegation split, probably with King and Gerry voting nay.

Thus, in exchange for tying taxation to representation, which it was assumed would throw the greater financial burden on the South when it became, as expected, the dominant power in government, the North gave way on the three-fifths formula and on a mandatory census, which would force the Congress to give the South its majority when its population had increased sufficiently.

But according to Staughton Lynd's thesis, the bargain was a good deal more complicated than that. There was—it appears—a second compromise interlocked with the first; for the next day, July 13, back in New York, the old Congress passed the Northwest Ordinance, which settled the problem of the western lands *north* of the Ohio River. And remarkably enough, a Congress controlled at the moment by the South voted to *exclude* slavery from any future states in the Northwest Territory. It is Lynd's suggestion that a deal had been made and brought to Philadelphia by Hamilton and Cutler. In this case, half of it was put through Congress sitting in New York, and half of it at the Convention sitting in Philadelphia.

What were the terms of the whole complex deal? The North, most significantly, got a prohibition of slavery in the Northwest Territory.

Another factor that Lynd does not suggest might well have played a significant part in persuading at least some members of both bodies to support the various elements of the compromise. Even if few southern land speculators were as rapacious as William Blount, many of them had very great holdings and depended on congressional and state concert to protect their claims. The new Northwest Ordinance was passed at the urging of landholders who feared the loss of their property to the tens of thousands of squatters filling the West.

Congress, of course, needed to sell the land to pay its debts, and the Ohio Company offered not only to provide money for a large piece of the Territory but also to organize it. In addition, Cutler put tremendous pressure on Congress to sell by threatening to break off negotiations unless his terms were met, and to make proposals to state governments instead. New York, Massachusetts, and Connecticut, he reported, were all ready to sell at half a dollar an acre. Arranging the terms of the sale and the terms of the Ordinance to suit Cutler and his New England partners would take much force from the factions opposed to letting Virginia, North Carolina, and Georgia deal with their own speculators. It would set up a concordance between southern speculators and those from New England.

When Cutler's deal was finally approved by Congress on July 27, he exulted, "By this Ordinance, we obtained the grant of near 5,000,000 of acres of land," a half million of which were open "for a private speculation, in which many of the principal characters in America are concerned." Thus, a quid pro quo between major land speculators allowed New Englanders a large share of the action in exchange for their acquiescence in a southern free hand in the area south of the Ohio.

But the southerners also insisted on and got a remedy to one of their most troubling interstate problems under the Articles: an explicit statement of their right to cross state lines when pursuing fleeing slaves. The Ordinance of 1787 provided that any fugitive from another state where his "labor or service is lawfully claimed . . . may be lawfully reclaimed." The Constitution of 1787 provides also that such fugitives "be delivered up on Claim of the party to whom . . . labor may be due." These fugitive-slave clauses were a sticking point to the nascent abolitionist movement in Massachusetts and Pennsylvania and were the grounds for charges that the Constitution was a pact with the devil. But they were a major part of the price paid to gain acquiescence in perhaps the largest private real-estate deal of all time and to give northern pioneers a clean bed, as Abraham Lincoln later put it, with no snakes in it. And from the South's point of view, as one North Carolina congressman told his governor, the welfare of the southern settlers in the west "has at length from a variety of circumstances unnecessary as well perhaps as improper to relate been put in a better situation than before."

It is impossible to guess at how widespread slavery would have become in the Northwest Territory had it been allowed there. Some people believed that slave economies worked only in warmer climates; there would therefore have been little incentive to import slaves north across the Ohio River. Yet when Indiana and Illinois became states, slavery was kept out only with great difficulty, and Illinois actually permitted it under the guise of indentures. And in Kentucky, just south of the Ohio, the number of slaves grew from 2,500 in 1770 to 40,000 in 1800.

Nobody could predict what might happen. But the delegates knew that, whatever the future brought, the decision to bar slavery from the Northwest Territory would have the immediate effect of placating the abolitionists back home when it came time to ratify the Constitution. It became, furthermore, an essential precedent that helped to confine slavery to the South for the rest of that institution's life in America.

The prohibition of slavery in the Northwest Territory was, then, the first major advantage the North gained from this complex deal. The second was the agreement that the Northwest Territory would be divided into no more than five states, instead of the relatively large number—ten or fourteen—suggested by earlier congressional committees. (In the end it became Ohio, Illinois, Indiana, Michigan, and a part of Wisconsin.) This was something the northerners wanted, because they feared a flood of new states would destroy their majority in the Senate, which they expected to be their counterweight against future southern majorities in the lower house, produced by rising population in the South. The South, assuming that many of the new states would be slave states, had no quarrel with a large number of new states, which might give slavery a majority in the Senate. The final compromise on this issue therefore favored the North.

In exchange, nothing whatever was said about slavery south of the Ohio River. This was understood to mean that slavery would be permitted there. This area had once belonged to Virginia, North Carolina, and Georgia, and it would continue to be open to slavery.

The South also got its three-fifths formula, a measure that Lynd says "sanctioned slavery more decidedly than any previous action at a national level." It also got a relatively low population requirement for admission of new states, which it wanted because it expected them to be southern in their politics. It got a mandatory census, which it wanted so that a Congress dominated by northerners, as it would be at the start, could not refuse to reapportion. And finally, it got clauses included in both the Constitution and the Ordinance that required the return of fugitive slaves escaped into the North—something that had not been sanctioned under the old Articles of Confederation.

What is the evidence that the passage of interlocking measures by the Congress sitting in the New York and the Convention in Philadelphia was not merely coincidental? For one thing, there is the uncharacteristic willingness of southern congressmen to prohibit slavery in the Northwest. According to Ulrich Phillips, for a generation America's premier southern historian, the Ordinance was "the first and last antislavery achievement by the central government" before the Civil War. For another, Lynd has turned up a statement James Madison's secretary, Edward Coles, made years later. "The distracting question of slavery was agitating and retarding the labors of both [Convention and Congress], and led to conferences and intercommunications of the members, which resulted in a compromise by which the northern or anti-slavery portion of the country agreed to incorporate, into the Ordinance and Constitution, the provision to restore fugitive slaves." For a third, over a quarter of the delegates to the Convention were also congressmen, including such influential men as Madison, Charles Pinckney, William Samuel Johnson, and both Nathaniel Gorham and Rufus King from Massachusetts. These men could not only find out what was going on in both bodies but also act as go-betweens, and perhaps most important, influence the proceedings in either. Once more, the otherwise unexplained arrival of Manasseh Cutler and Alexander Hamilton in Philadelphia at so critical a moment is certainly suggestive. And finally, Gouverneur Morris, who had closed the session of July 11 with a strong anti-southern speech, opened the next day's session with his representation-tied-to-taxation proposal, which bridged the North-South conflict. This swift shift of position suggests that something had been worked out overnight.

As Lynd points out, this is speculative: there is no hard-and-fast proof. Yet the conclusion is inescapable that once the big-state–small-state battle over proportional representation was settled, the major movement at the Constitutional Convention was a series of complex and intricately intermeshed deals struck between North and South, with some of the most illustrious names in American history acting as negotiators.

Once again we must be cautious of viewing this horse-trading too cynically. Without question the North and South were wary of each other, and each was keeping a sharp eye out for its own welfare; and without question they were, from a modern viewpoint, far too ready to trade away the interests of blacks in making their arrangements. But behind everything was a sense most of the delegates had that the crucial thing was to create a new government for what they hoped would be a great American nation. They knew that in order to accomplish that, no faction could leave Philadelphia feeling it had got the short end of the bargain. What they must aim for was a result that would leave everybody reasonably content; and that, inevitably, would require some very fine balancing of interests. Nothing else would do if they were to accomplish the great work that had been given them.

But the bargaining was not yet over, and before we can assess the Convention's treatment of the slavery problem, we must turn to yet another difference in interest between North and South.

Chapter Sixteen

Another Trade-off

The bargaining between the North and South, as must now be abundantly clear, was enormously convoluted, with the main deals being continually modified by subbargains, which were in turn further adjusted with yet other bargains. This was certainly the case with yet one more of these horse trades, a bargain in which the South made concessions on certain commercial matters in exchange for further protections for slavery. One of the principal causes of the American Revolution had been the effort by the British to control the trade of the colonies to its own benefit. In general, the British in London did not want the colonies trading independently with foreign nations. They wanted instead to force the trade to pass through England, where it could be taxed, and middleman profits could be extracted. They also required that colonial goods be shipped in British or colonial ships. In exchange, the colonies were given trading advantages with the mother country and each other over foreign competitors.

Parliament began passing the so-called navigation acts as early as 1650, and continued to pass them virtually up to the moment of the Revolution. The acts were not always seen as burdensome by Americans, because they did help to keep down foreign competition, especially in the lucrative West Indies trade. But in the years leading up to the Revolution they were increasingly resented, and were got around whenever possible. Many Americans favored the moves toward independence primarily to escape British regulation of their trade.

The term "navigation acts" thus was a loaded one, and the whole question of how foreign trade was to be regulated proved thorny right from the moment the colonies achieved their freedom. The problem, as was so frequently the case in the union, was that the different states had different commercial interests. Pennsylvania, New York, Virginia, and Massachusetts imported great quantities of goods, a substantial proportion of which were passed along to neighboring states, such as New Hampshire, Maryland, New Jersey, and Delaware. It was to the advantage of the big importing states to levy for themselves high import taxes, which could be collected from the ultimate consumers in other states.

The major importers were not averse to taxes on exports, either. Export taxes were standard among commercial nations in the eighteenth century and had been for some time. Indeed, it was more usual to tax exports than imports, because export taxes could be passed along to customers in other nations, while import taxes would be borne at home. All the big trading states, of course, exported, but the largest portion of any export taxes would be collected on the products of the southern states, whose economy was built around exporting tobacco, rice, and indigo. Such taxes would raise the prices of their exports and reduce their markets.

The big importing states also had a strong interest in gaining trading privileges from foreign nations. In order to negotiate trade treaties they needed to present a unified front. But under the Articles of Confederation, which left most commercial matters in the hands of the individual states, a coordinated policy was difficult to put together. As a consequence, in 1785, when New Hampshire, Massachusetts, and Rhode Island passed laws restricting British trade, in hopes of forcing commercial concessions from the British, Connecticut refused to go along, planning to draw off British trade to itself, and the effort collapsed. This inability to coordinate commercial policy moved one British observer to refer to the "dis-united states." Trade with the West Indies dried up, and since this consisted in large measure of foodstuffs, including livestock and fish, farmers and fishermen suffered along with sailors, shipbuilders, and merchants.

The major trading states, thus, wanted a government with substantial powers to regulate foreign trade and negotiate trade treaties. The small states, too, wanted a firm national control over trade, but for somewhat different reasons. They assumed that a government with power to regulate trade would take the power to tax imports away from the individual states, and use the duties for the benefit of all.

The interests of the southerners, however, were different. They were afraid that a national government with a free hand to regulate commerce might levy export taxes on the produce that was central to their economy. They also did not want a national government that could require them to use American bottoms, which would effectively give northerners a monopoly on shipping.

And because the North would initially have a majority in both houses of Congress, southerners considered it essential to build into the Constitution some limitations on what the national government could do in respect to trade, or "navigation," as they usually termed it.

To sum up a rather complex question, then, both North and South had very strong reasons for not wanting the other section to control commerce; but for the North it was especially critical to establish a national government that could, and would, manage trade.

The North-South battle over navigation acts began on July 24 with the appointment by the Convention of what came to be known as the Committee of Detail. This committee was handed the task of going through the resolutions passed by the Convention and bringing some sort of order to them—dealing with contradictions, clarifying the language, and in general tying up loose ends. It did not seem like a terribly significant task. The delegates at this point felt that they had worked out the major issues and the committee needed only to tidy things up a bit.

The delegates were wrong. Some of the loose ends that the Committee of Detail was charged with tying up were not only very loose, but touched on matters of considerable significance. The committee would be making decisions on very important questions. It was, in fact, to write a draft of a Constitution.

Its membership, therefore, is a matter of a good deal of interest. It comprised two northerners, two southerners, and one man from the middle states. One of the northerners was Nathaniel Gorham of Massachusetts, a nationalist who had just served a term as president of the old Congress, and a businessman who had become modestly wealthy through commerce. The other was the snuff-taking Connecticut lawyer Oliver Ellsworth, who operated under the influence of Roger Sherman. The southerners were the politically sharp John Rutledge and Edmund Randolph of Virginia, a careful politician who in the end refused to sign the Constitution because he was afraid his Virginia constituents would not like it. The man from the middle states was James Wilson, a business ally of Rutledge's, whom Rutledge lived with for the first three weeks of the Convention, and who had been Madison's major supporter in putting together the Big Three–Deep South alliance.

In picking this committee, the Convention made a misstep. Congressional control over commerce, then, was of great interest to Southerners, but it was vital to Northerners—as vital as slavery was to Southerners. According to Donald Robinson, who has studied the matter closely, "The Convention could not have produced at this critical point an intersectional committee in whose hands the interests of slave owners would have been safer." Randolph and Rutledge were totally committed to the defense of slavery, Wilson had accepted it as the price of Deep South support for proportional representation, and Ellsworth was part of the Connecticut–South Carolina axis. Only Nathaniel Gorham was likely to protest against slavery, and he could hardly prevail alone.

And in fact he did not. The Convention adjourned from July 27 to August 6 to allow the Committee of Detail to do its work. When it gave its report on Monday, August 6, it was immediately clear to at least some of the northerners that they had been sold out. Robinson says, "The report of the Committee of Detail was a monument to Southern craft and gall."

The key portions of the report read:

> No tax or duty shall be laid by the legislature on articles exported from any states; nor on the migration or importation of such persons [i.e., black slaves] as the several states shall think proper to admit; nor shall such migration or importation be prohibited. . . . No capitation tax shall be laid, unless in proportion to the census. . . . No navigation act shall be passed without the assent of two thirds of the members present in each House.

The Committee of Detail had given the South everything it wanted. There would be no export taxes on their rice and indigo. The Constitution would forbid the new government from ending the hated foreign slave trade. There would be no "capitation," or head, taxes on the slaves, and the two-thirds requirement for passage of navigation acts would give the South an effective veto over them.

It is difficult to understand why the northerners on the committee had given in so completely to southern demands: they may simply have been persuaded that such was the price for bringing the Deep South into the union. It is even harder to understand why they thought they could drive these clauses past the other northern men at the Convention. In any case, they did not. When the report was read out, the portions dealing with slavery so dismayed at least some of the delegates that they made an effort to adjourn the Convention for a day so that they could mount a counterattack. Virginia and Maryland were particularly upset by the lack of limitations on the slave trade, which many of the delegates, including Washington, Mason, and Madison, intensely disliked. But the delegates by this time were tired and eager to get finished. They voted down the adjournment, and proceeded to take up the draft Constitution of the Committee of Detail, step by step.

In the normal course of the discussion they would not have gotten to the slavery clauses for some days, but northern hostility to them was boiling over, and at the earliest opportunity, August 8, the independent-minded Rufus King of Massachusetts leapt ahead to what he considered the central issues. The admission of slaves was a most grating "circumstance," he announced. He had agreed to the three-fifths formula, he said, because he had assumed that in return for this concession, the South would agree to accept a strong national government, free to make decisions on other matters as it saw fit. But in this report, "In two great points the hands of the legislature were absolutely tied. The importation of slaves could not be prohibited—exports could not be taxed." As the black population rose, there would be increasing danger of slave insurrections, which foreign nations were certain to take advantage of. Northerners would have to help defend white southerners against these attacks, and that being the case, shouldn't southern export wealth be taxed to help pay for defense? "There was so much inequality and unreasonableness in all this," said King, "that the people of the northern states could never be reconciled to it. . . . He had hoped that some accommodation would have taken place on this subject; that at least a time would have been limited for the importation of slaves. He never could agree to let them be imported without limitation and then be represented in the National Legislature. . . . Either slaves should not be represented, or exports should be taxable."

A deal, in other words, was a deal, King insisted. But it is apparent some other deal had been struck, because as soon as King sat down, Roger Sherman rose and gently pointed out that King was out of order, and the points he had raised must be debated in their proper place. Sherman would support the South on the issue.

But other northerners were not having it. Gouverneur Morris immediately rose and gave by far the strongest antislavery speech of the Convention, an angry peroration in which he said that slavery

> was a nefarious institution . . . the curse of Heaven on the states where it prevailed. . . . Upon what principle is it that the slaves shall be computed in the representation? Are they men? Then make them citizens and let them vote. . . . The admission of slaves into the representation when fairly explained comes to this: that the inhabitant of Georgia and South Carolina who goes to the Coast of Africa, and in defiance of the most sacred laws of humanity tears away his fellow creatures from their dearest con-

nections and damns them to the most cruel bondages, shall have more votes in a government instituted for protection of the rights of mankind, than the citizen of Pennsylvania or New Jersey who views with a laudable horror so nefarious a practise.

Morris may have been taking an extreme position for bargaining purposes, or just exhibiting some of the rhetorical flamboyance for which he was noted. But he went on to say that the northern states were going to be taxed to pay for the defense of the South against slave insurrections. The legislature would be able to tax imports, and the North got a considerable part of its living by importing goods, which it sold to the South. But the national government would not be able to tax exports, by which the South made its living. "The bohea tea used by a northern freeman will pay more tax than the whole consumption of the miserable slave." And he concluded by saying that he would rather be taxed to buy all American slaves free than "saddle posterity with such a Constitution" as the Committee of Detail had brought in.

King and Morris were in the minority. Only Dayton of New Jersey spoke in their support. Sherman got up and said he did not see what the problem was, and Wilson, who had been on the committee, thought that the debate was premature. The Convention went on to other aspects of the committee's report, and it was not until two weeks later, on August 21, that it finally reached the critical issues that had so angered Morris, King, and some others.

The issue was forced when the Convention began to debate the clause in the committee's report that prohibited taxes on exports. Moderates in the North believed that export taxes might be necessary at some point and certainly should not be flatly prohibited. Even James Madison argued that the national government's hands should not be tied, and in one of the few instances in which Washington's vote was recorded, he agreed. But the South hated and feared the possibility of an export tax, and it voted as a solid bloc for not permitting it. Virginia, despite the influence of Madison and Washington, voted with the rest of the South. Two northern states did so, too. One was Massachusetts, where Gorham, who had been on the committee, presumably brought his fellow delegates into camp. The other, of course, was Connecticut. The prohibition on export taxes was carried.

However, the moment it was, Luther Martin got up and insisted that the resolution be amended to allow either prohibition of the importation of slaves, or at least a tax on them if importation was permitted. Slavery presented a danger to one part of the union, which the other part would have to defend, and besides, "it was inconsistent with the principles of the Revolution and dishonorable to the American character to have such a feature in the Constitution."

The only effect of this speech was to cause the southerners to become more obdurate. Rutledge said flatly that "religion and humanity had nothing to do with this question. Interest alone is the governing principle with nations. The true question at present is whether the Southern states shall or shall not be parties to the union." And Charles Pinckney said even more flatly that "South Carolina can never receive the plan if it prohibits the [foreign] slave trade." Then, to mollify the northern delegates a little, he added that if South Carolina was left to decide for itself, it might eventually abolish the importation of slaves, as Virginia and Maryland had done.

Once again it was the Connecticut men who broke ranks with their northern neighbors. At the close of debate on August 21 Oliver Ellsworth, who had been on the Committee of Detail, said, "The morality or wisdom of slavery are considerations belonging to the states themselves." And the first thing the next morning, August 22, Roger Sherman said that although he disapproved of the slave trade, the "public good" did not require its prohibition, and he "thought it best to leave the matter" as it was, in order not to drive the South out of the union. He added that slavery was dying out anyway and would by degrees disappear. Connecticut would continue to support the Deep South.

It was a Virginian, the prickly George Mason, who rose to make a strong speech against the slave trade. Mason owned scores of slaves and was not seeking the abolition of slavery; but the Virginians generally opposed the slave *trade,* in part because they felt it degraded master as well as servent, but also because the ending of slave importation would increase the value of Virginia's surplus slaves. Motives, once again, were mixed.

And yet once again the Connecticut men rose to support the South Carolinians. Ellsworth pointed out that Virginia could well oppose the slave trade, as it would only make their surplus blacks more valuable. "Let us not intermeddle," he said. "Slavery in time will not be a speck in our country."

Sherman, too, spoke in favor of allowing the Deep South to continue to import slaves. He said that "it was better to let the southern states import slaves" than to lose their support. And when Read of Delaware then suggested that the question ought to be handed over to another committee, Sherman responded that "the clause had been agreed to and therefore could not be committed."

But despite the support of Connecticut, the men from the Deep South were beginning to realize that they had better give ground somewhere. They recognized, as Randolph said, that slave importation "would revolt the Quakers, Methodists, and many others in the states having no slaves." In other words, at least Pennsylvania, and possibly others of the northern states, would refuse to ratify a Constitution that left the slave trade untouched. So the southerners backed off a little: Charles Cotesworth Pinckney suggested that a committee be put together to consider whether new slaves coming into the country should be taxed as other goods would be, "which he thought right and which would remove one difficulty that had been started." Rutledge seconded the motion; and Morris immediately said that he "wished the whole subject to be committed, including the clauses relating to taxes on exports and to a navigation act. These things may form a bargain among the Northern and Southern states." Ellsworth spoke against the idea of a committee, saying that he was "for taking the plan as it is. This widening of opinions has a threatening aspect. If we do not agree on this middle and moderate ground," the union might lose two states—Georgia and South Carolina. But the Convention voted solidly in favor of the committee.

The composition of the new committee, one of a number called the Committee of Eleven, is, as usual, of considerable interest. (Yates and Lansing of New York left on July 10; John Langdon and Nicholas Gilman of New Hampshire arrived on July 23). Its members were, in the main, conciliatory men, a number of whom had spoken little on the issue and had given no indication of strong feeling one way or another—William Livingston of New Jersey, George Clymer of Pennsylvania, Hugh Williamson of North Carolina. It also included some of the men who had already indicated that they were prepared to bargain —Charles Cotesworth Pinckney and John Langdon of New Hampshire.

On Friday, August 24, the Committee of Eleven brought in its report, which contained four provisions:

Congress could prohibit the importation of slaves after 1800.

Imported slaves could be taxed.

No exports could be taxed.

Navigation acts could be passed by simple majorities in Congress.

A complex bargain, modifying the report of the Committee of Detail, which had been so favorable to southerners, had been struck. In essence, the southerners, in order to hang on to the prohibition against export taxes, had given in to the northerners on other kinds of navigation acts, which northern majorities in Congress would now be able to pass as they liked. The South had also accepted what at the time seemed a very minor limitation on the slave trade

—the proviso that the new government could not interfere with it until 1800. Much later, as David Davis points out, when the issue of slavery began to tear at the country, Charles Pinckney called this clause a "negative pregnant." It forbade action for a time, and did not require any afterward, leaving open the possibility of the growth and expansion of the slave population. It was generally assumed, of course, that by 1800 the South might well have a majority in the House of Representatives and would be able to forestall congressional action on the slave trade.

The report was debated on August 25. Immediately Charles Cotesworth Pinckney arose and moved that the slave trade should be allowed to continue not merely until 1800 but for a full twenty years. How many of the northern delegates grasped this we do not know, but only James Madison spoke against extending the life of the slave trade. On August 25 he said that "twenty years will produce all the mischief that can be apprehended from the liberty to import slaves. So long a term will be more dishonorable to the national character than to say nothing about it in the Constitution." The clear-eyed Madison, as he so frequently did, prophesied accurately: the South never did get its majority in Congress, and in 1808 the slave trade was prohibited, but by that time slavery had become deeply entrenched all through the lower half of the United States and was spreading into the newly purchased Louisiana Territory. Between 1803 and 1808 South Carolina alone imported 40,000 slaves. The consequences in the 1860s would be terrible.

But few others thought it was a serious matter. Gorham seconded Pinckney's motion, and it passed, aided by the alliance of the New England and Deep South states. Immediately after the vote the middle states tried to fight back. Gouverneur Morris of Pennsylvania offered a motion to limit slavery specifically to the Deep South. It was an interesting idea, and if it had worked to confine slavery to the modern Southeast it might have prevented the Civil War, because the slave states would have been too few to take on the rest of the nation. But nobody liked the idea: among other things, there was the fear that if slavery was specifically permitted in any terms by the Constitution, it would only make people who disliked slavery more hostile to the final document. Then John Dickinson, a leading member of the Delaware delegation and a man widely respected in the nation, offered a compromise: perhaps importation of slaves could be prohibited to states that had already stopped the trade, assuring that they at least would not begin it again. But this motion failed.

Next the Convention took up the second part of the bargain, that slaves could be taxed. A number of people spoke against it, including Roger Sherman, who said that he was against "acknowledging men to be property, by taxing them as such." But King of Massachusetts and Langdon of New Hampshire pointed out that a deal was a deal, and a tax on slaves was "the price" of permitting the slave trade to continue for so long. The South Carolinian Charles Cotesworth Pinckney "admitted that it was so." Nonetheless, southerners managed to get a limitation of ten dollars for each imported slave. In view of the fact that a healthy slave was worth several hundred dollars, the tax was only a sop. But the northerners accepted it.

The third part of the deal, the prohibition on export taxes, was not even debated, as it was understood by the northern delegates that it was the quid pro quo for the time limit on the slave trade.

Debate on the fourth item, the simple majority for navigation acts, was postponed, exactly why we do not know. But it was clear that some people wanted time to do a little talking. Three days later, on August 28, the Convention began debating the question of the extradition of criminals from one state to another. In the course of the debate the South Carolinians Butler and Pinckney proposed to add to the extradition clause a clause that would "require fugitive slaves and servants to be delivered up like criminals." There was resistance to the idea—Wilson said that the cost would fall on the taxpayers, and Sherman said he "saw no more propriety in the public seizing and surrendering a slave or a servant, than a horse."

The southerners withdrew the motion for the moment and went off to do some more talking. The next day the Convention returned to the subject of navigation acts, which the Committee of Eleven had decided should be passed by simple majorities, as the North wished. Now the maverick Charles Pinckney offered a motion reintroducing the requirement of a two thirds majority for passage of navigation acts, which would effectively give the South a veto. Very quickly his cousin Charles Cotesworth Pinckney rose and said:

> . . . it was the true interest of the southern states to have no regulation of commerce; but considering the loss brought on the commerce of the eastern states [i.e., New England] by the Revolution, their liberal conduct towards the views of South Carolina, and the interest the weak southern states had in being united with the strong eastern states, he thought it proper that no fetters should be imposed on the power of making commercial regulations; and that his constituents though prejudiced against the eastern states, would be reconciled to this liberality. He had himself, he said, prejudices against the eastern states before he came here, but would acknowledge that he had found them as liberal and candid as any men whatever.

This series of exchanges makes it abundantly clear that the Connecticut men and the South Carolinians had a firm understanding; and it also makes it clear that the young Pinckney was not going along with the leaders of his own delegation, his cousin Charles Cotesworth Pinckney and the politically shrewd John Rutledge.

Several northerners followed, insisting on the importance of navigation acts to them, and speaking against the requirement of two-thirds majorities for them. They were supported by the South Carolinian Pierce Butler, who also wanted to keep the deal intact. He announced that he, too, despite his antipathy to navigation acts was "desirous of conciliating the affections of the east," and would vote against the two-thirds requirement. It was a signal: when the vote came, South Carolina was the only southern state to vote with the North in killing the two-thirds requirement.

And in virtually the next breath South Carolina's Butler rose and offered this motion:

> If any person bound to service or labor in any of the United States shall escape into another state he or she . . . shall be delivered up to the person justly claiming their service or labor.

This was the same as the fugitive slave clause that had been written into the Northwest Ordinance in July by the old Congress sitting in New York, as part of the price for prohibiting slavery north of the Ohio River. In Philadelphia on this August 29 it was written into the Constitution in part payment for allowing simple majorities for passage of navigation acts. It is almost as if the actors in the drama were following a script. First Charles Pinckney demands two-thirds majorities; then the other South Carolinians contradict him, saying they are "desirous of conciliating the affections of the New Englanders" for "their liberal conduct toward the views of South Carolina." Pinckney's call for two-thirds majorities is duly rejected without debate or a vote, and immediately Pierce Butler proposes the fugitive slave clause, which is duly accepted by general assent without a debate or a vote. The machinery constructed by Connecticut and South Carolina in early July was by the end of August running without a squeak or a hitch.

And this now brings us to the question that still haunts our thinking about the Constitutional Convention: could the northern delegates have put closer limits on slavery, perhaps sparing the country the disastrous Civil War, and the racial animosities that have dogged it ever since?

To begin with, virtually no one, North or South, was advocating immediate abolition. Nor was there any possibility of even a phased abolition stretching out for decades. The white voters of the Deep South would never have ratified a constitution calling for abolition, and it would have been impossible to get such a constitution through Virginia, too. New York and Rhode Island, hostile to the whole idea of a new constitution, would have used the defection of the southern states as reason for not joining—Rhode Island failed to join the union until conditions forced it to do so, and New York ratified only by the slimmest of margins. In sum, if the North had pressed for the abolition of slavery, there would have been no Constitution, and everybody at the Convention knew it.

Nonetheless, the Deep South states were in a poor position to go it alone. Georgia was desperately underpopulated and defenseless against Spanish, Indians, and their own blacks, numbers of whom had found safe harbor with Florida Indians. North Carolina was not much more populous, and South Carolina, while richer and more peopled, had nonetheless succumbed rapidly to the British during the Revolution. It is difficult to see how the three states of the Deep South could have survived long in isolation against the array of enemies set against them—the states to the north; foreign nations with substantial fleets and greedy eyes alit at the sight of southern agricultural wealth; Indians; their own slaves. And most of these Deep South delegates knew better than anyone else just how vulnerable they were: some of them had been in British prison camps not many years before.

It is our belief that by playing on these very real fears, the northern delegates could have forced into the Constitution stricter limits on slavery. The South would probably have accepted the 1800 end to the slave trade proposed by the Committee of Eleven. This would at least have prevented the importation of tens of thousands of slaves and slowed the spread of slavery. It is also possible that the North could have secured prohibitions against slavery in *any* new states, north or south. There had not been much opposition to this idea when Thomas Jefferson and his committee had proposed it to the old Congress in 1784. It would not have been popular in the South; but the southerners might have been forced to swallow it by a determined northern coalition. Indeed, some southerners were willing to limit the spread of slavery in order to prevent competition in growing hemp, tobacco, and other staples. These two measures alone would have had the effect of confining slavery to the Southeast, and would perhaps have prevented the Civil War.

Finally, the North almost certainly could have fought off the fugitive slave clause. In fact, the effect of the act was more symbolic than real. It was always difficult for plantation owners from Georgia or Virginia to trace and recapture slaves who had run into Massachusetts or upstate New York. The fugitive slave act would have been useful mainly to slave owners on the borders of the Ohio River, who could chase slaves attempting to swim to freedom. As it worked out, the real effect of the fugitive slave act was to allow man-stealers to go into northern states and kidnap free blacks, under the pretense that they were escaped slaves. Unfortunately, black freedmen usually had only their friends and family to help them, and tens of thousands of freedmen were kidnapped into slavery under the fugitive slave act. If nothing else, defeat of this article would have saved these thousands of humans from lives of misery.

But the men of the North did not make the fight. They did not because most of them genuinely believed that blacks were inferior and, even as freedmen, could work only at menial labor. Furthermore they felt that slavery was bound to die out anyway, especially as the slave trade seemed likely to end. Even though most of the northern delegates believed that slavery was wrong in theory, they did not see it as a central issue of the time, as we tend to see racial friction today. As Madison's secretary said, it was a "distracting question," which was "retarding the labors" of the Convention. As a consequence, few northerners were prepared to risk jeopardizing the union in a battle over the happiness of blacks. What mattered to the North primarily was fear of southern dominance of a new government. And the result was that the blacks became bargaining chips in a set of complex compromises, which were meant to adjust the delicate balance of North and South in the new government.

In what they did and what they left undone, the delegates to the Convention were reflecting the opinions of most Americans. At the ratifying conventions later there would be little outcry against the delegates' decisions about slavery. That the 20 percent of the population that was black were used as pawns with no rights the white man was bound to respect only means that the Founders were living in the eighteenth century, not the twentieth. They committed one of the worst mistakes in American history, but that can be seen better under twentieth-century illumination than it could by the light of eighteenth-century ideological lamps. With hindsight, we can see that the Founding Fathers might have provided for the phasing out of slavery over a relatively long term, principally by confining it geographically. But they saw things, as we all do, according to their lights, and they acted on their own vision.

And of course the irony of it all was that the South gave up power to the North because it expected it would soon be dominant anyway, and the North gave up slavery to the South because it thought it would die out anyway, and both were wrong. The final lesson, then, may be that institutions, once established, are not easily changed.

Part IV

THE QUESTION OF POWER

Chapter Seventeen

Balancing Act

When the delegates to the Constitutional Convention reached Philadelphia, few of them expected that the small-state–big-state issue would so dominate the early stages of the meeting. Some may have been aware that conflicts of interest between North and South might cause trouble, but it is doubtful that many expected them to raise as much dust as they ultimately did. In general, these fifty-five men, from North and South, big states and small, felt that their own positions on these issues were so reasonable that their opponents would quickly be converted to their side. As a consequence, most of them were startled to find these two great issues so divisive.

What they had expected to fight over was the whole broad question of the distribution of power: how much would remain with the states, how much would be given to the new government, how it would be distributed among various branches of the government, who finally would wield it. Lying underneath this problem was a basic question that any democracy must answer: how can government be made effective without infringing on the liberties of the people?

The delegates began fencing over this fundamental question almost from the outset, but they could not really confront it until the troublesome conflicts between the big and small states and the North and South were settled. But finally they came to it; and now we will begin to deal with the crux of what the Constitutional Convention was all about.

Let us recall Madison's famous statement from *Federalist* No. 51:

> If men were angels, no government would be necessary. If angels were to govern men, neither external nor internal controls on government would be necessary. In framing a government which is to be administered by

men over men, the great difficulty lies in this: you must first enable the
government to control the governed; and in the next place oblige it to
control itself.

Most of the delegates agreed. William Paterson said (June 9), "The mind
of man is fond of power." Hamilton said, "Men always love power." As the
historian Bernard Bailyn puts it, these men saw society as "divided into
distinct, contrasting, and innately antagonistic spheres: the sphere of power
and the sphere of liberty or right. The one was brutal, ceaselessly active, and
heedless; the other was delicate, passive, and sensitive."

The problem was this: without government there would be anarchy, out of
which would inevitably emerge a demagogue who would arrogate all power
to himself. Therefore, you had to have sound and stable government. This
meant giving power to a body of men so they could govern. But because all
men love power, these men would take as much of it as they could, endangering
the liberties of the governed. They would have to be checked, therefore—but
not so much that the government would become impotent, as the old Congress
under the Articles had become.

The problems before the delegates were the obvious ones. Who was to check
the vagrant passions of a legislature? Should there be some sort of council with
review power? Should the executive have a veto? And if so, who—or what—
was to check the executive? It was all circular: you could move the checking
power around the board as you liked, but who was to check the checker?

These issues of control were considered, reconsidered, and considered again
that long, hot summer, and in the course of the arduous and sometimes
acrimonious debating, the Founding Fathers worked out on the Convention
floor a system for implementing a great principle of government, one that is
at the heart of the American Constitution: the separation of powers. To see
how it came about, we must once more go back to the beginning of the
Convention and watch the debate on the subject unfold.

One of the most basic questions facing the Framers, an issue that came up
May 31, the second day of the debate on the Virginia Plan, was exactly what
powers ought to be given to the new national government. It was this problem
—the lack of necessary power in the old government—that had brought them
to Philadelphia in the first place.

This was a novel question to confront people writing a constitution. By and
large, governments are vested with all powers—the right to do what they want
anywhere, except as limited by a national constitution. Even in modern democ-

racies it is taken for granted that the national government holds all political power and subgovernments are mere administrative units. But the United States, we remember, was to be a federation of states, and if the states were to have any function at all, there must be areas in which they could act and the national government could not. Indeed, at the Convention, even the most fervent advocates of a powerful national government recognized that, as a practical matter, many decisions would have to be left to the states, because of the difficulties of transportation and communication over the vast expanse of a half-settled country. The system would require, in large measure, voluntary compliance with the law. Such compliance would follow only if the laws fit the needs of the scattered local societies. Thus many men, like Roger Sherman, felt that the people of a locality knew best how they wanted things done, and insofar as possible should be left to decide for themselves.

So power must be divided between the states and the national government. As the delegates saw from the beginning, there were two ways of giving the national government power. One was through a *general* grant, which would authorize it to do whatever was necessary for the "happiness of the nation," or some such wording. The other was to list *specific* areas the national government could control—that is to say, it could legislate about interstate commerce, prepare for the defense of the country, provide for a national revenue, or whatever function seemed appropriate.

Each method had its drawbacks. Many of the delegates felt that a general grant, no matter how carefully phrased, would be too broad and too vague for safety. On the other hand, a list of specific powers—an enumeration, as it came to be called—might freeze the national government out of areas where it ought to be. Times change, and the Founding Fathers recognized that they could not, with the best will in the world, foresee every possible problem. In this respect, certainly, they were right: how, for example, could they have predicted the conflicts between labor unions and large corporations, struggles that have played so large a role in America? How could they have guessed at the battling that agitates us today over pollution controls or use of the airwaves?

A decision had to be made, and at the outset James Madison and the Virginians had chosen the general grant. The Virginia Plan said that the new Congress would have all the powers that the old Congress had, and would in addition be able to "legislate in all cases to which the separate states are incompetent, or in which the harmony of the United States may be interrupted by the exercise of individual legislation." This was a broad grant, but it was not infinitely broad: it would not, at the time, have been seen as allowing the national government to legislate about the militia or regulate the press in a given state, for instance. However, when the Virginia Plan was drawn up, it contained a national veto over state legislation, and in Madison's mind this veto would take care of exigencies not covered by the general grant.

But right from the start there was a good deal of feeling against the general grant. On May 31, when it was first debated as part of the Virginia Plan, Charles Pinckney and Rutledge immediately objected to the "vagueness of the term *incompetent,*" and said they would like to see exactly what the plan meant to include under this term. It is probable that the two South Carolinians had a more specific worry about the general grant: the fear that it would give the national government the power to interfere with slavery. But Edmund Randolph, despite the fact that he had helped shape the plan and had presented it to the Convention, said that he had no "intention to give indefinite powers to the national Legislature . . . and that he did not think any considerations whatever could ever change his determination." He had, in fact, always assumed that there would be an enumeration. And then Madison himself rose and said that he "had brought with him into the Convention a strong bias in favor of an enumeration and definition of the powers necessary to be exercised by the national legislature, but had also brought doubts concerning its practicability. His wishes remained unaltered; but his doubts had become stronger." It was just the problem we have discussed: an enumeration was certainly best as it would fix definite limits to the powers of the national government, but was it really possible to draw up a list which would cover enough ground without covering too much? The delegates were convinced, and they accepted the general grant contained in the Virginia Plan. Roger Sherman, not surprisingly, was the only delegate recorded as voting against it.

But there remained doubts. As we have repeatedly seen, the making of the Constitution was a kaleidoscopic process in which shifts in one place often produced changes in seemingly unrelated places. One of these crucial shifts, in which a good deal of the whole design abruptly changed, occurred on July 16, when equal voting was finally accepted for the Senate. The small states now had the protection they had fought so hard for; they would not have a majority in the Senate, but they would have something close to it and could hope for a veto power over issues that were important to them. Once they had some protection, it was to their interest to press for a strong national government, which would, for example, take the import taxes away from New York, Massachusetts, and Pennsylvania, and use them for the general good of all states; or take over the western lands and spread the benefits through the union. As Madison pointed out later, "as soon as the smaller states had secured more than a proportional share in the proposed government, they became favorable to an augmentation of its power."

Not all the small states' men came over: the intemperate Luther Martin remained a determined fighter for states' rights, and Roger Sherman continued to believe that states knew best what their people wanted. But in the main, the men from the small states, like Paterson of New Jersey, Read of Delaware, and Jenifer of Maryland, were ready for strong national government once they had the protection of equal voting in the Senate.

At the same time, the passage of equal voting did not make the nationalists any less eager for a strong central government. The net effect, then, of allowing equal voting in the Senate was dramatically to increase support for a strong national government.

Nonetheless, there remained a good deal of feeling that the general grant, which had passed so easily on May 31, was dangerous. And on July 16, when the proportional representation issue was finally settled and the Convention could begin to see the design of the government they were shaping, the issue of the general grant was raised again.

The debate that day began with Butler of South Carolina objecting to the term "incompetent," as too vague. His colleague Rutledge agreed, and asked for a committee to work out a more specific list of powers. These southerners were undoubtedly still concerned that the new government might try to limit slavery, and they wanted it made clear precisely what it could and could not do. But in the vote for a committee the Convention split, and the motion was lost: for a second time the delegates had chosen the general grant over an enumeration of powers.

The next morning Roger Sherman took up the question, and he once again made an effort to limit the power of the national government to meddle in what he considered state affairs. He moved that the national government be authorized to "make laws binding on the people of the United States in all cases which may concern the common interests of the Union; but not to interfere with the government of the individual states in any matters of internal police [i.e., regulation] which respect the government of such states only, and wherein the general welfare of the United States is not concerned."

Sherman's motion was opposed by Gouverneur Morris, who said that there were times when a national government *ought* to intermeddle in the affairs of the states, "as in the case of paper money and other tricks by which citizens of other states may be affected." The Convention could always be counted on to respond to the war cry of paper money, and Sherman's motion was soundly defeated.

Now the corpulent and impulsive Gunning Bedford of Delaware spoke, proposing that the government should be able to legislate "in all cases for the general interest of the union, and also in those to which the states are separately incompetent, or in which the harmony of the United States may be interrupted by the exercise of individual legislation."

Bedford was from a small state, and he was offering a much broader grant than had been in the Virginia Plan. Edmund Randolph was instantly up and denouncing Bedford's motion as "a formidable idea indeed. It involves the power of violating all the laws and constitutions of the states and intermeddling with their police." He was quite right about Bedford's proposal. Almost any act of the national legislature could be interpreted as being "for the general interest of the union."

At this point it might be well to look at the character of Edmund Randolph, governor of the powerful state of Virginia, friend and ally of James Madison, legal counsel to George Washington, the nation's first attorney general, and a person of consequence throughout the South. For curiously, despite his political alliance with Madison and Washington, both devoted advocates of strong national government, Randolph was essentially a states' righter at heart.

Randolph was almost an archetype for the Founding Fathers. Born in 1753, he was one of the "young men of the Revolution," who had come of age during the struggle against Great Britain. He once said, "I am a *child* of the Revolution." He was an aristocrat, a member of the Virginia establishment, which ran the state by birthright. His grandfather had been an attorney general of Virginia; so had his uncle, and his father had been clerk of Virginia's House of Burgesses. He was not raised on a plantation, as were Washington, Mason, Madison, and so many of the other southerners at the Convention, but in the capital town, Williamsburg. His family was deeply enmeshed in Virginia politics, and he was immersed in politics from his infancy. He studied law cursorily, then apprenticed at his father's law office, eventually holding on his own account what was said to be the largest law practice in Virginia. He grew up to be a tall, somewhat portly man with a commanding presence. He was on Washington's staff briefly during the siege of Boston, then returned home to deal with family problems, and began to move up in politics, serving both in the Virginia government and in the Continental Congress, and becoming governor of his state in 1786.

Edmund Randolph has not been given top grades by historians of the Constitution. He lacked both the high intellectualism of his colleague Madison and the certainty of character of his colleague Washington. Too often he allowed expediency to get the best of him. It was not so much that he was ambitious for high office: that was accepted behavior, and many of the men at the Convention were as ambitious as Edmund Randolph. It was more that he disliked doing anything that would offend the voters of Virginia. In the end, Edmund Randolph was one of three men who refused to sign the Constitution, and it is the opinion of his biographer John J. Reardon that he did so in order to dissociate himself from a document he was afraid Virginia's voters would not like because it gave too much of Virginia's power to the national government.

Randolph has frequently been seen as one of the Virginians who was working for a strong national government, largely because he presented the Virginia Plan, which was sometimes referred to as the Randolph Plan, although of course he had not been primarily responsible for drawing it up. But in truth, despite the fact that he was a friend and ally of Madison and Washington, he was consistently opposed to giving the national government too much strength.

It is not surprising, then, that Randolph spoke out strongly against Bedford's proposal to enlarge the general grant; nor is it surprising that when he got a chance to substitute an enumeration for it, he seized the opportunity.

His chance came on July 23, when the Convention established the Committee of Detail. Believing that the committee had little to do except to tidy up the Constitution and put it in good legal language, the delegates chose for it men of wide legal experience. Ellsworth of Connecticut, Gorham of Massachusetts, and Rutledge of South Carolina were all judges. James Wilson was considered perhaps the leading legal thinker in the United States. And Edmund Randolph had been a successful lawyer and attorney general of his state. Of the five, only Wilson was a strong nationalist from the Madison-Washington-Morris camp. Ellsworth took a middle position: Gorham and Rutledge were nationalists, but not strong ones. Randolph thus would not have to face strong nationalist opposition on the committee.

No record of the proceedings of the Committee of Detail were kept. However, from various drafts that emerged from the committee in the handwriting of Randolph, Rutledge, and Wilson, we are led to suspect that Randolph was primarily responsible for disregarding the Convention's explicit wishes on the general grant. The Convention had twice debated the merits of a general grant versus an enumeration, and twice had voted for the general grant. Why did the Committee feel it could simply disregard their instructions?

The answer is, first, that by this stage in the Convention the men on the committee had a clear sense of the way the delegates were thinking, and they recognized that regardless of how the delegates had voted, there was substantial fear of a general grant. Second, Randolph, Rutledge, Gorham, and Ellsworth almost certainly favored an enumeration: why not try it and see what happened?

The enumeration drawn up by the Committee of Detail contained a good many prescriptions that seem obvious to us today. The national government would have the power to tax, regulate commerce with foreign nations, coin money, to borrow, make war, raise armies, establish post offices, call out the militia, and a few other things. Some of these would prove controversial, and some would not. For the moment, however, we must deal with a short clause that the Committee of Detail, in the most casual fashion, added to the enumeration:

> And to make all laws that shall be necessary and proper for carrying into execution the foregoing powers, and all other powers vested, by this Constitution, in the government of the United States, or in any department or officer thereof.

None of them, it appears, thought that the clause was in any way exceptional. It meant to them simply that the government must be able to make laws necessary to the exercise of its powers. What use would it be, for example, to give the government the power to raise armies without allowing it to make laws regulating terms of enlistment, pay, and the like? But the word "necessary," put so casually into this clause, would prove to be a keg of dynamite with a very short fuse once the new government was established.

The debate over the enumeration produced by the Committee of Detail began on August 16. The Convention did not even question the abandonment of the principle of a general grant. The Committee of Detail had guessed correctly that the delegates wanted an enumeration. The specifics of the enumeration, however, were debated extensively over the next several days. On August 18 both Madison and Charles Pinckney brought in long lists of powers to be added to the enumeration, which were referred to the Committee of Detail for consideration. Pinckney brought in another great list two days later, and so did Gouverneur Morris. Finally, the Convention reached that pregnant "necessary and proper" clause. It was passed virtually without debate, by general consent, without a vote. Nobody saw the implications. Indeed, Madison and Pinckney moved to make the clause even stronger by giving Congress not only the power to "make all laws that shall be necessary and proper" but to "establish offices" for the purpose as well. But the Convention decided that the addition was redundant and rejected it. And that was the extent of the debate on the clause.

The enumeration of powers stands today as Section 8 of Article I of the Constitution of the United States. Though half its specific grants can be traced back to the Articles, its seventeen clauses represent a huge expansion of power over that delegated to the national government under the Articles of Confederation but still greatly less than what modern governments exercise. It was the eighteenth clause that gave Congress the flexibility to meet the social and technological changes of the past two centuries. It is difficult to see, for example, how the enumeration alone would have permitted the United States government to subsidize arts, letters, and scholarship; to support universities; to acquire huge pieces of wilderness for national parks (to say nothing of the huge Louisiana Purchase); to require controls on pollution of air, land, and water; to tax for the purpose of establishing a social security system, welfare payments for the poor, medical benefits for the elderly; to subsidize the building of a huge network of public highways; to regulate aviation and the railroads, and in general to establish independent agencies with vast power over whole industries; to subsidize agriculture; to protect consumers by imposing standards of manufacture; and much, much more.

What has allowed the United States government to do all this was that innocent little "necessary and proper" clause so casually tacked on to the end of the enumeration, where it now sits as the eighteenth clause of Section 8 of Article I, like a tiny light with an enormous beam falling on everything where it shines. It is not the only clause that has been interpreted broadly. Specifically, the clauses that empower the national government to legislate for the "general welfare" of the country and to regulate commerce have been taken as implying broad mandates. But neither of them has been driven so far beyond the Founders' expectations.

It is not necessary here for us to go into the long story of how the "necessary and proper" clause was used to interpret the Constitution in so broad a fashion. Suffice it to say that in 1790 Alexander Hamilton, Washington's secretary of the treasury, and a man long committed to strong national government, proposed that the government establish a national bank. Those opposed said flatly that the Constitution gave Congress no such power. That, Hamilton said, depended on how you define "necessary." And he chose to define it as meaning "conducive to." That is to say, anything that *worked toward* a certain goal could be seen as necessary. The national government had the specific power to "regulate commerce," both with foreign nations and between the states. If a national bank was "conducive to" regulating commerce, Hamilton argued, the government was empowered to establish one. In Hamilton's opinion, the bank did not have to be *essential* to the goal, but merely *helpful.*

This is not a definition of "necessary" that most people and most dictionaries would agree with, but it was widely accepted because it permitted the government to do a lot of things—such as establishing a national bank—that many people wanted the government to do. It became law in 1819 when John Marshall, Chief Justice of the Supreme Court, in the famous case of *M'Culloch* v. *Maryland,* said:

> Let the end be legitimate, let it be within the scope of the Constitution, and all means which are appropriate, which are plainly adapted to that end, which are not prohibited, but consist with the letter and spirit of the Constitution, are constitutional.

Not many of the men at the Constitutional Convention would have agreed with Marshall. Nor did a lot of people around the country when it came time to ratify the Constitution. The "necessary and proper" clause was too vague and too broad, and it became a focus of much opposition to the Constitution. As *M'Culloch* v. *Maryland* would show, these fears were justified. The effect, finally, was to expand immeasurably each of the seventeen specific powers in the enumeration—to give them what Edward S. Corwin, the great authority on the clause, has called their "second dimension." The necessary and proper clause thus works in tandem with the powers granted in the enumeration; and the clause it has most frequently been teamed up with to extend the powers of Congress has been the so-called commerce clause, put into the enumeration by the Committee of Detail.

We should understand that government control of commerce and industry is no modern invention. For centuries prior to 1787 it was taken for granted that governments—by and large monarchies—would, when necessary, set wages and prices, establish government monopolies over such industries as the mining of precious metals, and tax as many activities as they chose to.

In America during the eighteenth century the same belief prevailed. Colonial and state governments set toll fees, ferry fares, stage coach rates. There were limits on "engrossing"—that is, monopoly. In times of drought, states might fix wheat prices, and when there was a shortage of some particular skilled labor—carpenters, for example—they might fix wages. During the Revolution regional price-fixing conventions set prices for a broad range of goods and services. And of course state legislatures felt free to enact those notorious stay and tender laws, which interfered with private contracts. In general, eighteenth-century Americans took it for granted that the hand of government would be everywhere in commerce. There was at least as much control of trade then as there is today.

Most of the Founding Fathers came to Philadelphia expecting to write a document that would give the national government a good deal of power over commerce. Even states' righters like Sherman recognized that the national government had to be able to deal better with trade matters than it had done.

Given this, it is not surprising that there was relatively little conflict over economic policy at the Convention, and therefore a minimum of debate. Nor is it surprising that economic matters are first on the list of powers the Committee of Detail worked up. In final form the enumeration says that Congress shall have the power:

> To regulate Commerce with foreign Nations, and among the several States, and with the Indian Tribes.

This is a fairly sweeping statement. It is complemented mainly by another clause, which prohibits state governments from "impairing the Obligation of Contracts"; this essentially was aimed at those stay and tender laws which "impaired" the contract between creditors and debtors. As written, the commerce clause was wide open to interpretation, and when used in tandem with the clause that made U.S. law supreme over state laws, it was even wider open.

The net effect was to turn the United States into a huge free-trade zone, at the time the largest one in the western world. The consequences were enormous, for the abolition of interstate restrictions on commerce allowed the development of the American economic system, which was, by the twentieth century, to become the dominant one in the world. Without free trade, few states would have permitted entrepreneurs from other states to run railroad lines across their terrain, sell steam engines, harvesting machines, cloth, and dishware in their towns and cities, without extracting some price. Only because the Convention turned the nation into a free-trade zone was the American industrial machine able to develop as it did.

But interestingly enough, although most of the men at the Convention would have, in 1787, objected strenuously to Marshall's broad interpretation of the "necessary and proper" clause, those who lived on to see the country develop over the next several decades did not object when Hamilton put forward his expansive definition in 1791 and when Marshall incorporated it into law in 1819 because they wanted the dynamic and growing economy that it produced. (A major exception is Madison during the 1790s, when he was attempting to counter Hamilton's centralizing programs.) The interpretation is not infinitely broad; there are limits to laws Congress can pass. As Corwin has pointed out, the Supreme Court has generally kept Congress within the limits of the enumerated powers. It took amendments to the Constitution to curb the states' right to allow slavery and to qualify their control over voting rights, for example. Nonetheless, the "necessary and proper" clause remains one of the most critical—and some would say the most fruitful—delegations of power in the Constitution of the United States. Its effect has been to give the Constitution the elasticity to fit changes in social thinking, advances in technology, altered views about the balance of power between the national and state governments, and the international context of American politics.

Chapter Eighteen

Curing the Republican Disease

The Constitutional Convention was called because of a general recognition that the national government formed under the Articles of Confederation was weak and ineffective. The root cause of this ineffectiveness, most of the delegates agreed, was the habit the states had of disregarding the demands placed upon them by the national government or actually passing laws of their own contrary to national ones. Even worse, in the view of many of the delegates, was the way states so frequently passed laws that encroached on the rights of their own citizens—in particular, ramming paper money down creditors' throats. James Madison, especially, viewed these depredations against property with fear and loathing; he said that "the evils issuing from these [state] sources contributed more to that uneasiness which produced the Convention and prepared the public mind for a general reform, than those which accrued to our national character." Madison was not alone. Randolph, in his opening speech, insisted that the Confederation "could not defend itself against the encroachments from the states." Gouverneur Morris said that "the public liberty was in greater danger from legislative usurpations than from any other source." Dickinson of Delaware said that "all were convinced of the necessity of making the general government independent of the prejudices, passions, and improper views of the state legislature." John Francis Mercer of Maryland said that the "corruption and mutability of legislative Councils of the states" had brought about the Convention in the first place.

The most extreme example of what troubled Madison and the others was the case of Rhode Island, a state that flatly refused to send anybody to the Convention and did not join the union until after Washington became president. In Rhode Island a legislature dominated by small farmers, who were invariably in the debtor class, had instituted paper money. Creditors, recognizing that it would depreciate quickly, refused to take it in payment for debts, whereupon the legislature made acceptance of it mandatory. To avoid taking paper money, many creditors fled Rhode Island into neighboring states. In response, the legislature passed laws allowing the debtors to pay money into courts, which would hold it for the creditors, legally canceling the debt. However, many judges, who tended to side with creditors anyway, refused to enforce the law; so the legislature turned them out of office. Needless to say, the fracas threw the finances of Rhode Island into utter confusion.

Legislatures had not gone so far in other states, but where paper money did not exist, the demand that it be issued was a constant threat. Thus, the problem was not merely that state legislatures frequently flouted the authority of the national government; it was also that they frequently passed what the Framers saw as unwise and unjust laws against their own citizens.

To James Madison, one of the most important things a new government must do was curb scoundrelly legislatures. He put into the Virginia Plan a clause authorizing the national government "to negative all laws passed by the several states, contravening in the opinion of the national legislature the articles of Union." This was not quite the same as giving the national government the right to veto *any* state laws, but the clause was sweeping enough.

According to Charles Hobson, who has made a study of the matter, "Of the reforms he offered at the Convention . . . none in Madison's view was more important than the one to vest the national legislature with the power to negative state laws."

Yet despite the strong feeling in Madison and some of the others that the bad habits of states had to be curbed, the "negative" over state laws was a risky thing to propose. It had an ancestor in "disallowance"—the English king's authority to veto colonial legislation. Needless to say, this power was hated by the Americans.

Moreover, Madison's negative once again brought up the question of states' rights. Clearly enough, everybody at the Convention, even the pugnacious Luther Martin, recognized that states could not be allowed to legislate against the laws of the national government. But there was considerable question in the minds of many as to how far national supremacy ought to be carried. The men from the Deep South, obviously, did not want to empower the national government to overthrow its laws in regard to slavery; and others, like Roger Sherman, wanted any national government to "intermeddle" in local affairs as little as possible. There was a good deal of feeling, which would eventually emerge, against giving the national government too large a power to veto state laws.

Yet the astonishing fact is that when the veto was first raised as part of the Virginia Plan on May 31, it passed without a murmur—as Madison says, "without debate or dissent." Why? The answer in part is that these men were so disgusted by runaway legislatures that they were willing to go some distance to curb them. The historian Charles Warren says that we must "appreciate with what grave apprehension the unwise and unjust legislation of the States had been regarded, and to what an extent it had been a factor in bringing about the Convention." However, it is probable that the resolution passed so easily largely because of the way it was phrased: it seemed to apply only to state laws that contravened the Constitution itself.

The issue was then dropped until June 7, when Charles Pinckney moved that it be reconsidered the next day. He offered a sweeping resolution which said that the "national legislature should have authority to negative all [state] laws which they should judge to be improper." Pinckney, alone in his own delegation, had been fighting for a strong national government for at least four years. Under his resolution the Congress would, without doubt, have been able to override any state law whatever. This was precisely what Pinckney intended. He said, "The States must be kept in due subordination to the nation . . . this universal negative was in fact the corner stone of an efficient national government."

Despite his intense personal dislike of Pinckney, Madison immediately rose to second the motion, saying:

> He could not but regard an indefinite power to negative legislative acts of the States as absolutely necessary to the perfect system. Experience had evinced a constant tendency in the States to encroach on the federal authority; to violate national treaties; to infringe the rights and interests of each other; to oppress the weaker party within their respective jurisdictions. A negative was the mildest expedient that could be devised for preventing these mischiefs.

This position was precisely in line with Madison's desire to check power wherever he found it, and we are entitled to suspect that he had originally put a universal negative in the Virginia Plan, but that it had been subsequently modified by others of the Virginia delegation. Edmund Randolph especially, with his unwillingness to give offense to his Virginia constituents, could not have liked it very much.

James Wilson, another high nationalist, supported Pinckney's motion. When the confederation had been formed, he said, there had been an exfoliation of good feeling, and everybody had viewed everybody else as "brethren." "The tables at length began to turn. No sooner were the State Governments formed than their jealousy and ambition began to display themselves. Each endeavored to cut a slice from the common loaf, to add to its own morsel, till at length the confederation became frittered down to the impotent condition in which it now stands."

But the Pinckney resolution went too far for most of the delegates. For one thing, some of the men from the Deep South felt that so sweeping a negative could be used by the North against slavery. For another, the states' righters were against it on principle. For a third, many delegates of all persuasions were afraid that such a powerful attack on states' rights would turn their constituents against the Constitution. Williamson of North Carolina, Gerry of Massachusetts, Sherman of Connecticut, Bedford of Delaware, and Butler of South Carolina spoke against it. Gunning Bedford was particularly vehement. He pointed out that under proportional representation, which at that point was still part of the Plan, the big states could use the negative to make virtual prisoners of the small ones. "Will not these large states crush the small ones whenever they stand in the way of their ambitions or interested views. . . . It seems as if Pennsylvania and Virginia by the conduct of their deputies wished to provide a system in which they would have an enormous and monstrous influence."

Whether or not Bedford was right about the big states, only the Big Three voted for Pinckney's resolution. Everybody else voted against it, including two Virginians, Randolph and Mason. So the clause was left as it stood, giving the national government a negative only over state laws contravening the articles of union.

Over the next few weeks, as the Committee of the Whole continued to debate the Virginia Plan, the question of the negative over state laws surfaced occasionally, usually as part of the general question of states' rights. For example, on June 11, it was implied throughout the debate over whether state officials ought to swear allegiance to the United States as well as to their own states. Sherman, Gerry, and Luther Martin spoke against the resolution, but the motion carried by the alliance of the Big Three and the Deep South over the small-states bloc.

On June 20 John Lansing of New York once again made the states' rights case, this time singling out the negative over state laws specifically. He pointed out that the national legislature would hardly have time to review the legislative acts of all thirteen states; and beyond that, "Will a gentleman from Georgia be a judge of the expediency of a law which is to operate in New Hampshire?" He offered a sweeping resolution that would have kept the old Congress, with its strong states' rights bias, going.

Roger Sherman seconded the motion. He said, "Each state, like each individual, had its peculiar habits, usages and manners, which constituted its happiness. It would not therefore give to others a power over this happiness, any more than an individual would do, when he could avoid it." But once again the states' righters lost on a close vote, with the Big Three and the Deep South alliance prevailing.

On July 7 Gouverneur Morris made a long speech in support of a strong national government, saying, "It had been one of our greatest misfortunes that the great objects of the nation had been sacrificed constantly to local views; . . . particular states ought to be injured for the sake of a majority of the people, in case their conduct should deserve it." And that seemed to be the way the majority of the delegates felt.

But then, on the morning of July 17, after equal suffrage in the Senate had won, the Convention tackled first the question of the general grant of power to the national government, and then turned once more to the negative over the states' laws. Morris now spoke against it, "as likely to be terrible to the states," and Martin said the power was "improper and inadmissible." Roger Sherman made what would be the crucial point. The legislative veto was unnecessary, "as the courts of the states would not consider as valid any law contravening the authority of the union."

This was the first mention at the Convention of what would come to be a central aspect of the American system of government: the power of the courts to strike down state laws that they deem unconstitutional. The old government under the Articles of Confederation had no standing courts, and no power of judicial review of either state or United States laws, except in admiralty cases —that is, cases concerning crimes committed on the high seas. However, state courts were beginning, somewhat tentatively, to refuse to enforce laws they thought were contrary to state constitutions, and the concept of judicial review was known to most of the delegates at the Convention. Sherman thus was suggesting that a kind of judicial review would be practiced by state courts in deference to the national constitution, and that therefore the government did not need any other veto power over state laws.

But James Madison was determined that the national government have the veto power. He made a long speech in its favor, saying that "the negative on the laws of the states [was] essential to the efficacy and security of the general government. The necessity of a general government proceeds from the propensity of the states to pursue their particular interests in opposition to the general interest. This propensity will continue to disturb the system, unless effectively controlled. Nothing short of a negative on their laws will control it." And he went on to contest Sherman's opinion that the courts would fill the gap. "Confidence cannot be put in the state tribunals as guardians of the national authority and interests. In all the states these are more or less dependent on the legislatures. . . . In Rhode Island the judges who refused to execute an unconstitutional law were displaced, and others substituted, by the legislature, who would be willing instruments of the wicked and arbitrary plans of their masters."

He was answered by Morris—usually a strong nationalist—who again said that a congressional veto over state legislation "would disgust all the states," the implication being that it would make it difficult to get the Constitution ratified. Sherman insisted that the veto involved "a wrong principle, to wit, that a law of a state contrary to the articles of the union, would, if not negatived, be valid and operative." He would rely on the courts to overturn such acts. Pinckney, as expected, spoke in support of Madison, but when the vote was taken, the negative on state laws *lost,* with only Virginia and North Carolina voting for it.

Why had the Convention made this sudden about-face? Like many other decisions taken at the Convention, it was the result of several diverse pressures bearing on a single point. Coloring everything, however, was the fact that the proportional representation issue had been settled. There was a sense, suddenly that morning of July 17, that the worst was over. The Convention would succeed, and the document that came out of it would actually be presented to the voters of their states. The feeling was growing that what Gouverneur Morris was suggesting was right: Madison's negative was certain to be the focus of a lot of opposition at the ratifying conventions. Moreover, a Senate with a strong small-state minority would carry a lot of states' rights sentiment and would not be eager to strike down state laws. The strong nationalists realized that the veto would not be as effective as they had believed at first, and most of them were now less insistent on putting it into the Constitution.

Further, the slave states had sufficient reason for voting against the negative, for they had always, right from the start, been afraid that the negative could and would be used as a weapon against slavery. It had not generally been noticed that equal voting in the Senate strengthened not only the small states against the big ones but also the North against the South, for most of the small states were in the North. The North would control the Senate for a long time, and this, for the Deep South, was a fact to be kept in mind. Finally, the suggestion made by Sherman and Morris that conflicts between state and national law could be resolved in the courts made sense to the delegates. Conflicts would arise, certainly; but perhaps some mechanism could be put into the judiciary to cover such cases.

The defeat of the negative on state laws left the Constitution without any mechanism for arbitrating disputes between the national government and the states. Disputes certainly would arise; they had been one of the major reasons for the failure of the old government. Somebody would have to decide them. If it was not to be the national legislature through a veto, then it would certainly have to be the courts.

Nobody, however, expected that a resolution to that effect would come from the most fervent antinationalist at the Convention, Luther Martin. Immediately after the negative over state laws was voted down on July 17, he rose and offered a resolution that appeared to give the national government a tool for controlling state laws: acts of Congress and treaties, he moved, "shall be the supreme law of the respective states . . . and that the judiciaries of the several states shall be bound thereby in their decisions, anything in the respective laws of the individual states to the contrary not withstanding." The clause, virtually identical to one in the New Jersey Plan, was accepted without dissent or a vote. Why did the states' righter Luther Martin offer a resolution to make the national government "supreme" over the states?

In fact, as Martin made clear later, he was attempting to slip something by the Convention. His resolution made acts of Congress supreme over state *laws*, but it did not make them supreme over state *constitutions.* This was a loophole big enough to drive an ox cart through. State laws were limited by state constitutions, and without authority to measure state constitutions against the national constitution, courts would be hamstrung in their efforts to overturn state legislation. That, in any case, was Martin's intention. How Martin's system would have worked in practice we will never know, for he did not get away with it. When the Committee of Detail dealt with the clause, it changed it as follows:

> The acts of the legislature of the United States made in pursuance of this
> Constitution, and all treaties made under the authority of the United

States, shall be the supreme law of the several states, and of their citizens and inhabitants; and the judges in the several states shall be bound thereby in their decisions; anything in the Constitutions or laws of the several states to the contrary notwithstanding.

The language of this clause was subsequently modified somewhat, but its essence remained the same and became part of the American Constitution, known today as the "supremacy clause." Yet it really did not settle the question of who would actually overturn state laws that conflicted with national ones. There were at the Convention many old-fashioned republicans who firmly believed that sovereignty resided in the people, and that there ought to be no body higher than the people's representatives in their legislatures.

And in fact, the Convention never really did make a clear-cut decision on this point. The closest it came was on August 27, during the debate on the organization of the court system. The clause in question said that the Supreme Court would have jurisdiction over "cases arising under the laws passed by the legislature of the United States." The Connecticut jurist William Samuel Johnson offered an amendment to make it: "The jurisdiction of the Supreme Court shall extend to all cases arising under *this Constitution* and the laws passed by the legislature of the United States."

The intent of the wording was suggested by Madison, who was the only person to speak against the change. He said that he thought the resolution went too far. The Court ought to be limited to "cases of a judiciary nature. The right of expounding the Constitution in cases not of this nature ought not to be given to that department."

The statement is not as clear as we would like it to be. However, it has been taken to mean that in Madison's view, the rulings of the Court ought not to be general law but should apply only to the parties in the case in question. Consider, for example, the famous case of *Brown* v. *Board of Education,* in which the Supreme Court struck down state laws establishing segregated schools. Madison would have argued that a Court ruling of this kind could not be applied everywhere, but would be in effect only in the particular school district where the case was brought.

The delegates accepted Johnson's wording, but they did so, according to Madison, only because "it was generally supposed that the jurisdiction given was constructively limited to cases of a judiciary nature." We only have Madison's word, in his notes on the debate at this point, that this is what the delegates believed, but Constitutional historians generally agree that Madison was correct. "If the import of this passage is correct," wrote Alfred Kelly and Winfred Harbison in a standard text, "the delegates were generally agreed that the federal judiciary was not to possess the general right of expounding the Constitution. In other words, the right to declare void an unconstitutional federal law was not supposed to confer any general power to interpret the compact."

The men at the Convention, it is clear enough, assumed that the national government must have the power to throw down *state* laws that contradicted federal ones: it was obvious to them that the states could not be permitted to pass laws contravening federal ones. But there is substantial doubt that these men wanted the Supreme Court to be able to overturn laws passed by the national Congress. Most of these men at bottom felt that if there had to be some final power in government, it must be lodged in the legislature. The legislature represented the people, and the people would not, it was supposed, act against their own best interests. The same could not be said of a president, or even a group of appointed officials constituting a Supreme Court.

And yet, the truth is that the Convention never really did see the problem of unconstitutional national laws for the issue it became. As it finally appears in the Constitution the wording is "the judicial Power shall extend to all Cases, in Law and Equity, arising under this Constitution, the Laws of the United States, and Treaties made, or which shall be made, under their Authority." And the Constitution goes on to say that the "Supreme Court shall have appellate jurisdiction, both as to Law and Fact." In a sense, what the men at the Convention were attempting to do was what one railway official was supposed to have proposed when he was told that the most dangerous car on the train was the last: simply leave off the last car.

But there always has to be a last car: somebody had got to be able to interpret the Constitution. If not, Congress would be able to pass any laws it chose in defiance of the Constitution, and the document would then become meaningless. Of course the president is obligated to veto bills that he believes violate the Constitution. But to give him an absolute veto on those grounds would be to create the potential for the very tyranny the Framers were so determined to avoid. Congressmen should be presumed to vote against bills that they see as unconstitutional, but in recent history they have tended too often to leave that concern to the courts. The Supreme Court became and remains the final arbiter of the meaning of the Constitution.

It did not take long for the supremacy of the Supreme Court to become clear. Shortly after the new government was installed under the new Constitution, people realized that the final say had to be given to somebody, and the Connecticut jurist and delegate to the Convention Oliver Ellsworth wrote the Judiciary Act of 1789, which gave the Supreme Court the clear power of declaring state laws unconstitutional, and by implication allowed it to interpret the Constitution. The power to overturn laws passed by Congress was assumed by the Supreme Court in 1803 and became accepted practice during the second half of the nineteenth century. The crucial decision in 1803 came in the famous case of *Marbury* v. *Madison,* when John Marshall asserted, "It is emphatically the province and duty of the judicial department to say what the law is. Those who apply the rule to particular cases must of necessity expound and interpret that rule." By the early twentieth century Chief Justice Charles Evans Hughes could proclaim—though admittedly somewhat hyperbolically—that "the Constitution is what the Supreme Court says it is."

Yet even though in the nature of things this assumption of large powers by the Supreme Court may have been inevitable, there is no doubt that most of the Founding Fathers would have been stunned and dismayed to see federal courts, for example, administering city school systems, dictating the hiring policies of municipal fire departments, deciding at what stage of pregnancy abortions become illegal, and taking on countless other legislative and administrative functions. Whether or not the Supreme Court has arrogated to itself too much power—is itself behaving unconstitutionally—is a matter for debate.

It should be emphasized, however, that judicial review of *state* legislation has in practice taken the place of a congressional or executive veto of such laws. Since Madison desired that veto largely to protect minorities and individuals from oppression by legislatures, the substitution of a judicial veto has worked relatively well. It has been the Court more than the Congress that has risen to succor persecuted minorities and individuals.

For the nationalists, the supremacy clause was a great victory, but not just because it became the basis for judicial review of state legislation. More fundamentally, the supremacy clause made the Constitution not only a document constituting a government, but also a body of law enforceable on individuals. Thus the federal judiciary and executive can arrest, try, and jail those people who violate acts of Congress, and also those who violate rules established in the Constitution. Further, state judges are required by the Constitution to swear an oath upholding that document and laws made under it, even above their own state constitutions.

The critical wording, as it finally appears in Article VI of the Constitution, is this:

This Constitution, and the Laws of the United States which shall be made in Pursuance thereof; and all Treaties made, or which shall be made, under the Authority of the United States, shall be the supreme Law of the Land; and the Judges in every State shall be bound thereby, any Thing in the Constitution or Laws of any State to the Contrary notwithstanding.

The defeat of the nationalists' beloved veto over state legislation appeared at the time to be a victory for the states' righters. But in fact, through later interpretations of the language of Article VI, the nationalists won a victory the effects of which none of them could have anticipated, and most of them would not have liked. Yet it is because of the flexibility that later generations found in Article VI that the Supreme Court was able to void state regulation of commerce and industry, to end segregation in the schools, protect the rights of people arrested by police, expand the meaning of freedom of speech and the press, and bring about other changes that Americans today so value.

Chapter Nineteen

James Wilson,
Democratic Nationalist

Of all of the problems that confronted the Convention, the one the delegates found most difficult to solve was that of the "executive," the branch of government we today call the presidency. The trouble was that the delegates had exceedingly ambivalent feelings about what sort of an executive the new government should have. They wanted one strong enough to supply "energy," as they said, to the government, and to act as some kind of check on the legislature. At the same time they wanted an executive whose powers were sufficiently limited so that he could not turn himself into a tyrant.

This ambivalence about the executive was a direct result of the recent history of the United States. Under the British, most of the colonies had been ruled by a governor appointed by the Crown, a lower house elected locally, and an upper house occasionally elected but usually appointed by the governor. The governor had substantial power. He was usually able to veto legislation, and in theory at least could prorogue and dissolve the legislature as he chose and try to rule by proclamation. Over the decades colonial legislatures managed to get a measure of control over the governors, by refusing to approve taxes necessary to the running of government, by refusing to raise troops, and similar devices. In particular, during the French and Indian War of the 1750s, when the governors needed large levies of both money and men from the colonies, the legislatures made substantial gains in getting greater control of the system.

However limited, the royal governors continued to dominate, and where they could not get what they wanted by law, they frequently resorted to guile, corrupting influential legislators by offering them judgeships, government contracts, and other forms of patronage.

Back in the mother country a similar situation had prevailed. King George III was intensely jealous of his power, and he had managed, also through offers of government contracts, cabinet posts, and jobs in which a man might get rich, to sidestep Parliament. This had obvious corrupting effects: a legislator beholden to a governor for his job as, say, a tax collector, would be under considerable pressure to vote as the governor wanted; and furthermore, he could hardly vote disinterestedly when tax matters came up. The whole political experience of America prior to the Revolution, as well as their wide reading of history, had taught them to beware of tyrants—kings and governors who would, through force and guile, set themselves up as arbitrary rulers of the country. It also taught them that protection for the people lay in the legislature, a body elected by the people, from the people, which the people could upset at the next election.

As a consequence, when Americans began to write their own constitutions after the Declaration of Independence in 1776, they created governments dominated to one degree or another by legislatures. According to Gordon Wood, in an important study of the matter, governors became "little more than chairmen of their executive boards." Although the rules varied from state to state, in general, legislatures made most major appointments, including judicial ones, elected the executive, and even tried certain kinds of cases in their own chambers. Government was concentrated in one branch, and we have seen what happened: legislatures kept running from one extreme to the next according to the passions of the day, establishing paper money, putting in stay and tender laws, and in general behaving erratically, often dominated by minority factions. Or so, at least, most of the men at the Convention believed.

Nonetheless, the memory of King George and his royal governors was only twelve years old. Many of the men at the Convention had lived under tyrannical governors longer than they had under fickle legislatures. They were not about to substitute one tyranny for another. And thus the ambivalence on the subject of the executive most delegates brought to the Convention: they had suffered under strong executives, suffered under weak ones, and they wanted neither. A balance would have to be struck. And in the course of striking that balance they worked out a way, there on the Convention floor, to put into practice the idea that is at the heart of the American Constitution, the theory of the separation of powers. The recent authority on the subject, Gordon Wood, writes, "Perhaps no principle of American constitutionalism has attracted more attention than that of separation of powers. It has in fact come to define the very character of the American political system."

As the Founders eventually came to understand it, the doctrine of the separation of powers required the government to be split into several branches or departments, each with its own rights and prerogatives, worked out in such a way that no man, or group of men, would be able to rule by fiat. The Founders found inspiration in a famous passage in Montesquieu's *L'Esprit des Lois*, with which they were all familiar. The passage is worth quoting at length.

> The political liberty of the subject is a tranquility of mind, arising from the opinion each person has of his safety. In order to have this liberty, it is requisite the government be so constituted as one man need not be afraid of another.
>
> When the legislative and executive powers are united in the same person, or in the same body of magistracy, there can be no liberty; because apprehensions may arise lest the same monarch or senate should enact tyrannical laws, to execute them in a tyrannical manner.
>
> Again, there is no liberty, if the power of judging be not separated from the legislative and executive powers. Were it joined with the legislative, the life and liberty of the subject would be exposed to arbitrary control; for the judge would then be the legislator. Were it joined to the executive power, the judge might behave with all the violence of an oppressor.
>
> Miserable indeed would be the case, were the same man, or the same body, whether of the nobles or of the people, to exercise those three powers, that of enacting laws, that of executing the public resolutions, and that of judging crimes or differences of individuals.

The idea was not entirely original with Montesquieu. John Locke and others had made similar suggestions. But Montesquieu's was the form in which it was best known to the delegates.

However, as the Convention was coming together in May of 1787 the doctrine of the separation of powers was not well understood by many of them and was even disliked by a few. (Although it was referred to directly in four state constitutions, it had not really been followed in practice subsequently.)

Roger Sherman in particular was convinced that all power ought to reside in a legislature, which, after all, represented the people. On June 1, only his third day at the Convention, he said that he considered "the executive magistracy as nothing more than an institution for carrying the will of the legislature into effect, that the person or persons ought to be appointed by and accountable to the legislature only, which was the depository of the supreme will of the society." Later the same day he again insisted, "An independence of the executive on the supreme legislative was in his opinion the very essence of tyranny." And the next day he repeated his idea that "the national legislature should have the power to remove the executive at pleasure." Sherman was

clear and certain in his belief that government should be run by the representatives of the people, and that the executive, far from acting as a check on the
legislature, should be its servant.

There was another man at the Convention who had a deeper and more
abiding faith in the judgment of the people, and it was this man who would
lead the fight, with the support of James Madison and Gouverneur Morris, for
a strong executive.

If George Washington is badly understood and James Madison is hardly
understood at all, James Wilson is simply unknown. The name means nothing
to most Americans, even those who take an interest in their country's history;
indeed, most historians, specialists in the Constitution aside, would be hard put
to it to say exactly what role he played in Philadelphia.

Yet few of the great men whose names toll like bells in our minds did so
much to make America what it is today. He was, according to one recent
biographer, "widely acknowledged as the preeminent legal scholar of his generation." He sat on the first United States Supreme Court, and might well have
been his country's first chief justice had it not been for some unhappy financial
dealings he had got himself embroiled in. He signed the Declaration of Independence, was involved in the writing of the Articles of Confederation, was
a leading figure in the writing of the Constitution of the State of Pennsylvania,
and spoke as often at the Convention as any other man except Madison. His
influence at Philadelphia was immense. William Pierce said in his miniature
biography of him, "Mr. Wilson ranks among the foremost in legal and political
knowledge," and George Washington himself found him "as able, candid, and
honest a member as any at the Convention." Yet he was forgotten by everybody before his bones had begun to dry. If any man in American history
deserves the term unsung hero, it is James Wilson.

Two factors in Wilson's background stand out. The first is that he was a late
arrival to America, immigrating from Scotland in 1765, when he was already
twenty-four. A second is that he was one of the small handful of men at the
Convention who were lowborn.

But in this group James Wilson was an anomaly. As we have seen, these
risen men tended to have no high opinion of "the people." Hamilton was an
acknowledged monarchist; Paterson was ever fearful of the uncontrolled passions of fornicators and rebellious back-country mobs; Sherman and Martin
doubted the wisdom and even the good sense of the plain people. But James
Wilson, more than any other man at the Convention, trusted the people's good

instincts, and he fought for a truly democratic government, far closer to the present American system than that proposed by anybody else at the Convention.

James Wilson was born in 1742 in a part of the Scottish lowlands called the Fife, a chunk of raw, bleak land surrounded on three sides by the cold, blustery North Sea. In these southern lowlands the people lived by tough, hard, farming and fishing and learned endurance and frugality. In the highlands to the north, rude clans, led by rough chieftains who were virtually a law unto themselves in their tiny fiefdoms, lived by pillage and rape as much as by agriculture. Like the land and the climate, the Calvinism of the Scottish Kirk was harsh, offering little reward on earth and not much more elsewhere. There was an aristocracy of lairds and ladies, but these, for the most part, were so poor that ladies of the manor were regularly seen headed for market with baskets of eggs to sell. The clans to the north were well beyond the control of any sort of government to the south; and the Kirk would not brook interference from secular authorities. Most men considered themselves as good as anybody else, for the very sound reason that from top to bottom of the society there was only a short way to go. Everything about the culture tended to produce a sturdy, toughminded spirit of democracy.

By the time of James Wilson's birth, however, Scotland was undergoing something of a renaissance, both economically and intellectually. The great David Hume was publishing the works that were to influence so strongly the thinking of Madison and others at the Convention, and along with Hume were others, such as Adam Smith and some lesser-known men, "making Edinburgh, for a generation or more, the greatest university in Christendom."

Wilson was born on a typical small farm, where the family scratched out a difficult living on a small piece of land. He was the first son, after three daughters, and clearly important to his parents. They were devout, like most of their neighbors, and they decided to educate James for the ministry.

It was not quite so unusual in Scotland for a poor boy to go on to a university as it was elsewhere, but it was unusual enough. As a boy James was excused from his farm work so he could study at the local grammar school, and at fourteen he passed a competitive scholarship examination for nearby St. Andrews University. Here he studied Latin, Greek, mathematics, and the usual courses in logic and philosophy, and which included what we might call the social sciences today. He also, says his biographer Charles P. Smith, inhaled the new humanistic spirit of Hume and the others, which, in its belief that the goal of human life was happiness, contradicted much of the Calvinism Wilson had learned at home. He was particularly influenced, Smith says, by the thinking of Thomas Reid, today seen as one of the lesser of the Scottish humanists, but then prominent. The basis of Reid's theories was the idea that truths which seem to us just "common sense" are in fact "intuitive beliefs implanted in our consciousness by God," or at any rate by the hand of nature. These commonsensical ideas are therefore available to everybody, rich or poor, ignorant or educated. This theory was obviously democratic in effect: if everybody, no matter how high or low, had equal access to God's wisdom, the sheep-herder was as qualified to vote as the squire. Thus, the rough democratic spirit that surrounded Wilson as he grew up was echoed by a philosophy that virtually made political democracy the will of God. James Wilson came to maturity a confirmed democrat in both heart and mind.

Around the time that James Wilson graduated from college his father died, leaving a widow and six children. Wilson decided to abandon the ministry, and went to work as a tutor. His teaching stint was relatively brief, and he went off to Edinburgh to study bookkeeping, and incidentally, learn to play a good game of golf. Once again it is important to note that most of the lowborn men —Wilson, Hamilton, Paterson, Sherman—had experience in commerce either as shopkeepers or in general trade.

But Wilson was ambitious; he had been marked by his parents for great things, and like Hamilton, clerking in that store in St. Croix, he chafed at his lowly circumstances. He decided to emigrate to America, and in the fall of 1765 Wilson arrived in New York.

Wilson was tall, stocky, growing stout, ruddy of face. He wore heavy glasses for nearsightedness, from which he had suffered since youth. He was far better educated than most Americans; in particular, he had breathed at first hand the ideas of the Scottish philosophers, which Madison and the others were getting only at a distance.

Yet it must be said that James Wilson's democratic ideals were expressed more in his theories than in his personal life. He was seen by his American contemporaries as aloof, reserved, even arrogant—the classic snob holding his skirts above the mud in which ordinary men labored. He was, a friend admitted, afflicted with "stiff reserve and awkward manners." And it seems clear that despite his commitment to democracy, Wilson did hold himself above the people he was eager to give power to, and did believe, along with most of the delegates to the Convention, that the people would have to elect their betters to run the government for them.

Yet good friends spoke of him with affection and remembered pleasant evenings at his dinner table, where there might be singing and port and pipes. (One friend ascribed Wilson's aristocratic bearing to an effort to keep his glasses from slipping off his nose.)

On arrival in New York, Wilson headed for Philadelphia, where he had no trouble getting a teaching job at the new College of Philadelphia. But this was not enough for him, and he decided to study law.

The extent to which lawyers dominated American affairs in the late eighteenth century cannot be overestimated. It is fair to say that the role of the legal profession today, acting, as it does, as arbiter in virtually every important facet of ordinary life, was built on foundations laid in the Revolutionary era. As Wilson's biographer points out, when the Puritans first came to the New World, they were determined to construct a society built around God's word. To a large degree they rejected the English legal system and attempted to draw their laws from the Bible, or failing that, from a consensus of the religious leaders of the society. (Outside of New England there was a larger dependence on the British system, but nonetheless, before the Revolution, lawyers were generally suspected by the common people everywhere.) Lawyers were seen as mere agents of the hated English system, and "had less status than honest artisans, and indeed constituted in colonial eyes a pariah caste." Lawrence Friedman, a leading historian of the American bar, points out that the colonial governing class distrusted lawyers and feared their influence; while the lower classes came to identify lawyers with the aristocracy. "Some hatred surely was there," he says and quotes Daniel Boorstin's statement that "ancient English prejudice against lawyers gained new strength in America," where "distrust of lawyers became an institution."

But as the society grew more complex and the old religious oligarchy lost its hold on the people, lawyers began to edge into more prominent roles. The country was beset by laws that conflicted from state to state, by endless crossclaims to huge tracts of land, by complex cases involving shipping, and by the rapidly pyramiding structure of debt and credit that, after the break with England, floated over a commerce unsupported by sound currency. Americans were constantly racing into court over their claims and counterclaims: it is safe to say that nowhere in the world were ordinary people so at home before judge and jury. Inevitably, the importance of the legal profession grew, until by the time of the Revolution lawyers were a major—perhaps the major—component of the American establishment, both in an official capacity as office-holders, and unofficially as shapers of law in the give and take of courts. Thirty-one of the fifty-five men at the Convention had been trained in the law. It is a commonplace among historians that the American Revolution was a "revolution of lawyers," who built their demands for freedom on legal theorizing.

In America, as James Wilson quickly saw, the way to rise was through the law. With financial help from a cousin living in Pennsylvania, he apprenticed himself to John Dickinson, one of the country's best-known lawyers, an ardent patriot, and eventually a delegate to the Constitutional Convention. Wilson practiced first in western Pennsylvania, and then in Philadelphia. Like Luther Martin and William Paterson, he became wealthy and well known during the Revolution through the law. He married into the rich and prominent Bird family, got involved in the politics of his state, and served in the Continental Congress.

Unfortunately, as he rose into prominence and began to earn a substantial income from his legal fees, his ambitions began, bit by bit, to push him into ventures that would ultimately break him financially, ruin his reputation, and finally kill him. He became, like so many other Americans, infected with land fever. He had grown up in a land-starved Old World, and the vast reaches of empty land around him in western Pennsylvania dazzled his normally clear mind. He began borrowing to buy land; and then, his appetite unslaked, started pyramiding his debts to buy more and more. He was able to do so because, through his marriage, he had become a good friend of Robert Morris, the financial genius who built one of the great American fortunes of the time. Morris knew everybody, and very quickly Wilson moved into the highest financial circles, which unhappily gave him access to more credit than he could sensibly manage. Over time he bought at least four million acres, an area larger than Connecticut or Maryland, worth on paper almost any amount that could be dreamed of, and under the circumstances, as likely to vanish as quickly as the dream. But the troubles were not yet come. In 1787 James Wilson was considered one of the leading Pennsylvanians, a man not universally loved but respected everywhere for his learning and his legal skills.

But Wilson was no rabid partisan of his state. He had grown up elsewhere, and he tended to think nationally. It is not surprising, then, that he fell into the strong nationalist camp, along with Madison, Hamilton, Robert Morris, Washington, Gouverneur Morris, Pinckney, and the others.

But there was a subtle difference to his thinking. The other nationalists believed, generally, that government must be built on "the people," but "the people" was an abstraction to them, a philosophic idea. In reality, few of the delegates—nationalists and states' righters alike—had much faith in the ability of the people to govern themselves. The people were given to anarchy, to the blandishments of demagogues, to heedlessly driving through their legislatures intemperate laws, which they just as heedlessly contradicted with other laws. James Wilson, however, had faith that the people could run their own governments.

Wilson saw the people as the ultimate repository of sovereignty. They held all power and could distribute it as they liked, dividing it among whatever governments they saw fit to construct. Wilson's view of the matter was not clear to the other delegates at first. They had grown up believing in a somewhat different principle of government, the idea of the social contract, which said that government was a bargain between the rulers and the ruled. The people, in essence, agreed to accept the overlordship of their kings and governors; in return, the rulers agreed to respect certain rights of the people.

But as the debate progressed, a new concept of government began more and more to be tossed around. It abandoned the whole idea of the contract between rulers and the ruled as the philosophic basis for government. It said instead that as power resided solely in the people, they could delegate as much as they wanted to, and withdraw it as they saw fit. All members of the government, not just legislators, would represent the people. The Constitution, thus, was not a bargain between the people and whoever ran the new government, but a delegation of certain powers to the new government, which the people could revise whenever they wanted. Wilson, in a major speech defending the new Constitution at the Pennsylvania ratifying convention, would say, "The congressional power is to be collected . . . from the positive grant expressed in the instrument of the union." He added that the social contract concept is dangerous, because once entered into, "a contract cannot be altered but by the mutual consent of both parties." Under the new idea, the governors are not partners, but the servants of the governed. The people could alter the arrangement; the government could not.

Gordon Wood says, "For the Federalists the historic distinction between rulers and the people, governors and representatives, was dissolved, and all parts of the government became rulers and representatives of the people at the same time."

In Wilson's view, this new theory required direct election of as many officials as possible, and at the Convention he consistently fought to let the people participate as fully as they could in the machinery of government. As a consequence, he pushed for election of the executive by the people, not by legislators, and thus became the inventor of our electoral college.

Why, then, has James Wilson fallen through the sieve of history? The answer lies in the fact that he died in disgrace. In the years just after the Convention Wilson was at the peak of his fame. He was asked to give the Fourth of July oration in Philadelphia in 1788, one of the highest honors the city could bestow. The College of Philadelphia chose him to give a series of lectures on the basic principles of law, and Washington appointed him to the first Supreme Court. He was, by 1790, one of the most eminent men in America.

But unfortunately, by this time rumors were beginning to circulate that he had overextended himself in his speculation in western lands. Wilson's land schemes had a somewhat visionary aspect to them. He reasoned that the Old World was filled with landless poor, and the New World was filled with empty land. It would be a service to both to bring the surplus population to the surplus land. He proposed to supply clean, uncrowded ships to bring over the immigrants, and build little communities for them in the wilderness. It was an audacious, even noble, scheme, and although it would enrich Wilson, it would benefit humanity as well.

So he pyramided his debts, and by the mid-1790s the structure was bearing more weight than it could stand. The collapse that followed was not entirely Wilson's fault. Many other men had been doing precisely as Wilson had, and they, too, were in trouble. Robert Morris, the financier of the Revolution, would land in debtors' prison, and in 1796 there was a general panic in America among speculators. But a lot of Wilson's troubles were of his own making.

His first wife had died, and he had, in 1793, courted and married a nineteen-year-old Bostonian named Hannah Gray, some thirty-two years his junior. Even as the marriage was being celebrated, the wolves were gathering. Wilson borrowed, juggled his credit, temporized. Nothing worked. In the winter of 1796–1797 a hundred and fifty businesses went under in Philadelphia alone, and sixty-four men were jailed for debt. And by the spring of 1797, even as he was traveling on the Supreme Court circuit as one of the highest judges in the land, Wilson had constantly to look over his shoulder for the sheriff. Finally, in the summer, he and the loyal Hannah were forced to hide from creditors in "a dirty, drafty inn" in Bethlehem. Back home in Philadelphia "the larder was empty . . . the children threadbare." Finally the strain proved too much for Hannah and she went to Boston to visit relatives. Wilson slipped up to Burlington, New Jersey. Here the sheriff caught up with him and he was jailed for debt. He managed to raise bail and, desperate, fled south. He was, mind you, a Justice of the United States Supreme Court and a shaper of the American Constitution. The loyal Hannah came back to Philadelphia, but when it was clear that Wilson could not possibly come home, she decided to join him. By the time she reached him, in Edenton, North Carolina, he had once again managed to get out, and was living in a dreary local tavern.

> He was shockingly changed from the man she had last seen. Gaunt, listless, his clothes ragged and stained, he sat staring interminably out of the window of his room over the waters of Albemarle Sound.

It was, in any case, almost over. In July Wilson suffered from an attack of malaria, which almost killed him. He recovered, and seemed to be improving, for the first time in months growing a little optimistic that he could resolve his problems somehow. Then in August he suffered a stroke. With Hannah hovering over him, he "raved deliriously about arrest, bad debts, and bankruptcy." Then he died, aged fifty-six, and was buried in a simple ceremony in an obscure plot on the estate of a friend. James Wilson died an embarrassment to his friends, and in particular to his Federalist party, led by President John Adams. He was a stench, misshapen, and he was hustled offstage as quickly as possible, and allowed to disappear from history.

The first biography of Wilson was written more than a hundred and fifty years after his death, and the only subsequent work about him has been a long monograph on his political ideas by Geoffrey Seed. In part the problem lies in the shortage of colorful details about his early life: there is not much on record of his years in Scotland, which constituted nearly half his life, and owing to his reserve, he did not write long gossipy letters about his personal affairs. In addition, he had few close, warm friends to defend him in later years, when the surviving members of the Convention were gathering around themselves a blaze of glory. Nonetheless, he was one of America's first great democratic theorists and he deserves more from the people whose cause he so eloquently served.

Chapter Twenty

In the Shadow of Washington

Unlike the other men at the Convention, James Wilson saw what Americans take for granted today, that the president could be a "representative" of the people as a whole, and would be just as protective of the people's liberties as the legislature. But this could be true only if the people had the power to turn the president out of office if he displeased them, and this meant that they had to elect him directly. Wilson would fight hard to see that they did.

But at the outset his was distinctly a minority view—a minority of one, at first. The theory of separation of powers did not require direct election of the president; it required only that a president be somehow able to check the legislature at points, regardless of how he was elected. When the delegates came to look at the whole question of the executive, they found themselves confronted by three separate considerations. One was what shape the executive function would take. Would it be a single person or a committee? If a single person, would he be encumbered by a council or a cabinet of some kind?

The second question was how it was to be elected: by the people, the legislature, the governors of the states, the state legislatures, or in some other fashion?

The third was the question of what powers it would be given. Would it or Congress control the military? Would it have a veto over legislation? Would it appoint ambassadors, judges, heads of departments, or would this be done by the legislature after the manner of the old Congress?

Once again, we can best understand how the idea of our presidency was developed by pulling the debates apart and following each thread separately. To begin with, the executive that James Madison put into the Virginia Plan was a shadowy and unimpressive figure. This was not only because Madison was fearful of a strong executive, but also because he was unable to make up

his mind about what kind he wanted. Before the Convention he wrote to
Washington, "I have scarcely ventured as yet to form my own opinion either
of the manner in which [the executive] ought to be constituted or of the
authorities with which it ought to be clothed." The Virginia Plan did not
specify how long the executive's term should be or whether there would be one
man or several, and it left the executive powers vague. He or they would,
however, be elected by the Congress, and would serve on a council of revision,
along with Supreme Court justices, who together would have an absolute veto
over legislation. Here we see in fullest flower James Madison's propensity to
check power wherever it lay.

The debate on the executive began on June 1. It was immediately clear that
many delegates strongly favored a single executive rather than a small committee. The old Congress had had executive committees, and most of the men at
the Convention recognized that the system had not worked. One of the greatest
problems was that it left Congress itself to actually manage things—that is, not
merely to authorize the government to buy so many muskets, but to pick a gun
maker, haggle over prices, and supervise quality. Thomas Jefferson wrote,
"Nothing is so embarrassing as the details of execution. The smallest trifle
. . . occupies so long as the most important action of legislation and takes place
of everything else." The old Congress had come to realize this fairly quickly,
and had appointed a secretary of war, of the treasury, and of foreign affairs
to take over some of the detail. But there remained a widespread feeling of
dissatisfaction with the committee system.

Not surprisingly, James Wilson made the motion for a single executive, and
not surprisingly Roger Sherman objected, on grounds that the executive
should do no more than carry out the will of the legislature, and that therefore
the Congress ought to be able to make it one or several as it suited them at
the moment. It is obvious how different a government we would have today
had Sherman's idea prevailed.

But Wilson answered immediately, saying that a single magistrate would
give the "most energy, dispatch, and responsibility to the office." Randolph
then said that he was "strenuously opposed" to a single executive, which he
regarded "as the fetus of monarchy." Wilson immediately answered that
"unity in the executive instead of being the fetus of monarchy would be the
best safeguard against tyranny."

The battle lines were being drawn. Throughout the entire debate over the
executive, in a broad sense, the states' righters, like Sherman, Martin, and
Randolph, wanted a weak executive under the control of Congress. The propo-

nents of strong national government, like Madison, Washington, Wilson, and Morris, wanted to install a strong executive independent of Congress to one degree or another. The arguments over the executive, however, were frequently so vague and winding that it is difficult to make safe generalizations. In any case, on June 1 there was no consensus on the question of a single or plural executive, and debate on Wilson's motion was postponed.

They got back to the problem the next day, Saturday, June 2, when Rutledge and Charles Pinckney of South Carolina moved for the single executive. Once again Randolph "opposed it with great earnestness, declaring that he should not do justice to the country [i.e., Virginia] which sent him if he were silently to suffer the establishment of a unity in the executive department." Randolph, as governor of Virginia, was a "single executive" himself and could hardly have believed that there was anything essentially wrong with the idea. It seems clear enough that he was objecting primarily to get himself on the record in case his constituents back home did not like the scheme. His argument was that a single executive was more likely to become a tyrant than a committee was, and he suggested an executive of three members, each drawn from "different portions of the country."

The debate was put off over Sunday, and was opened again on June 4 by Wilson. He said that the main thrust of Randolph's argument was "not so much against the measure itself, as against its unpopularity." He then pointed out that all thirteen states had single executives—it was an accepted practice in America. More important, a single executive would not only supply more "vigor" to the government but would avoid the contention that was certain to ensue in an executive committee. "In courts of justice there are two sides only to a question. In the legislative and executive departments questions have commonly many sides. Each member therefore might espouse a separate one and no two agree."

The argument convinced at least Roger Sherman, who said that he would support a single executive, if there was some sort of council that he would have to consult before he acted. But Wilson did not want a council, "which oftener serves to cover, than prevent, malpractices." The Convention then voted for the single executive, seven to three, with New Jersey not recorded as voting. This was another of the rare instances in which we know Washington's vote, and not surprisingly, he voted for a single executive.

This left the question of a council unresolved. All states had councils of some kind, with greater or lesser control over their executives. The state governments had been organized at a moment when there was strong feeling all across the United States for curbing the power of executives, and these councils were seen as a means of doing just that. In the Virginia Plan, the executive was to have a council of revision, composed of "the executive and a convenient number of the national judiciary," which could veto legislative acts. Elbridge Gerry, however, raised a critical point. He doubted that the judiciary ought to be part of any council of revision, as they would already have the power to decide on a law's constitutionality. Gerry's fellow delegate from Massachusetts, Rufus King, said the same: "Judges ought to be able to expound the law as it should come before them, free from the bias of having participated in its formation."

They were now toying with the concept of the separation of powers. It is impossible to know how many of the men at the Convention were convinced of the wisdom of this concept. It is clear that Roger Sherman had no interest in it, and was not even troubled by the idea of legislators holding other government jobs: it was done all the time in Connecticut.

Yet to many of the delegates the idea of the separation of powers was immensely attractive, because—if one assumed it would actually work—it seemed a way around one of the central dilemmas they were facing: how to keep either the legislature or the executive from taking over the government. From this point on, we shall see that appeals to the separation of powers were usually convincing to the delegates.

And it was so in the case of the debate over the executive council. The delegates voted to postpone a decision, which in effect killed the council. It did not die entirely; from time to time, virtually to the end of the Convention, one or another delegate would raise the idea again. But the delegates had in the main decided that a council would handcuff the executive too much and upset the balance between him and the legislature. It was an important decision: in omitting an executive council, the Founders were casting aside a well-established American practice and opening space for the development of the cabinet as we know it today, an institution not mentioned in the Constitution.

Thus, fairly early in the Convention and without too much difficulty, the delegates decided to abandon the committee system and establish a single executive with at least some authority to act on his own. But nothing else about the executive was settled easily. The delegates now had to decide upon the length of his term, who was to elect him, and whether he could be reelected. These issues were so intermeshed that they cannot be considered separately, but must be seen as a clockwork, where if one part moves, so must all the rest.

The point was this: if the executive was chosen by the Congress, he was likely to become its servant. To make him more immune from their blandishments, it would be necessary to limit him to one term so that he would not campaign for reelection by approving legislators' favorite bills or appointing their friends and relatives to office. This being the case, he ought to be given a fairly long term; otherwise the government would be subject to too frequent transitions. However, if his term was to be long, he certainly ought to be impeachable so that if, for example, he was caught taking bribes from foreign nations, he could be removed from office.

On the other hand, if he was elected in some other manner, especially if he was elected by the people as a whole, the danger would be that the executive would not be sufficiently checked. In that case, he ought to be "reeligible" and his term short so that he could be judged by the people fairly frequently. Under those conditions impeachment might not be necessary, as he could be put out of office reasonably quickly in any case. Or so went the thinking of the delegates. And we can see, as we follow the debate on this aspect of the presidency, how closely tied these considerations were.

The executive Madison put into the Virginia Plan was, in all probability, the sort of executive the delegates had expected, a weak one chosen by the legislature. He would, however, have somewhat more independent strength, in order to check the legislature, than had been the case with the governors of states. Madison's executive would be elected for seven years and would be ineligible for a second term, so he would not be tempted to curry favor with the legislature.

The debate on the executive reached the question of how he should be elected toward midday on June 1. James Wilson was the first to speak. He said:

> He was almost unwilling to declare the mode which he wished to take place, being apprehensive that it might appear chimerical. He would say however, at least that in theory he was for an election by the people. Experience, particularly in New York and Massachusetts, showed that an election of the first magistrate by the people at large, was both a convenient and successful mode. The objects of choice in such cases must be persons whose merits have general notoriety.

Wilson's reluctance to declare the mode he wanted stemmed from the fact that in practice it was impracticable. The Founders did not envision a two-party nominating system. They disliked parties as they had seen them operate in England, where Whigs and Tories seemed always to be fighting for the advantage of their own party, to the detriment of the country as a whole. The old Congress had not been divided into parties, as we understand them today. Congressmen had simply been chosen by their legislatures or the voters, without party organization. Nor was the congressional caucus, which nominated our first six presidents, envisioned at the Convention. Thus the idea of direct election stumbled at the threshold; how would the voters, scattered from Georgia to New Hampshire, know who to vote for in the first place? A presidential election would have to be managed by a small group of people who could keep nominations to a reasonable number, and who could go through a series of ballots efficiently and swiftly. Wilson, of course, knew what the problems were, but his belief in basing the government on the people was strong, and he was determined to make a fight: somehow, a way around the obvious difficulty could be found.

But the other delegates considered the idea hopeless and did not discuss it. Sherman, as he would all along, spoke in favor of election by the Congress in order to make the executive "absolutely dependent on that body." Wilson was still hoping for popular election, and he spoke for a three-year term and reeligibility; Sherman also was for a three-year term and reeligibility so that a good man, who would be dependent on the legislature anyway, would not be put out of office after a single term. Mason wanted a seven-year term and no reeligibility. Bedford thought seven years was far too long. A man could be impeached only for misfeasance, and if he was simply incompetent, the country would be stuck with him. Better a three-year term with two reelections allowed. The vote for a seven-year term was exceedingly close—five yes, four no, with Massachusetts divided. (Maryland did not vote.) The composition of the vote is interesting: Connecticut and the Deep South voted no, the middle states and Virginia yes. This was long before the Connecticut–South Carolina axis was formed, and it is obvious the delegates were torn on the issue and were voting independently out of their own convictions as to where it was safest to lodge power.

Then, late on June 1 Wilson repeated his call for election by the people. He "wished to derive not only both branches of the legislature from the people, without the intervention of the state legislatures, but the executive, also; in order to make them as independent as possible of each other, as well as of the states." Wilson was now putting in explicit terms the idea of the separation of powers, and once again it had an appealing ring to the delegates. Mason said that he favored the idea, but thought it impractical. Nonetheless, he moved that a vote be postponed to see if Wilson could come up with a method for solving the problem.

And so, Wilson went home and thought about it, and on Saturday, June 2, brought in a scheme for election of the president by the people. Wilson's idea was that the states should be divided into relatively large districts, which would each choose an elector; the electors would meet at a specified time and elect a president, who could not be one of them. This was, minor details aside, the first proposal for the electoral college, by which Americans still elect their presidents. But the idea was too novel for the Convention, and they voted it down, with only Maryland and Wilson's Pennsylvania voting aye. The Convention then voted to have the executive chosen by Congress, and it went on, later in the day, to make the executive ineligible to run again, and impeachable for malpractice or neglect of duty.

But the delegates were still left uneasy. The idea of the separation of powers was being talked about more and more. Two of the most influential men at the Convention, James Madison and James Wilson, had made it the keystone of their thinking about the Constitution. The idea made sense, and it was clear that if the Congress elected its own president and could impeach him for "neglect of duty," which fundamentally meant failing to do what the Congress told him to do, he would hardly be an independent arm of government.

But over the weeks following the early June votes on the executive, the Convention was plagued by issues of states' rights, slavery, and proportional representation. It was not until that critical July 17, when the proportional representation issue was finally resolved and so many other things fell into place, that the Convention really got back to reconsideration of the executive. The delegates swiftly agreed again that the executive should be a single person but did not so quickly agree on how he should be chosen. Gouverneur Morris was the first to speak. He said that he was "pointedly against" the executive being chosen by the Congress. "He will be the mere creature of the legislature if appointed and impeachable by that body." And he went on to move that the executive be chosen by the "citizens of the United States." Sherman objected: The people "will never be sufficiently informed of characters" to make a good choice, "and besides will never give a majority of votes to any one man."

In response Wilson said that where a majority was lacking, the national legislature could choose among the contenders, as was done in gubernatorial elections in Massachusetts. "This would restrain the choice to a good nomination at least." Pinckney and Mason spoke against election by the people, and Morris and Wilson fought back. But the proposal for popular election lost heavily, with only Pennsylvania voting for it, and it was again agreed that Congress should elect the president. The delegates then struck out the ineligibility clause, on the theory that a president who could run for office again would have a motive for doing a good job. That was exactly opposite to the theory held in June, that a president who could succeed himself would attempt to bribe the legislature with job offers. One of the delegates who saw this was Dr. James McClurg, the delegate from Virginia who had been the last-minute substitute for Patrick Henry. McClurg pointed out that an executive who could be reelected time and again by Congress would become "dependent forever on the legislature." And he suggested that the executive be allowed to continue in office "during good behavior"—that is to say, he could be removed only for dereliction, by impeachment proceedings. Gouverneur Morris, who all along had wanted a very strong executive, was delighted with the idea. "This was the way to get a good government. . . . He was indifferent how the executive should be chosen, provided he held his place by this tenure." Jacob Broom of Delaware, like McClurg, a quiet delegate, said that he "highly approved the motion. It obviated all difficulties."

The Convention was in reality toying with the idea of a president for life— the very monarch so many of them had feared. But the more cautious delegates were not having it. Sherman said that he "considered such a tenure as by no means safe or admissible. . . . If he behaves well, he will be continued; if otherwise, displaced, on a succeeding election." Sherman, of course, had been pushing for an executive wholly dependent on the legislature, and as matters stood, he was very close to getting it, if he could fend off the proposal for a lifetime executive.

Sherman was followed by James Madison, who immediately appealed to the necessity of the separation of powers, referring directly to the authority of Montesquieu. Allowing an executive to remain in office on good behavior would also allow him to be pulled up or down by the legislature as it saw fit; he was wholly against the idea.

A third Virginian, George Mason, was also against good-behavior tenure, but for exactly the opposite reason: it would inevitably lead to an executive who held office for life, and from there it "would be an easy step to hereditary monarchy." McClurg, however, stuck to his guns: only by allowing the executive to continue in office during good behavior could he be made sufficiently independent of the legislature. It is some measure of the delegates' confusion over the issue of the executive that individuals could speak on the same side but for opposite reasons.

McClurg's proposal was, in any case, voted down. The Convention then voted to reconsider the whole matter of the executive's term.

So it was all still up in the air, for if the Convention changed the term, it would change other things as well. The debate that followed has an almost Alice in Wonderland quality to it. The delegates appeared to be struggling to create an executive who could be strong without being strong. Over the week the Convention reversed itself again and again. On July 17 it constructed a weak executive dominated by Congress. On the nineteenth and twentieth it created a strong executive independent of Congress. On July 24 it went back to the executive chosen by Congress. At various times it was suggested that his term be eight, fifteen, and even, though the proposal was facetious, thirty, years. All sorts of odd expedients for electing him were offered. But it should be noted that for a brief period of two days, the Convention accepted Wilson's idea of election by the people through a system of electors, an idea they had refused even to debate a few weeks earlier. It was a harbinger.

Finally, on July 26, Mason took the Convention right back to square one with a motion that the executive be elected by the legislature for a seven-year term, that he be ineligible for a second term, and that he be impeachable. The motion passed the Committee of the Whole six to three, with Virginia divided and Massachusetts absent—if out of disgust, nobody would have blamed them. Then the Convention turned the whole business over to the Committee of Detail, which must have wondered exactly what its mandate was.

The Committee of Detail, we remember, was supposed only to write a draft of the Constitution, but it made a good many important decisions on its own. It was composed of jurists, who as a group were leery of too strong a national government, but one of them was James Wilson, and Wilson—borrowing from Pinckney, who had modeled his executive on the New York governor—wrote the section pertaining to the president.

The Committee of Detail made its report on August 6. In respect to the executive it said:

> The executive power of the United States shall be vested in a single person. His stile [title] shall be "The President of the United States," and his title shall be "His Excellency." He shall be elected by ballot by the legislature. He shall hold his office during the term of seven years; but shall not be elected a second time.

He could, in addition, be impeached by the House of Representatives and tried by the Supreme Court. This was a president who would be to some extent independent of Congress, but not entirely so. As appealing as the idea of the separation of powers was to the delegates, considerable feeling still remained among them that the legislature ought to have the edge in power.

The Convention did not get to this part of the committee's report until August 24, when the men were growing tired and eager to get home to their families. However, they still could not find a handle to the problem of the election of the executive. The resolution brought in by the Committee of Detail merely said that the executive was to be elected "by ballot by the legislature." The phrase had deliberately been left vague because it was a hot potato. If the House of Representatives was to choose the president, the Big Three could pick more or less whomever they wanted, shutting the small states out. Conversely, if the Senate chose, the small states would have a say out of all proportion to their populations. Would the two houses of Congress somehow vote separately? What would be done if they failed to agree on a candidate? So Rutledge moved to amend the resolution by adding the word "joint" before "ballot." His idea was that the two houses would vote together, as if all the members belonged to a single body. The effect of this would be to give an advantage to the more numerous lower house, where the strength of the large states lay. The delegates from the small states, however, could add and subtract; Roger Sherman immediately protested, and so did Dayton and Brearley of New Jersey. But the amendment carried by a vote of seven to four.

Then Morris, Wilson, and some others made one more attempt to put through the idea of election by the people. The attempt failed, but the vote was six to five, indicating that there was still a good deal of feeling for popular election of the executive. There was also a good deal of confusion: once again the Convention could not settle anything about length of term and reeligibility, and both questions were postponed.

But they could not be postponed forever. On August 31 Roger Sherman moved that these important questions, and other loose strings, be handed over to another one of those committees composed of one man from each state. With no doubt a sigh of relief, the Convention agreed. The committee was a strong one, including King, Sherman, Gouverneur Morris, Madison, Dickinson, and Baldwin—"almost the ablest men from each state," according to historian Charles Warren. It was also one with a nationalist bent: all but Sherman and Brearley favored a strong central government.

The committee applied to the executive the term he is now known by, *president.* The word had been used for the presiding officer of the old Congress and was a familiar one. They recommended that the president be chosen by electors "equal to the whole number of Senators and members of the House of Representatives." The electors themselves were to be chosen in any manner the individual state legislatures wished. This was something that Sherman and the states' righters in general wanted. It would allow the states to leave the choice of the president, in effect, in the hands of state legislatures, or even state governors, if they wished. It was not a mandate for election by the people. Nonetheless, it left the door open for the popular election that James Wilson wanted—yet another of the bargains made to see that everybody got a little something.

According to the system worked out by the committee, each elector would vote for two people, at least one not from his own state. If there was a tie, or nobody received a majority, the Senate would make the final choice. We must understand that the delegates expected that George Washington would be elected president unanimously for as many terms as he wished. They did not anticipate the rise of the two-party system, of course, and they took for granted that after Washington, it would be rare that anybody got a clear-cut majority on the first ballot. In effect, then, they assumed that the electors would be presenting the Senate with a set of nominations. (Actually, for reasons we will see shortly, the final choice was shifted from the Senate to the House.)

This distribution of electors among the states was not proportional to the population, nor of course would a final choice by the Senate reflect state populations. The system was worked out very carefully to strike a balance between the interests of big and small states. In a direct popular election the big states' votes would drown the votes of the small states, a situation the small states could hardly permit; but the big states could not allow the small states to have a disproportionate say in electing the chief executive. In the proposed system, the large states would have the greatest weight in votes of the electors; the small states would have an advantage if or when the choice was thrown to the Senate.

We must understand, then, that the American electoral college system of choosing a president is a Rube Goldberg machine. It was jerry-rigged out of odds and ends of parliamentary junk pressed together by contending interests. And the question that inevitably comes up is whether it ought to be abandoned.

The decision, made so late in the day, to have the president elected by a body other than Congress, was a direct reflection of the growing acceptance by the delegates of the doctrine of the separation of powers. It is probable that none of them, with the exception of James Wilson, had come to Philadelphia believing that allowing the people to choose the president was wise, or in any case, feasible. The largest number of them assumed that power in government should reside in the legislature; legislators, whatever their faults, represented the people, and would therefore not act against the people's best interests.

But wayward legislatures had always been a concern of many of the delegates, and there had been from the start an undercurrent of feeling that perhaps the president ought to have some way of controlling sudden bursts of hasty legislation by Congress. And slowly, over that hot summer, the delegates began to see that the doctrine of the separation of powers provided the answer. The result was a broad movement toward increasing the strength of the president so he could act as a check on the Congress. And by the end of August they had come to conclude that election of the president by the people was wise, and could be made feasible.

But in creating a president so much stronger than any of them had anticipated, the delegates had awakened old fears of a tyrant. It was therefore essential for them to spell out the power of the president exactly, so that there could be no chance that he might come to dominate the legislature, instead of simply balancing it.

To see how the powers of the presidency, so central to the American political system, evolved, we must once again travel back to the last days of May, when Edmund Randolph was presenting the Virginia Plan. The essential question, really, was how power would be divided between the president and Congress. The chief executive who emerged from the Virginia Plan was given only "the executive rights vested in Congress by the Confederation," which were few, and a veto, in concert with the Supreme Court, over acts of Congress. This was a very weak presidency, nothing at all like the presidency we have today. The executive was not given power to make appointments, to run foreign policy, to command the armies. These things would all be done by the Congress, as was the case under the Articles of Confederation.

During the course of the debate on the Virginia Plan the executive was strengthened slightly. He was given power to veto acts of Congress, although he could be overridden by a two-thirds majority; and he could "appoint to offices in cases otherwise not provided," which in practice meant very few. The legislature would appoint Supreme Court justices and judges to lower courts.

We remember that the delegates were very conscious of how King George had manipulated Parliament, and the royal governors the colonial legislatures, by dangling lucrative appointments before influential politicians. In order to prevent this, the Virginia Plan expressly forbade congressmen from holding other public offices. Nonetheless, a president could easily get around this provision by offering plums to family or friends of congressmen; it seemed best to the delegates to limit his appointing power as sharply as possible.

Thus matters rested until the critical July 17, when the Convention got back to debating the executive. This was the day when it was decided, following the Virginia Plan, that the executive would be chosen by the national legislature. And he was once again given only the powers to "carry into execution the national laws," "to appoint to offices in cases not otherwise provided for," and to veto legislation on his own.

But then on the nineteenth and twentieth the delegates turned in their traces and created that much stronger executive, who would be independent of the legislature. Now, somewhat unnerved, they turned back to the idea of hedging his power by requiring a council of some sort to approve his vetoes—what they called a council of revision. The debate on this point suggests how divided in their minds the delegates were on the subject of the executive. Some of them spoke *for* the idea of the council, because they felt that joining the judges with the executive would give him *strength* against the legislature; others spoke *for* it because they believed that the council would act as a *check* on the executive; some spoke *against* it because it would make him too *strong,* still others because it was contrary to the theory of the separation of powers. And over the whole debate hung the unanswerable question of how the public back home would take the idea of a strong executive. Those independent farmers, the delegates knew, had no love of strong government to begin with, and they tended to put their trust in legislatures, which they could sometimes control. The vote on a council to act with the president shows just how ambivalent the delegates were: Pennsylvania and Georgia split, and the other states went four to three against, with Massachusetts, Delaware, and the Carolinas against, Connecticut, Maryland, and Virginia for; New Jersey was not present. As was the case with much of the voting on the executive, none of the natural alliances at the Convention held: the delegates were voting from gut feeling about a strong presidency.

So the executive was left with an independent veto power, which could be overturned by a two-thirds majority in Congress, but at this point he remained relatively weak. Then the whole matter was given over to the Committee of Detail. The committee, we remember, created an executive who would be elected by the legislature, as he had been in the Virginia Plan. They also enlarged his powers. The president would "give information to the legislature, of the state of the union," and recommend legislation. He had his veto power. He could convene the legislature in emergencies, and he could adjourn it if the two houses failed to agree on a time for adjournment. He could commission all the "officers of the United States" and make appointments not otherwise provided for, receive ambassadors, and correspond with other heads of state. He would be commander in chief of the armed forces. And he would have no council looking over his shoulder. But the Senate would appoint judges and ambassadors, and make treaties, effectively keeping foreign policy out of the president's hands. Congress as a whole had the power to raise armies, build fleets, make war, and raise the militia. It also had the power to "regulate commerce with foreign nations," to constitute inferior courts, to appoint the treasurer of the United States.

Over the next three weeks the power of the presidency was modified. The majority needed to override his veto was raised to three-quarters, which would have made an override nearly impossible. He was allowed to receive "other public ministers" as well as ambassadors, but an effort by Read of Delaware to allow him to appoint the treasurer was rejected. The Convention wanted anything to do with money firmly in the hands of the Congress. His appointing power was spelled out more precisely, to read that the president "shall appoint to all offices established by this Constitution, except in cases herein otherwise provided for, and to all offices which may hereafter be created by law."

This, then, was the presidency that was turned over to the Grand Committee of Eleven on August 31. The Convention was nearing its conclusion, and most of the delegates believed that their job was almost done. The president they had lodged in the Constitution at that late date was extremely weak—a creature of the legislature, who could not run foreign policy, appoint judges, ambassadors and even his own treasury head. Needless to say, the American government would be strikingly different if the secretary of the treasury were controlled by Congress, and foreign affairs were conducted by the Senate through a "State Department" it appointed itself.

But the committee included a number of men who were convinced of the necessity for a separation of powers, among them Gouverneur Morris and James Madison. The stage, then, was set for some intricate give and take. The power of the small states of course lay in the Senate, and the committee was insistent that the Senate should play an important role in government. And as we have seen, through the complex device of the electoral college, the small states had gotten—so they thought—the final choice of a president by the Senate.

As the small states now felt that they could have a substantial say in the choice of the president, they were willing to go along with the idea of strengthening him at the expense of Congress, especially the Senate, where their strength lay. And this allowed the committee to embed in the Constitution the theory of the separation of powers, which so many of the delegates had come to believe in.

So they set about increasing the executive's powers. He would, they decided, appoint justices of the Supreme Court, ambassadors, ministers, as well as other officers already provided for—with the advice and consent of the Senate. He would also make treaties—with the consent of two-thirds of the Senate. In turn, the Senate, instead of the Supreme Court, would try impeachment proceedings. Taken as a whole the power of the president was increased at the expense of the Senate, but for the moment the Senate was given a major part in electing him and bringing him down if he misbehaved.

The debate on the Convention floor that followed the committee's expansion of presidential powers concentrated on two points. One was a prolonged and persistent attempt by James Wilson to eliminate the "advice and consent" clause, which allowed the Senate to veto treaties and major presidential appointments. Giving the Senate even this power, which was substantially less than it had had heretofore, had "a dangerous tendency to aristocracy." The Senate would have "the appointment of the President, and through his dependence on them, the virtual appointment to offices." The small states, in Wilson's view, still had too much power. But Wilson was able to get nowhere with his arguments.

The other focal point of the debate was the treaty-making power. We remember the furor that had been going on through the spring and summer over the attempts by the North to swap with Spain rights to the Mississippi for a trade treaty. There was considerable concern among the delegates to make sure that the treaty-making power was carefully hedged. But a deal had been made: in exchange for a strong president, the Senate, in which the small states had a strong voice, was to have some control over him, and the deal stuck.

What is surprising about this debate is how little complaint there was that this new scheme had created a presidency much too strong. The main objectors were Edmund Randolph and George Mason, both from Virginia, both of whom would refuse to sign the Constitution. The majority of the delegates were now prepared for a stronger presidency, and although there was considerable debate over the scheme worked out by the committee and many amendments were proposed, the Convention accepted nearly everything that the committee had done with respect to the presidency. There was only one change of consequence. A number of delegates from the large states were unhappy at the extent of the Senate's control of the presidency. To tamp down feeling against the report, that great compromiser Roger Sherman proposed that when there was no majority for a presidential candidate, the House of Representatives would choose, with each state having one vote. This was Sherman at his cleverest: the small states would still have a disproportionate say, but at least the power to choose the president would be taken from the Senate.

There are certain things, finally, to be said about the winding debate on the presidency, which so often looped back over itself. One is that bloc voting, so evident at many moments at the Convention, broke down in respect to the constructing of the presidency. In this regard the delegates were expressing their own inner fears about monarchy, about rampaging legislatures—about the conflicting demands of power and liberty. Each delegate had his own idea how things should be done, and the consequence was split delegations, close votes, flip-flops, and speeches favoring certain proposals for diametrically opposed reasons. The debate over the presidency shows just how much these men were moved by their own deeply rooted attitudes. Sherman and Martin, for instance, who had come out of the people, did not trust them, but wanted them to hold power against potential tyrants through their legislators. Madison and Morris, who were born rich, could not have understood the common people in the way Sherman and Martin did but nonetheless trusted them; and yet they wanted their legislators to be prevented by a strong president from responding to every popular demand. These men could think and reason, but they could also feel. And feelings counted.

What they wanted, in essence, was the separation of powers. They did not realize it at first, and they came to understand what it was only slowly, and its usefulness even more slowly. Over the course of the Convention, the delegates, bit by bit, saw how a separation of powers, as part of a larger system of checks and balances, could ensure that no one in the government would be able to run away with power. This is today at the heart of American democracy. Should the walls break down, the entire system would be in danger. Today, in particular, the risk is that a president with a popular mandate may arrogate to himself powers that belong to Congress, as some recent presidents have done. The potential for this is especially great, as we shall shortly see, in respect to the war-making power. But the risk can run in the other direction, too, as when Congress, responding to popular demand, forces injudicious legislation past a presidential veto. In 1867 an overbearing Congress, for instance, railroaded legislation designed to set up Andrew Johnson for impeachment and reduced the number of Supreme Court justices so as to deprive him of a chance to fill a vacancy. Once any branch of government is able to rule by itself, democracy will be threatened at the root. And it is one of the most important signs of the collective genius of the Constitutional Convention that the delegates could not only define for themselves this critical theory of political science but had the courage to put it in place.

Chapter Twenty-one

Elbridge Gerry's War
Against the Army

Power, wherever it lies, ultimately has to be backed by force. Nations need military forces to protect themselves against intruders threatening their integrity, and they need an internal police force to put down disorder and make people obey the law. The delegates to the Convention took this as a matter of course. There was little sense among them that human beings would live in peace and brotherhood if left to themselves. Without physical might, they were certain, the new nation would not last long.

Indeed, there was a certain measure of siege mentality in the United States in 1787. Most of the delegates had experienced firsthand the efforts by the British to bring them to heel, and many of them had actually been in the fighting. Many of them, too, could remember the efforts of the French some twenty-five years earlier to move into the Ohio River area. In 1787, the British, disregarding the Treaty of Paris, still occupied four military posts on the northern border of New York, and two in what is now Michigan. They arrogantly forbade American ships to use the Great Lakes, and had established a customs office at Oswego, New York.

The Spanish were dug in deeply in Florida and along much of the coast of the Gulf of Mexico. They were encouraging the Creek Indians to hold the line against the Americans, and had even paid an American general, James Wilkinson, to start a secessionist movement in what is now Tennessee, Mississippi, and Alabama. The Spanish, for the moment, also controlled Louisiana, and had closed the Mississippi River to American traffic. Given the least chance, both English and Spanish would have attacked, the one in the north, the other in the south, and rapidly dismembered the new nation. Once trouble had started, France and Holland, both entrenched in the Caribbean, might have been tempted to try to carve off slices for themselves, too.

The Indians remained an omnipresent threat, not just in the Deep South, but everywhere along the huge American frontier. In 1787 the two cultures were in an almost constant state of warfare at the borders. The Indians could hardly drive across the Alleghenies and swoop down on New York or Boston, but they could and did burn settlements and kill their inhabitants less than thirty miles from Philadelphia. In sum, as Richard H. Kohn, an authority on the American military says, "At birth, the United States was a large, rich nation with a great military potential, but also with its long coastline, seaborne commerce, vast frontier, and hostile European-held territory nearby, a nation immensely vulnerable to surprise attack and invasion."

Nor was the enemy only on the outside. As the delegates in Philadelphia saw it, the nation was threatened by at least three sets of internal enemies. The least threatening of these were a substantial number of Indians living in the settled parts of the United States, who might join an enemy should it come to war. Certainly far more ominous were the roughly 600,000 black slaves, most of whom were collected in groups in the Deep South, in many places outnumbering the whites. The slaves were not docile; there had been slave revolts and rumors of slave revolts almost since slavery was established in the seventeenth century in Virginia. How much of a threat the slaves actually were is hard to determine: serious revolts in 1800, 1822, and 1831 were fairly swiftly put down, although in the last case with many deaths on both sides. No doubt the fear of slave uprisings was exacerbated by emotions about blacks that teemed in the white unconscious. Nonetheless, there was a real feeling throughout the United States that slave rebellion was a constant danger.

Finally, there was Daniel Shays hiding out in upstate New York, even as the Convention was sitting. While the Shaysites had been closing courts and fighting battles with the militia, the national government had been virtually helpless to intervene. Edward Carrington, a former army officer and at the time of Shays' Rebellion a congressman, spoke for many people when he wrote from New York that "there is the imbecility [weakness], the futility, the nothingness of the federal powers; The U S have no troops, nor dare they call into action what is called the only safe guard of a free government, the militia of the state, it being composed of the very object of the force." The Shaysites had been defeated, but everywhere in the United States there were disaffected groups capable of rebellion—mobs of riffraff in the city streets, westerners across the mountains unwilling to take orders from the eastern capitals, debtors facing sheriffs' actions in every state.

Related to all these questions involving an army was the whole problem of how a new government would enforce its laws. It is exceedingly important for us to bear in mind that the United States in 1787 did not possess a standing army worth the name; instead, the population itself was armed. In this respect the nation was unique. Everywhere else governments had standing armies officered by members of the hereditary ruling class, made of well-trained men equipped with the best weapons. They could put down insurrections by force, collect taxes by force, march into unruly villages and arrest mayors, councillors, private citizens by force.

The United States had a few hundred troops on short enlistments stationed at frontier posts, and the states, of course, had their militias, which could be called up to put down insurrections, as they did in the case of Shays' Rebellion.

Making enforcement difficult was the fact that American citizens were armed to an extent that would have astonished Europeans, both nobles and peasants. Not every household owned a gun, but certainly on the frontier, where the danger of Indian attack was real, every farmer did. Even in more settled areas farmers usually had a musket or rifle for hunting and for killing wolves and foxes that preyed on livestock. The American citizenry, potentially, constituted an army of its own, and if any substantial proportion of it chose to face down a militia, it probably could. Americans, unlike most people elsewhere, could not be governed without their own consent.

The delegates were filled with a very real sense of the nation's vulnerability: the enemies were there, waiting to pounce. We should understand, as Reginald C. Stuart says, that "the Revolutionary generation did not identify sharp dividing lines between war and peace." Nations were always taking umbrage at one thing or another, and sending out troops. A nation simply had to be prepared to fight, and the United States was not.

The new country must be able to defend itself, obviously. But there was a countervailing idea held by the delegates—and the country as a whole. That was hatred of the standing army—the permanent force ready to fight at an instant. Kohn says flatly, "No principle of government was more widely understood or more completely accepted by the generation of Americans that established the United States than the danger of a standing army in peacetime." Indeed, antiarmy feeling had a long English heritage. The standing army of professional soldiers, usually drawn from the dregs of society and held under tight control by harsh discipline, had been developed in Europe in the seventeenth century. During the colonial period, the British had used troops on occasion to impose order as they wanted, and in an era when barracks were not widely used, citizens were often forced to billet them in their homes. Then, in 1770, came the Boston Massacre, in which British troops fired on an American mob. As events rolled toward the Revolution, it was the British standing army that was the enemy.

Even Madison, the proponent of strong national government, had his fears. He said, "In time of actual war, great discretionary powers are constantly given to the executive magistrate. Constant apprehension of war, has the same tendency to render the head too large for the body. A standing military force with an overgrown executive will not long be safe companions to liberty. . . . Throughout all Europe, the armies kept up under the pretext of defending, have enslaved the people." Americans saw a standing army not so much as a force to defend them, but as a force to be used against them by whatever tyrant would get control of it. The country, many people believed, could defend itself with civilian armies—a militia composed of the able-bodied males of each locality, organized into companies and brigades and led by officers appointed by their own state governments, or even elected by the troops. The militia would never attempt to enslave the people, because they *were* the people.

However, not everybody agreed that the militia could be an effective force in war. The state militias had not proven to be very good troops during the Revolution. Washington had become completely disgusted with them. He said, "They come in you cannot tell how, go you cannot tell when, and act you cannot tell where, consume your provisions, exhaust your stores, and leave you at last in a critical moment." Washington eventually stopped depending on them and, with the help of Baron Steuben, built a disciplined regular army, which eventually won the war. Many other delegates had themselves had experience with the militias, and they agreed with Washington that the militia was not a reed to lean on in a crisis. Furthermore, what use would the militia be in putting down insurrections of their friends and neighbors? Even though it had been the militia that destroyed Shays' army, many of the men at the Convention—one-third of whom had been Continental Army officers—did not trust them.

The men coming to the Convention, thus, had mixed feelings, as they had on so many things, about the need for a standing army. On the one hand, they feared the power of an army in the hands of a tyrant, or worse, the chance that an army might take over the government, as some of the officers of Washington's army had wanted to do at the Newburgh crisis. On the other hand, they did not see a good alternative. It was the old story: how do you establish necessary power without giving away too much? In this fear they were certainly wise. How many would-be democracies around the world have, in just the past few decades, been taken over by their own armies?

The battle over the American army and the war-making power in general draws in several related questions. Should there be a standing army, or could the militia be made adequate for the national defense? What control would the national government have over the state militias? Would it appoint the officers, for example? Would it take the militias over entirely? What role would Congress play in making war? Who would be commander in chief? How would war be declared? Few of the delegates had clear ideas on these questions. One who did, however, was Elbridge Gerry, from Massachusetts.

Gerry played an important role in the debate over the American war-making power. He is a clear example of a man who was motivated not by his pocketbook or the interest of his section of the country, but by deeply held personal attitudes, beliefs so strong that in the end they prevented him from signing the Constitution.

Elbridge Gerry has generally received a bad press from historians. The formidable Charles Beard insisted that as the largest holder of government bonds at the Convention, he was interested mainly in setting up a government that would pay them off. Samuel Eliot Morison, noticing a certain ambivalence in his positions, called him "schizophrenic." He is remembered best today for contributing his name to the term "gerrymander."

But his more recent biographer, George A. Billias, etches a different portrait. The Gerrys (it is pronounced with a hard G, as in Gary) were not an old New England family. Gerry's father, Thomas, was a seaman who arrived in Massachusetts in 1730. He settled in Marblehead, a seafaring town on a spit of land sticking out into the Atlantic Ocean, a place so hard and rocky that visitors often wondered how Marbleheaders buried their dead. Exposed to the weather and making their living fishing for cod in rough, cold seas or on trading ships that were gone for months or even years at a stretch, the men of Marblehead were as rugged as the spit of land they lived on. Somewhat isolated on their little peninsula, facing the sea rather than the inland towns, they tended to be suspicious and clannish: it is reported that they had a custom of stoning strangers who appeared in their town.

In this milieu Thomas Gerry thrived as a merchant and ship captain, and by the time Elbridge, the third surviving son, was born in 1744, Thomas was one of the leading men in the community. Marblehead at the moment was prospering on commerce and cod, which was sold in the Caribbean and even

Spain. Elbridge Gerry grew up in comfortable circumstances, as did the other men of the establishment who dominated the Convention. For reasons unknown, his father singled him out for an education. He went to Harvard College, where he earned both Bachelor's and Master's degrees. He was especially interested in the study of political philosophy, or as we would term it, political science.

But though Thomas Gerry was willing to educate Elbridge, he was no indulgent father. He was a man of strong, indeed puritanical, convictions, who ran, according to Billias, a pious and austere home. Possibly because his father demanded it, young Gerry came into the family business after graduation, rather than going into one of the professions, as many college graduates did. He grew into a rather curious and paradoxical adult. He was, on the one hand, tough and outspoken. Once the Gerrys fell into a feud with another Marblehead family. Two of the enemy broke into the Gerry house one evening and threatened the father, then sixty-eight. In response, Elbridge and one of his brothers beat up one of the men and his wife, and then "gladly paid their fines." He was, furthermore, a resourceful and clever businessman, and by the time of the Convention he had made himself rich.

Yet on the other hand, according to Billias, "A nervous and birdlike little person, he stammered and developed a 'singular habit of contracting and expanding the muscles of his eye,' which gave him an air of unusual sternness." William Pierce gives a similarly contradictory picture of him:

> Mr. Gerry's character is marked for integrity and perseverence. He is a hesitating and laborious speaker;—possesses a great deal of confidence and goes extensively into all subjects that he speaks on, without respect to elegance or flower of diction. He is connected and sometimes clear in his arguments, conceives well, and cherishes as his first virtue, a love for his country [i.e., Massachusetts].

Gerry in certain respects reminds us of Madison: the shy, nervous speaker who is nonetheless independent in his thinking and dogged in action.

Yet despite his manner and his obduracy in some circumstances, Gerry was admired by his contemporaries for his intelligence and respected for his integrity. He served in Congress and eventually as minister to France and vice president of the United States under Madison. He was a close friend of both Thomas Jefferson and John Adams, neither of whom was in the habit of befriending stupid or self-serving men. Adams, while serving in the old Congress with Gerry, said that he was "a man of immense worth. If every man here was a Gerry, the liberties of Americans would be safe against the gates of Earth and Hell."

We cannot accept simplistic notions that Gerry was "schizophrenic" or that he was at the Convention solely to see that his investments were safe. He was too complex for that. Billias sees as a basic element in Gerry's character an instinctive trust of the American spirit—the "genius" of the people, Gerry would have said. Unlike the citizens of the corrupt Old World, who had fallen into depravity, Americans would make sound judgments and behave honorably—although they would need their betters to lead them.

But above everything, Billias believes, was an enormous fear of power. "His distrust of uncontrolled centralized power remained the main motivation behind Gerry's thought and behavior not only during the Revolutionary crisis but throughout his life. . . . One of the key ideas in Gerry's concept of a 'free state' was the way in which political power might be blunted or mitigated." There were, Gerry believed, two ways in which political power might be curbed. One was through the machinery of the separation of powers. The second was by basing the government on the smallest possible unit in which there would be "a commonality of interest between the ruler, or representative, and those ruled: those governing would hardly pass iniquitous laws because they would be legislating against their own self-interest."

But Gerry, as a member of the Massachusetts legislature, had been one of those who had had to deal directly with Shays' Rebellion. It had troubled him, and it had, at least for the moment, tempered his democratic instincts. Surely there had to be enough power somewhere to prevent disorders of this sort. On May 31, shortly after he arrived at the Convention, he stated his position to his fellow delegates exactly. He had "been too Republican heretofore: he was still however Republican, but had been taught by experience the danger of the levelling spirit." Thus the dualism in his attitudes: he was all for preventing governments from intruding on private liberties; but on the other hand, there should never be another Shays' Rebellion.

The Convention was slow to tackle the problem of an army, defense, and internal police. The Virginia Plan said nothing about a standing army, but it did say that the national government could "call forth the force of the union against any member of the union failing to fulfill its duty under the articles thereof." The delegates had expected to discuss something like this clause, for one of the great problems had been the inability of the old Congress to enforce its laws. Surely it should be able to march troops into states when necessary to get state governments to obey.

But in the days before the Convention opened Madison had been thinking it over, and he had concluded that the idea was a mistake. You might well march your troops into Georgia or Connecticut, but then what? Could you really force a legislature to disgorge tax money at bayonet point? "The use of force against a state," Madison said, as the debate started on May 31, "would be more like a declaration of war, than an infliction of punishment, and would probably be considered by the party attacked as a dissolution of all previous compacts by which it might be bound." Although he did not say so at the moment, he had in mind another way of enforcing national law, which not only would be more effective, but was philosophically sounder. As the government was to derive its power from the people, it ought to act on the people directly. Instead of trying to punish a state, which was, after all, an abstraction, for failure to obey the law, the U. S. government could punish *individuals* directly. Some person—a governor, a tax collector, a state treasurer—would be held responsible for failure to deliver the taxes. Similarly, the national government would not punish a state government for allowing, say, illegal deals with Indians over western lands, but would directly punish the people making the deals. All of this seemed eminently sensible to the Convention, and early in the debate on the Virginia Plan the power of the national government to "call forth the force of the union" against disobedient states was dropped. And so the idea that the government should be able to coerce states disappeared from the Convention. It is rather surprising, in view of the fact that the Convention had been called mainly to curb the independence of the states, that the concept went out so easily. The explanation is, in part, that the states' righters were glad to see it go; and in part that Madison's logic was persuasive: it is hard to arrest an abstraction.

The Convention, preoccupied with proportional representation, slavery, and other matters, took some time to return to the question of an army and the national defense. It was finally brought back to the Convention's attention by the August 6 report of the Committee of Detail. The committee had, of course, abandoned the idea of a "general grant," empowering the national government to "legislate in all cases to which the separate states are incompetent"—which would certainly have included the power to raise an army for the country's defense. It now had to include specific war-making powers in the enumeration of powers to be granted the national government. It thus gave the new Congress power "to subdue a rebellion in any state, on the application of the legislature; to make war; to raise armies; to build and equip fleets; to call forth the aid of the militia, in order to execute the laws of the Union, enforce treaties, suppress insurrections and repel invasions."

This clause said nothing about a standing army, but it did not rule one out. The Committee of Detail, we remember, which included Edmund Randolph, was somewhat states' rights in tone, and this cautious resolution, which neither authorized a standing army nor forbade one, would have been typical of Randolph. On August 18, George Mason, the bristly Virginia aristocrat who was always fearful of national power, protested that he "hoped there would be no standing army in time of peace, unless it might be for a few garrisons." And he went on to suggest that military appropriations be limited to a certain period, so they could be cut off by the Congress if necessary. This the Convention quickly approved.

Shortly afterward Gerry took up the attack. "There was no check here against standing armies in time of peace. . . . The people were jealous on this head, and great opposition to the plan would spring from such an omission. . . . He thought an army dangerous in time of peace and could never consent to a power to keep up an indefinite number." And he went on to propose that any standing army be limited to two or three thousand troops.

Madison's notes give no indication of any response to Gerry's statement, but there is a tradition that Washington then said, in a stage whisper, that the Constitution should also include a rule limiting invading forces to the same number. In any case, the convention attempted to ignore Gerry and to take up the question of the power to build fleets, but Gerry would not be ignored. He and Luther Martin, the rabid states' righter, now moved specifically that in peacetime the army be limited to a few thousand men. Charles Cotesworth Pinckney made the obvious response that the nation could hardly wait until it was attacked before it raised an army. But Gerry was obstinate. The strength of his feeling against a standing army is revealed in a remark ascribed to him by historian Samuel Eliot Morison. A standing army, Gerry said, is like a standing member: an excellent assurance of domestic tranquillity, but a dangerous temptation to foreign adventure. If there were no restrictions on a standing army, he told the Convention, the representatives of a few states in Congress "may establish a military government." But the Convention did not agree, and Williamson reminded Gerry that the necessity for getting frequent congressional approval of funds for the military would effectively curb it. There was a clear consensus against limiting any standing army, and the Convention negatived the motion of Gerry and Martin.

There would be a standing army, then; and in that case what should be done about the militia? The delegates knew that they could not abolish the state militias, for too many of the people saw these citizen armies as their defense against tyranny. Besides, in time of war militias might be necessary. But they clearly had to be made more effective than they were. The question was first raised on August 18 by Mason, who "considered uniformity as necessary in the regulation of the militia throughout the Union," and wanted national control of them. But there the Convention was divided. There was an uneasy sense that the states would fight against giving up control of their own militias. On this point Gerry was adamant. In line with his wariness of power, he could not trust the national government with control of the militia. "If this be agreed to by the Convention, the plan will have as black a mark as was set on Cain. He had no such confidence in the general government as some gentlemen professed, and believed it would be found that the states have not." In reality, Gerry was envisioning a time when the states might need their militias to fight off a tyrannous national government. As ever, he wanted power dispersed and localized as much as possible.

This time he had support from men in the states' rights camp. Sherman pointed out that the states might need control of their militias "for defense against invasions and insurrections and for enforcement of obedience to their laws." Mason now said that he "thought there was great weight in the remarks of Mr. Sherman," and moved that each state might hold out for its own use a certain portion of its militia. So the Convention decided to turn the matter back to one of its several committees of eleven, which were redoing much of the work of the Committee of Detail.

But in this brief debate on control of the militia the Convention had touched on a central issue, which had faced it from opening day. Gerry had said that he "had no such confidence in the general government as some gentlemen professed." His opponents took exactly the opposite position. John Langdon of New Hampshire "saw no more reason to be afraid of the general government than of the state governments." Pinckney agreed. Madison said that "if the states would trust the general government with a power over the public treasure, they would from the same consideration of necessity grant it the direction of the public force."

This was the essence of it. It was one thing to give the government certain powers on paper: it was entirely different to equip it with armed might. Could the government, even with the safeguards they had so painstakingly built into it, really be trusted not to enslave the people? On this great issue, opinions were not based on sectional, economic, or class interests: each man at the Convention responded from the gut on an individual and emotional basis.

Let us consider John Langdon, who told Gerry and the Convention that he saw no reason to be afraid of giving the national government armed might. He was one of the two New Hampshire men who arrived so late. He was, however, the reason that they arrived at all, for when the parochial New Hampshire legislature, suspicious of what was going on in Philadelphia, refused week after week to allocate to their delegates the expenses for the trip, Langdon decided to pay the expenses for himself and his fellow delegate, Nicholas Gilman. Langdon came from a farming family but had gone to sea, as the extra sons of New England farmers frequently did, had become a merchant, and had quickly made himself wealthy and an important man in his state. He had commanded troops during the Revolution and been a member of Congress; as a merchant dealing in the West Indies, he had a far wider experience of the broad world than most of his fellow New Hampshire citizens. "Affable, handsome, a good liver and a gracious entertainer, Langdon was a man of whom New Hampshire could be proud. While he reciprocated this feeling of pride in full measure, he was not blind to the fact that the future of his doughty state was bound up closely with the cause of union." Specifically, as a merchant and member of the creditor class, he was eager to see a well-regulated national system of commerce, and an end to paper money. His state had felt the threat of Shays' Rebellion nearby, and he wanted a government able to deal with this kind of disorder.

Langdon, in other words, was a sophisticated and experienced man, and it was he who had pushed the New Hampshire delegation into the nationalist camp, somewhat to the surprise of Sherman and other states' rights men, who had thought they would have New Hampshire with them. The contrast with Gerry is striking, because the two men came from such similar backgrounds. Langdon was one of nine children, Gerry one of five. Gerry had grown up in Marblehead, Langdon in Portsmouth, a similarly tough New England port town on the same rocky Atlantic coast fifty miles further north. Both men had become wealthy as merchant shippers. Both had been ardent patriots during the war; both had been in the old Congress. Further, both held substantial amounts of public securities. Coming out of the same world, with the same economic and sectional interests, they should have been political allies, fighting the good fight together. And yet on many central issues they were at opposite poles.

Why? It is simply because, beneath their sectional loyalties, beneath their concern for their pocketbooks, lay different human cores, that in the end overrode the more superficial interest in money or in the welfare of New England. The one was a cheery, openhanded man; the other nervous, birdlike, afflicted by a stammer and a tic. How could they not view the world differently? Once again we see that we cannot truly understand why the Founding Fathers constructed the instrument they did simply by reference to economic, political, or sectional interests.

All of these men brought to the Convention their conscious and unconscious attitudes toward power. Madison mistrusted it, and tried to check it everywhere. Washington chafed under control, but liked strength. Hamilton was attracted to power and put himself at the service of powerful men. Paterson feared chaos more than power. Langdon was unafraid of power. And Elbridge Gerry, who had seen chaos marching in the streets of his own state, was nonetheless ready to risk disorder rather than set too much power in one place.

But Gerry was fighting a losing battle. On Thursday, August 23, the Committee of Eleven proposed that the government could

> Make laws for organizing, arming and disciplining the militia, and for governing such part of them as may be employed in the service of the United States, reserving to the states respectively, the appointment of the officers, and the authority of training the militia according to the discipline prescribed.

It was another federal compromise, sharing power over the militia between the state and the national government, and in the debate that followed most of the delegates were concerned only with making minor adjustments in the language for clarity and to make sure the states were protected from too much government control. But Gerry was against the whole thing. Giving the national government any say in the militia "would be regarded as a system of despotism." Langdon answered him, saying that he "could not understand the jealousy expressed by some gentlemen. The general and state governments are not enemies to each other, but different institutions for the good of the people of America. . . . In transferring power from one to the other, I only take out of my left hand what it cannot so well use, and put it into my right hand where it can be better used."

Not so, Gerry immediately insisted. "Will any man say that liberty will be as safe in the hands of eighty or a hundred men taken from the whole continent [the Congress], as in the hands of two or three hundred taken from a single state [the state legislatures]." Martin was with him, but nobody else was.

A little later in the day Madison proposed that generals in the state militia be appointed by the national government. Gerry rose to reply sarcastically, "Let us at once destroy the state governments, have an executive for life or hereditary, and a proper senate, and then there would be some consistency in giving full powers to the general government. . . . He warned the Convention against pushing the experiment too far. Some people will support a plan of vigorous government at every risk. Others of a more democratic cast will oppose it with equal determination, and a civil war may be produced by the conflict." This time, however, Sherman came to Gerry's support, and the Convention voted to keep appointment of militia generals in the states. But the rest of what Gerry so disliked, a measure of control over the militias by the national government, went through. From these militias, of course, have descended our national guards.

On September 5 the Committee of Eleven gave the Congress the right "to grant letters of marque and reprisal," by which private ships were allowed to prey on enemy shipping; put in a two-year limit on military appropriations; and following an earlier suggestion of Madison's, gave the government the power to acquire land for the purpose of building forts, arsenals, and the like, and to exercise authority over such areas—the jurisdiction that the government has today over army camps and naval bases.

Still Gerry fought on. He wanted the military appropriations limited to one year instead of two. He did not want to give the national government the right to control the land under its forts because "this power might be made use of to enslave any particular state by buying up its territory, and that the strongholds proposed would be a means of aweing the state into an undue obedience to the general government." Gerry was now fighting alone. He was seeing enemies behind every bush. The Convention was not with him. The delegates were tired, they wanted to go home, and they were not interested in the obsessions of this too-vehement New Englander. But still Gerry would not give in, and on the next to the last day of the Convention, September 15, he announced that he could not sign the Constitution, because it had placed too much power in the national government.

But despite him, there would be a standing army, and there would be nationally regulated state militias which could easily fall under the control of the national government. That left one remaining set of questions in respect to the military: who would control the army? Who would have the right to put it in action? Who could tell it where to march, and who to shoot at? It is a critical issue; witness the struggle between recent presidents and Congress to control the war-making power. It is thus vital for us to know what the Founders thought.

To begin with, they did not envision an American army setting out for conquest. They could not foresee an American army wresting Texas from Mexico or policing the Caribbean. They saw an American army as purely a defensive force, to be called into action only when the country was attacked, or at least provoked. It would be used, thus, principally in an emergency, not for aggrandizement, as European armies were.

The Virginia Plan said nothing whatever about who could declare war. Neither did the Paterson Plan. The matter was first brought up by the Committee of Detail, which, in the course of working out its enumeration, specifically gave Congress the power to "make" war. It also said the executive would be "commander in chief of the Army, and Navy of the United States, and of the militia of the several states."

The debate on the war-making power began on August 17, with Pinckney suggesting that the lower house worked too slowly, and that the power to make war ought to be given to the Senate alone, which would be "more acquainted with foreign affairs, and most capable of proper resolutions." Pierce Butler of South Carolina responded that the Senate would work no faster than the legislature as a whole, and suggested that the president should be able to decide.

This, however, smacked too much of King George for most of the men present. Yet it was obvious that somebody must be able to move swiftly in an emergency. So Madison and Gerry moved to change the wording from "make" war to "declare" war. This phrasing, Madison, said, would leave to "the executive the power to repel sudden attacks." Sherman agreed, saying that "the executive should be able to repel and not commence war." Gerry added that he "never expected to hear in a republic a motion to empower the executive alone to declare war."

That was the beginning and end of it. There was virtually no other important question on which the Convention was so solidly in agreement as that the power to declare war be exercised by the Congress, and not the president. The president, of course, would have to be able to send the army out to fight off a surprise attack, but these men wanted to give him little more power than that. For example, on August 24, in debating the entirely separate question of what officials the president could appoint, Sherman swiftly moved to modify the language to make it clear that Congress, not the president, would appoint all army officers. He said, "If the executive can model the army, he may set up an absolute government, taking advantage of the close of a war and an army commanded by his creatures." Sherman was thinking of James II of England, who "was not obeyed by his officers because they had been appointed by his predecessors, not by himself," but it is not hard to find more recent examples in South America, Africa, the Middle East. The change was agreed to without debate. As a consequence, officers in the military still get their commissions from the Congress of the United States.

On July 27, the president's power over the military was further hedged when Sherman proposed that he should command the militia only when it was actually called up for national service. And on August 27, the Convention without debate accepted the wording that the president should be "Commander in Chief of the Army and Navy of the United States."

What, finally, would the Founders have thought of the tendency of recent American presidents to commit troops to battle without formal permission from Congress? They would almost certainly have been astonished and outraged. They were determined not to give a potential tyrant an armed force to use as he wished. Had they seen a president sending troops out on his own in pursuit of his foreign policy objectives they would have taken immediate steps to stop him.

Chapter Twenty-two

George Mason and the Rights of Man

Undoubtedly, to most Americans, the best-known and most important part of the Constitution is the Bill of Rights. Probably few of them could recite in detail what it actually contains, but almost all would know that it guarantees freedom of religion, freedom of speech, freedom of the press, the right to a fair trial, and some other freedoms about which they might be somewhat more vague. And from a certain point of view the Bill of Rights *is* the most important part of the Constitution, because it sets marked and dramatic limits to what the American government can do, limits that in 1787 were found on no other government in the world. Even today there are few countries that so sharply constrain their national governments from interfering in private liberties. Americans are justly proud of the Bill of Rights, for it is this section of the Constitution, more than any other, that has been a rallying cry for people all around the world.

In view of this, it remains astonishing that the great majority of the delegates to the Convention thought a Bill of Rights not merely unnecessary but unwarranted, and they refused to put one into the Constitution. It was a grave mistake from a number of viewpoints, so clearly a mistake that one of the first things the new government did was to start the amendment process to add a Bill of Rights. How could the Founders have made so grievous and obvious an error?

The idea that human beings have "natural rights" given by God or simply arising from the nature of things has a long history, dating back to the days of ancient Greece and Rome. It was, however, given currency in the seventeenth and eighteenth centuries by political philosophers—especially John Locke, writing as the colonies were gathering settlers in the late seventeenth century, and Jean-Jacques Rousseau, writing as the conflict with England was aborning. The concept of natural rights was familiar to most Americans who took an interest in politics, and was taken as a self-evident truth by the men who led the Americans into the Revolution.

In fact, a lack of a schedule of guaranteed rights was the basic reason for the split with England. According to Sam Adams, one of the most determined fighters for independence, if the colonies and the mother country could "agree in one general Bill of Rights, the dispute might be settled on the principles of equity, and harmony restored between Britain and the colonies." So much were natural rights on the minds of the colonists that in 1774 at the First Continental Congress, called to work out a unified response to British measures, the delegates made a point of drawing up a declaration of rights. Had Britain accepted it, or some version of it, the American states might still be individual parts of the British system—after all, the British Empire was the most powerful political organization on earth and there were many advantages in belonging to it. But Americans did object to being summarily arrested, having their homes searched without warrants, being taxed without having a role in setting those taxes, and being tried in admiralty courts without juries.

Guaranteed rights, then, were exceedingly important to Americans through the 1770s and 1780s. They were, in essence, what the country had fought the Revolution for. More, they were a rallying cry to which men around the world could respond, would actually risk death for. These rights were not abstractions, resounding words on paper, but something Americans believed in deeply, passionately. As a consequence, when the colonies started to set up their own individual governments after the Declaration of Independence, they took it for granted that a state constitution should include a bill of rights.

One of the first states to write one was Virginia. In 1776, as fighting broke out, Virginia quickly called a convention and established a committee to work out a government for the state. The committee included some familiar names: James Madison, Edmund Randolph, George Mason. Although a number of men on the committee had ideas about what should go into a bill of rights, it was a draft produced by George Mason that was adopted by the committee almost *in toto*. The Virginia Bill of Rights eventually became a major model for the national bill, and as a consequence George Mason is sometimes referred to as the father of the Bill of Rights. Mason is today not considered one of the great figures at the Convention, but, says Robert Rutland in his study of the Bill of Rights, his contemporaries "held his abilities in high esteem."

George Mason was, however, an odd duck. Born into one of the wealthy and aristocratic families that ran Virginia, he behaved more like a New England

Calvinist than the mythic southern rakehell dedicating his life to drink, women, and fast horses. According to his biographer Helen Hill Miller, "He was abstemious—he drank little and ate with moderation." (This was by the standard of the times, of course: Mason usually had a toddy before dinner and two or three glasses of wine with the meal.) He shaved his head and doused it in cold water every morning, and at the Convention—his puritanism overcoming his libertarianism—he was the lone delegate in favor of sumptuary laws designed to control people's drink, dress, and deportment.

He was born in 1725 and was thus considerably older than most of the men at Philadelphia—seven years older than Washington, twenty-five years older than Madison. His father died when he was ten and he was "plunged into an early maturity." Despite the age gap, he was in adolescence a chum of a neighboring youth who had also lost a father: George Washington. He grew up to be something of a loner, who preferred the quiet of his study to trafficking in politics, as people of his class were expected to do. He undertook public office reluctantly and only occasionally, and he rarely traveled beyond Virginia: that summer at the Convention was his first long trip out of his own state. Characteristically, after his first wife died when Mason was forty-eight, he waited seven years to remarry, and then, instead of taking a young bride, as Madison, Gerry, Wilson, and other men of his class did, married a spinster of fifty. His mansion, Gunstun Hall, was much smaller than what he could have afforded, and he ran it himself, without the help of the managers and secretaries other rich men hired. He was good at it, too: he was born rich and became substantially richer, eventually owning 75,000 acres of land and ninety black slaves.

At the core of George Mason's personality was a deep-seated mistrust of other people. He depended on himself alone. Rutland says that he was "above all things a manager who liked to control his affairs down to the last detail." He could be humorous, but his wit was sarcastic. He did not like socializing. During that—for Mason, endless—summer in Philadelphia he wrote, "It is impossible to judge how long we shall be detained here, but from present appearances I fear until July, if not later. I begin to grow heartily tired of the etiquette and nonsense so fashionable in this city. It would take me months to make myself master of them, and that it should require months to learn what is not worth remembering in as many minutes, is to me so discouraging a circumstance as determines me to give myself no trouble about them."

In sum, Mason was crusty, arrogant, and misanthropic. And yet on the other side, he was honest, reliable, consistent, a careful student of politics, and one of the clearest and most precise thinkers at the Convention. He spoke frequently on the Convention floor, usually briefly and to the point, and the other men there forgave his crustiness out of respect for his genuine abilities.

It is hardly surprising, given Mason's suspicious and misanthropic nature, that at the Convention he devoted his strength to putting hedges around power. He was endlessly doubtful of the "easterners," those merchant shippers of the northern states, and fought to require the two-thirds majority for navigation laws. Although he owned slaves, he hated slavery, as many Virginians did. The institution "made petty tyrants" of slaveholders, and he fought for the abolition of the slave trade, which left him against both sides of the North-South bargain. He fought for broad impeachment powers, and against a standing army in peacetime. Again and again, as on July 26, he insisted that he had "for his primary object, for the polestar of his political conduct, the preservation of the rights of the people." Although he frequently sounded like a states' righter, he was really not so much that as a determined and consistent libertarian who was concerned that no government meddle in the lives of its citizens. It is thus hardly surprising that George Mason believed a bill of rights to be essential to the Constitution, and he made it his central concern.

The bill of rights that he had designed for the state of Virginia contained some ideas that will be very familiar to Americans. It began by saying that all men were created free and equal, and were entitled to "the enjoyment of life and liberty, with the means of acquiring and possessing property, and pursuing and obtaining happiness and safety." It went on to list other individual rights: it forbade cruel and unusual punishments and provided that no citizen could be compelled to testify against himself. It called for speedy trial by an impartial jury, prohibited unreasonable search and seizure, called for jury trial in civil cases, prescribed freedom of religion, and generally guaranteed the people's freedom against the government.

Mason wanted something along these lines for the United States. At the Convention, however, he found himself virtually alone. None of the early plans suggested anything like a bill of rights, and for a long time neither did any of the delegates. Finally, on August 20, Charles Pinckney brought in a long list of proposals for consideration by the Committee of Detail. Among the items on the list were some that might go into a bill of rights if there was one: liberty of the press, suspension of habeas corpus under extreme circumstances only, no quartering of troops in private houses during peacetime. The Committee of Detail did nothing with these suggestions, so on August 28 Pinckney proposed that the Constitution include a clause providing that habeas corpus "should not be suspended but on the most urgent occasions, and then only for a limited time, not exceeding twelve months." In the brief debate that followed, John Rutledge said that he "was for declaring habeas corpus inviolable," and Morris supported Pinckney's proposal with a motion saying that habeas corpus could not be suspended except "where in cases of rebellion or invasion or the public safety may require it." The motion was quickly agreed to. Finally, the delegates put into the Constitution the clause that "no bill of attainder [that is, legislation punishing an individual for acts not forbidden by law] shall be passed, nor any ex post facto law." These three items were the beginning and end of the delegates' concern for guaranteed rights.

But Mason would not give up. On September 8, the Convention, now satisfied that the Constitution they had been writing was about complete, established a Committee of Style to rewrite the resolutions that had been passed in so piecemeal a fashion, to give it order, clarity, and elegance. The committee consisted of Alexander Hamilton, James Madison, Rufus King, and Gouverneur Morris, all nationalists, and William Samuel Johnson, who sometimes supported the nationalist position. It has generally been agreed, even by Madison, that the final draft of the American Constitution was written by that rake Gouverneur Morris. On September 12 the committee brought the draft back to the Convention for approval. The delegates had worked hard and long. They were tired and eager to go home. In the main they were pleased with the result, and suffused with relief that they had finally done it. The last thing they wanted was to have issues raised again that had long since been decided, in many cases several times. But such issues did get raised. The Convention voted to reduce the three-quarters majority needed to override a presidential veto to two-thirds, and took up and dropped one or two other small matters.

Finally George Mason rose and said that he "wished the plan had been prefaced with a bill of rights and would second a motion if made for the purpose. It would give great quiet to the people; and with the aid of the state declarations a bill might be prepared in a few hours." The implication was that Mason would have no difficulty designing one along the lines of the one he had written for Virginia eleven years earlier.

Not surprisingly, it was Elbridge Gerry who supplied the motion Mason wanted. Mason seconded it. Only Sherman spoke. He said, "The state Declarations of Rights are not repealed by this Constitution; and being in force are sufficient." The national legislature could not impinge on the rights of the people because its powers were limited to those enumerated. Mason protested that the new government would be paramount to the state constitutions and could override state bills of rights. Nobody agreed. On the vote, the state delegations voted unanimously against a bill of rights. Neither Gerry nor Mason could carry with them the delegates from their own states.

Why, then, did the delegates so adamantly reject a bill of rights? There are several reasons for it. For one, the Southerners had a special problem about it. When the lack of a bill of rights was raised during the fight for ratification in South Carolina, Charles Cotesworth Pinckney pointed out, "Such bills generally begin with declaring that all men are by nature born free. Now, we should make that declaration with very bad grace when a large part of our property consists in men who are actually born slaves."

Second, the state constitutions had their own bills of rights attached, and the states' righters especially felt that they should remain binding. As Sherman said, the state bills "were not repealed" by the new Constitution. (In fact, Sherman was probably wrong and Mason right: the new government would certainly have been able to override state bills under the authority that made the new constitution "supreme" over state constitutions.)

Third, some delegates feared that a new government might feel free to go ahead and do anything that was not explicitly prohibited; that is to say, rights not specifically stated might be taken not to exist. Later Hamilton said that a bill of rights "would contain various exceptions to powers which are not granted; and on this account would afford a colorable pretext to claim more than were granted."

Finally, by this point in the Convention the delegates were aware that they had produced a finely tuned instrument that could collapse if they began shifting bits and pieces around. They did not want to risk this by starting what could be a lengthy debate over a bill of rights.

Thus, for a variety of reasons, some of them not very profound, the men at Philadelphia refused Mason's pleas and left out of their Constitution any basic list of guaranteed rights.

The Committee of Style brought in its report on September 12. Over the next few days the delegates went through it, making minor changes, and turning down other suggestions. Finally, on September 15, they were done. But there were some who were not yet finished. Edmund Randolph, still desperately concerned about how the document would be received back home in Virginia, rose to announce that he had strong doubts about the new Constitution, and hoped that the states could offer amendments to it, and that these could be taken up at a second convention. Otherwise, "It would . . . be impossible for him to put his name to the instrument. Whether he should oppose it afterwards he would not then decide but he would not deprive himself of the freedom to do so."

Randolph was followed by George Mason, who put his objections much more forcefully: as it stood, the Constitution was likely to produce "monarchy, or a tyrannical aristocracy," and he would neither sign it nor support it at home. Finally Elbridge Gerry rose to announce that unless some provision was made for a second convention, he, too, would not sign the document. And then, at six o'clock at the end of a long day, the Convention voted to "agree to the Constitution as amended. All the states aye."

That was a Saturday. Over the weekend the finished document was written out in the version we know, and on Monday, September 17, the delegates once again assembled. The Constitution was read through one more time, and then Benjamin Franklin rose and gave to James Wilson to read a long speech, which said in essence:

> Mr. President, I confess that there are several parts of this constitution which I do not approve, but I am not sure that I shall never approve them. For having lived long, I have experienced many instances of being obliged by better information, or fuller consideration, to change opinions even on important subjects, which I once thought right, but found to be otherwise. . . . I doubt too whether any other convention we can obtain may be able to make a better constitution. . . . It therefore astonishes me, Sir, to find this system approaching so near to perfection as it does; and I think it will astonish our enemies. . . . Thus I consent, Sir, to this constitution because I expect no better, and because I am not sure that it is not the best.

Gouverneur Morris proposed that all the delegates sign, as witnesses to the unanimous consent of the states to the Constitution, in hopes of bringing Randolph, Mason, and Gerry around. But the tactic did not work. And just as they were about to sign Nathaniel Gorham moved that the ratio for representation in the House of Representatives be reduced from one congressman for each 40,000 population to one for each 30,000. The delegates were at this point startled to see Washington rise in support of the change and make his first speech at the Convention. Such was his influence that it was instantly agreed to. Then they signed. While they were doing so, Benjamin Franklin, in a famous incident, said that throughout the Convention he had looked at the sun painted on the back of the chair Washington had been seated in as president of the Convention. "I have, said he, often and often in the course of the session, and the vicissitudes of my hopes and fears as to its issue, looked at [the painted sun] behind the president without being able to tell whether it was rising or setting: But now at length I have the happiness to know that it is a rising and not a setting sun."

So they were done, and they went off to the City Tavern for dinner, where, no doubt, they were cheerful, pleased with themselves, and flushed with good fellowship. Then they all went home to see if they could get their handiwork ratified by the citizens of their respective states.

They were fully aware that they had a tough and possibly hopeless fight ahead of them to get ratified the Constitution that they had made with such difficulty. Many of them had serious doubts that they would succeed. George Washington, writing to his beloved Lafayette, when it appeared that the Constitution would actually be ratified after all, said that it was "beyond any thing we had a right to imagine or expect eighteen months ago, that it will demonstrate as visibly the finger of Providence as any possible event in the course of human affairs can ever designate it." And as it turned out, what nearly sank the Constitution was the lack of a bill of rights. Those opposed to the Constitution (the antifederalists, as historians call them) used it as a center point of their attacks.

The nationalists were forced to respond. For their main argument they fell back on the new concept of government that had emerged from the Convention—the idea that it was not a compact between the people and the governing body, but a delegation of powers by the people, which could be withdrawn at any time. The nationalists argued that as the people could take back delegated powers, there was no risk that the government could overreach, and therefore no need of a bill of rights. For example, if the government began closing down newspapers, the people could step in and, through one Constitutional device or another, order the government to desist.

The argument that no bill of rights was necessary because the people could withdraw power from the government was somewhat specious: would the people in fact have been able to stop a government determined, as in our example, to close down opposition newspapers? Yet in another sense, the use of this particular argument was a sound one, because it lay at the heart of the essential difference in viewpoint between the nationalists and the antifederalists. This difference has been carefully examined by the historian Cecelia Kenyon, in a widely quoted study called "Men of Little Faith," first published in 1955. Kenyon says:

Advocates and opponents of ratification may have belonged to different economic classes and been motivated by different economic interests. But they shared a large body of political ideas and attitudes, together with a common heritage of political institutions. For one thing, they shared a profound distrust of man's capacity to use power wisely and well. They believed self-interest to be the dominant motive of political behavior, no matter whether the form of government be republican or monarchical, and they believed in the necessity of constructing political machinery that would restrict the operation of self-interest and prevent men entrusted with political power from abusing it. This was the fundamental assumption of the men who wrote the Constitution, and of those who opposed its adoption, as well.

Kenyon then goes on to say, "The fundamental issue over which Federalists and Anti-Federalists split was the question of whether republican government could be extended to embrace a nation, or whether it must be limited to the comparatively small political and geographical units which the separate American states then constituted."

The antifederalists believed that unless the voters knew their representatives personally, and remained close enough to keep a watch on them, the representatives were bound to turn themselves into autocrats and enslave the people.

Implicit in the antifederalist position was a belief in the old idea of the social contract. The antis never really grasped the new idea that there was no contract between governors and governed but only a delegation of powers by the people to their representatives, and that those powers could be withdrawn at any moment. The antis were not at all sure that once the government got some power, the people would or could control it. To put it simply, thinkers on both sides mistrusted human nature; but the antis mistrusted it more. Further, they did not believe that sufficient control over government could be brought about through the extended republic, the internal mechanism of checks and balances, or the idea of a sovereign people in complete command of a servant government.

These people believed the new government could be far too strong. A president who could be reelected would manage, perhaps by underhanded means, to be reelected over and over again. The Senate had far too much power and would become an aristocracy. The Senate and the president were not separate enough, and would combine to control everything. The Constitution would give the new government the right to set up a capital, and it would become a fortified city from which the government would send forth its standing army to enslave the people. Many of the objections were simply "imaginary horribles" thrown up as scare tactics, but there were also a good many more reasonable fears: it did seem to many people that the new government would be a very powerful institution.

Feeling against the Constitution was, thus, genuine and widespread. It is probable that, at the outset, a *majority* of the people in many states were opposed to it. And yet, despite this, and despite the determined attacks of the antifederalists, the ratification process went ahead with astonishing swiftness. Delaware and New Jersey ratified quickly, a good indication of how much the little states wanted a strong national government, as long as they were assured some protection against the big states. Pennsylvania also ratified before 1787 was out, after a rough battle. Georgia ratified on January 2 of the next year, and Connecticut a week later. Massachusetts—where there was also a tough fight—followed in early February. That made six of the nine states required by Article VII, which provided that the Constitution would go into effect among those that ratified as soon as nine had done so.

There was a pause. Then, in April delegates to the Maryland convention ratified 63 to 11, and the next month South Carolina came in 149 to 73. Only one more state was needed; and in late June both New Hampshire and Virginia ratified, also after much battling and close votes. That left New York as the only important state outside the union, and it finally consented, again after a bitter fight, on July 26, by a vote of 30 to 27. The remaining two states, North Carolina and Rhode Island, held out until after the new government of the United States was established and George Washington was president; then they were forced to capitulate.

The turning points came with the Massachusetts and Virginia votes. Had both these two large and economically important states failed to ratify, it is unlikely that the union would have been formed. In Massachusetts opposition had come particularly from those western farmers, many of whom had fought with Daniel Shays only months before. They were suspicious of governments in any form and saw no good in a novel and powerful one. The key to the state lay in the hands of Governor John Hancock, a shrewd and vain politician, who stayed away from the ratifying convention pleading a convenient attack of gout, in order not to commit himself until he saw which way the people were leaning. He was finally persuaded to support the Constitution when it was hinted that if Virginia did not come in, as seemed entirely possible at that moment, Hancock instead of Washington might become president. Hancock's support was important in bringing around reluctant voters. Also important was the suggestion that the ratifying convention might recommend amendments to the Constitution for consideration by the new government. This device helped to allay fears on the part of the antis that they were being cast powerless into the hands of an aristocracy intending to turn them into serfs. Nationalists elsewhere quickly saw the value of this device and used it to get acceptance of the Constitution in their own states.

In Virginia the battle was even hotter than it was in Massachusetts. The antifederalists were led by Patrick Henry, generally regarded as the finest American orator of his day, or perhaps any day, who harangued the crowd for hours at a stretch and built a solid antifederalist camp at the ratifying convention. Although New Hampshire had provided the critical ninth ratification, the Virginians did not yet know that, and they felt that theirs was the crucial vote. New York was tending toward not ratifying, and if Virginia held out, New York would almost certainly have done so too. But on June 25 Virginia ratified, 89 to 79. And a month later the New York antifederalists saw that the game was over, and on the promise that amendments would be submitted to the new government, New York also ratified.

Why, then, considering the strong and emotionally committed opposition to the Constitution, did the nationalists triumph in eleven of thirteen states? There were several reasons. For one, the nationalists were led, in most states, by the very men who had written the Constitution—Madison in Virginia, Wilson in Pennsylvania, Hamilton in New York, Sherman in Connecticut. These men had for weeks been over every inch of the battleground again and again. They knew every argument for and against every comma in the Constitution. Furthermore, they went out knowing they were going to meet determined opposition, and they prepared themselves to run astute and carefully thought-out political campaigns. Without exception they handled themselves brilliantly in debate. Luther Martin and Patrick Henry would throw up oratorical fireworks, and in answer Madison, Wilson, Hamilton, Sherman, and the rest bore back relentlessly with carefully reasoned and usually unanswerable arguments. And if they did not have the answers, they could find them in a series of newspaper articles appearing in New York under the signature Publius—the famous *Federalist Papers,* written by Madison, Hamilton, and John Jay. The *Federalist Papers* were literary and closely reasoned, and did not have a large popular readership, but they made available to the nationalists brilliant and succinct answers to the arguments of the antis. The careful reasoning of the nationalists in state ratifying conventions wore away at the opposition. A Patrick Henry might raise vague specters of monarchy, but men are sometimes as susceptible to reason as to prejudice, and the antis never really did present a good case.

And this is a second reason why the antis failed in the end. The nationalists had something to offer and the antis did not. It was clear enough that the old government was finished. If the Constitution was not ratified, the union would dissolve, with what result nobody could calculate. As a consequence, the antifederalists could not simply ask for a vote of no on the Constitution, for that way lay possible disaster. Instead, they were forced to offer a call for a round of state conventions to propose changes to the Constitution, followed by a second convention like the one that had just concluded in Philadelphia. In response the nationalists could and did argue that this plan was absurd: it had been hard enough to get a Constitution through once; it would never happen a second time.

The argument told, because there were a great many people in the country who, however unnerved they might have been by the novelty of the proposed government, were far more unnerved by the prospect of disunion. Georgia, for example, had ratified quickly for precisely this reason. As Washington said at the time, ". . . if a weak state with Indians on its back and Spaniards on its flank does not see the necessity of a general government there must, I think, be wickedness or insanity in the way." Similarly, the small states saw the Constitution as their chance, perhaps their last one, to secure themselves against their monstrous neighbors. In New England, where much of the economy was based on fishing, shipping, and trading, there was recognition of the need for a sound government that could pay its debts and negotiate trade treaties. Both North and South wanted to see the British West Indies reopened to American trade. And of course the fear of another Shays' Rebellion was constantly in the minds of many people. In other words, the anxieties that had impelled Americans to send delegates to Philadelphia in the first place were still there.

A nice sense of how such people felt is offered by a speech given at the Massachusetts ratifying convention by a politically minded farmer named Jonathan Smith of Lanesboro in the western part of the state, who would no doubt be flabbergasted to know that his words have been reprinted many times for two hundred years. He was responding to a violently antinational speech by a man similar to himself named Amos Singletary. Smith said:

> Mr. President, I am a plain man and get my living by the plow. I am not
> used to speak in public, but I beg your leave to say a few words to my

brother plow joggers in this house. I have lived in a part of the country where I have known the worth of good government by the want of it. There was a black cloud that rose in the east last winter, and spread over the west [Shays' Rebellion]. . . . Now, Mr. President, when I saw this Constitution, I found that it was a cure for these disorders. I got a copy of it and read it over and over. I had been a member of the Convention to form our own state constitution, and had learnt something of the checks and balances of power, and I found them all there. I did not go to any lawyer to ask his opinion. We have no lawyers in our town, and we do well enough without. I formed my own opinion, and was pleased with this Constitution. My honorable old dady [*sic*] there [Amos Single-tary] won't think that I expect to be a Congressman, and swallow up the liberties of the people. I never had any post, nor do I want one. But I don't think worse of the Constitution because lawyers and men of learning, and moneyed men, are fond of it. I don't suspect that they want to get into Congress and abuse their power. . . . Some gentlemen think that our liberty and property are not safe in the hands of moneyed men, and men of learning. I am not of that mind. . . . Some gentlemen say, don't be in a hurry. Take time to consider, and don't take a leap in the dark. I say, take things in time, gather fruit when it is ripe. There is a time to sow and time to reap. We sowed our seed when we sent men to the Federal Convention. Now is the harvest. Now is the time to reap the fruit of our labor. And if we don't do it now, I am afraid we shall never have another opportunity.

The attitude of Jonathan Smith, Massachusetts farmer, proved, once the Constitution had become familiar to people, to be the majority one. Yes, there was always risk in delegating great powers; but the Constitution, with its system of checks and balances, offered as much protection as a reasonable man could expect. Even the Founding Fathers admitted that it was not exactly what any of them would have preferred; but it was the best that could be done, and on the whole it seemed good enough.

There was, however, one need that had to be supplied: a bill of rights. The demand for a bill of rights was voiced by convention after convention, and even before the ninth state had ratified the Constitution, it was obvious that one would be added. It was, thus, the people of the United States who put the Bill of Rights in the Constitution.

What remains surprising is how quickly antifederalist feeling died out once the new government was in place. Many of those who had been most vociferous in fighting it were ready to join it. James Monroe later became president. George Clinton and Elbridge Gerry became vice presidents, the latter under James Madison. Edmund Randolph became attorney general and later secretary of state. The unanimity was extraordinary. There were no antifederalist attempts to carry on the fight, no suggestions of secession, no bitter underground cabals. When the ninth state ratified, all across the union there were enormous celebrations, parades, fireworks, bonfires, huge ship models twenty and thirty feet long towed through the streets, speeches, joy. There was a sense everywhere among Americans that they had done something grand and glorious, something that would endure and light a lamp for the rest of the world to follow.

And they had.

Chapter Twenty-three

"The Most Remarkable Work"

Democracy is an exceedingly fragile instrument. In the years since 1787 it has failed far more frequently than it has succeeded. In this century alone democracy has gone under at one time or another in Germany, Spain, Italy, Russia; in numerous of the new nations in Africa and Asia; in many of the older nations of South America. Human beings continue to find it difficult to work out ways of governing themselves, and even today the majority of them live under autocratic governments, which reach deep into their daily lives. Democracy, with its attendant freedoms, has generally proven hard to achieve and even more difficult to maintain.

The American society that grew out of the Constitutional Convention is by no means perfect. The country is cursed with racial friction, which seems almost irradicable. It suffers from a painful knot of poor who, despite the honest efforts of several presidents, and huge sums of money, remain poor and suffering. Crime has reached epidemic proportions in the country's inner cities, and neither harsh tactics nor lenient ones have done much to diminish it. The nation has, in recent decades, shown too great a willingness to throw guns and bombs at foreign problems rather than to search rationally for more fruitful solutions, as the Founders would have done. And to some observers at least, the citizens of the country appear to be devoted far too much to a restless superficiality—the "California syndrome"—rather than to finding meaningful things to do with their lives.

Measured against an ideal, thus, the United States has fallen far short. Especially in the area of race relations did the Constitution, and subsequently the nation, fail to meet the ideals that the Founders professed. The generalizations we make here must always be qualified in that respect. But when we measure the United States against reality—the other nations of the world—

we are amazed at how well it has worked, for it is certainly the most prosperous nation in the world, and a case can be made that it is the freest. It is one of the few nations that do not require their citizens to carry identification papers. It is perhaps the only nation anywhere in which a group of ordinary people can run one of their own for public office with a realistic chance of getting a hearing. It is one of a very few nations in which it is virtually impossible to sustain for very long policies that the people do not want: the voice of the people, for better or worse, speaks louder in the United States than it does elsewhere.

Thus, without overlooking the suppurating wounds, especially poverty and racism, that continue to stain the American fabric, it is fair to say that the United States has gone a long way toward becoming what the men at Philadelphia wanted it to be: a prosperous, orderly nation in which no man need fear the arbitrary hand of a capricious government.

What, then, was it about the American Constitution that allowed American democracy not merely to survive but to thrive? Were the men who wrote that document as virtuous and wise as has been said, or was it all just a matter of chance?

The American Constitution works not for one single reason, but for several. The first of these is that the men at Philadelphia drew their document out of the American spirit. As Charles Pinckney said explicitly, and the other delegates quickly understood, this was to be an American document, for the American people. (This helps to explain why attempts to use it in other cultures have not always worked.) The men at the Convention understood their people. Most of the delegates had spent years in politics, and they knew how Americans thought and felt: they were a practical, commonsensical, and above all independent-minded people who wanted to get on with their lives with as little government interference as possible. Americans believed in God, but they were more materialistic than spiritual in their approach to life. They wanted a government that was practical and commonsensical, and that was precisely what the Founding Fathers gave them. The American Constitution was written not by ideologues tied to a theory, but by men with vast experience in politics, and it was drawn up to reflect political realities, not only as they saw them in 1787, but also as they thought they might be generations later.

Even if the Founding Fathers had wanted to ignore the American spirit— by following Hamilton's lead, for instance—they knew they could not, because, as should be sufficiently clear at this point, Americans would not and therefore could not be governed except by their own consent. James Madison and his supporters, especially James Wilson, were absolutely right when they insisted on building the new government on the people; and they were absolutely right when they replaced the old notion of the social contract with the new theory that said the people could delegate power any way they liked. Most of the men at Philadelphia were wise enough to agree with Madison and Wilson. In some cases it took them time to come to this conclusion, but in the end they voted to involve the people as closely in their own government as was believed practical at the time. They proposed direct elections for their representatives, the widest suffrage practiced anywhere in 1787, ratifying conventions based on broad popular participation, and perhaps most important, the chance for the people themselves to force policy on their government through frequent elections and the amendment machinery. They wanted a government that would, in the end, belong to the people, and therein lies one of the great strengths of American democracy.

Second, the American Constitution has worked because the men who wrote it had got human nature right. They believed that human beings had much good in them, but they also were sure that it was the bad that you had to watch out for. Almost all politically minded Americans of the day were profoundly distrustful of man's capacity to exercise power wisely or well. Self-interest, it was generally agreed, was the dominant determinant of human behavior. This, we also believe, is so, if we take "self-interest" in its broadest sense. Perhaps a time will come when people will often be willing to sacrifice their own best interest for the general good, but we do not expect it to be soon.

The Constitution, then, reflects the reality of human nature. It takes it for granted that the voters will not always make wise choices. It takes it for granted that people in government will frequently put their own interests above those of the people they are governing. The American government is made to work not only when good people are in power but also when it is in the hands of fools, knaves and ignoramuses, as it often has been.

Third, the Constitution permits a government that is strong enough to get done what has to be done. Some of the delegates had come hoping to establish a strong central government, but many others had to be convinced. As cautious as they were about giving the new government too much power, they were realistic enough to see that it had to have real authority; and they were able to give it that authority because they came to understand the concept of separation of powers, with its system of checks and balances, and to have faith that it would work.

Fourth, the Founding Fathers were very much concerned with the rights of minorities. They were concerned in part because they saw themselves and people like them as members of a creditor minority that the debtor majority would inevitably try to "oppress." But beyond their own self-interest, they recognized that the country even then was a collection of minorities. No section, no church, no occupational group really dominated.

There is nothing in the Constitution that says anything specific about minorities, but because the Founders were always conscious of the problem, they built protections for them into the entire fabric of the document. Most basic is the fact that in a Congress drawn from all over the nation, majorities would inevitably be collections of minorities, and it behooved everybody to be cautious about attacking any minority, for who knew whose turn it would be next? This was not necessarily the case in smaller jurisdictions, even ones as large as states, which tended to be homogeneous and might have majorities made of people from the same ethnic stock, the same church, the same occupations. A majority of Congregationalists might, for example, decide to pay their ministers, but nobody else's, out of everybody's taxes. But in a Congress where the membership was drawn from all over James Madison's extended republic, no single faction could dominate, and minorities would be safe.

A very important effect of the arrangement implicit in the extended republic and the diverse society it would house was the necessity for compromise. In the United States, nobody can have it all his own way. Just as the Founders were forced at every step of the way to make trades, so must American governments work in a spirit of give and take. The consequence has been that no single ideology has ever been able to dominate an American government. In short, American government under the Constitution is good for minorities.

In establishing protections for minorities the Founders at the same time built in a great deal of freedom for individuals. As a consequence, the American Constitution allows free rein to independent action, ambition, and the aggressive materialism that is a hallmark of the American character. The divided and checked government they created has difficulty interfering with these traits. Optimism and faith in the future are inherent in the American experience in part because the government can impose so few constraints on the people.

Finally, it was crucially important to the success of the document that these men were neither ideologues nor crass pragmatists. Beneath the theories, the sectional and economic interests that the delegates fought to promote, were deeply felt human emotions. While one feared too much authority, another shrank from the threat of anarchy. While one strove to create an orderly society, another struggled to allow free play of human interests. The Constitution, beyond all else, was forged in the heat of human emotion. In the end it reflected, for good or ill, the human spirit. It worked because it was made by human beings for the use of human beings, not as we might wish them to be, but as they really were.

The result has been a government that is more responsive to the people than most governments elsewhere. The American people, *when* sufficiently concerned and sufficiently aroused, can repair deficiencies in the social system. The machinery to do so is embedded in several places in the Constitution— in the fact that officials must stand for reelection and will obey popular mandates when made clear enough; in the people's power to make their feelings known through such civil rights as freedom of speech, the right of assembly, the right to petition; and finally in the power to amend the Constitution.

It is true enough that the people are frequently slow to become aroused, and slower to act. But we should remember that it was the people, finally, not governments, who forced the abolition of slavery, and impelled the government to regulate the corporations, give unions legal weapons, take a stand against pollution, end the Vietnam War, guarantee women the vote, and much else. These things were not done without a struggle, and it took perhaps too much time to get them done. But in the end the government of the United States is always responsive to public pressure when it is applied firmly enough for a long enough time. And this, too, was the wish of the Founding Fathers: they wanted a government that was responsive to the will of the people, but they did not want one that tacked from port to starboard in response to every vagrant wind the people blew.

It has been argued that, yes, the people *can* redress grievances when they perceive them, but that they frequently fail to perceive injuries done to them because their minds are clouded by news media held captive by various interests. It is, of course, perfectly true that the major newspapers, magazines, and broadcasting services are largely supported by industry and are unlikely to launch attacks on industrial capitalism.

Yet if the people are deluded, it is their own doing. A variety of political viewpoints and an enormous mass of information on every subject of consequence are readily available to anyone willing to make the effort to go to a library. It is hardly the fault of the Founding Fathers that most people would rather watch a situation comedy or a football game than *Meet the Press*.

The critical point is that the American people can force their government into action when they decide to. As a consequence American society is not riddled with caverns and tunnels filled with explosive gases—again excepting the racial problem. Only a few times since 1787 have Americans resorted to violence to get what they want; they can usually gain their ends through political means when they really want a change and are willing to work for it.

The delegates to the Constitutional Convention, clearly, made some very wise and rather sophisticated decisions on some very basic questions. It was one of the most extraordinary intellectual adventures ever undertaken by a group of human beings. To be sure they made their deals; to be sure they were guided by self-interest, temperament, the needs of their constituents. But they were also struggling with concepts, ideas, abstractions. There, on the Convention floor, they adapted the idea of the separation of powers to the American situation. There they wrestled with the concept of federalism and the implications growing out of the theory that all power was derived from the people. And despite their clashing interests and temperaments, they were determined to apply reason to the affairs of men. And the most remarkable thing is the extent to which they succeeded.

But they were human beings, and it seems to us that in four areas they failed to think their way through to the best solution. The first of these, as we have seen in some detail, was their refusal to see the racial problem for what it was. In viewing blacks as innately inferior to whites, they were behaving like men of their own time, but the result was to leave American society with a sore that continues to fester. Their failure to develop a more humanitarian policy toward the Indians is a little easier to understand: they saw the Indian tribes as "foreign nations," with whom the government would make treaties. As the United States ended at the Mississippi, it was assumed that it would be centuries before there would be any shortage of living space for Indians in the west, and we cannot reasonably expect the delegates to have considered what would happen when the whites had taken over the whole continent.

A second problem they did not fully understand is what we might call the "federal ambiguity." As we have seen, some of the delegates, such as Madison, Wilson, and Hamilton, would have reduced the powers of the states markedly; but the consensus of the Convention was that the states ought to be left a good deal of authority to run their own affairs, where no national interest was involved. The consequence has been a dual system in which congressmen are frequently torn between national and local interest. For example, regardless of what a congressman from Iowa believes about farm subsidies, he cannot possibly vote against them if he is to remain in office. A further consequence is that he may have to trade away his vote on, say, subsidies for mass transit, in order to get big-city congressmen to vote for his farm supports. He may thus be driven by the needs of his constituency to vote for a whole array of bills that he believes in his heart are not good national policy. The result is that Congress finds it very difficult to work out a consistent national policy on many basic issues, leaving a vacuum which most presidents are happy to fill. The Founding Fathers, we believe, should have been able to anticipate this problem, because they were faced with it at the Convention, where most of the delegates had positions that they could not abandon without risk that their home states would refuse to accept the document. Whether they could have done anything about this federal ambiguity is another question. Perhaps they could not have. In any case they never really addressed the problem, and provided no guidance to the congressman anguishing over his divided loyalties.

Third, it is our belief that the Convention failed adequately to deal with the question of judicial review. The delegates recognized that somebody would have to settle disputes between the states, and that somebody would have to decide when laws were in conflict with the Constitution. They assumed it would be the courts. But the idea of specifically giving any one body the last word troubled a good many of them, and in the end they deliberately left the matter vague.

The result was that the Supreme Court arrogated these functions to itself. In general, this was a good thing. If the Convention had dealt with the problem of judicial review, it would almost certainly have limited the power of the Court to interpret the Constitution as broadly as it has done in, for example, ending segregation, reapportioning state legislatures, or defining the powers of Congress and the president.

The power of the Supreme Court to interpret the Constitution is what has given the document the flexibility necessary to deal with changing conditions. Yet it is certain that the delegates would have been horrified to see how broadly the Court has used its interpreting power. They believed, at bottom, that if final power had to lie anywhere, it ought to be in the legislature, which they saw as the primary voice of the people. They certainly did not expect the judiciary to be dealing with day-to-day details of school systems, prisons, and fire departments as they do today.

We are inclined to agree. It seems to us that the Supreme Court is setting national policy on a wide variety of issues that ought properly to be decided by Congress—issues like abortion, women's rights, pornography, and others. In general, the Supreme Court has over the years reflected public opinion fairly well, but that is no guarantee that it will continue to do so. A president who by chance is able to make a number of appointments to the Court may well leave a Court with a social philosophy which a decade later may be wholly out of tune with the wishes of the people. (The Congress, of course, has constitutional authority to take back control in most of these areas, but without a wide popular mandate it is unlikely to make the effort.)

Finally, we believe, as we have said earlier, that the institution of the electoral college ought to be discarded. Few Americans realize that under the U. S. Constitution to this day, each state legislature may decide how presidential electors are chosen. Throughout much of our early history the legislatures themselves chose the electors. In some cases they were even appointed by the governor. There is nothing in the Constitution that prevents a return to such methods, though for political reasons it is highly unlikely. The real danger of the electoral system lies elsewhere, that is, in the possibility that even in a two-way race, the candidate with the smaller number of popular votes will receive a majority of the electoral votes. Neal R. Peirce has carefully studied the statistical chances of a popularly elected front-runner coming out second in the electoral college. Peirce says, "The experience of the past 50 years, . . . shows that in an election as close as that between Kennedy and Nixon, there is no better than a 50–50 chance that the electoral vote will agree with the popular vote as to the winner." Even with leads of over one percent, there would still be a one in four chance that the wrong candidate would win, this study says. A shift of one percent in the voting in a few pivotal states, caused by something as irrelevant as heavy rainstorms in areas where one party dominates, is all it would take to produce a minority president. It has happened, and it is certain to happen again. It might be worth trying to find another way of doing things before we get into difficulties.

That still leaves us with the question of whether or not the Constitution was just a happy accident. There are influential historians who think so—who believe that the delegates were mainly trying to devise a government that would allow them to line their own pockets, or that they were simply shrewd politicians who wanted a government that would keep the people in their place, but who had to compromise in order to sell the new government to their constituents.

We do not agree. This was, to begin with, an astonishing group of men. At least four of them were among the most remarkable men of modern times. There was Washington, who defeated the world's mightiest fighting force with his scrappy, ill-armed troops, and would go on to run a model presidency.

There was James Madison, one of America's keenest political thinkers of any age. There was Alexander Hamilton, who would in large measure design the American economic system. There was Benjamin Franklin, old and infirm, but nonetheless considered by all one of the great men of his time.

Just a cut below them was a group of brilliant, clear-thinking, and far-sighted men: Roger Sherman, Charles Pinckney, George Mason, James Wilson, Gouverneur Morris, and perhaps one or two others. And they were surrounded by another dozen or so men of high intelligence, who would have shone in any company but this one: William Paterson, John Dickinson, Robert Morris, C. C. Pinckney, John Rutledge, Oliver Ellsworth, William Samuel Johnson, Edmund Randolph, Elbridge Gerry, Rufus King, and more. There was among them at least one outright scoundrel, William Blount, and a few others of only moderate talent, like Gunning Bedford and John Francis Mercer. But at least twenty of these fifty-five men were remarkable people by any standard.

It is not surprising, then, that they were virtuous to a degree that we find exceeding rare in public personages today. For one thing, they truly and deeply believed in the concept of liberty. They were not willing to extend that liberty to blacks. But the idea of freedom meant something real to them, and if they did not plan to overturn society and put the bottom at the top, they at least would make a society in which the liberties of the bottom would be protected, and room would be made for the bottom to rise, with skill and industry.

For a second thing, they avoided a temptation that few designers of governments have resisted: to seize the opportunity to create a system that would leave them in charge. We need only look at recent governments all over the world to see how frequently this temptation has been given in to. Many of the delegates, certainly, expected to play roles in the new government, as so many of them had in the old. But they did not arrange things so that they would come to power automatically. Not all people would have done the same.

The writers of the American Constitution were not angels. They made mistakes: they left out a bill of rights, they did not confront the question of judicial review, and most tragically, they were so much people of their time that they could not see that blacks were as human as they were.

But withal, they rose above themselves far more than most men would have done in their place. And the generations of Americans who have grown up under the Constitution they struggled so hard to make are eternally in their debt.

Appendix A

THE ARTICLES OF CONFEDERATION
AGREED TO BY CONGRESS NOVEMBER 15, 1777
RATIFIED AND IN FORCE MARCH 1, 1781

To ALL TO WHOM these Presents shall come, we the undersigned Delegates of the States affixed to our Names send greeting. Whereas the Delegates of the United States of America in Congress assembled did on the fifteenth day of November in the Year of our Lord One Thousand Seven Hundred and Seventy seven, and in the Second Year of the Independence of America agree to certain articles of Confederation and perpetual Union between the States of New-hampshire, Massachusetts-bay, Rhodeisland and Providence Plantations, Connecticut, New York, New Jersey, Pennsylvania, Delaware, Maryland, Virginia, North-Carolina, South-Carolina and Georgia in the Words following, viz. "Articles of Confederation and perpetual Union between the states of Newhampshire, Massachusetts-bay, Rhodeisland and Providence Plantations, Connecticut, New-York, New-Jersey, Pennsylvania, Delaware, Maryland, Virginia, North-Carolina, South-Carolina and Georgia.

Art. I. The Stile of this confederacy shall be "The United States of America."

Art. II. Each state retains its sovereignty, freedom and independence, and every Power, Jurisdiction and right, which is not by this confederation expressly delegated to the United States, in Congress assembled.

Art. III. The said states hereby severally enter into a firm league of friendship with each other, for their common defence, the security of their Liberties, and their mutual and general welfare, binding themselves to assist each other, against all force offered to, or attacks made upon them, or any of them, on account of religion, sovereignty, trade, or any other pretence whatever.

Art. IV. The better to secure and perpetuate mutual friendship and inter-
course among the people of the different states in this union, the free inhabitants of each of these states, paupers, vagabonds and fugitives from Justice
excepted, shall be entitled to all privileges and immunities of free citizens in
the several states; and the people of each state shall have free ingress and
regress to and from any other state, and shall enjoy therein all the privileges
of trade and commerce, subject to the same duties, impositions and restrictions
as the inhabitants thereof respectively, provided that such restriction shall not
extend so far as to prevent the removal of property imported into any state,
to any other state of which the Owner is an inhabitant; provided also that no
imposition, duties or restriction shall be laid by any state, on the property of
the united states, or either of them.

If any Person guilty of, or charged with treason, felony, or other high
misdemeanor in any state, shall flee from Justice, and be found in any of the
united states, he shall upon demand of the Governor or executive power, of
the state from which he fled, be delivered up and removed to the state having
jurisdiction of his offence.

Full faith and credit shall be given in each of these states to the records, acts
and judicial proceedings of the courts and magistrates of every other state.

Art. V. For the more convenient management of the general interests of the
united states, delegates shall be annually appointed in such manner as the
legislature of each state shall direct, to meet in Congress on the first Monday
in November, in every year, with a power reserved to each state, to recal its
delegates, or any of them, at any time within the year, and to send others in
their stead, for the remainder of the Year.

No state shall be represented in Congress by less than two, nor by more than
seven Members; and no person shall be capable of being a delegate for more
than three years in any term of six years; nor shall any person, being a delegate, be capable of holding any office under the united states, for which
he, or another for his benefit receives any salary, fees or emolument of any
kind.

Each state shall maintain its own delegates in a meeting of the states, and
while they act as members of the committee of the states.

In determining questions in the united states, in Congress assembled, each
state shall have one vote.

Freedom of speech and debate in Congress shall not be impeached or
questioned in any Court, or place out of Congress, and the members of congress shall be protected in their persons from arrests and imprisonments,

during the time of their going to and from, and attendance on congress, except for treason, felony, or breach of the peace.

Art. VI. No state without the Consent of the united states in congress assembled, shall send any embassy to, or receive any embassy from, or enter into any conference, agreement, or alliance or treaty with any King, prince or state; nor shall any person holding any office of profit or trust under the united states, or any of them, accept of any present, emolument, office or title of any kind whatever from any king, prince or foreign state; nor shall the united states in congress assembled, or any of them, grant any title of nobility.

No two or more states shall enter into any treaty, confederation or alliance whatever between them, without the consent of the united states in congress assembled, specifying accurately the purposes for which the same is to be entered into, and how long it shall continue.

No state shall lay any imposts or duties, which may interfere with any stipulations in treaties, entered into by the united states in congress assembled, with any king, prince or state, in pursuance of any treaties already proposed by congress, to the courts of France and Spain.

No vessels of war shall be kept up in time of peace by any state, except such number only, as shall be deemed necessary by the united states in congress assembled, for the defence of such state, or its trade; nor shall any body of forces be kept up by any state, in time of peace, except such number only, as in the judgment of the united states, in congress assembled, shall be deemed requisite to garrison the forts necessary for the defence of such state; but every state shall always keep up a well regulated and disciplined militia, sufficiently armed and accoutred, and shall provide and constantly have ready for use, in public stores, a due number of field pieces and tents, and a proper quantity of arms, ammunition and camp equipage.

No state shall engage in any war without the consent of the united states in congress assembled, unless such state be actually invaded by enemies, or shall have received certain advice of a resolution being formed by some nation of Indians to invade such state, and the danger is so imminent as not to admit of a delay, till the united states in congress assembled can be consulted: nor shall any state grant commissions to any ships or vessels of war, nor letters of marque or reprisal, except it be after a declaration of war by the united states in congress assembled, and then only against the kingdom or state and the subjects thereof, against which war has been so declared, and under such regulations as shall be established by the united states in congress assembled, unless such state be infested by pirates, in which case vessels of war may be fitted out for that occasion, and kept so long as the danger shall continue, or until the united states in congress assembled shall determine otherwise.

Art. VII. When land-forces are raised by any state for the common defence, all officers of or under the rank of colonel, shall be appointed by the legislature of each state respectively by whom such forces shall be raised, or in such manner as such state shall direct, and all vacancies shall be filled up by the state which first made the appointment.

Art. VIII. All charges of war, and all other expences that shall be incurred for the common defence or general welfare, and allowed by the united states in congress assembled, shall be defrayed out of a common treasury, which shall be supplied by the several states, in proportion to the value of all land within each state, granted to or surveyed for any Person, as such land and the buildings and improvements thereon shall be estimated according to such mode as the united states in congress assembled, shall from time to time direct and appoint. The taxes for paying that proportion shall be laid and levied by the authority and direction of the legislatures of the several states within the time agreed upon by the united states in congress assembled.

Art. IX. The united states in congress assembled, shall have the sole and exclusive right and power of determining on peace and war, except in the cases mentioned in the sixth article—of sending and receiving ambassadors—entering into treaties and alliances, provided that no treaty of commerce shall be made whereby the legislative power of the respective states shall be restrained from imposing such imposts and duties on foreigners, as their own people are subjected to, or from prohibiting the exportation or importation of any species of goods or commodities whatsoever—of establishing rules for deciding in all cases, what captures on land or water shall be legal, and in what manner prizes taken by land or naval forces in the service of the united states shall be divided or appropriated.—of granting letters of marque and reprisal in times of peace —appointing courts for the trial of piracies and felonies committed on the high seas and establishing courts for receiving and determining finally appeals in all cases of captures, provided that no member of congress shall be appointed a judge of any of the said courts.

The united states in congress assembled shall also be the last resort on appeal in all disputes and differences now subsisting or that hereafter may arise between two or more states concerning boundary, jurisdiction or any other cause whatever; which authority shall always be exercised in the manner following. Whenever the legislative or executive authority or lawful agent of any state in controversy with another shall present a petition to congress, stating the matter in question and praying for a hearing, notice thereof shall be given by order of congress to the legislative or executive authority of the other state in controversy, and a day assigned for the appearance of the parties by their lawful agents, who shall then be directed to appoint by joint consent, commissioners or judges to constitute a court for hearing and determining the matter in question: but if they cannot agree, congress shall name three persons out of each of the united states, and from the list of such persons each party shall alternately strike out one, the petitioners beginning, until the number shall be reduced to thirteen; and from that number not less than seven, nor more than nine names as congress shall direct, shall in the presence of congress be drawn out by lot, and the persons whose names shall be so drawn or any five of them, shall be commissioners or judges, to hear and finally determine the controversy, so always as a major part of the judges who shall hear the cause shall agree in the determination: and if either party shall neglect to attend at the day appointed, without shewing reasons, which congress shall judge sufficient, or being present shall refuse to strike, the congress shall proceed to nominate three persons out of each state, and the secretary of congress shall strike in behalf of such party absent or refusing; and the judgment and sentence of the court to be appointed, in the manner before prescribed, shall be final and conclusive; and if any of the parties shall refuse to submit to the authority of such court, or to appear to defend their claim or cause, the court shall nevertheless proceed to pronounce sentence, or judgment, which shall in like manner be final and decisive, the judgment or sentence and other proceedings being in either case transmitted to congress, and lodged among the acts of congress for the security of the parties concerned. provided that every commissioner, before he sits in judgment, shall take an oath to be administered by one of the judges of the supreme or superior court of the state, where the cause shall be tried, "well and truly to hear and determine the matter in question, according to the best of his judgment, without favour, affection or hope of reward:" provided also that no state shall be deprived of territory for the benefit of the united states.

All controversies concerning the private right of soil claimed under different grants of two or more states, whose jurisdictions as they may respect such lands, and the states which passed such grants are adjusted, the said grants or either of them being at the same time claimed to have originated antecedent to such settlement of jurisdiction, shall on the petition of either party to the congress of the united states, be finally determined as near as may be in the same manner as is before prescribed for deciding disputes respecting territorial jurisdiction between different states.

The united states in congress assembled shall also have the sole and exclusive right and power of regulating the alloy and value of coin struck by their own authority, or by that of the respective states—fixing the standard of weights and measures throughout the united states.—regulating the trade and managing all affairs with the Indians, not members of any of the states, provided that the legislative right of any state within its own limits be not infringed or violated—establishing and regulating post-offices from one state to another, throughout all the united states, and exacting such postage on the papers passing thro' the same as may be requisite to defray the expences of the said office—appointing all officers of the land forces, in the service of the united states, excepting regimental officers.—appointing all the officers of the naval forces, and commissioning all officers whatever in the service of the united states—making rules for the government and regulation of the said land and naval forces, and directing their operations.

The united states in congress assembled shall have authority to appoint a committee, to sit in the recess of congress, to be denominated "A Committee of the States," and to consist of one delegate from each state; and to appoint such other committees and civil officers as may be necessary for managing the general affairs of the united states under their direction—to appoint one of their number to preside, provided that no person be allowed to serve in the office of president more than one year in any term of three years; to ascertain the necessary sums of Money to be raised for the service of the united states, and to appropriate and apply the same for defraying the public expences—to borrow money, or emit bills on the credit of the united states, transmitting every half year to the respective states an account of the sums of money so borrowed or emitted,—to build and equip a navy—to agree upon the number of land forces, and to make requisitions from each state for its quota, in proportion to the number of white inhabitants in such state; which requisition shall be binding, and thereupon the legislature of each state shall appoint the regimental officers, raise the men and cloath, arm and equip them in a soldier like manner, at the expence of the united states, and the officers and men so cloathed, armed and equipped shall march to the place appointed, and within the time agreed on by the united states in congress assembled: But if the united states in congress assembled shall, on consideration of circumstances judge proper that any state should not raise men, or should raise a smaller number than its quota, and that any other state should raise a greater number of men than the quota thereof, such extra number shall be raised, officered, cloathed, armed and equipped in the same manner as the quota of such state, unless the legislature of such state shall judge that such extra number cannot be safely spared out of the same, in which case they shall raise officer, cloath, arm and equip as many of such extra number as they judge can be safely spared. And the officers and men so cloathed, armed and equipped, shall march to the place appointed, and within the time agreed on by the united states in congress assembled.

The united states in congress assembled shall never engage in a war, nor grant letters of marque and reprisal in time of peace, nor enter into any treaties or alliances, nor coin money, nor regulate the value thereof, nor ascertain the sums and expences necessary for the defence and welfare of the united states, or any of them, nor emit bills, nor borrow money on the credit of the united states, nor appropriate money, nor agree upon the number of vessels of war, to be built or purchased, or the number of land or sea forces to be raised, nor appoint a commander in chief of the army or navy, unless nine states assent to the same: nor shall a question on any other point, except for adjourning from day to day be determined, unless by the votes of a majority of the united states in congress assembled.

The congress of the united states shall have power to adjourn to any time within the year, and to any place within the united states, so that no period of adjournment be for a longer duration than the space of six Months, and shall publish the Journal of their proceedings monthly, except such parts thereof relating to treaties, alliances or military operations as in their judgment require secresy; and the yeas and nays of the delegates of each state on any question shall be entered on the Journal, when it is desired by any delegate; and the delegates of a state, or any of them, at his or their request shall be furnished with a transcript of the said Journal, except such parts as are above excepted, to lay before the legislatures of the several states.

Art. X. The committee of the states, or any nine of them, shall be authorised to execute, in the recess of congress, such of the powers of congress as the united states in congress assembled, by the consent of nine states, shall from time to time think expedient to vest them with; provided that no power be delegated to the said committee, for the exercise of which, by the articles of confederation, the voice of nine states in the congress of the united states assembled is requisite.

Art. XI. Canada acceding to this confederation, and joining in the measures of the united states, shall be admitted into, and entitled to all the advantages of this union: but no other colony shall be admitted into the same, unless such admission be agreed to by nine states.

Art. XII. All bills of credit emitted, monies borrowed and debts contracted by, or under the authority of congress, before the assembling of the united states, in pursuance of the present confederation, shall be deemed and considered as a charge against the united states, for payment and satisfaction whereof the said united states, and the public faith are hereby solemnly pledged.

Art. XIII. Every state shall abide by the determinations of the united states in congress assembled, on all questions which by this confederation are submitted to them. And the Articles of this confederation shall be inviolably observed by every state, and the union shall be perpetual; nor shall any alteration at any time hereafter be made in any of them; unless such alteration be agreed to in a congress of the united states, and be afterwards confirmed by the legislatures of every state.

AND WHEREAS it hath pleased the Great Governor of the World to incline the hearts of the legislatures we respectively represent in congress, to approve of, and to authorize us to ratify the said articles of confederation and perpetual union. KNOW YE that we the under-signed delegates, by virtue of the power and authority to us given for that purpose, do by these presents, in the name and in behalf of our respective constituents, fully and entirely ratify and confirm each and every of the said articles of confederation and perpetual union, and all and singular the matters and things therein contained: And we do further solemnly plight and engage the faith of our respective constituents, that they shall abide by the determinations of the united states in congress assembled, on all questions, which by the said confederation are submitted to them. And that the articles thereof shall be inviolably observed by the states we respectively represent, and that the union shall be perpetual. In Witness whereof we have hereunto set our hands in Congress. Done at Philadelphia in the state of Pennsylvania the ninth Day of July in the Year of our Lord one Thousand seven Hundred and Seventy-eight, and in the third year of the independence of America.

Appendix B

THE CONSTITUTION OF THE UNITED STATES

WE THE PEOPLE of the United States, in Order to form a more perfect Union, establish Justice, insure domestic Tranquility, provide for the common defence, promote the general Welfare, and secure the Blessings of Liberty to ourselves and our Posterity, do ordain and establish this Constitution for the United States of America.

ART. I

Sec. 1. All legislative Powers herein granted shall be vested in a Congress of the United States, which shall consist of a Senate and House of Representatives.

Sec. 2. The House of Representatives shall be composed of Members chosen every second Year by the People of the several States, and the Electors in each State shall have the Qualifications requisite for Electors of the most numerous Branch of the State Legislature.

No Person shall be a Representative who shall not have attained to the Age of twenty five Years, and been seven Years a Citizen of the United States, and who shall not, when elected, be an Inhabitant of that State in which he shall be chosen.

Representatives and direct Taxes shall be apportioned among the several States which may be included within this Union, according to their respective Numbers, which shall be determined by adding to the whole Number of free Persons, including those bound to Service for a Term of Years, and excluding Indians not taxed, three fifths of all other Persons. The actual Enumeration shall be made within three Years after the first Meeting of the Congress of the United States, and within every subsequent Term of ten Years, in such Manner as they shall by Law direct. The Number of Representatives shall not exceed one for every thirty Thousand, but each State shall have at Least one Representative; and until such enumeration shall be made, the State of New Hampshire shall be entitled to chuse three, Massachusetts eight, Rhode-Island and Providence Plantations one, Connecticut five, New-York six, New Jersey four, Pennsylvania eight, Delaware one, Maryland six, Virginia ten, North Carolina five, South Carolina five, and Georgia three.

When vacancies happen in the Representation from any State, the Executive Authority thereof shall issue Writs of Election to fill such Vacancies.

The House of Representatives shall chuse their Speaker and other Officers; and shall have the sole Power of Impeachment.

Sec. 3. The Senate of the United States shall be composed of two Senators from each State, chosen by the Legislature thereof, for six Years; and each Senator shall have one Vote.

Immediately after they shall be assembled in Consequence of the first Election, they shall be divided as equally as may be into three Classes. The Seats of the Senators of the first Class shall be vacated at the Expiration of the second Year, of the second Class at the Expiration of the fourth Year, and of the third Class at the Expiration of the sixth Year, so that one third may be chosen every second Year; and if Vacancies happen by Resignation, or otherwise, during the Recess of the Legislature of any State, the Executive thereof may make temporary Appointments until the next Meeting of the Legislature, which shall then fill such Vacancies.

No Person shall be a Senator who shall not have attained to the Age of thirty Years, and been nine Years a Citizens of the United States, and who shall not, when elected, be an Inhabitant of that State for which he shall be chosen.

The Vice President of the United States shall be President of the Senate, but shall have no Vote, unless they be equally divided.

The Senate shall chuse their other Officers, and also a President pro tempore, in the Absence of the Vice President, or when he shall exercise the Office of President of the United States.

The Senate shall have the sole Power to try all Impeachments. When sitting for that Purpose, they shall be on Oath or Affirmation. When the President of the United States is tried, the Chief Justice shall preside: And no Person shall be convicted without the Concurrence of two thirds of the Members present.

Judgment in Cases of Impeachment shall not extend further than to removal from Office, and disqualification to hold and enjoy any Office of honor, Trust or Profit under the United States: but the Party convicted shall nevertheless be liable and subject to Indictment, Trial, Judgment and Punishment, according to Law.

Sec. 4. The Times, Places and Manner of holding Elections for Senators and Representatives, shall be prescribed in each State by the Legislature thereof; but the Congress may at any time by Law make or alter such Regulations, except as to the Places of chusing Senators.

The Congress shall assemble at least once in every Year, and such Meeting shall be on the first Monday in December, unless they shall by Law appoint a different Day.

Sec. 5. Each House shall be the Judge of the Elections, Returns and Qualifications of its own Members, and a Majority of each shall constitute a Quorum to do Business; but a smaller Number may adjourn from day to day, and may be authorized to compel the Attendance of absent Members, in such Manner, and under such Penalties as each House may provide.

Each House may determine the Rules of its Proceedings, punish its Members for disorderly Behaviour, and, with the Concurrence of two thirds, expel a Member.

Each House shall keep a Journal of its Proceedings, and from time to time publish the same, excepting such Parts as may in their Judgment require Secrecy; and the Yeas and Nays of the Members of either House on any question shall, at the Desire of one fifth of those Present, be entered on the Journal.

Neither House, during the Session of Congress, shall, without the Consent of the other, adjourn for more than three days, nor to any other Place than that in which the two Houses shall be sitting.

Sec. 6. The Senators and Representatives shall receive a Compensation for their Services, to be ascertained by Law, and paid out of the Treasury of the United States. They shall in all Cases, except Treason, Felony and Breach of the Peace, be privileged from Arrest during their Attendance at the Session of their respective Houses, and in going to and returning from the same; and for any Speech or Debate in either House, they shall not be questioned in any other Place.

No Senator or Representative shall, during the Time for which he was elected, be appointed to any civil Office under the Authority of the United States which shall have been created, or the Emoluments whereof shall have been encreased during such time; and no Person holding any Office under the United States, shall be a Member of either House during his Continuance in Office.

Sec. 7. All Bills for raising Revenue shall originate in the House of Representatives; but the Senate may propose or concur with Amendments as on other Bills.

Every Bill which shall have passed the House of Representatives and the Senate, shall, before it become a Law, be presented to the President of the United States; If he approve he shall sign it, but if not he shall return it, with his Objections to that House in which it shall have originated, who shall enter the Objections at large on their Journal, and proceed to reconsider it. If after such Reconsideration two thirds of that House shall agree to pass the Bill, it shall be sent, together with the Objections, to the other House, by which it shall likewise be reconsidered, and if approved by two thirds of that House, it shall become a Law. But in all such Cases the Votes of both Houses shall be determined by yeas and Nays, and the Names of the Persons voting for and against the Bill shall be entered on the Journal of each House respectively. If any Bill shall not be returned by the President within ten Days (Sundays excepted) after it shall have been presented to him, the Same shall be a Law, in like Manner as if he had signed it, unless the Congress by their Adjournment prevent its Return, in which Case it shall not be a Law.

Every Order, Resolution, or Vote to which the Concurrence of the Senate and House of Representatives may be necessary (except on a question of Adjournment) shall be presented to the President of the United States; and before the Same shall take Effect, shall be approved by him, or being disapproved by him, shall be repassed by two thirds of the Senate and House of Representatives, according to the Rules and Limitations prescribed in the Case of a Bill.

Sec. 8. The Congress shall have Power To lay and collect Taxes, Duties, Imposts and Excises, to pay the Debts and provide for the common Defence and general Welfare of the United States; but all Duties, Imposts and Excises shall be uniform throughout the United States;

To borrow Money on the credit of the United States;

To regulate Commerce with foreign Nations, and among the several States, and with the Indian Tribes;

To establish an uniform Rule of Naturalization, and uniform Laws on the subject of Bankruptcies throughout the United States;

To coin Money, regulate the Value thereof, and of foreign Coin, and fix the Standard of Weights and Measures;

To provide for the Punishment of counterfeiting the Securities and current Coin of the United States;

To establish Post Offices and post Roads;

To promote the Progress of Science and useful Arts, by securing for limited Times to Authors and Inventors the exclusive Right to their respective Writings and Discoveries;

To constitute Tribunals inferior to the supreme Court;

To define and punish Piracies and Felonies committed on the high Seas, and Offences against the Law of Nations;

To declare War, grant Letters of Marque and Reprisal, and make Rules concerning Captures on Land and Water;

To raise and support Armies, but no Appropriation of Money to that Use shall be for a longer Term than two Years;

To provide and maintain a Navy;

To make Rules for the Government and Regulation of the land and naval Forces;

To provide for calling forth the Militia to execute the Laws of the Union, suppress Insurrections and repel Invasions;

To provide for organizing, arming, and disciplining, the Militia, and for governing such Part of them as may be employed in the Service of the United States, reserving to the States respectively, the Appointment of the Officers, and the Authority of training the Militia according to the discipline prescribed by Congress;

To exercise exclusive Legislation in all Cases whatsoever, over such District (not exceeding ten Miles square) as may, by Cession of particular States, and the Acceptance of Congress, become the Seat of the Government of the United States, and to exercise like Authority over all Places purchased by the Consent of the Legislature of the State in which the Same shall be, for the Erection of Forts, Magazines, Arsenals, dock-Yards, and other needful Buildings;—And

To make all Laws which shall be necessary and proper for carrying into Execution the foregoing Powers, and all other Powers vested by this Constitution in the Government of the United States, or in any Department or Officer thereof.

Sec. 9. The Migration or Importation of such Persons as any of the States now existing shall think proper to admit, shall not be prohibited by the Congress prior to the Year one thousand eight hundred and eight, but a Tax or duty may be imposed on such Importation, not exceeding ten dollars for each Person.

The Privilege of the Writ of Habeas Corpus shall not be suspended, unless when in Cases of Rebellion or Invasion the public Safety may require it.

No Bill of Attainder or ex post facto Law shall be passed.

No Capitation, or other direct, Tax shall be laid, unless in Proportion to the Census or Enumeration herein before directed to be taken.

No Tax or Duty shall be laid on Articles exported from any State.

No Preference shall be given by any Regulation of Commerce or Revenue to the Ports of one State over those of another: nor shall Vessels bound to, or from, one State, be obliged to enter, clear, or pay Duties in another.

No Money shall be drawn from the Treasury, but in Consequence of Appropriations made by Law; and a regular Statement and Account of the Receipts and Expenditures of all public Money shall be published from time to time.

No Title of Nobility shall be granted by the United States: And no Person holding any Office of Profit or Trust under them, shall, without the Consent of the Congress, accept of any present, Emolument, Office, or Title, of any kind whatever, from any King, Prince or foreign State.

Sec. 10. No State shall enter into any Treaty, Alliance, or Confederation; grant Letters of Marque and Reprisal; coin Money; emit Bills of Credit; make any Thing but gold and silver Coin a Tender in Payment of Debts; pass any Bill of Attainder, ex post facto Law, or Law impairing the Obligation of Contracts, or grant any Title of Nobility.

No State shall, without the Consent of the Congress, lay any Imposts or Duties on Imports or Exports, except what may be absolutely necessary for executing it's inspection Laws: and the net Produce of all Duties and Imposts, laid by any State on Imports or Exports, shall be for the Use of the Treasury of the United States; and all such Laws shall be subject to the Revision and Controul of the Congress.

No State shall, without the Consent of Congress, lay any Duty of Tonnage, keep Troops, or Ships of War in time of Peace, enter into any Agreement or Compact with another State, or with a foreign Power, or engage in War, unless actually invaded, or in such imminent Danger as will not admit of delay.

ART. II

Sec. 1. The executive Power shall be vested in a President of the United States of America. He shall hold his Office during the Term of four Years, and, together with the Vice President, chosen for the same Term, be elected, as follows

Each State shall appoint, in such Manner as the Legislature thereof may direct, a Number of Electors, equal to the whole Number of Senators and Representatives to which the State may be entitled in the Congress: but no

Senator or Representative, or Person holding an Office of Trust or Profit under the United States, shall be appointed an Elector.

The Electors shall meet in their respective States, and vote by Ballot for two Persons, of whom one at least shall not be an Inhabitant of the same State with themselves. And they shall make a List of all the Persons voted for, and of the Number of Votes for each; which List they shall sign and certify, and transmit sealed to the Seat of the Government of the United States, directed to the President of the Senate. The President of the Senate shall, in the Presence of the Senate and House of Representatives, open all the Certificates, and the Votes shall then be counted. The Person having the greatest Number of Votes shall be the President, if such Number be a Majority of the whole Number of Electors appointed; and if there be more than one who have such Majority, and have an equal Number of Votes, then the House of Representatives shall immediately chuse by Ballot one of them for President; and if no person have a Majority, then from the five highest on the List the said House shall in like Manner chuse the President. But in chusing the President, the Votes shall be taken by States, the Representation from each State having one Vote; A quorum for this Purpose shall consist of a Member or Members from two thirds of the States, and a Majority of all the States shall be necessary to a Choice. In every Case, after the Choice of the President, the Person having the greatest Number of Votes of the Electors shall be the Vice President. But if there should remain two or more who have equal Votes, the Senate shall chuse from them by Ballot the Vice President.

The Congress may determine the Time of chusing the Electors, and the Day on which they shall give their Votes; which Day shall be the same throughout the United States.

No Person except a natural born Citizen, or a Citizen of the United States, at the time of the Adoption of this Constitution, shall be eligible to the Office of President; neither shall any Person be eligible to that Office who shall not have attained to the Age of thirty five Years, and been fourteen Years a Resident within the United States.

In Case of the Removal of the President from Office, or of his Death, Resignation, or Inability to discharge the Powers and Duties of the said Office, the Same shall devolve on the Vice President, and the Congress may by Law provide for the Case of Removal, Death, Resignation or Inability, both of the President and Vice President, declaring what Officer shall then act as President, and such Officer shall act accordingly, until the Disability be removed, or a President shall be elected.

The President shall, at stated Times, receive for his Services, a Compensation, which shall neither be encreased nor diminished during the Period for which he shall have been elected, and he shall not receive within that Period any other Emolument from the United States, or any of them.

Before he enter on the Execution of his Office, he shall take the following Oath or Affirmation:—"I do solemnly swear (or affirm) that I will faithfully execute the Office of President of the United States, and will to the best of my Ability, preserve, protect and defend the Constitution of the United States."

Sec. 2. The President shall be Commander in Chief of the Army and Navy of the United States, and of the Militia of the several States, when called into the actual Service of the United States; he may require the Opinion, in writing, of the principal Officer in each of the executive Departments, upon any Subject relating to the Duties of their respective Offices, and he shall have Power to grant Reprieves and Pardons for Offences against the United States, except in Cases of Impeachment.

He shall have Power, by and with the Advice and Consent of the Senate, to make Treaties, provided two thirds of the Senators present concur; and he shall nominate, and by and with the Advice and Consent of the Senate, shall appoint Ambassadors, other public Ministers and Consuls, Judges of the supreme Court, and all other Officers of the United States, whose Appointments are not herein otherwise provided for, and which shall be established by Law: but the Congress may by Law vest the Appointment of such inferior Officers, as they think proper, in the President alone, in the Courts of Law, or in the Heads of Departments.

The President shall have Power to fill up all Vacancies that may happen during the Recess of the Senate, by granting Commissions which shall expire at the End of their next Session.

Sec. 3. He shall from time to time give to the Congress Information of the State of the Union, and recommend to their Consideration such Measures as he shall judge necessary and expedient; he may, on extraordinary Occasions, convene both Houses, or either of them, and in Case of Disagreement between them, with Respect to the Time of Adjournment, he may adjourn them to such Time as he shall think proper; he shall receive Ambassadors and other public Ministers; he shall take Care that the Laws be faithfully executed, and shall Commission all the Officers of the United States.

Sec. 4. The President, Vice President and all civil Officers of the United States, shall be removed from Office on Impeachment for, and Conviction of, Treason, Bribery, or other high Crimes and Misdemeanors.

ART. III

Sec. 1. The judicial Power of the United States, shall be vested in one supreme Court, and in such inferior Courts as the Congress may from time to time ordain and establish. The Judges, both of the supreme and inferior Courts, shall hold their Offices during good Behaviour, and shall, at stated Times, receive for their Services, a Compensation, which shall not be diminished during their Continuance in Office.

Sec. 2. The judicial Power shall extend to all Cases, in Law and Equity, arising under this Constitution, the Laws of the United States, and Treaties made, or which shall be made, under their Authority;—to all Cases affecting Ambassadors, other public Ministers and Consuls;—to all Cases of admiralty and maritime Jurisdiction;—to Controversies to which the United States shall be a Party;—to Controversies between two or more States;—between a State and Citizens of another State;—between Citizens of different States,—between Citizens of the same State claiming Lands under Grants of different States, and between a State, or the Citizens thereof, and foreign States, Citizens or Subjects.

In all Cases affecting Ambassadors, other public Ministers and Consuls, and those in which a State shall be Party, the supreme Court shall have original Jurisdiction. In all the other Cases before mentioned, the supreme Court shall have appellate Jurisdiction, both as to Law and Fact, with such Exceptions, and under such Regulations as the Congress shall make.

The Trial of all Crimes, except in Cases of Impeachment, shall be by Jury; and such Trial shall be held in the State where the said Crimes shall have been committed; but when not committed within any State, the Trial shall be at such Place or Places as the Congress may by Law have directed.

Sec. 3. Treason against the United States, shall consist only in levying War against them, or in adhering to their Enemies, giving them Aid and Comfort. No Person shall be convicted of Treason unless on the Testimony of two Witnesses to the same overt Act, or on Confession in open Court.

The Congress shall have Power to declare the Punishment of Treason, but no Attainder of Treason shall work Corruption of Blood, or Forfeiture except during the Life of the Person attainted.

ART. IV

Sec. 1. Full Faith and Credit shall be given in each State to the Public Acts, Records, and judicial Proceedings of every other State. And the Congress may by general Laws prescribe the Manner in which such Acts, Records and Proceedings shall be proved, and the Effect thereof.

Sec. 2. The Citizens of each State shall be entitled to all Privileges and Immunities of Citizens in the several States.

A Person charged in any State with Treason, Felony, or other Crime, who shall flee from Justice, and be found in another State, shall on Demand of the executive Authority of the State from which he fled, be delivered up, to be removed to the State having Jurisdiction of the Crime.

No Person held to Service or Labour in one State, under the Laws thereof, escaping into another, shall, in Consequence of any Law or Regulation therein, be discharged from such Service or Labour, but shall be delivered up on Claim of the Party to whom such Service or Labour may be due.

Sec. 3. New States may be admitted by the Congress into this Union; but no new States shall be formed or erected within the Jurisdiction of any other State; nor any State be formed by the Junction of two or more States, or Parts of States, without the Consent of the Legislatures of the States concerned as well as of the Congress.

The Congress shall have Power to dispose of and make all needful Rules and Regulations respecting the Territory or other Property belonging to the United States; and nothing in this Constitution shall be so construed as to Prejudice any Claims of the United States, or of any particular State.

Sec. 4. The United States shall guarantee to every State in this Union a Republican Form of Government, and shall protect each of them against Invasion; and on Application of the Legislature, or of the Executive (when the Legislature cannot be convened) against domestic Violence.

ART. V

The Congress, whenever two thirds of both Houses shall deem it necessary, shall propose Amendments to this Constitution, or, on the Application of the Legislature of two thirds of the several States, shall call a Convention for proposing Amendments, which, in either Case, shall be valid to all Intents and Purposes, as Part of this Constitution, when ratified by the Legislatures of three fourths of the several States, or by Conventions in three fourths thereof, as the one or the other Mode of Ratification may be proposed by the Congress; Provided that no Amendment which may be made prior to the Year One thousand eight hundred and eight shall in any Manner affect the first and fourth Clauses in the Ninth Section of the first Article; and that no State, without its Consent, shall be deprived of it's equal Suffrage in the Senate.

ART. VI

All Debts contracted and Engagements entered into, before the Adoption of this Constitution, shall be as valid against the United States under this Constitution, as under the Confederation.

This Constitution, and the Laws of the United States which shall be made in Pursuance thereof; and all Treaties made, or which shall be made, under the Authority of the United States, shall be the supreme Law of the Land; and the Judges in every State shall be bound thereby, any Thing in the Constitution or Laws of any State to the Contrary notwithstanding.

The Senators and Representatives before mentioned, and the Members of the several State Legislatures, and all executive and judicial Officers, both of the United States and of the several States, shall be bound by Oath or Affirmation, to support this Constitution; but no religious Test shall ever be required as a Qualification to any Office or public Trust under the United States.

ART. VII

The Ratification of the Conventions of nine States, shall be sufficient for the Establishment of this Constitution between the States so ratifying the Same.

Done in Convention by the Unanimous Consent of the States present the Seventeenth Day of September in the Year of our Lord one thousand seven hundred and Eighty seven and of the Independence of the United States of America the Twelfth. In witness whereof We have hereunto subscribed our Names,

G⁰ WASIIINGTON—Presidᵗ
and deputy from Virginia

New Hampshire	JOHN LANGDON		
	NICHOLAS GILMAN		GEO: READ
			GUNNING BEDFORD jun
		Delaware	JOHN DICKINSON
			RICHARD BASSETT
Massachusetts	NATHANIEL GORHAM		JACO: BROOM
	RUFUS KING		
			JAMES MᶜHENRY
Connecticut	Wᴹ Samᴸ JOHNSON	Maryland	DAN OF Sᵀ Thoˢ JENIFER
	ROGER SHERMAN		Danᴸ CARROLL
New York	ALEXANDER HAMILTON	Virginia	JOHN BLAIR—
			JAMES MADISON JR.

New Jersey	WIL: LIVINGSTON DAVID BREARLEY W^M PATERSON JONA: DAYTON	North Carolina	W^M BLOUNT RICH^D DOBBS SPAIGHT HU WILLIAMSON

Pennsylvania	B. FRANKLIN THOMAS MIFFLIN ROB^T MORRIS GEO. CLYMER THO^S FITZSIMONS JARED INGERSOLL JAMES WILSON GOUV MORRIS	South Carolina	J. RUTLEDGE CHARLES COTES- WORTH PINCKNEY CHARLES PINCKNEY PIERCE BUTLER
		Georgia	WILLIAM FEW ABR BALDWIN

Citations to Sources

This book is written largely from Madison's "Notes of Debates in the Federal Convention of 1787," of which there are several versions. The most complete edition is that of Max Farrand, published in 1911 as *The Records of the Federal Convention of 1787* and revised and reprinted in 1937. In most instances, our quotations are taken from a one-volume edition prepared by Adrienne Koch. Another work of constant reference is Charles Warren's *The Making of the Constitution*.

We also made use of a vast body of scholarly—and some popular—books and essays, which are listed in the bibliography. The citations that follow provide sources for quotations only. However, quotations from Madison's "Notes" and from Georgia delegate William Pierce's "Notes," which are also found in Farrand's *Records*, are not cited, but our text will reveal the day from which we drew speeches; thus they can be readily located.

In the notes below we have listed the principal sources for each chapter. The full data for the abbreviated bibliographic citations is included in the bibliography that follows. The bibliography is selected. Many works of a general nature or those from which we took certain factual, descriptive information are omitted: e.g., *The Dictionary of American Biography, The Statistical History of the United States,* Commager's *Documents of American History*.

I A Nation in Jeopardy

This chapter is drawn largely from Gordon Wood's *The Creation of the American Republic,* Merrill Jensen's *The New Nation,* E. James Ferguson's "The Nationalists of 1781–1783," Edmund Cody Burnett's *The Continental Congress,* and Jackson Turner Main's *The Sovereign States*. Particular sections rely on Samuel Flagg Bemis on the Algerian pirates, David Szatmary on Shays' Rebellion, Peter Onuf on the western lands, Frederick Marks on foreign relations, and especially, Madison's "Vices," found in *The Papers of James Madison*.

PAGE 3   "to avert the humiliating": Warren, *Making of the Constitution*, p. 34.

PAGE 3   "We shall be one of the most": Burnett, *Letters* VIII:333.

PAGE 3   "How to strengthen": Warren, *Making*, p. 14.

PAGE 3   "If the present paroxysm": Ibid., pp. 15–16.

PAGE 3   "show to the nations of the Earth": Wood, *Creation*, p. 118.

PAGE 5   "The Americans were received": Abernethy, *Western Lands*, p. 267.

PAGE 7   "If therefore": Burnett, *Letters* VIII:458.

PAGE 7   "no treaty can be made": Lord Sheffield, quoted in Marks, *Independence on Trial*, p. 55.

PAGE 8   "and bloodshed would": Burnett, *Letters* VIII:318.

PAGE 9   "The Articles of Confederation": Onuf, *Origins of the Federal Republic*, p. 179.

PAGE 9   "as different as the interests": Bowen, *Miracle*, p. 92.

PAGE 9   "different from each other": Farrand, *Records* III:270.

PAGE 9   "in many ways": Ferguson, "Nationalists of 1781," p. 241.

PAGE 10   £150,000 in Massachusetts: Szatmary, *Shays' Rebellion*, p. 26 and passim.

II   America in 1787

This description of the United States in 1787 is drawn from a great many sources. Most useful have been Ralph Brown, *Mirror for Americans*; Jackson Turner Main, *The Social Structure of Revolutionary America* and *The Sovereign States*; Lester Cappon, ed., *Atlas of Early American History*; Alice Hanson Jones, *Wealth of a Nation-to-Be*; Edwin J. Perkins, *The Economy of Colonial America*; Merrill Jensen, *The New Nation*; Curtis Nettels, *The Emergence of a National Economy*; and *The Statistical History of the United States* prepared by the U.S. Bureau of the Census. We used excerpts from Henry Adams' monumental work on the administrations of Jefferson and Madison, a fragment of which is published as *The United States in 1800*. Mark Lender and James K. Martin's *Drinking in America* and Russel Nye's *Cultural Life of the New Nation* provided information on their subjects.

PAGE 19   "near the biological maximum": Perkins, *Economy of Colonial.*
           pp. 146–47. Other data from Robert Wells, *Population,* pp. 268–69.

PAGE 20   Perkins, *Economy:* p. 146, 148; pork consumption, Szatmary,
           Shays' Rebellion, p. 2.

PAGE 20   English visitor, Volney, and quote from Adams, *United States in
           1800,* pp. 30–32.

PAGE 21   Mark Lender and J. K. Martin, *Drinking in America,* p. 14.

PAGE 22   "The material standard": Perkins, *Economy,* p. 145.

PAGE 23   Nye, *Cultural Life,* p. 43.

III   The Mind of James Madison

Irving Brant's six volumes on Madison are highly partisan, but nonetheless an
excellent biography. We have used them, volumes IX and X of *The Papers of
James Madison,* edited by Hutchinson and Rachal, and Robert Rutland's
excellent short sketch, *James Madison and the Search for Nationhood* for our
biographical material. Douglass Adair's two essays, "That Politics May Be
Reduced to a Science," and "The Tenth *Federalist* Revisited," and one by
Lance Banning, "James Madison and the Nationalists," along with Edward
McNall Burns, *James Madison: Philosopher of the Constitution,* illuminate
Madison's attitudes and intellect.

PAGE 25   "profoundly disappointed": Madison, *Papers* X:205; "neither
           effectually answer": Ibid.

PAGE 26   "no bigger than . . . soap": Bowen, *Miracle,* p. 13.

PAGE 26   On epilepsy, see Brant, *Madison* I:106–7. Brant says it was epilept-
           oid hysteria.

PAGE 27   Hat anecdote: Richard Morris, *Seven Who Shaped,* p. 208.

PAGE 27   "a gloomy, stiff, creature": Brant, *Madison* II:33.

PAGE 27   Pierce's "Notes" have been printed in many places. We used
           Charles C. Tansill, ed., *Documents Illustrative of the Formation of
           the Union of the American States.*

PAGE 27   On Madison's romantic attachments, see Brant, *Madison* II:283–
           87; III:401–29; and passim.

PAGE 28   "injure his feelings": Brant, *Madison* II:17.

PAGE 28   "A few hours": Moore, *Dolley Madison,* pp. 192–95.

PAGE 29   Lance Banning, "James Madison and the Nationalists, 1780–1783."

PAGE 29   Madison's "Vices" are published in full in Madison, *Papers*
           X:345–58.

CITATIONS TO SOURCES

IV   The Unbelievable George Washington

Irving Brant's biography of Madison continued to serve us in this chapter. Douglas Southall Freeman's biography of Washington is indispensable, but James Thomas Flexner's is shorter and more interestingly written. Marcus Cunliffe's *George Washington, Man and Monument* is perhaps the best one-volume study. We used Richard H. Kohn's *Eagle and Sword* on the Newburgh Conspiracy. Douglass Adair's famous essay "Fame and the Founding Fathers" informs our understanding of many of the Convention delegates, but most particularly Washington.

PAGE 31   "This was the precipitating step": Brant, *Madison* II:376.

PAGE 31   "Though my wishes": Mitchell, *Biography of the Constitution,* p. 17.

PAGE 32   "Abraham Clark": Mitchell, *Hamilton,* p. 143.

PAGE 32   "meet at Philadelphia": Burnett, *Continental Congress,* p. 668.

PAGE 33   "Every hero becomes a bore at last" is from Emerson's *Representative Men: The Uses of Great Men.*

PAGE 33   "Washington had quantities": Flexner, *Washington* I:236–37.

PAGE 34   "The familiar faces": Ibid. II:507.

PAGE 34   "And then suddenly": Ibid.

PAGE 34   "There was something so natural": Josiah Quincy, ed., *The Journal of Major Samuel Shaw,* p. 104.

PAGE 35   "have learnt": Morris, *Seven Who Shaped,* p. 50.

PAGE 35   had not dined alone: Cunliffe, *Washington,* p. 106.

PAGE 39   "failed to acquire": Freeman, *Washington* II:378.

PAGE 39   "led by the man": Flexner, *Washington* I:222–23.

PAGE 39   "Only when physically": Ibid. II:412–13.

PAGE 40   Franklin in his *Autobiography* lists, as the thirteenth virtue to cultivate, Humility: imitate Jesus and Socrates.

PAGE 40   Douglass Adair, "Fame and the Founding Fathers," in *Fame and the Founding Fathers.*

PAGE 40   "egotism transmuted gloriously": Adair, "Fame," p. 36.

PAGE 41   "The confidence and affection": Flexner, *Washington* I:176.

PAGE 41   he "has a dignity which forbids": Flexner, *Washington* II:541.

PAGE 42   "they descried an amazing sight": Flexner, *Washington* II:443.

V   Madison Plans a Government

Descriptions of Philadelphia as it was in 1787 are found in John F. Watson, *Annals of Philadelphia and Pennsylvania*; Ellis Paxson Oberholtzer, *Philadel-*

phia: A History of the City and Its People; and the journals of Manasseh Cutler, edited by William and Julia Cutler. The works by Adair and Burns (especially the latter's Chapter II, "General Theory of the State") noted in connection with Chapter IV; Madison's "Vices"; letters to Jefferson and Washington in *The Papers of James Madison;* and *Federalist*s 51 and 55, are the principal sources of this chapter.

PAGE 44   "Would it not" Warren, *Making,* pp. 66–67.

PAGE 44   "The political existence": Warren, *Making,* pp. 92–93.

PAGE 45   "a large pile": Cutler, *Cutler* I:253.

PAGE 46   "load you with the most": Ibid., p. 263.

PAGE 46   Madison's "Vices" is in Madison, *Papers* IX:345–58. The quotation is on p. 346.

PAGE 47   "Human beings": Burns, *Madison,* p. 30.

PAGE 47   *Federalist*s 55 and 51; quotations from Hume are from Adair, "Politics May be Reduced," p. 497.

PAGE 47   "As there is a degree of depravity": *Federalist* 55.

PAGE 48   Madison quotations are from Burns, *Madison,* p. 37.

PAGE 51   "a consolidation of the whole": Madison, *Papers* IX:383.

PAGE 51   These quotations are from the Convention debates of July 9, June 6 and 8.

PAGE 53   Bailyn, *Pamphlets,* pp. 38–39.

VI Alexander Hamilton and The British Model

Biographies by Broadus Mitchell and James Thomas Flexner, and an analysis of Hamilton's political thought by Gerald Stourzh, inform our discussion of Alexander Hamilton. We have also had recourse to *The Papers of Alexander Hamilton,* edited by Harold Syrett. The concept of mixed government and its American permutation is thoroughly elaborated by Gordon Wood in *The Creation of the American Republic.* Another essay by Douglass Adair, "Experience Must Be Our Only Guide," provides much insight into the Framers' thinking.

As noted above, quotations from Madison's "Notes of Debates" are taken from the version edited by Adrienne Koch and can be checked by reference to the date of the debate under discussion, which we have tried to indicate in every case. Yates' "Notes" of the debates is in Farrand's *Records* and Tansill's *Documents.*

PAGE 57   "extreme views": Mitchell, *Hamilton,* p. 149.

PAGE 58   The Washington-Hamilton anecdote is from Flexner, *Hamilton,*
            pp. 331–32.

PAGE 59   "Never did the megalomania": Ibid., p. 335.

PAGE 59   "Despite his marked abilities": Koch, *Power, Morals,* p. 66.

PAGE 59   "You know the opinion": Flexner, *Hamilton,* p. 27.

PAGE 60   "went beyond the ideas": In Convention, June 18.

PAGE 60   "lessons from the antique": Adair, "Experience," p. 398.

PAGE 63   "perhaps the most important": Syrett, ed., *Papers of Alexander*
            Hamilton IV:178.

PAGE 63   "probably the greatest": Stourzh, *Hamilton.* p. 49.

PAGE 63   "praised by everybody": Yates' "Notes" of the Convention de-
            bates, June 21.

VII   The Puzzle of Charles Pinckney

The detective work on the Pinckney Plan was done largely by J. Franklin
Jameson and Andrew McLaughlin early in the twentieth century. A more
recent partison of Pinckney is S. Sidney Ulmer, whose claims for his subject
seem exaggerated but are on the whole a useful corrective to the conventional
wisdom on the question. There is no modern biography of Charles Pinckney.
The reconstructed Pinckney Plan is printed in Farrand's *Records.*

PAGE 64   "a sponger . . . plagiarist": Brant, *Madison* III:28.

PAGE 65   Pinckney quotations from Ulmer, "Madison and the Pinckney
            Plan," p. 419; Sparks quotation, Ibid., p. 422.

PAGE 65   "Several rough draughts": Ulmer, "Madison," p. 423.

PAGE 66   McLaughlin, "Sketch of Pinckney's Plan," p. 741; "Madison's
            objectivity": Ulmer, "Pinckney, Father," p. 245.

PAGE 66   Madison's and Yates' "Notes" are compared in Arnold A.
            Rogow, "The Federal Convention: Madison and Yates."

PAGE 67   "There is an *esprit de corps*": Yates' "Notes," June 21.

PAGE 68   The article in the *Dictionary of American Biography* was written
            by J. Harold Easterby.

PAGE 69   Singer, *South Carolina,* p. 83.

PAGE 69   "The movement within Congress": Madison, *Papers* IX:56 n. 3.

PAGE 69   Washington and Madison: Madison, *Papers* X:204, 225.

PAGE 69   Pinckney laid his plan before the Convention on May 29: Ulmer,
            "Madison and the Pinckney Plan," pp. 416–17.

PAGE 70   Van Doren, *Great Rehearsal,* p. 97; Warren, *Making,* p. 239.

PAGE 71   "no more heard of": Jared Sparks quoting Madison, Farrand, *Records* 3:479.

PAGE 71   Yates filled with errors: Rogow, "Federal Convention," p. 324.

PAGE 72   "Into the debates": Warren, *Making,* p. 239.

PAGE 73   "From the time": Ibid., p. 240.

VIII   Men, Manners, and Rules: The Convention Begins

As explained above, we have used an edition of Madison's "Notes of Debates" edited by Adrienne Koch, but provide no citations beyond indicating the date of speeches from which quotations have been taken. We have modernized spelling and punctuation. Yates' and Pierce's notes are printed in Farrand's *Records* and Tansill's *Documents.*

PAGE 76   Rossiter, *1787,* p. 150: "at least one team, and perhaps two, that would have been no less eminent and capable."

PAGE 77   "handsome and ambitious": Ernst, *King,* p. 37.

PAGE 77   "Unequalled" as an orator: *DAB.*

PAGE 77   "agreeable and easygoing": Pierce's "Notes."

PAGE 77   "Of simple, engaging": *DAB.*

PAGE 80   "it is clear": Holcombe, "Roll of Washington," p. 322.

PAGE 80   "In short": Ibid., pp. 326–27, 332–33.

PAGE 80   Madison quotation is from his Preface to his "Notes."

PAGE 81   Yates' "Notes" are compared with Madison's in Arnold A. Rogow, "The Federal Convention: Madison and Yates."

PAGE 82   "such is my jealousy": Warren, *Making,* pp. 210, 211.

PAGE 82   "tired of continental gatherings": Rossiter, *1787,* p. 166.

PAGE 83   "The Doctor mentioned": Cutler, *Cutler* I:268–69.

PAGE 84   Pierce on secrecy: Warren, *Making,* p. 139.

IX   Roger Sherman and the Art of Compromise

In addition to Christopher Collier's biography of Roger Sherman, we have relied on Farrand's "Compromises of the Constitution." There have been several attempts to subject the voting at the Convention to numerical analysis by counting up how many times one delegation agreed with another. We have not found them convincing, though they do tend to substantiate state groupings discovered by more conventional scholarship. They are listed in our bibliography under Anderson, Jillson, Pomper, and Ulmer.

PAGE 95   Quotations from Adams, Henry, Jefferson, etc., are from Collier,
           Sherman, pp. 94, 193, 316, 229.
PAGE 98   "Sherman's air": Ibid., p. 129.
PAGE 98   he "rarely failed": Ibid., p. 64.
PAGE 99   "The vote should": Ibid., p. 262.

X William Paterson Picks a Fight

Our notes make clear our reliance on John O'Connor's biography of William
Paterson for an interpretation of his subject's character.
PAGE 102   "obedience to the law": O'Connor, p. 234.
PAGE 102   "For I so detest": Ibid., p. 24.
PAGE 102   "Luxury effeminates": Ibid., p. 59.
PAGE 103   "His position in the": Ibid., p. 249.
PAGE 103   Popularity "phenomenal": Ibid., p. 181.
PAGE 103   "looks bespeak talents": Pierce's "Notes."
PAGE 104   "manly . . . virtues": O'Connor, p. 16.
PAGE 104   "The decision for independence": Ibid., pp. 68–69.
PAGE 105   That Paterson avoided attendance at the Continental Congress for
           mercenary reasons is the view of Richard Haskett in "William
           Paterson."
PAGE 105   "In the present state": O'Connor, p. 93.
PAGE 106   Wood, *Creation,* pp. 171–75.
PAGE 108   "more nearly represented": Farrand, *Framing,* p. 89.

XI The Battle Joined

There are two major biographies of Gouverneur Morris: a scholarly one by
Max Mintz that focuses on his career through the Convention and then
sketches the rest of his life, and a popular but seemingly reliable one by
Howard Swigett that tells the whole, often amusing, story.
PAGE 110   "heard that Morris": Collier, *Sherman,* p. 12n.
PAGE 112   "Why," Washington responded: Farrand, *Records,* III:359.

XII Luther Martin and a Lost Opportunity

There is no really good biography of Luther Martin, but Clarkson and Jett
have described his legal career in one small volume. Martin's partial autobiography, *Modern Gratitude,* published in 1802, is accurate and is perhaps the best

guide to his character. Philip Crowl's work on Maryland during the revolutionary era explains the political background of the election of delegates in that state.

PAGE 117   "He was a familiar figure": Clarkson and Jett, *Martin,* p. 204.

PAGE 117   "middle size": Ibid., p. 279.

PAGE 118   "with a fixed determination": Farrand, "If James Madison Had Had a Sense of Humor," p. 138. Farrand in the same article puts forth the view that Martin was drunk at the Convention.

PAGE 118   "was regarded by": Crowl, *Maryland,* p. 120 n. 48.

PAGE 119   "to supply the amazing": Clarkson and Jett, *Martin,* p. 196.

PAGE 120   "might have continued": "The Landholder X," in Ford, ed., *Essays,* p. 183.

XIII   "The Most Serious and Threatening Excitement"

Kenneth Coleman tells the story of Georgia during the revolutionary era, but there is no full-scale, modern biography of Abraham Baldwin; but that by Henry White published in 1927 is serviceable.

PAGE 124   Bedford's heated speech: Yates' "Notes," June 30.

PAGE 125   Washington "much dejected": Jared Sparks, quoted in Warren, *Making,* p. 284.

PAGE 129   "Is the science of government": Ibid., p. 269.

PAGE 132   "how difficult a part": Farrand, *Records* III:71.

PAGE 132   "raise a standard": Warren, *Making,* p. 106.

PAGE 133   "the most serious and threatening excitement": *Life and Writings of Sparks* II:228.

XIV   A New Alliance

There is a large scholarly literature about the relationship between slavery and the Constitution. David B. Davis' work forms the background against which all other scholars write. We have depended on volumes by Jordan and Robinson listed below, as well as many others not focused specifically on the late eighteenth century. Stanley Elkins and Eric McKitric's essay on "Young Men of the Revolution" informs our discussion of Oliver Ellsworth, as it has of other delegates of a similar age. There is a good biography of C. C. Pinckney by Marvin Zahniser and a very bad one of Rutledge by Richard Barry. The life of W. S. Johnson has been ably told recently by Elizabeth McCaughey and a generation ago by George Groce. Ellsworth's standard biography is still that

by W. G. Brown. Jay Sigler's piece on the Three-Fifths Clause was especially
helpful.

PAGE 138   The statistics are from Jones, *Wealth,* pp. 51–54 and Cappon,
            Atlas, p. 67.

PAGE 139   "The way west": Jordan, *White Over Black,* p. 318.

PAGE 140   "not a brilliant lawyer": *DAB.*

PAGE 141   Franklin on blacks quoted in Lynd, "Slavery and the Founding
            Fathers," pp. 129–30.

PAGE 144   Ellsworth "tall, dignified": *DAB*; surrounded by snuff: Smith,
            Wilson, p. 177; Ellsworth "unimaginative," voted with Sherman:
            Littieri, *Ellsworth,* pp. 37, 43; took Sherman for his model: Brown,
            Ellsworth, pp. 37–38.

PAGE 145   "British supremacy": McCaughey, *Johnson,* p. 170; "fall into fac-
            tions": Benton, *Whig-Loyalism,* p. 160.

PAGE 145   "I must live in peace": Groce, *Johnson,* p. 94.

PAGE 145   *"tout ensemble"*: Ibid., p. viii.

PAGE 147   "The ruler was dominant": Barry, *Rutledge,* p. 324; "Care not":
            Ibid., p. 14.

PAGE 147   Adams on Rutledge: Ibid., p. 159.

PAGE 148   "The Constitution as agreed to": Warren, *Making,* p. 584.

XV   The Western Lands

On the western lands question we have relied on works by Merrill Jensen and
T. P. Abernethy, and on J. P. Boyd's discussion in relevant sections of his
edition of *The Papers of Thomas Jefferson.* We have accepted much of Staughton Lynd's still controversial thesis about the relationship of the western lands
to slavery and of the debates in Congress and in the Convention. Cutler's
journal is useful in that matter. Frederick Marks and S. F. Bemis are excellent
on the Jay-Gardoque Mississippi negotiations. There is a full-scale biography
of Blount by William Masterson.

PAGE 154   Population figures for the southwestern territories are from *Statis-
            tical History of the United States* (1976), pp. 1168, 35.

PAGE 157   "throw the weight": Burnett, *Letters of Members* VIII:425.

PAGE 159   "employ who you wish": Masterson, *Blount,* p. 62; "upwards of
            100,000 acres": Ibid., p. 141; "businessman in politics": Ibid., p.
            349.

PAGE 159   "make use of any name": Ibid., pp. 90–91.

PAGE 160   Lynd on three-fifths clause: *Class Conflict,* p. 185.
PAGE 162   "By this Ordinance": Cutler, *Cutler* I:305.
PAGE 163   "has at length from a": Burnett, *Letters of Members* VIII:619.
PAGE 164   "sanctioned slavery": Lynd, *Class Conflict,* p. 185.
PAGE 164   "the first and last": Ibid., p. 185.
PAGE 164   "The distracting question": Ibid., p. 189.

XVI   Another Trade-off

The general sources for this chapter are the same as those listed for the previous chapter.

PAGE 168   "The Convention could not": Robinson, *Slavery in the Structure,*
            p. 217.
PAGE 169   "The report . . . craft and gall": Ibid., p. 218.
PAGE 174   "negative pregnant": Davis, *Problem of Slavery,* p. 126. Hamilton
            used the term in *Federalist* No. 32.
PAGE 178   "distracting question": Lynd, *Class Conflict,* p. 189.

XVII   Balancing Act

John Reardon has written a good biography of Edmund Randolph. Edward Corwin treats the "necessary and proper" clauses in *The Constitution and What It Means Today.*

PAGE 184   "Men always love power": Yates' "Notes," June 18.
PAGE 184   "divided into distinct": Bailyn, *Pamphlets,* p. 39.
PAGE 187   Madison on smaller states. Letter of March, 1836 in Farrand,
            Records III:538.
PAGE 188   "I am a *child*": Reardon, *Randolph,* p. 141. Emphasis added.
PAGE 189   Randolph equivocates on the Constitution: Ibid., p. 119.
PAGE 192   Hamilton on "necessary": *Federalist* No. 33 and his "Opinion on
            the Constitutionality of The Bank."
PAGE 192   "second dimension": Corwin, *The Constitution,* p. 38. See also pp.
            122–24.

XVIII   Curing the Republican Disease

Madison's failure in the matter of negativing state laws is dealt with by Charles Hobson. The literature on judicial review is enormous. A short summary of the controversy can be found in Alan F. Westin's introduction to Beard's *The*

Supreme Court and the Constitution, but interested investigators will want to consult some of the eighty-eight items listed under "Judicial Review" in A. T. Mason and D. G. Stephenson's bibliography *American Constitutional Development.* But see in particular Edward S. Corwin's *The Doctrine of Judicial Review.* For judicial activities of Congress under the Articles, see Henry Bourguignon's *The First Federal Court.*

PAGE 195   "the evils issuing": Madison, *Papers* X:212.

PAGE 196   "Of the reforms": Hobson, "Negative on State Laws," p. 218.

PAGE 197   "appreciate . . . grave apprehension": Warren, *Making,* p. 165.

PAGE 203   "If the import": Kelly and Harbison, *American Constitution,* p. 133. The most recent edition of that text, rewritten by Herman Belz, includes only the last quoted sentence, p. 104.

PAGE 204   Justice Hughes' remark is discussed in his *Autobiographical Notes,* p. 143.

XIX   James Wilson, Democratic Nationalist

Gordon Wood, in *Creation of the American Republic,* is especially useful on the separation of powers, and the new theory of social contract. See also the essay by George Carey listed in the bibliography below. Our comments on lawyers are drawn from Lawrence Friedman's *History of American Law.* There are biographies of James Wilson by Charles P. Smith and Geoffrey Seed, and excellent commentary is presented by Wilson's editor, Robert G. McCloskey. Andrew C. McLaughlin has also written a useful piece about him.

PAGE 207   "little more than chairmen": Wood, *Creation,* p. 138.

PAGE 207   "Perhaps no principle": Ibid., p. 151.

PAGE 208   The quotation from *L'Esprit des Lois* is from Book XI, Ch. 6, p. 202, of the reprint of the first English edition, edited by David Wallace Carrithers.

PAGE 209   "widely acknowledged": McCloskey, in Wilson, *Works,* p. 37.

PAGE 209   Washington on Wilson: Smith, *Wilson,* p. 265.

PAGE 210   "making Edinburgh": Ibid., p. 5.

PAGE 211   The Reid quotations are from Ibid., p. 321.

PAGE 211   "stiff reserve": Ibid., p. 100.

PAGE 212   Smith on lawyers: Ibid., p. 317.

PAGE 212   Friedman on lawyers: *American Law,* pp. 81–83.

PAGE 212   Thirty-one delegates were lawyers: Ibid., p. 88.

PAGE 214   "The congressional power": Wilson quoted in Wood, *Creation*, p. 539.

PAGE 214   "For the Federalists": Ibid., p. 546.

PAGE 216   "He was shockingly changed": Smith, *Wilson*, p. 386.

XX   In the Shadow of Washington

We have used Charles C. Thach and Edward S. Corwin on the creation of the presidency. Neal Peirce's book on the electoral college includes an analysis of its pitfalls in the context of modern presidential elections.

PAGE 218   "I have scarcely ventured": Madison, *Papers* IX:385.

PAGE 218   "Nothing is so embarrassing": Peirce, *People's President*, p. 31.

PAGE 226   "almost the ablest men": Warren, *Making*, p. 621n.

XXI   Elbridge Gerry's War Against the Army

George Billias's excellent biography provides material for an analysis of Gerry's character. Richard Kohn and Reginald C. Stuart were our sources for the military matters we discuss.

PAGE 235   "At birth, the United States": Kohn, *Eagle and Sword*, p. 288.

PAGE 235   "there is the imbecility": Burnett, *Letters of Members* VIII:517.

PAGE 236   "the Revolutionary generation": Stuart, *War in American Thought*, p. 62.

PAGE 236   "No principle of government": Kohn, *Eagle and Sword*, p. 2.

PAGE 237   "They come in you cannot tell how": Ibid., p. 9.

PAGE 237   One-third of delegates had been Continental officers: Ibid., p. 77.

PAGE 238   "schizophrenic": Morison, "Elbridge Gerry, Gentleman-Democrat."

PAGE 239   "A nervous and birdlike": Billias, *Gerry*, p. 7.

PAGE 239   "a man of immense worth": Ibid., p. 70.

PAGE 240   "His distrust"; "commonality of interest": Ibid., p. 21.

PAGE 242   The Washington anecdote is passed on from Paul Wilstach's *Patriots off Their Pedestals* by Warren in *Making*, p. 483.

PAGE 242   The Gerry comment about a standing army is in Morison, *Oxford History*, pp. 308–9.

PAGE 244   "Affable, handsome": Rossiter, *Grand Convention*, p. 82.

XXII   George Mason and the Rights of Man

Robert Rutland on George Mason and on the Bill of Rights has been very useful. There are longer useful biographies of Mason by Helen Miller and Kate M. Rowland. Cecelia Kenyon's essay on the antifederalists as "men of little faith" informs this chapter, but we believe that the Federalists had little more faith in human nature or man-made institutions than did their opponents. Gordon Wood's analysis, "The Primal Powers of the People," in his *Creation of the American Republic,* underlies much of our discussion.

PAGE 250   Sam Adams quoted in Rutland, *Birth of the Bill of Rights,* p. 35.

PAGE 250   "held his abilities in high esteem": Ibid., p. 42.

PAGE 251   "He was abstemious": Miller, *Mason,* p. 43.

PAGE 251   "above all things": Rutland, *Mason,* p. 14.

PAGE 251   "It is impossible": Miller, *Mason,* p. 235.

PAGE 254   "Such bills generally": Zahniser, *Pinckney,* p. 99.

PAGE 254   Hamilton on bills of rights is from *Federalist* No. 84.

PAGE 256   "beyond any thing we had a right": Van Doren, *Great Rehearsal,* p. 216.

PAGE 257   The quotations from Kenyon are on pp. 37–38.

PAGE 260   "if a weak state": Van Doren, *Great Rehearsal,* p. 193.

PAGE 260.   "Mr. President, I am a plain man": Bowen, *Miracle,* p. 287.

XXIII   "The Most Remarkable Work"

PAGE 270.   "The experience of the past": Peirce, *People's President,* p. 31.

Selected Bibliography

Abernethy, Thomas Perkins. *Western Lands and the American Revolution.* New York: Russell and Russell, 1959 (1937).

Adair, Douglass G. "Experience Must Be Our Only Guide: History, Democratic Theory, and the United States Constitution." In *The Reinterpretation of Early American History: Essays in Honor of John Edwin Pomfret.* Edited by Ray Allen Billington. New York: W. W. Norton, 1968 (1966).

————. *Fame and the Founding Fathers.* Edited by Edmund P. Willis. Bethlehem, Pa.: Moravian College, 1967. This is the transcript of a talk. The essay has been widely anthologized.

————. "The Tenth *Federalist* Revisited," *William and Mary Quarterly.* 3rd series, 8 (January 1951).

————. "That Politics May Be Reduced to a Science: David Hume, James Madison, and the Tenth *Federalist.*" *Huntington Library Quarterly* 20 (August 1957). Reprinted in *The Reinterpretation of the American Revolution, 1763–1789.* Compiled by Jack P. Greene. New York: Harper and Row, 1968.

Adams, Henry. *The United States in 1800.* Ithaca, N.Y.: Cornell University Press, 1964.

Anderson, Thornton, and Jillson, Calvin. "Realignment in the Convention of 1787: The Slave Trade Compromise." *Journal of Politics* 39 (August 1977).

————. "Voting Bloc Analysis in the Constitutional Convention: Implications for an Interpretation of the Connecticut Compromise." *Western Political Quarterly* 31 (December 1978).

Appleby, Joyce. "The Social Origins of American Revolutionary Ideology." *Journal of American History* 64 (March 1978).

————. "What Is Still American in the Political Philosophy of Thomas Jefferson?" *William and Mary Quarterly,* 3rd series, 39 (April 1982).

Austin, James T. *The Life of Elbridge Gerry. With Contemporary Letters. To the Close of the American Revolution.* 2 vols. Boston: Wells and Lilly, 1829.

Bailyn, Bernard. *Pamphlets of the American Revolution, 1750–1776.* Cambridge: Harvard University Press, 1965.

Baker, William Spohn. *Washington After the Revolution.* Philadelphia: J. B. Lippincott Co., 1898.

Banning, Lance. "James Madison and the Nationalists, 1780–1783." *William and Mary Quarterly,* 3rd series, 40 (April 1983).

————. "Republican Ideology and the Triumph of the Constitution, 1789 to 1793." *William and Mary Quarterly,* 3rd series, 31 (April 1974).

Barrett, Jay Amos. *The Evolution of the Ordinance of 1787.* New York: Arno Press, 1971 (1891).

Barry, Richard. *Mr. Rutledge of South Carolina.* New York: Buell, Sloan and Pearce, 1942.

Beard, Charles A. *The Supreme Court and the Constitution.* Edited by Alan Westin. New York: Prentice Hall, 1962.

Benton, William A. *Whig Loyalism: An Aspect of Political Ideology in the American Revolutionary Era.* East Brunswick, N.J.: Fairleigh Dickinson University Press, 1968.

Bemis, Samuel Flagg. *A Diplomatic History of the United States.* 3rd. ed. New York: Henry Holt and Company, 1950.

Bethea, Andrew J. *The Contribution of Charles Pinckney to the Formation of the American Union.* Richmond, Va.: Garrett and Massie, Inc., 1937.

Billias, George Athan. *Elbridge Gerry: Founding Father and Republican Statesman.* New York: McGraw-Hill, 1976.

Birkby, Robert H. "Politics of Accommodation: The Origin of the Supremacy Clause." *Western Political Quarterly* 19 (March 1966).

Blount, John Gray. *The John Gray Blount Papers.* Edited by Alice Barnwell Keith. 2 vols. Raleigh, N.C.: State Department of Archives and History, 1952.

Bourguignon, Henry J. *The First Federal Court.* Philadelphia, American Philosophical Association, 1977.

Bowen, Catherine Drinker. *Miracle at Philadelphia: The Story of the Constitution, May to September, 1787.* Boston: Little, Brown, 1966.

Boyd, William K. *History of North Carolina.* 6 vols. Chicago and New York: The Lewis Publishing Co., 1919.

Brant, Irving. *The Bill of Rights: Its Origin and Meaning.* Indianapolis: Bobbs-Merrill, 1965.

———. *James Madison.* 6 vols. Indianapolis: Bobbs-Merrill, 1941–61.

Brown, Ralph H. *Mirror for Americans: Likeness of the Eastern Seaboard, 1810.* New York: American Geographic Society, 1943.

Brown, Richard D. "The Founding Fathers of 1776 and 1787: A Collective View." *William and Mary Quarterly,* 3rd series, 33 (July 1976).

Brown, William Garrott. *The Life of Oliver Ellsworth.* New York: The Macmillan Company, 1905.

Burnett, Edmund Cody. *The Continental Congress.* New York: The Macmillan Company, 1941.

———. *Letters of Members of the Continental Congress.* 8 vols. Washington: Carnegie Institute, 1936.

Burns, Edward McNall. *James Madison: Philosopher of the Constitution.* New Brunswick, N.J.: Rutgers University Press, 1938.

Burrows, Edwin G. "Military Experience and the Origins of Federalism." In *Aspects of Early New York Society and Politics.* Edited by Jacob Judd and Irwin H. Polishook. Tarrytown, N.Y.: Sleepy Hollow Restoration, 1974.

Butzner, Jane, comp. *Constitutional Chaff: Rejected Suggestions of the Convention of 1787, with Explanatory Argument.* New York: Columbia University Press, 1941.

Cappon, Lester J., ed. *Atlas of Early American History: The Revolutionary Era 1760–1790.* Princeton, N.J.: Princeton University Press, for the Newberry Library and the Institute of Early American History and Culture, 1976).

Carey, George W. "Separation of Powers and the Madisonian Model: A Reply to the Critics." *American Political Science Review* 72 (March 1978).

Clarkson, Paul S., and Jett, R. Samuel. *Luther Martin of Maryland.* Baltimore: Johns Hopkins Press, 1970.

Coleman, Kenneth. *The American Revolution in Georgia 1763–1789.* Athens, Ga.: University of Georgia Press, 1958.

Collier, Christopher. *Roger Sherman's Connecticut: Yankee Politics and the American Revolution.* Middletown, Conn.: Wesleyan University Press, 1971.

Conrad, Henry C. "Gunning Bedford, Junior." *Papers of the Historical Society of Delaware* 26 (1900).

Corwin, Edward S. *American Constitutional History: Essays by Edward S.*

Corwin. Edited by Alpheus T. Mason and Gerald Garvey. New York: Harper and Row, 1964.

―――. *The Constitution and What It Means Today.* Revised by Harold W. Chase and Craig R. Ducat. 14th ed. Princeton, N.J.: Princeton University Press, 1978.

―――. *The Doctrine of Judicial Review, Its Legal and Historical Basis, and Other Essays.* Princeton, N.J.: Princeton University Press, 1914.

―――. *The President, Office and Powers, 1787–1948: History and Analysis of Practice and Opinion.* 3rd ed., rev. New York: New York University Press, 1948.

Crosskey, William W. *Politics and the Constitution in the History of the United States.* Chicago: University of Chicago Press, 1953.

Crowl, Philip A. *Maryland During and After the Revolution: A Political and Economical Study.* Baltimore: The Johns Hopkins Press, 1943.

Cunliffe, Marcus. *George Washington: Man and Monument.* Boston: Little, Brown and Company, 1958.

Cutler, William Parker, and Cutler, Julia Perkins. *Life, Journals and Correspondence of Rev. Manasseh Cutler, LL.D.* 2 vols. Cincinnati: R. Clarke and Co., 1888.

Daniell, Jere R. *Experiment in Republicanism: New Hampshire Politics and the American Revolution, 1741–1794.* Cambridge, Mass.: Harvard University Press, 1970.

Davis, David Brion. *The Problem of Slavery in the Age of Revolution, 1770–1823.* Ithaca, N.Y.: Cornell University Press, 1975.

Davis, S. Rufus. *The Federal Principle: A Journey Through Time in Quest of a Meaning.* Berkeley: University of California Press, 1978.

Dennison, George M. "The 'Revolutionary Principle': Ideology and the Constitution in the Thought of James Wilson." *Review of Politics* 39 (April 1977).

Diamond, Martin. "The Declaration and the Constitution: Liberty, Democracy, and the Founders." *The Public Interest* 41 (Fall 1975).

―――. "Democracy and *The Federalist:* A Reconsideration of the Framers' Intent." *American Political Science Review* 53 (March 1959).

Diggins, John Patrick. "Power and Authority in American History: The Case of Charles A. Beard and His Critics." *American Historical Review* 36 (October 1981).

Donahue, Bernard, and Smelser, Marshall. "The Congressional Power to

Raise Armies: The Constitutional and Ratifying Conventions." *Review of Politics* 33 (April 1971).

Dumbauld, Edward. *The Constitution of the United States.* Norman: University of Oklahoma Press, 1964.

Eckenrode, H. J. *The Randolphs: The Story of a Virginia Family.* Indianapolis and New York: The Bobbs-Merrill Company, 1946.

Eidelberg, Paul. *The Philosophy of the American Constitution: A Reinterpretation of the Intentions of the Founding Fathers.* New York: Free Press, 1968.

Elkins, Stanley, and McKitrick, Eric. "The Founding Fathers: Young Men of the Revolution." *Political Science Quarterly* 76 (June 1961).

Elsmer, Jane Shaffer. *Justice Samuel Chase.* Muncie, Ind.: Janevar Pub. Co., 1980.

Ernst, Robert. *Rufus King, American Federalist.* Chapel Hill: University of North Carolina Press, for the Institute of Early American History and Culture at Williamsburg, Va., 1968.

Farrand, Max. "Compromises of the Constitution." *American Historical Review* 9 (April 1904).

———. *The Fathers of the Constitution: A Chronicle of the Establishment of the Union.* New Haven: Yale University Press, 1921.

———. *The Framing of the Constitution of the United States.* New Haven: Yale University Press, 1913.

———. "If James Madison Had Had a Sense of Humor." *Pennsylvania Magazine of History and Biography* 62 (April 1938).

———. *The Records of the Federal Convention of 1787.* 4 vols. New Haven: Yale University Press, 1937.

Ferguson, E. James. *The American Revolution: A General History, 1763–1790.* Homewood, Ill.: Dorsey Press, 1974.

———. "The Nationalists of 1781–1783 and the Economic Interpretation of the Constitution." *Journal of American History* 56 (September 1969).

———. *The Power of the Purse: A History of American Public Finance, 1776–1790.* Chapel Hill: University of North Carolina Press, for the Institute of Early American History and Culture, 1961.

———. "Political Economy, Public Liberty, and the Formation of the Constitution." *William and Mary Quarterly,* 3rd series, 40 (July 1983).

Fitzpatrick, John Clement, ed. *The Diaries of George Washington, 1748–1799.* 4 vols. Boston and New York: Houghton Mifflin Company, 1925.

———, ed. *The Writings of George Washington from the Original Manuscript*

Sources, 1745–1799. 39 vols. Washington, D.C.: U.S. Government Printing Office, 1931–44.

Flexner, James Thomas. *George Washington.* 4 vols. Boston: Little, Brown and Company, 1965–69.

————. *George Washington: The Indispensable Man.* Boston: Little, Brown and Company, 1969.

————. *The Young Hamilton: A Biography.* Boston: Little, Brown and Company, 1978.

Flower, Milton E. *John Dickinson: Conservative Revolutionary.* Charlottesville: University Press of Virginia, for the Friends of the John Dickinson Mansion, 1983.

Ford, Paul Leicester, ed. *Essays on the Constitution of the United States, Published During Its Discussion by the People 1787–1788.* Brooklyn, N.Y.: Historical Printing Club, 1892.

————. *Pamphlets on the Constitution of the United States, Published During Its Discussion by the People, 1787–1788.* Brooklyn, N.Y.: The Historical Printing Club, 1888.

Freehling, William W. "The Founding Fathers and Slavery." *American Historical Review* 77 (February 1972).

Freeman, Douglas S. *George Washington: A Biography.* 7 vols. New York: Scribner, 1948–57.

Friedman, Lawrence M. *A History of American Law.* New York: Simon and Schuster, 1973.

Gerlach, Larry R. "Toward a More Perfect Union: Connecticut, the Continental Congress, and the Constitutional Convention." *Bulletin of the Connecticut Historical Society* 34 (July 1969).

Goddard, Henry P. "Luther Martin: The 'Federal Bull-dog.' " In *A Sketch of the Life and Character of Nathaniel Ramsey,* by W. F. Brand. Maryland Historical Society Fund Publication No. 24. Baltimore: J. Murphy & Co., 1887.

Goldwin, Robert A., ed. *A Nation of States: Essays on the American Federal System.* Chicago: Rand McNally, 1963.

Greene, Jack P., comp. *The Reinterpretation of the American Revolution, 1763–1789.* New York: Harper & Row, 1968.

Groce, George C., Jr. *William Samuel Johnson: a Maker of the Constitution.* New York: Columbia University Press, 1937.

Hamilton, Alexander. *The Papers of Alexander Hamilton.* Edited by Harold C. Syrett. Vol. IV. New York: Columbia University Press, 1961–1979.

Haskett, Richard C. "William Paterson, Attorney General of New Jersey." *William and Mary Quarterly,* 3rd series, 7 (January 1950).

Hendrick, Burton J. *Bulwark of the Republic: A Biography of the Constitution.* Boston: Little, Brown and Co., 1937.

Hobson, Charles F. "The Negative on States Laws: James Madison and the Crisis of Republican Government." *William and Mary Quarterly,* 3rd series, 36 (April 1979).

Hockett, Homer Carey. *The Constitutional History of the United States, 1776–1826: The Blessings of Liberty.* 2 vols. New York: The Macmillan Co., 1939.

Hoffer, Peter Charles. *Revolution and Regeneration: Life Cycles and the Historical Vision of the Generation of 1776.* Athens: University of Georgia Press, 1983.

Holcombe, Arthur N. "The Role of Washington in the Framing of the Constitution." *Huntington Library Quarterly* 19 (August 1956).

Hubbard, F. M. "William R. Davie." In *The Library of American Biography,* 2nd series, vol. 5. Edited by Jared Sparks. Boston: Hilliard, Gray and Co., 1834–48.

Hunt, Gaillard, and Scott, James Brown. *Debates in the Federal Convention of 1787.* Washington, D.C.: Carnegie Institution, 1920.

Hughes, Charles Evans. *The Autobiographical Notes of Charles Evans Hughes.* Edited by D. J. Danelski and J. S. Tulchin. Cambridge: Harvard University Press, 1973.

Hutchinson, William T. "Unite to Divide; Divide to Unite: The Shaping of American Federalism." *Mississippi Valley Historical Review* 46 (June 1959).

Hutson, James H. "County, Court, and Constitution: Antifederalism and the Historians." *William and Mary Quarterly,* 3rd series, 38 (July 1981).

―――. "The Creation of the Constitution: Scholarship at a Standstill." *Reviews in American History* 12 (December 1984).

―――. "John Dickinson at the Federal Constitutional Convention." *William and Mary Quarterly,* 3rd series, 40 (April 1983).

Jameson, J. Franklin. "Portions of Charles Pinckney's Plan for a Constitution, 1787." *American Historical Review* 8 (April 1903).

Jefferson, Thomas. *The Papers of Thomas Jefferson.* Edited by Julian Boyd, et al. Princeton, N.J.: Princeton University Press, 1950–.

Jensen, Merrill. "The Cession of the Old Northwest." *Mississippi Valley Historical Review* 23 (June 1936).

————. "The Creation of the National Domain, 1781–1784." *Mississippi Valley Historical Review* 26 (December 1939).

————. "The Idea of a National Government During the American Revolution." *Political Science Quarterly* 58 (September 1943).

————. *The New Nation: A History of the United States During the Confederation, 1781–1789.* New York: Knopf, 1950.

————. *The Making of the American Constitution.* New York: Van Nostrand & Reinhold, 1964.

Jillson, Calvin C. "Constitution-Making: Alignment and Realignment in the Federal Convention of 1787." *American Political Science Review* 75 (September 1981).

————. "The Representation Question in the Federal Convention of 1787: Madison's Virginia Plan and Its Opponents." *Congressional Studies* 8 (1981).

————. "Voting Bloc Analysis in the Constitutional Convention: Implications for an Interpretation of the Connecticut Compromise." *Western Political Quarterly* (December 1978).

Jillson, Calvin C., and Anderson, Thornton. "Realignments in the Convention of 1787: The Slave Trade Compromise." *Journal of Politics* 39 (August 1977).

Jones, Alice Hanson. *Wealth of a Nation-to-Be: The American Colonies on the Eve of the Revolution.* New York: Columbia University Press, 1980.

Jordan, Winthrop P. *White Over Black: American Attitudes Toward the Negro 1550–1812.* Chapel Hill: University of North Carolina Press, for the Institute of Early American History and Culture, 1968.

Kelly, Alfred H., and Harbison, Winfred A. *The American Constitution: Its Origins and Development.* 5th ed. New York: W. W. Norton & Company, 1976.

Kenyon, Cecelia M. "Alexander Hamilton: Rousseau of the Right." *Political Science Quarterly* 73 (June 1958).

————. "Men of Little Faith: The Anti-Federalists and the Nature of Representative Government." *William and Mary Quarterly,* 3rd series, 12 (January 1955).

King, Charles R., ed. *The Life and Correspondence of Rufus King; Comprising his Letters, Private and Official, His Public Documents, and his Speeches.* 6 vols. New York: G. P. Putnam's Sons, 1894–1900.

Koch, Adrienne. *Power, Morals and the Founding Fathers: Essays in the Inter-

pretation of the American Enlightenment. Ithaca, N.Y.: Great Seal Books, 1961.

————, ed. *Notes of Debates in the Federal Convention of 1787 by James Madison.* Athens: Ohio University Press, 1966.

Kohn, Richard H. *Eagle and Sword: The Beginnings of the Military Establishment in America.* New York: Free Press, 1975.

————. "Rebuttal to C. Edward Skeen, 'The Newburgh Conspiracy Reconsidered.'" *William and Mary Quarterly,* 3rd series, 31 (April 1974).

Konkle, Burton Alva. *James Wilson and the Constitution.* Philadelphia: The Law Academy of Philadelphia, 1907.

Lander, Ernest M., Jr. "The South Carolininas at the Philadelphia Convention, 1787." *South Carolina Historical Magazine* 57 (July 1956).

Lefler, Hugh Talmage, and Newsome, Albert Ray. *North Carolina: The History of a Southern State.* Chapel Hill: University of North Carolina Press, 1954.

Lender, Mark Edward, and Martin, James Kirby. *Drinking in America: A History.* New York: Free Press, 1982.

Levy, Leonard W., ed. *Essays on the Making of the Constitution.* New York: Oxford University Press, 1969.

Littieri, Ronald John. *Connecticut's Young Man of the Revolution: Oliver Ellsworth.* Hartford: American Revolution Bicentennial Commission of Connecticut, 1978.

Lynd, Staughton. *Class Conflict, Slavery and the United States Constitution: Ten Essays.* Indianapolis: Bobbs-Merrill, 1967.

————. "Slavery and the Founding Fathers." In Melvin Drimmer, ed. *Black History: A Reappraisal.* Garden City: Doubleday and Co., 1968.

Lovejoy, Arthur O. "The Theory of Human Nature in the American Constitution and the Method of Counterpoise." In *Reflection on Human Nature.* Baltimore: Johns Hopkins Press, 1961. Reprinted in *The Reinterpretation of the American Revolution, 1763–1789,* compiled by Jack P. Greene. New York: Harper and Row, 1968.

McCaughey, Elizabeth P. *From Loyalist to Founding Father: The Political Odyssey of William Samuel Johnson.* New York: Columbia University Press, 1980.

McDonald, Forrest. *E Pluribus Unum: The Formation of the American Republic, 1776–1790.* Boston: Houghton Mifflin, 1965. Reprinted as *The Formation of the American Republic, 1776–1790.* Baltimore: Penguin Books, 1965.

——. *We the People: Economic Origins of the Constitution.* Chicago: University of Chicago Press, 1958.

McGuire, Robert A., and Ohfeldt, Robert L. "Economic Interests and the American Constitution: A Quantitative Rehabilitation of Charles A. Beard." *Journal of Economic History* 44 (June 1984).

McLaughlin, Andrew Cunningham. *The Confederation and the Constitution, 1783–1789.* New York: Collier Books, 1962 (1905).

——. *A Constitutional History of the United States.* New York and London: D. Appleton-Century Co., Inc., 1935.

——. "James Wilson in the Philadelphia Convention." *Political Science Quarterly* 12 (March 1897).

——. "Sketch of Charles Pinckney's Plan for a Constitution, 1787." *American Historical Review* 9 (July 1904).

Madison, James. *The Papers of James Madison.* Edited by William T. Hutchinson and William M. E. Rachal. Chicago: University of Chicago Press, 1962–. 14 vols. to date.

Main, Jackson Turner. *The Antifederalists, Critics of the Constitution, 1781–1788.* Chapel Hill: University of North Carolina Press, for the Institute of Early American History and Culture, 1961.

——. *Political Parties Before the Constitution.* Chapel Hill: University of North Carolina Press, for the Institute of Early American History and Culture, 1973.

——. *The Social Structure of Revolutionary America.* Princeton: Princeton University Press, 1965.

——. *The Sovereign States, 1775–1783.* New York: New Viewpoints, 1973.

Marks, Frederick W., III. *Independence on Trial: Foreign Affairs and the Making of the Constitution.* Baton Rouge: Louisiana State University Press, 1973.

Martin, Luther. *Modern Gratitude in Five Numbers: Addressed to Richard Raymond Keene, esq. concerning family marriage.* Baltimore, 1802.

Masterson, William H. *William Blount.* Baton Rouge: Louisiana State University Press, 1954.

Meigs, William M. "The Relation of the Judiciary to the Constitution." *American Law Review* 174 (1885).

Miller, Helen Hill. *George Mason: Gentleman Revolutionary.* Chapel Hill: University of North Carolina Press, 1975.

Mintz, Max M. *Gouverneur Morris and the American Revolution.* Norman: University of Oklahoma Press, 1970.

Mitchell, Broadus. *Alexander Hamilton: A Concise Biography*. New York: Oxford University Press, 1976.

Mitchell, Broadus, and Mitchell, Louise Pearson. *A Biography of the Constitution of the United States: Its Origin, Formation, Adoption and Interpretation*. 2nd ed. New York: Oxford University Press, 1975.

Montesquieu, Charles de Secondat, Baron de. *The Spirit of Laws: A Compendium of the First English Edition*. Edited by David W. Carrithers. Berkeley: University of California Press, 1977.

Moore, Virginia. *The Madisons*. New York: McGraw-Hill Company, 1979.

Morgan, Robert J. "Madison's Analysis of the Sources of Political Authority." *American Political Science Review* 75 (September 1981).

Morison, Samuel E. "Elbridge Gerry, Gentleman-Democrat." *New England Quarterly* 2 (January 1929).

————. *The Oxford History of the American People*. New York: Oxford University Press, 1965.

Morris, Richard B. *Seven Who Shaped Our Destiny: The Founding Fathers as Revolutionaries*. New York: Harper and Row, 1973.

Morse, Jedidiah. *The American Geography; or, A View of the Present Situation of the United States of America: . . . .* 2nd ed. London: J. Stockdale, 1792.

Murphy, William P. *The Triumph of Nationalism: State Sovereignty, the Founding Fathers and the Making of the Constitution*. Chicago: Quadrangle Books, 1967.

Murrin, John M. "The Great Inversion, or Court Versus Country: A Comparison of the Revolutionary Settlements in England (1688–1721) and America (1776–1816)." In *Three British Revolutions: 1641, 1688, 1776*, edited by J. G. A. Pocock. Princeton, N.J.: Princeton University Press, 1980.

Nettels, Curtis P. *The Emergence of a National Economy, 1775–1815*. New York: Holt, Rinehart and Winston, 1962.

Nott, Charles C. *The Mystery of the Pinckney Draft*. New York: The Century Co., 1908.

Nye, Russel Blaine. *The Cultural Life of the New Nation, 1776–1830*. New York: Harper, 1960.

Oberholtzer, Ellis Paxson. *Philadelphia: A History of the City and Its People*. 3 vols. Philadelphia: J. S. Clarke, n.d.

O'Connor, John E. *William Paterson, Lawyer and Statesman, 1745–1806*. New Brunswick, N.J.: Rutgers University Press, 1979.

Ohline, Howard A. "Republicanism and Slavery: The Origins of the Three-

Fifths Clause." *William and Mary Quarterly,* 3rd series, 28 (October 1971).

Onuf, Peter S. *The Origins of the Federal Republic: Jurisdictional Controversies in the United States: 1775–1787.* Philadelphia: University of Pennsylvania Press, 1983.

———. "Towards Federalism: Virginia, Congress, and the Western Lands." *William and Mary Quarterly,* 3rd series, 34 (July 1977).

Pease, Theodore C. "The Ordinance of 1787." *Mississippi Valley Historical Review* 25 (September 1938).

Peirce, Neal R. *The People's President: The Electoral College in American History and the Direct-Vote Alternative.* New York: Simon and Schuster, 1968.

Perkins, Edwin J. *The Economy of Colonial America.* New York: Columbia University Press, 1980.

Phillips, Ulrich B. "The South Carolina Federalists." *American Historical Review* 14 (April 1909); continued in 15 (July 1909).

Pocock, J. G. A., ed. *Three British Revolutions: 1641, 1688, 1776.* Princeton, N.J.: Princeton University Press, 1980.

———. "Virtue and Commerce in the Eighteenth Century." *Journal of Interdisciplinary History* 3 (Summer 1972).

Pomper, Gerald M. "Conflict and Coalitions at the Constitutional Convention." In *The Study of Coalition Behavior, Theoretical Perspectives and Cases from Four Continents.* Edited by S. O. Groennings, et al. New York: Holt, Rinehart and Winston, 1970.

Poole, William Frederick. *The Ordinance of 1787 and Dr. Manasseh Cutler as an Agent in its Formation.* Cambridge, Mass.: Welch, Bigelow, and Co., 1876.

Prescott, Arthur Taylor, comp. *Drafting the Federal Constitution; a Rearrangement of Madison's Notes, Giving Consecutive Developments of Provisions in the Constitution of the United States, ...* Baton Rouge, La.: Louisiana State University Press, 1941.

Pritchett, C. Herman. *The American Constitution.* New York: McGraw-Hill, 1959.

Quincy, Josiah, ed. *The Journals of Major Samuel Shaw, the First American Consul at Canton.* Boston: W. Crosby and H. P. Nichols, 1847.

Rakove, Jack N. *The Beginnings of National Politics: An Interpretative History of the Continental Congress.* New York: Knopf, 1979.

Reardon, John J. *Edmund Randolph: A Biography*. New York: Macmillan, 1974.

Riemer, Neal. "The Republicanism of James Madison." *Political Science Quarterly* 69 (March 1954).

Riken, William H. "The Heresthetics of Constitution-Making: The Presidency in 1787, with Comments on Determinism and Rational Choice." *American Political Science Review* 78 (March 1984).

Robinson, Blackwell P. *William R. Davie*. Chapel Hill: University of North Carolina Press, 1957.

Robinson, Donald L. *Slavery in the Structure of American Politics, 1765–1820*. New York: Harcourt Brace Jovanovich, 1971.

Roche, John P. "The Founding Fathers: A Reform Caucus in Action." *American Political Science Review* 15 (December 1961).

Rogers, George C., Jr. *Charleston in the Age of the Pinckneys*. Norman: University of Oklahoma Press, 1969.

Rogow, Arnold H. "The Federal Convention: Madison and Yates." *American Historical Review* 60 (January 1955).

Roll, Charles W., Jr. "We, Some of the People: Apportionment in the Thirteen State Conventions Ratifying the Constitution." *Journal of American History* 56 (June 1969).

Rossiter, Clinton. *Alexander Hamilton and the Constitution*. New York: Harcourt, Brace and World, 1964.

———. *1787: The Grand Convention*. (New York: Macmillan, 1966).

Rothman, Rozann. "The Impact of Covenant and Contract Theories on Conceptions of the U.S. Constitution." *Publius* 10 (Fall 1980).

Rowland, Kate Mason. *The Life of George Mason, 1725–1792*. 2 vols. New York and London: G. P. Putnam's Sons, 1892.

Rutland, Robert Allen. *The Birth of the Bill of Rights, 1776–1791*. Chapel Hill: University of North Carolina Press, for the Institute of Early American History and Culture, 1955.

———. *George Mason: Reluctant Statesman*. Williamsburg, Va.: Colonial Williamsburg, 1961.

———. *James Madison and the Search for Nationhood*. Washington, D.C.: Library of Congress, 1981.

Schachner, Nathan. *The Founding Fathers*. South Brunswick, N.J.: H. S. Barnes, 1970 (1954).

Seed, Geoffrey. *James Wilson*. Millwood, N.Y.: KTO Press, 1978.

Shalhope, Robert E. "Republicanism and Early American Historiography." *William and Mary Quarterly*, 3rd series, 39 (April 1982).

———. "Toward a Republican Synthesis: The Emergence of an Understanding of Republicanism in American Historiography." *William and Mary Quarterly*, 3rd series, 29 (January 1972).

Sigler, Jay H. "Rise and Fall of the Three-Fifths Clause." *Mid-America* 48 (October 1966).

Silverman, Kenneth. *A Cultural History of the American Revolution: Painting, Music, Literature and the Theatre in the Colonies and the United States from the Treaty of Paris to the Inauguration of George Washington, 1763–1789.* New York: T. Y. Crowell, 1976.

Singer, Charles Gregg. *South Carolina in the Confederation.* Philadelphia: University of Pennsylvania, 1941.

Smith, Charles Page. *James Wilson: Founding Father, 1742–1798.* Chapel Hill: University of North Carolina Press, for the Institute of Early American History and Culture, 1956.

Sparks, Jared. *The Life and Writings of Jared Sparks.* Herbert B. Adams, ed. 2 vols. Boston: Houghton, Mifflin and Co., 1893.

———, ed. *The Library of American Biography.* 25 vols. Boston: Hilliard, Gray and Co., 1934–48.

Stourzh, Gerald. *Alexander Hamilton and the Idea of Republican Government.* Stanford: Stanford University Press, 1970.

Stuart, Reginald C. *War in American Thought.* Kent, Ohio: Kent State University Press, 1982.

Swigett, Howard. *The Extraordinary Mr. Morris.* Garden City, N.Y.: Doubleday, 1952.

Szatmary, David P. *Shays' Rebellion: The Making of an Agrarian Insurrection.* Amherst: University of Massachusetts Press, 1980.

Tansill, Charles C., ed. *Documents Illustrative of the Formation of the Union of the American States.* Washington, D.C.: U.S. Government Printing Office, 1927.

Thach, Charles C., Jr. *The Creation of the Presidency, 1775–1789: A Study in Constitutional History.* Johns Hopkins University Studies in History and Political Science Series XL, no. 4. Baltimore: The Johns Hopkins Press, 1922.

Thayer, James B. "The Origin and Scope of the American Doctrine of Constitutional Law." *Harvard Law Review* 7 (1893).

Turner, Lynn Warren. *The Ninth State: New Hampshire's Formative Years.* Chapel Hill: University of North Carolina Press, 1983.

Ulmer, S. Sidney. "Charles Pinckney: Father of the Constitution?" *South Carolina Law Quarterly* 10 (Winter 1958).

———. "James Madison and the Pinckney Plan." *South Carolina Law Quarterly* 9 (Spring 1957).

———. "Subgroup Formation in the Constitutional Convention." *Midwest Journal of Political Science* 10 (August 1966).

Van Doren, Carl. *Benjamin Franklin.* New York: The Viking Press, 1938.

———. *The Great Rehearsal.* New York: The Viking Press, 1948.

Walther, Daniel. *Gouverneur Morris, Witness of Two Revolutions.* New York and London: Funk and Wagnalls Co., 1934.

Warren, Charles. *The Making of the Constitution.* Boston: Little, Brown, and Co., 1928.

———. *The Supreme Court and the Sovereign States.* Princeton: Princeton University Press, 1924.

Washington, George. *George Washington's Rules of Civility and Decent Behavior.* Edited by John Allen Murray. New York: G. P. Putnam's Sons, 1942.

Watson, John F. *Annals of Philadelphia and Pennsylvania.* 3 vols. Philadelphia: Whiting and Thomas, 1856.

Wells, Robert V. *The Population of the British Colonies in America Before 1776: A Survey of Census Data.* Princeton: Princeton University Press, 1975.

White, Henry Clay. *Abraham Baldwin, One of the Founders of the Republic, and Father of the University of Georgia, the First of American State Universities.* Athens, Ga.: The McGregor Co., 1926.

Wiecek, William M. *The Sources of Antislavery Constitutionalism in America, 1760–1848.* Ithaca: Cornell University Press, 1977.

———. "The Statuary Law of Slavery and Race in the Thirteen Mainland Colonies of British America." *William and Mary Quarterly,* 3rd series, 34 (April 1977).

Wilson, James. *The Works of James Wilson.* Edited by Robert Green McCloskey. 2 vols. Cambridge: Harvard University Press, Belknap Press, 1967.

Wisenhunt, Donald W., ed. *Delegate from New Jersey: The Journal of John Fell.* Port Washington, N.Y.: Kennikat Press, 1973.

Wood, Gordon S. "Conspiracy and the Paranoid Style: Causality and Deceit in the Eighteenth Century." *William and Mary Quarterly,* 3rd series, 39 (July 1982).

————. *The Creation of the American Republic, 1776–1787.* Chapel Hill: University of North Carolina Press, for the Institute of Early American History and Culture, 1969.

Wright, J. Leitch, Jr. *Britain and the American Frontier, 1783–1815.* Athens: University of Georgia Press, 1975.

Zahniser, Marvin R. *Charles Cotesworth Pinckney: Founding Father.* Chapel Hill: University of North Carolina Press, for the Institute of Early American History and Culture, 1967.

Abolition, 176; in Mass., 141, 161, 163
Adair, Douglass, 40, 60
Adams, Abigail, 40
Adams, Henry, quoted, 20
Adams, John, 44, 59, 76, 95, 99, 144, 216; *Defense of Constitutions,* 60; on Gerry, 239; on Rutledge, 147; on Sherman, 195, 198
Adams, John Quincy, 65, 66
Adams, Samuel, 76, 77, 249; quoted, 3
Admiralty courts, 4
Agriculture, 17–20
Alabama, 138, 154
Alexandria, Va., 30
Algiers, 6
Allegheny Mts., 153, 154
Anglican Church, 144–146
Annapolis Conference, 31–32, 44, 69, 75
Antifederalists. *See* Antinationalists
Antinationalists, 77–78, 106–09, 143, 257–60; die out, 261; oppose Constitution, 256
A Pilgrim's Progress, 22
Appropriations. *See* Money bills
Aristotle, 40
Army, 190, Ch. 21 passim; standing, 5, 236, 237. *See also* Militia
Articles of Confederation, 46, 69, 72, 74, 95, 209; amendment of, 4, 113; commercial policy, 167; equal voting under, 82, 92, 98–99, 133; no executive, 228; fugitive slaves, 163–64; powers continued in Constitution, 66, 67, 191; and ratifying conventions, 53; state sovereignty, 9; text of, 273–80; unicameral house, 109
Ayershire, Scotland, 57

Bacon, Francis, 40
Bailyn, Bernard, 53; quoted, 184
Baldwin, Abraham, 127–29, 157, 160, 226; sketch, 126–27; for equality in Senate, 128
Baltimore, 16, 117
Banning, Lance, 29
Beard, Charles, 238
Bedford, Gunning, 188–89, 198, 222, 271; on proportional representation, 124; threatens small-state union, 124–25
Bethlehem, Penna., 215
Bicameralism, 109–10
Billias, George A., 238–40
Bill of Rights, 261, 271; Ch. 22 passim; of Virginia, 250
Blacks, 22–23, 268; free, kidnapped, 178. *See also* Slavery
Blair, John, 55
Blount, William, 157, 158–60, 162, 271; biog., 158–59; goes to N.Y.C., 125
Boston, Mass., 15, 37, 39, 146, 154; port of, 7; slave trade, 141
Boorstin, Daniel, 212
Brant, Irving, on C. Pinckney, 64; quoted 26–27, 31
Brant, Joseph, 5
Brearley, David, 93, 226
Broom, Jacob, 224
Brown v. *Board of Education,* 202
Burlington, N.J., 215
Burnett, Edmund Cody, 293
Burr, Aaron, 59, 104, 144
Butler, Pierce, 175–76, 187, 198, 247; on North-South differences, 9

Caesar, 40
Campbell, James, 129–30
Canada, 153
Canals, 30–31, 37
Caribbean, 156, 234, 247
Carrington, Edward, 235
Catholics, 16, 76
Charleston, S.C., 139, 147; port of, 7
Chase, Samuel, 118
Checks and balances. *See* Separation of powers
Chesapeake Bay, 15, 42
Chester, Penna., 42
China, 18
Cicero, 40, 158
City Tavern, 256
Civil War, 137, 164, 174, 176, 177
Clark, Abraham, 32
Clarkson, Paul, 117
Class, economic, 48, 111; social, 17
Clinton, George, 78
Clymer, George, 173
Coinage, 10
Coles, Edward, 164
College of New Jersey, 103, 104, 117, 144; Madison attends, 26
College of Philadelphia, 212, 215
Colonial government, 4, 206, 207
Columbia University. *See* Kings College
Commerce, foreign, 8, 10, 108, 137–38, 142, 146, 149, 156–57, 190, Ch. 16 passim; export taxes prohibited, 175; import taxes, 108, 186; regulation of, 193
Commerce, interstate, 8, 106, 142; regulation of 193
Commerce, intrastate, 10, 137–38
Committee of Detail, 72, 169–73, 189–90, 192–93, 201, 226; and Bill of Rights, 252; descr., 168; on executive, 225, 229; on military, 241–42; supremacy clause, 201–2.
Committee of Eleven, 175, 177, 230; on military, 245; several such committees, 173
Committee of Style, 253; reports, 254
Committee of the Whole, system adopted, 84–85; explained, 90; use of, 100
Common law, 60
Common Sense, 23
Congress, Confederation, 44, 142, 157, 159–65, 176, 222, 235, 240; executive in, 218
Congress, U.S., 98, 155. *See also* Legislature
Connecticut, 15, 100, 127, 145, 149, 162, 171, 220; alliance with S.C., 146–48, 161, 169, 172, 176; descr., 19, 96, 146; gradual abolition in, 141; politics in, 144; population, 19; ratifies, 258; refuses tax payments, 123; trade, 6, 8, 146; vote, 99; war with Penna., 8, 153
Connecticut Compromise, 95, 98–100, 114, 143, Ch. 13 passim; accepted, 132; in Grand Committee, 129–30
Constitution, U.S., text 282–92
Continental Army, 105
Continental Congress, 4, 95, 98, 99, 105, 147, 250; weakness of, 9
Cornwallis, Charles, Lord, 42
Corwin, Edward S., 192, 194
Council of Revision, 219–20
Creditors, public, 47
Creek Indians, 127, 234
Crowl, Philip A., 118
Custis, Martha. *See* Washington, Martha
Cutler, Manasseh, 45, 46, 83, 160, 162, 165

Davie, W. W., 161; on proportional representation, 124
Davis, David B., 174
Dayton, Jonathan, 119, 124, 171, 226; youngest member, 68
Debt, public, 138
Declaration and Resolves (1774), 95
Declaration of Independence, 4, 26, 27, 95, 105, 144, 207, 250; signers at Convention, 76
Delaware, 149, 167; delegates' instructions, 82; landless, 154; and Penna., 100, 113; population, 91; ratifies, 258; rejects proportional representation, 93
Delaware Indians, 5
Delaware River, 15, 42
Delegates, collective descr., 76–77, 270–71; credentials, 81–82
Dickinson, John, 82, 271; on Cmte. of Detail, 226; descr., 213; as nationalist, 195; on slave trade, 174; in small-state camp, 106, 120; and states' rights, 122
Division of power. *See* Federalism
Duties. *See* Commerce, foreign
Dwight, Timothy, 98

Economy, U.S., Ch. 2 passim; occupations, 17; sectional, 137–38
Edenton, N.C., 216
Edinburgh, Scotland, 210
Edinburgh, University of, 211
Eisenhower, Dwight D., 42
Electoral College, 214, 223, 226–28, 270
Ellsworth, Oliver, 104, 123, 129, 173, 271; on Cmte. of Detail, 168, 189; and Conn. Compromise, 121, 123; in Conn.–S.C. alliance, 169;

Ellsworth, Oliver (*cont.*)
favors enumeration, 190; and Judiciary Act of 1789, 204; nationalism of, 145; sketch, 144; on slavery, 172; in small-state camp, 120; and three-fifths compromise, 142
England, 14; in Canada, 153; at Great Lakes, 9; government of, 60–61, 72; political parties, 221; trade with, 166–67; troops in N.Y., 234
Emerson, Ralph Waldo, 33
Epidemic of 1793, 46
L'Esprit des Lois, quoted, 208
Europe, 141, 146
Executive, 89, Chs. 19 and 20 passim; appointive power, 230–31; commander-in-chief, 248; election, 222–24, 226–28, 232; impeachment, 223, 225, 231; called president, 226; term, 220–22, 224–25; in Va. Plan, 55; veto, 184, 229–30
Extended republic, 49–50, 53, 112, 266

Factions, 47
Fairfax, Lord, 7
Fairfax, Sally, 35
Families, 19
Farrand, Max, on L. Martin, 118, 119, 301; on N.J. Plan, 108
Federalism, 91–95, 268, Chs. 17 and 18 passim; large-state–small-state conflict, 106–9; Madison on, 50–51; negative on states, 196–97; under Articles, 133
Federalist Papers, 47–49, 57, 259; No. 32, 303; No. 33, 303; No. 51, 48–49, 184; No. 84, 306
Ferguson, E. James, quoted, 9
Few, William, 126, 157, 160; goes to N.Y.C., 125
Flexner, James T., 39; quoted, 42, 59; on Washington, 33, 34
Florida, 127, 153, 159, 177, 234
Floyd, Kitty, 27
Food and drink, descr., 20–22
Foreign affairs, 5; secretary for, 4, 157
Foreign trade. *See* Commerce, foreign
France, 16, 234
Franklin, Benjamin, 22, 89, 102, 122, 160, 271; biog., 78–79; closing speech, 255–56; descr., 83, on Grand Cmte., 129–30; land speculator, 155; on Negroes, 141; oldest delegate, 126; plainness of, 23; proposes prayer, 121; state representation, 99
Fraunces, Samuel, 20
Freeman, Douglas Southall, quoted, 39
French and Indian War, 37, 206
Friedman, Lawrence, 212
Frontier, 16, 72. *See also* Western lands

Gates, Horatio, 39
George III, 206, 207, 228, 247
Georgia, 15, 124, 138, 162, 164, 173, 177, 178; delegation divided, 126–28; and Indians, 7, 8; in large-state bloc, 91, 107; political concerns, 127; population, 127; ratifies, 258, 260; weakness, 177; western lands, 7, 154
Germany, 16, 263
Gerry, Elbridge, xii, 77, 161, 220, 251, 254; biog., 238–40; contrasted to Langdon, 244; financial interests, 132; Grand Cmte., 128–30; moves Bill of Rights, 253; opposes national negative, 198; opposes standing army, 243–47; rejects Constitution, 254, 271; U.S. Vice President, 261; voting inconsistent, 131
Gerry, Thomas, 238
Gilman, Nicholas, 173, 244
Gladstone, William Ewart, quoted, ix
Goldberg, Rube, 227
Gorham, Nathaniel, 164, 171, 174, 189; on Cmte. of Detail, 168; on cmte. on representation, 150; descr., 77; favors enumeration, 190; moves to reduce ratio of representation, 255; nationalist, 129; on N.J. trade, 8; opposes equal vote, 131; and slavery, 169
Grasse, François, Comte de, 42
Gray, Hannah. *See* Wilson, Hannah
Grayson, William, quoted, 3
Great Britain. *See* England.
Great Lakes, 5, 234; British at, 7, 9
Greece, 60, 249
Gulf of Mexico, 153

Habeas corpus, 253
Harbison, Winfred, quoted, 203
Hamilton, Alexander, 54, 55, 64, 72, 73, 77, 89, 102, 158, 211, 213, 264, 271; aide to Washington, 39; and Annapolis Confr., 31–32; opposes bill of rights, 254; biog., 56–60; on Cmte. of Style, 253; duel with Burr, 59; writes *Federalist*, 259; on human nature, 62; monarchist, 209; nationalist, 30, 259, 268; on "necessary," 191–92, 194; on power, 62, 184, 245; for proportional representation, 121; and slavery compromise, 160, 162, 165
Hamilton, Elizabeth, 58
Hamilton, James, 57
Hamilton, Rachel Faucette, 57
Hamilton Plan, 60–64, 69
Hampshire County, Mass., 11
Hancock, John, 3, 258
Harvard College, 77, 239
Hawkins, Benjamin, 160

Henry, Patrick, 28, 44, 223; antinationalist, 77; does not attend, 55, 76; opposes Constitution, 249; "smelt a rat," 55; on R. Sherman, 95

Hobson, Charles, quoted, 196

Holcombe, Arthur N., 80

Holland, 14, 234

House, Mary, 46, 54

House of Commons, 61

House of Lords, 61, 62, 72, 109

House of Representatives, named, 71. *See also* Legislature

Housing, 20

Houstoun, William, 127, 129

Hudson River, 15

Human nature, 47, 264

Hume, David, 26, 47–49, 158, 210

Hunterdon County, N.J., 104

Illinois, 163

Import duties. *See* Commerce, foreign

Independence Hall. *See* State House

Indiana, 163

Indian Queen, 45, 84

Indians, 5, 16, 72, 127, 153, 154, 177, 193, 234–36, 268

Interstate trade. *See* Commerce, interstate

Iowa, 268

Italy, 263

Jackson, Andrew, 73

Jackson, William, 65, 81, 119

Jameson, J. F., 66

James II, 248

Jay, John, 44, 76, 157; writes *Federalist,* 259

Jefferson, Thomas, 16, 25, 46, 59, 239; absent, 44, 76; on executive, 218; on foreign trade, 6; friend of Madison's, 27; on Mason's refusal to sign, 148; and Northwest Ordinance, 156, 177; on R. Sherman, 95

Jenifer, Daniel of St. Thomas, 121, 128, 187; misses vote, 126; sketch, 125–26

Jensen, Merrill, 293

Jett, R. Samuel, 117

Jews, 16

Johnson, Andrew, 232

Johnson, William Samuel, 271; amends supremacy clause, 202; biog., 144; on Cmte. of Style, 253; on Hamilton's speech, 63; messenger from Congress, 147, 164; owned slaves, 146; on slave representation, 161

Jordan, Winthrop, quoted, 139

Judicial review, 199, 202–4, 269

Judiciary, in Va. Plan, 55. *See also* Judicial review; Supreme Court, U.S.

Judiciary Act of 1789, 204

Kelly, Alfred, quoted, 203

Kennedy, John, 270

Kentucky, 138, 154, 156, 158; slaves in, 163

Kenyon, Cecelia, quoted, 256–57

King, Rufus, 129, 161, 164, 226, 253; answers Bedford, 125; on Cmte. of Style, 271; descr., 77, 131; on judicial review, 220; on North-South balance, 150, 151; opposes equality in Senate, 99, 123–24, 131; on slavery, 170, 171, 175; on Spanish relations, 7

Kings College, 58, 145

Knox, Henry, 5

Koch, Adrienne, quoted, 59

Kohn, Richard H., quoted, 235, 236

Lafayette, Marquis de, 39, 256

Langdon, John, xii, 173, 174, 243, 245; sketch, 244

Lansing, John, 57, 128; antinationalist, 107, 114, 198–99; leaves Convention, 173; moves equality in House, 119; supports N.J. Plan, 113

Laurens, John, 39

Lawyers, 212–13

League of Nations, 4

Lee, Henry, 104

Lee, Richard Henry, 77

Lee, Robert E., 42

Legislature, 89, 109–10; direct election of, 112; to elect executives, 227; powers of, Ch. 17 passim; proportional representation compromised, 129–30; reapportionment, 151; in Va. Plan, 55; war-making power, 247; HOUSE: 121, 122, 143, 150, 174; SENATE: 72, 110, 112, 151, 164, 187, 200, 257; equal suffrage in, 126, 187; named, 17; members to vote individually, 133

Lender, Mark, quoted, 21

Lexington and Concord, Battle of, 104

Life expectancy, 22

Lincoln, Benjamin, 12

Livingston, William, 102, 173

Locke, John, 26, 120, 208, 249

London, England, 4, 76

Long Island Sound, 15

Louisiana Purchase, 191

Louisiana Territory, 153, 234; slavery in, 174

Loyalists, 105; property of, 7

Lynd, Staughton, 160, 162, 164, 165

McClurg, James, 55, 224
McCulloch v. *Maryland,* 192
McGillivray, Alexander, 5
McLaughlin, Andrew C., 66
Madison, Dolley, 28
Madison, James, 3, 30, 35, 59, 64, 66, 68, 73, 74, 89, 97, 100, 103, 105, 111, 114, 120, 142, 149, 158, 164, 168, 171, 188, 189, 209, 211, 213, 239, 261, 264, 268, 271; Annapolis Confr., 31–32; as antinationalist, 194; arrives in Phila., 46; biog., 25–29; opposes coercing states, 241; collapse of large-state alliance, 128–29, 131, 132, 148; on Cmte. of Style, 253; attacks Conn., 123; disappointed in Convention, 25; on direct election of legrs., 112; friend of Ellsworth's, 144; adds to enumerated powers, 190; opposes established church, 53–54; on executive, 218, 221; on evils of states, 196–97; extended republic, 49–51; on factions, 48; Father of Constitution, 25; writes *Federalist,* 259; and general grant, 185–86; on human nature, 47–50; on military, 241, 243, 246; on negative on states, 185–86, 196, 199–200; on N.J. Plan, 113; "Notes," 62, 80–81, 293; philosophy of government, 48–50; on Pinckney Plan, 65, 69, 70–72; on power, 49–53, 151, 219, 245; on proportional representation, 91–92, 113, 121, 122, 124, 128–29, 131, 133; leads ratification fight, 259; on sections, 138; on separation of powers, 223, 224, 230; and Shays' Rebellion, 13; on slave trade, 169, 174; on small states' nationalism, 187; on Va. bill of rights, 250; "Vices," 29, 294; on war-making powers, 247; on Washington, 44
Magna Carta, 60
Mail service, 15, 190
Main, Jackson Turner, 17
Marblehead, Mass., 238
Marbury v. *Madison,* 204
Marriage, 21–22
Marshall, John, 192, 194, 204
Martin, Denny *(Martin* v. *Hunter's Lessee),* 7
Martin, James, quoted, 21
Martin, Luther, xii, 76, 103, 107, 115, 128, 196, 209, 213, 246; arrives, 93; biog., 116–18; on compromise cmte., 129; for Conn. Compromise, 126; distrusts the people, 232; drunk, 119, 301; for legis. equality, 121, 124, 131; friend of Paterson's, 104, 144; moves to limit army, 242; against national negative, 198, 199; opposes Constitution, 259; against slave trade, 171; states' rights, 106, 107, 118–20, 126, 187;

proposes supremacy clause, 201; wants weak executive, 218
Maryland, 149, 167, 169, 172; debtors in, 11; landless, 154; ratifies, 258; vote of, 99
Mason, George, xii, 188, 271; and Bill of Rights, 251; biog., 250–51; descr., 54–55; on executive, 223, 224, 231; on Grand Cmte., 129; against national negative, 198; on New England/Southern Alliance, 148; on proportional representation, 130; rejects Constitution, 148, 254; on slave trade, 169, 172; on standing armies, 242; and Va. Bill of Rights, 250, 252
Massachusetts, 17, 108, 162, 166, 167, 171, 178, 186, 221; abolition in, 141, 161, 163; constitution of, 67; delegates, 77; excludes foreign imports, 6; on proportional representation, 131; ratifies, 258, 260; in Revolution, 37; and Shays' Rebellion, 10–13
Masterson, William H., quoted, 159
Mediterranean trade, 6
Mercer, John Francis, 196, 271
Methodists, 173
Mexico, 247
Michigan, 163, 234
Middle Temple, London, 55, 140
Mifflin, Thomas, and secrecy rule, 84
Military. *See* Army
Militia, 190, 237, 240–46. *See also* Army
Miller, Helen Hill, 251
Mississippi, 138, 154, 234
Mississippi River, 5, 16, 153, 154, 157, 160, 231, 234
Mississippi Valley, 154
Mitchell, Broadus, 57; quoted, 32
Mixed government, 61–62, 72
Mohawk Indians, 5
Money bills, 130
Monroe, James, 3, 157, 261
Montesquieu, Charles de Secondat, 50, 224; quoted 208
Morocco, 6
Morris, Gouverneur, xii, 97, 128, 150, 151, 160, 161, 165, 189, 209, 213, 219, 230, 232, 271; antisouthern sentiment, 165; attacks small states, 130, 31; on class system, 111; on cmte. to proportion states, 150; on election of exec., 223–24, 226; adds to enumeration, 190; fear of legislatures, 195; on Grand Committee, 230; supports habeas corpus, 253; suggests judicial review, 201; opposes national negative, 200; as nationalist, 187, 199; proposes North-South bargain, 173; on proportional repre-

sentation, 93, 122, 130–31; sketch, 110; suggests mode of signing, 255; on slave trade, 170–71, 174; proposes taxation/representation plan, 160–61; on upper house, 111; writes Constitution, 253

Morris, Robert, 54, 58, 94, 125, 155, 213, 215, 271; nominates Washington, 79

Morrison, Samuel Eliot, 238, 242

Mount Vernon, 30, 35, 37

Mount Vernon Conference, 30–31

Natchez, 5

Nationalism, 50–53

Nationalists, 9, 32, 133; defeated on Senate, 133; and general grant, 186–87

Natural rights. *See* Bill of Rights.

Navigation Acts, 166

Navy, 247

Necessary and proper clause, 190–94

Nevis, W.I., 57

Newburgh, N.Y., 237

Newburgh Conspiracy, 34

New Hampshire, 167; delegates, 123, 244; excludes foreign imports, 6; ratifies, 258, 259

New Haven, Conn., 97, 127

New Jersey, 102, 149, 167; at Annapolis Conference, 32; debtors in, 11; delegates arrive, 75; landless, 154; C. Pinckney on, 113; ratifies, 258; relative population, 94; in Revolution, 103–5; trade, 8, 106

New Jersey Plan, 60, 64, 69, 71, 109, 113, 201; descr., 108; introduced, 108; loses to Va. Plan, 114; as stalking horse for equal rep., 108

New Milford, Conn., 97

New Orleans, 5, 160

Newport, R.I., slave trade, 141

New York, 100, 108, 162, 166, 177, 178, 186, 221; absent, 131; British forts in, 234; constitution of, 67; delegates, 56; import duties, 8; ratifies, 258, 259; in small-state bloc, 107; loses Vt., 8

New York City, 104, 106, 146, 157; Congress at, 44; population, 17; port of, 7

Nixon, Richard, 270

North Carolina, 15, 124, 138, 162, 164, 177; congressmen as delegates, 159; against Conn. Compromise, 126; ignores Indian treaties, 7; on proportional representation, 131–32; ratifies, 258; for equality in Senate, 131–32; supports national veto, 200; western lands, 154

Northwest Ordinance, 162, 163, 176

Northwest Territory, 5, 153–57, 160–65

Nye, Russel B., quoted, 23

O'Connor, John E., 108; quoted 103, 104

Ohio Company, 160, 162

Ohio River, 16, 30, 37, 154, 156, 162, 163, 164, 176, 178, 234

Onuf, Peter, quoted, 9

Orange County, Va., 25

Oswego, N.Y., 234

Oxford University, 140, 145

Paine, Thomas, quoted, 23

Paper money, 8, 47, 187–88, 196–97

Paris, 76

Parliament, 4, 61, 109, 207, 228

Paterson, Richard, 103

Paterson, William, 77, 103–9, 120, 126, 211, 213, 271; avoids attending Continental Congress, 300; biog., 102–5; and Conn. Compromise, 99; on cmte. to compromise, 129; descr., 209; friend to L. Martin, 116, 117, 118; to O. Ellsworth, 144; introduces N.J. Plan, 107, 113; on power, 184, 245; on proportional representation, 93–94; requests recess, 101; on slavery, 150; state rights, 122

Peale, Charles Willson, 26, 44

Peirce, Neal R., 270

Pennsylvania, 15, 108, 146, 166, 186; abolitionists, 163 (*see also* Quakers); debtors to, 10, 11; Conn. war, 153; Indian raids, 5; large-state alliance, 91; ratifies, 258; and slavery, 173; State House, 46

Pennsylvania, University of. *See* College of Philadelphia

Pericles, 60

Perkins, Edwin, J., 20, 22

Pershing, John J., 42

Philadelphia, 4, 15, 104, 106, 215; descr., 44–46; population, 17; port of, 7; spiritual capital, 44

Philadelphia, College of, 212

Phillips, Ulrich, 164

Pierce, William, 126, 157, 160; on Bedford, 124; on Gerry, 239; on Madison, 27; on Martin, 117; on Paterson, 103; on Wilson, 209; goes to N.Y.C., 125; "Notes," 293; on secrecy rule, 84

Pinckney, Charles, 55, 89, 164, 186, 213, 243; Americanism, 72–73, 264; and bill of rights, 252; biog., 67–69; descr., 64; democracy of, 109; adds to enumeration, 190; on executive, 219, 223; initiates movement for Convention, 69; introduces his plan, 65; Madison on, 81; nationalist, 197; and national negative, 197, 198, 200; characterizes N.J., 113; on classes of

Pinckney, Charles (*cont.*)
  states in Senate, 128, 131; on slave trade, 172,
  174; speech of, 72–73; on war powers, 247
Pinckney, Charles Cotesworth, 271; on army,
  242; against bill of rights, 254; biog., 139–40;
  on slave trade, 161, 173, 174, 175; on Southern
  equality, 151; suggests compromise cmte., 128
Pinckney Plan, 64, 67, 69–72; outlined, 71
Pirates, 6
Pittsburgh, Penna., 15
Plato, 40
Political parties. *See* Factions.
Polybius, 40
Population, ethnic, 16; family size, 18; New
  York City, 17; Philadelphia, 44; urban, 17;
  western, 154. *See also* individual states
Portsmouth, N.H., 244
Post offices, 15, 190
Potomac River, 30, 37
President. *See* Executive
Princeton, Battle of, 58
Princeton, N.J., 103
Princeton University. *See* College of New Jersey
Property, definition, 48; Paterson on, 106; in
  slaves, 142, 150, 161
Proportional representation, 82, 91–93, 99, 112–
  13, 121, 142–43, 149, Chs. 12 and 13 passim. *See
  also* Connecticut Compromise; Virginia
  Plan.
Prostitution, 22
Publius. See *Federalist Papers*
Putnam, Israel, 39

Quakers, 76; and slavery, 141, 173

Randolph, Edmund, 128, 228, 271; antinationalism of, 186, 188; on Cmte. of Detail, 242;
  descr., 168, 189; favors enumeration, 190; on
  executive, 218, 219, 231; against national negative, 198; refuses to sign, 168, 189, 254–55,
  271; sketch, 188; on slavery, 169, 173; tempo-
  rizer, 189, 197; on Va. Bill of Rights, 250; Va.
  atty. genl. and sec. of state, 261; proposes Va.
  Plan, 90, 133
Ratification, 53, 177, 178, 257–61, 264. *See also*
  individual states
Read, George, 69, 106, 230; on equal vote, 82,
  92–93; nationalism of, 172, 187; and western
  lands, 82
Reid, Thomas, 211
Religion, 137, 145. *See also* individual denomi-
  nations

Republic, defined, 49
Revolutionary War, 27, 37–38, 58, 104, 140, 145,
  166, 177, 193, 250; debt of, 8, 155
Rhode Island, 100, 167, 177, 196–97, 200; aboli-
  tion in, 141; does not attend, 44; excludes for-
  eign imports, 6; ratifies, 258
Robinson, Donald, 168; quoted, 169
Rome, Italy, 40, 60, 249
Rossiter, Clinton, 76
Rousseau, Jean-Jacques, 249
Rules of Convention, 83
Rush, Benjamin, 76
Russia, 263
Rutland, Robert, 250, 251
Rutledge, Andrew, 146
Rutledge, John, 68, 140, 149, 151, 186, 189, biog.,
  146–47; on Cmte. of Detail, 168; on cmte. to
  compromise representation, 150; favors sin-
  gle executive, 219; on election of executive,
  226; favors enumeration, 187, 190; on habeas
  corpus, 253; nationalist, 189; favors propor-
  tional representation, 130; and slavery, 147,
  169, 172, 173; and S.C.–Conn. alliance, 176

St. Croix, W.I., 57, 58
Scandinavians, 16
Schuyler, Elizabeth. *See* Hamilton, Elizabeth
Schuyler, Philip, 39
Schuyler family, 56
Schuylkill, 45
Scotland, 209, descr., 210
Secrecy rule, 83–84
Sectionalism, 15, 52, 91, 132, 133, 137–52, 156,
  160–65
Seed, Geoffrey, 216
Senate. *See* Legislature
Separation of powers, 50, 53, 184, 220, 223, 228,
  232, 268, Ch. 19 passim
Sergeant, Jonathan Dickinson, 104
Sex, 21–22
Shays, Daniel, 12, 235, 237, 258
Shays' Rebellion, 10–13, 23, 29, 32, 44, 62, 235,
  236, 240, 244
Sherman, Roger, xii, 74, 76, 103, 115, 117, 120,
  144, 147, 158, 171, 193, 211, 259, 271, Ch. 13
  passim; against bill of rights, 253–54; biog.,
  95–98; on commercial policy, 149; and
  Conn.–S.C. alliance, 152, 170, 172; influences
  O. Ellsworth, 168; on executive, 208, 218, 219,
  222, 223, 224, 226, 227, 232; against general
  grant, 186; on judicial review, 200, 201; on
  legislatures, 112, 114, 151; for limited reform,
  89; on military, 243, 247–48; on G. Morris,

110–11; on national negative, 198; forced toward nationalism, 145; distrusts people, 73,
209; on guarding rights, 121; on separation of
powers, 220; on slavery, 143, 172, 174–75; in
small-state caucus, 106; on state rights, 107,
185, 187, 196, 199
Singletary, Amos, 260
Slavery, 22–23, 91, 92, 107, 137–52, 161–65, 170–
79, 200–1, 235; abolition, 176 (*see also* indi-
vidual states); descr., 139; fugitive, 142, 163,
175–78; in Northwest Territory, 156; revolts,
235
Slave trade, 138, 139, 141, 174, 175
Small-state–large-state conflict. *See* Federal-
ism
Smith, Adam, 210
Smith, Charles P., 210
Smith, Jonathan, 260–61
Spain, 5, 16, 231, 263; on frontier, 6, 7, 9; in
Florida, 234; on Ga. border, 127; in La., 153;
treaty with, 156–57, 160
Sparks, Jared, 65
Springfield, Mass., and Shays' Rebellion, 12–13
Social contract, 47, 214
Society, stratified, 16. *See also* Class
Somerset County, N.J., 104
South America, 263
South Carolina, 15, 124, 138, 172, 173, 177;
against Conn. Compromise, 126; in alliance
with Conn., 146, 147–48, 161, 169, 172, 176;
debtors in, 11; descr., 146; export trade, 146; in
large-state bloc, 91, 107; life-style, 67; politics
in, 68; slaves in, 139
Sovereignty, 4, 214; state, 9, 52. *See also* Feder-
alism
Standard of living, 17–22
State House, 78–83; descr., 75–76
State of the Union address, 71
States, evils of, 196–97; failure to pay quotas,
46; legislatures of, 110; relative populations,
82; descr., Ch. 2 passim
States' rights. *See* Federalism
Steuben, Friedrich Wilhelm von, 237
Story, Joseph, 117
Stoughton, Mass., 96
Stourzh, Gerald, quoted, 63
Strong, Caleb, 77, 128, 131, 132
Stuart, Reginald C., quoted, 236
Suffrage, 52
Supremacy clause, 201–2, 204, 205
Supreme Court, U.S., 102, 103, 144, 190–94,
202–4, 205, 215, 228, 232, 269–70; jurisdic-
tion, 202; in N.J. Plan, 108

Taxation, 160–61, 190; in Confederation, 4; in
N.J. Plan, 108
Temperance, 21
Tennessee, 138, 154, 156, 158, 159, 234; popula-
tion, 155
Texas, 247
Thompson, Charles, 160
Thorpe, Francis N., 73
Three-fifths compromise, 142, 143, 149–50, 152,
162, 164, 170
Thucydides, 60
Todd, Dolley Payne. *See* Madison, Dolley
Tories. *See* Loyalists
Trade. *See* Commerce
Transylvania, 158
Treaty-making power, 231
Treaty of Paris, 5, 7, 14, 153, 234
Trenton, Battle of, 58
Trenton, N.J., 104
Tripoli, 6
Tunis, 6

Ulmer, S. Sidney, 66, 70, 71
United States, geog. descr., 14; society, 16–17,
72; transportation, 14–15, 30, 46

Van Doren, Carl, quoted, 70
Vermont, 8
"Vices of the Political System of the United
States." *See* Madison, James, "Vices"
Virginia, 15, 100, 146, 149, 162, 164, 169, 171, 172,
177, 178, 189, 200, 219; Bill of Rights, 250, 252;
at Convention, 54; against Conn. Compromise, 126; debtors in, 11; elects delegates, 33;
in large-state alliance, 91; confiscates Loyalists' estates, 7; supports national veto, 200;
ratifies, 259; slaves in, 139; western lands, 154
Virginia Plan, 60, 64, 108, 128, 133, 145, 184, 188;
attacked by Bedford, 124; council of revision,
220; debate concluded, 100; defeats N.J.
Plan, 114; descr., 55; executive, 86, 89, 217,
221, 228, 229; Hamilton Plan distinguished,
63; introduced and adopted, 90, 113; legislative election, 112; military, 240–41; negative
on state legislation, 186, 196, 197; Paterson
postpones vote, 106; rivaled by Pinckney
Plan, 69; similarity to Pinckney Plan, 71; and
secrecy, 84; vote to adopt, 113

War, Secretary of, 4, 5
Ward, Joseph, 35
War-making power, 247–48
Warren, Charles, quoted, 70, 72, 197, 226

Washington, George, xii, 14, 16, 20, 21, 46, 51, 56, 68, 73, 94, 96, 97, 98, 102, 105, 110, 123, 125, 144, 158, 188, 189, 209, 213, 218, 270; and Annapolis Conference, 31; on limiting army, 242; biog., 33–42; on Constitution, 132; approves Constitution, 256; attends Convention, 43; President of Convention, 79; role at Convention; 79–80, descr., 245; wants strong executive, 219; votes for single executive, 219; French hero, 43; on frontier settlements, 6; on Georgia, 260; and Hamilton, 58–59; land speculator, 155; supports Madison, 129; friend of Madison's, 251; on militia, 237; nationalist, 54; as U.S. president, 227, 258; quoted, 3; saucer anecdote (Senate), 112; and secrecy rule, 84; and Shays' Rebellion, 13; and slavery, 23, 140, 169; speech of, 255; differences among states, 9; vote of, 171

Washington, Lawrence, 37

Washington, Martha, 28, 37

Washington, Mary, 36

Washington County, Penna., 5

Webster, Daniel, 77

Western lands, 8, 186–87, Ch. 15 passim; speculators, 155

West Indies, 6, 146, 166, 167, 260; British, 6; trade with, 9

Whatley, Mass. 20

Whiskey Rebellion, 103

Wilkes-Barre, Penna., 8, 153

Wilkinson, James, 6, 234

William and Mary College, 55

Williamsburg, Va., 188

Williamson, Hugh, 128, 132, 151, 173, 198, 242

Wilson, Hannah Gray, 215

Wilson, James, 66, 74, 111, 120, 124, 129, 149, 198, 251, 271; biog., 94, 209–16; on Cmte. of Detail, 171, 225; democratic, 109, 265; on executive, 217; election of executive, 221–24, 226, 227; for single executive, 218–19, 220–24; for strong executive, 219, 231; reads Franklin's speech, 255; on fugitive slaves, 175; land speculations, 155; as lawyer, 189; threatens union of large states, 113, 123; nationalist, 268; on proproportional representation, 94, 99, 121, 122, 123, 131; friend of Rutledge's, 147, 168; accepts slavery compromise, 169; proposes three-fifths compromise, 143

Witherspoon, John, 26

Wisconsin, 163

Wood, Gordon, 207, 214, 293; quoted, 106

Wyoming Valley, 8

Wythe, George, 55

Yale College, 97, 98, 127

Yankee-Pennamite War, 8, 151

Yates, Robert, antinationalist, 107; cmte. to compromise representation, 129; leaves Convention, 57, 173; on L. Martin, 120; "Notes," 66, 70, 71, 81

Yorkshire, England, 17

Yorktown, 38, 42

Zahniser, Marvin, quoted, 140

CHRISTOPHER COLLIER, professor of American history at the University of Connecticut and State Historian, has been Editor of Monographs in British History and Culture and Editor of the Public Records of the State of Connecticut. He has been visiting professor at Yale University, New York University, and elsewhere. He is the author of many books and articles on early American history, including *Roger Sherman's Connecticut: Yankee Politics and the American Revolution,* the standard work on its subject.

JAMES LINCOLN COLLIER is author of many books with historical and biographical subjects, including the highly acclaimed *The Making of Jazz.* He has also written widely on the social sciences, especially for American school systems. Together, the brothers have published six works of historical fiction for children, including the award-winning *My Brother Sam Is Dead.*

RENNER LEARNING RESOURCE CENTER
ELGIN COMMUNITY COLLEGE
ELGIN, ILLINOIS 60120